CLOSER THAN EVER

THE BROADWAY LEGACIES SERIES

Geoffrey Block, Series Editor

"South Pacific": Paradise Rewritten
Jim Lovensheimer

Pick Yourself Up: Dorothy Fields and the American Musical
Charlotte Greenspan

To Broadway, to Life! The Musical Theater of Bock and Harnick
Philip Lambert

Irving Berlin's American Musical Theater
Jeffrey Magee

Loverly: The Life and Times of "My Fair Lady"
Dominic McHugh

"Show Boat": Performing Race in an American Musical
Todd Decker

Bernstein Meets Broadway: Collaborative Art in a Time of War
Carol J. Oja

We'll Have Manhattan: The Early Work of Rodgers and Hart
Dominic Symonds

Agnes de Mille: Telling Stories in Broadway Dance
Kara Gardner

The Shuberts and their Passing Shows: The Untold Tale of Ziegfeld's Rivals
Jonas Westover

Big Deal: Bob Fosse and Dance in the American Musical
Kevin Winkler

"Pal Joey": The History of a Heel
Julianne Lindberg

"Oklahoma!" The Making of an American Musical, Revised Edition
Tim Carter

Sweet Mystery: The Musical Works of Rida Johnson Young
Ellen M. Peck

The Big Parade: Meredith Willson's Musicals from "The Music Man" to "1491"
Dominic McHugh

Everything is Choreography: The Musical Theater of Tommy Tune
Kevin Winkler

Yankee Doodle Dandy: George M. Cohan's Broadway and the Making of American Identity
Elizabeth T. Craft

Closer than Ever: The Unique Six-Decade Songwriting Partnership of Richard Maltby, Jr. and David Shire
Joshua Rosenblum

CLOSER THAN EVER

THE UNIQUE SIX-DECADE SONGWRITING PARTNERSHIP OF RICHARD MALTBY, JR. AND DAVID SHIRE

JOSHUA ROSENBLUM

OXFORD
UNIVERSITY PRESS

Oxford University Press is a department of the University of Oxford. It furthers the University's objective of excellence in research, scholarship, and education by publishing worldwide. Oxford is a registered trade mark of Oxford University Press in the UK and certain other countries.

Published in the United States of America by Oxford University Press
198 Madison Avenue, New York, NY 10016, United States of America.

Library of Congress Cataloging-in-Publication Data
Names: Rosenblum, Joshua, author.
Title: Closer than ever : the unique six-decade songwriting partnership of Richard Maltby, Jr. and David Shire / by Joshua Rosenblum.
Description: [First edition]. | New York, NY : Oxford University Press, 2024. | Series: [Broadway legacies] | Includes bibliographical references and index.
Identifiers: LCCN 2023054952 (print) | LCCN 2023054953 (ebook) | ISBN 9780197758236 (hardback) | ISBN 9780197758250 (epub) | ISBN 9780197758267
Subjects: LCSH: Shire, David. | Shire, David—Criticism and interpretation. | Maltby, Richard, Jr., 1937– | Maltby, Richard, Jr., 1937—Criticism and interpretation. | Musicals—United States—History and criticism.
Classification: LCC ML410.S52556 R67 2024 (print) | LCC ML410.S52556 (ebook) | DDC 782.1/40922—dc23/eng/20231219
LC record available at https://lccn.loc.gov/2023054952
LC ebook record available at https://lccn.loc.gov/2023054953

DOI: 10.1093/oso/9780197758236.001.0001

Printed by Sheridan Books, Inc., United States of America

For Joanne, Julian, and Phoebe—you are my blessings

CONTENTS

FOREWORD

In the course of preparing *Closer Than Ever: The Unique Six-Decade Songwriting Partnership of Richard Maltby, Jr. and David Shire*, Joshua Rosenblum interviewed the wizardly orchestrator Jonathan Tunick. Tunick has contributed to the scores of numerous popular and critically acclaimed shows, including all but two of Stephen Sondheim's musicals from *Company* through *Here We Are*, his last. One of these shows was the first Broadway musical by lyricist Maltby (b. 1937) and composer Shire (b. 1937), *Baby* (1983), with a score that musical theater critic Ken Mandelbaum assessed as "one of the best heard on Broadway in the 1980s." Perhaps surprisingly, Tunick told Rosenblum that he considered Shire "the outstanding musical theater composer of his generation," a judgment Tunick deemed valid since he considered Sondheim a member of the *previous* generation (despite being only seven years older than Shire). In a 2016 survey of writing teams from the past fifty years, the songwriter Noel Katz also embraced Shire's partner, concluding that "Maltby and Shire, I'd argue, are the best lyricist and best composer working today."

Starting Here, Starting Now (1977), which focused on the promise and disappointments of young love, has been lauded in *The TheaterMania Guide to Musical Theater Recordings* as "just about the best songwriter anthology ever created." Maltby and Shire's second major revue, *Closer Than Ever* (1989), with its emphasis on couples who have been around the block, prompted another *TheaterMania Guide* critic to praise that cast recording as "one of the best-sung albums of the decade." Those unfamiliar with these shows may wonder why the much-praised songwriting team of Maltby and Shire is less well known than Rodgers and Hammerstein, Lerner and Loewe, or Kander and Ebb. The short answer is that despite considerable critical acclaim, multiple Tony nominations, a long-lasting afterlife in regional theater both for *Baby* and for their less-acclaimed second Broadway show, *Big* (1996) (an adaptation of the 1988 hit movie starring Tom Hanks), and especially the high praise regularly bestowed on the two previously mentioned revues, Maltby and Shire as a team have neither savored a major hit show nor won coveted theater awards.

Their reputation is obscured by the reality that even masterful revues tend to have less cachet than book shows and are largely overlooked by Broadway historians. We can hope this will start to change for readers of Rosenblum, a composer, conductor, pianist, and music journalist, who teaches musical theater composition at Yale University and conducting at New York University. In addition to his exceptional analytical and critical acumen as a writer, Rosenblum has played or conducted for numerous Broadway shows, most recently as pianist and associate conductor for the 2022 revival of *Into the Woods*. Among Rosenblum's many compositions is *Fermat's Last Tango*, a musical about Andrew Wiles, the mathematician who proved Fermat's Last Theorem. The musical, written in collaboration with his wife, Joanne Sydney Lessner, who wrote the book and co-wrote the lyrics, premiered off-Broadway in 2000. In the years since, it has gained a significant following, including a March 2023 revival at Oxford University in the building named after Wiles.

Throughout *Closer Than Ever*, Rosenblum tells us what we need to know about Maltby and Shire's book shows and revues and how they work, appropriately placing his main emphasis on the songs. Some of these are epic in scope, such as "Life Story" and "One of the Good Guys" from *Closer Than Ever*, stories of a lifetime conveyed in about five minutes. Readers prepared for a good cry might listen to "If I Sing," also in *Closer*, with a rare lyric by composer Shire, a moving tribute to his and Maltby's fathers, both bandleaders: "If I sing, you are the music. / If I love, you taught me *how*. / Ev'ry day your heart is beating / In the man that I am *now*."

A good introduction to Rosenblum's approach is his analysis of the upbeat "Miss Byrd," also from *Closer*, a portrait of an unobtrusive office worker nobody notices as she confides her revelation over a catchy musical groove: "I sit here at my desk / And no one *knows* / Not twenty minutes ago / I was not wearing *clothes*." In his commentary, Rosenblum describes the ingenious way Maltby's lyrics employ "the metaphor of a bird making music and have it simultaneously work as a pun on the character's name . . . a bird that is bursting into song" from Miss Byrd's secret love nest.

Rosenblum then shows how "Shire does his part by opening out the vocal line, which has hitherto been primarily syncopated and composed of relatively rapid-fire eighth notes. Now, on the phrase '*This* bird [i.e., *Miss* Byrd] is singing,' the melody takes flight, with a broad sustained note on (appropriately enough) the syllable 'sing.'" Not only will "Miss Byrd" (assisted by Rosenblum) make listeners think a little more about "That little office temp / Who seems so *dumb* / How come a trip to McDonald's / Is making her *hum*?" If your response to Rosenblum's perceptive and readable commentary is anything like mine, I wouldn't be surprised if you stopped reading right now and found a way to experience this great song without further delay.

Rosenblum naturally focuses mainly on the songs and musicals Maltby and Shire wrote together "throughout their sixty-seven-year (and counting) partnership," which began when they were both undergraduates at Yale. Only Harvey Schmidt and Tom Jones (sixty-two years) and Betty Comden and Adolph Green (sixty-one years) come close. But Maltby and Shire also enjoyed highly successful, lucrative, and creative "day jobs," as Rosenblum makes abundantly clear.

In his creative life apart from Shire, Maltby is probably best known as a co-lyricist and director of the hit revue and Tony-winning Best Musical *Ain't Misbehavin'* (1978), based on the life and songs of Fats Waller, for which Maltby received a Tony as Best Director. After that, Maltby contributed English lyrics for the Broadway production of *Miss Saigon* (1991) and co-conceived and received a Tony nomination for his direction of *Fosse* (1999), another Best Musical Tony recipient. Meanwhile, Shire devoted a major portion of his career to the composition of roughly one hundred television scores (earning five Emmy nominations) and about fifty film scores, including the acclaimed *The Conversation*. His original musical contributions to the *Saturday Night Fever* soundtrack earned Shire a shared Grammy Award, and his song "It Goes Like It Goes" from *Norma Rae* received the Academy Award for Best Song.

Throughout this first book-length study of Maltby and Shire, Rosenblum takes great advantage of his access to interviews with his subjects as well as their manuscripts, drafts, and final versions, along with permission to reprint a generous number of lyrical and musical examples. To their credit, Maltby and Shire also granted Rosenblum permission to freely engage, discuss, evaluate, and analyze their creative process and product from a balanced critical distance. Building on their own penetrating reflections concerning their work, including disappointments and setbacks as well as critical triumphs and the joys of artistic collaboration, Rosenblum clearly, insightfully, and stylishly explains what this undervalued team was trying to do and how they did it. Although there is much more to their story, the gateway to understanding their work is the revue, a theatrical genre that, as Ethan Mordden observed, "allows them to write whole shows in a single song." Along these lines, at the end of his book, Rosenblum offers the following astute epiphany (sorry for the spoiler): "Thus, one might say Maltby and Shire are indisputably great musical theater songwriters whose primary legacy ultimately lies outside the Broadway musical, because so many of their best songs contain complete musical narratives in themselves. But it may be too soon to draw any sweeping conclusions. Clearly, for the time being, at least, their story goes on."

When Sondheim turned seventy in 2000, he included Maltby and Shire's early song "Travel," later incorporated into *Starting Here, Starting Now*, in

"Songs I Wish I'd Written (At Least in Part)." As readers of *Closer Than Ever* will discover, Maltby and Shire's longtime friendship with Sondheim receives its own well-deserved chapter. Later Rosenblum discusses Shire's contribution to Sondheim's *Company*, for which Shire penned the instrumental dance number "Tick-Tock." By then, Sondheim was already a fan of Shire's work, ever since he attended Maltby and Shire's early *The Sap of Life* at least three times in 1961.

After a performance of *The Sap of Life* in 2019, Maltby wrote to Sondheim to ask why he "kept coming back" to see the original production. In his response, Sondheim not only wrote that he "was knocked out by David's score, but I left the theater murmuring the lyrics." To Maltby's surprise (and wonder), Sondheim quoted a phrase from memory. Since this foreword has already revealed one of his final observations, the series editor has decided to make readers wait until they can get hold of Rosenblum's insightful and entertaining book to hear Maltby's memorable lyric, "a line which occurs to me [i.e., Sondheim] about once a week"—sixty years later.

Geoffrey Block
Series Editor, Broadway Legacies

PREFACE

The gifted songwriters, composer David Shire (b. 1937) and lyricist Richard Maltby, Jr. (b. 1937), are revered by many theater lovers for their Broadway musicals *Baby* and *Big*, as well as their groundbreaking off-Broadway revues *Starting Here, Starting Now* and *Closer Than Ever*. According to licensing agency Music Theater International, all the Maltby/Shire shows continue to be popular theatrical rentals worldwide. In addition, their songs are performed frequently in cabarets, auditions, student showcases, and musical theater master classes. Shire's peers regard him with awe for the richness of his harmonic vocabulary and his seemingly inexhaustible melodic inspiration, as well as his polish, sophistication, and facility in nearly any genre. Maltby is acknowledged as one of the great living wordsmiths (he also creates devilishly difficult cryptic puzzles for *Harper's* magazine) and an expert practitioner of songwriting as storytelling. Legendary Broadway orchestrator Jonathan Tunick considers Shire to be "the outstanding musical theater composer of his generation," comparing him to George Gershwin. Twelve-time Grammy-winning producer Thomas Z. Shepard says that even when he and Shire were both composition students at Yale, he was "knocked out" by Shire's music.

Yet Maltby and Shire, despite these and similar encomiums, have not fully received their due; they are certainly not household names like the most successful musical theater writers of their generation, such as Stephen Sondheim, John Kander and Fred Ebb, Charles Strouse, or Jerry Herman. By writing this book, I hope to increase appreciation for their marvelous body of work, explore the inner workings of their extraordinary long-running partnership, and establish their significance within the musical theater genre.

To those ends, this book details Maltby and Shire's sixty-seven-year (and counting) collaboration, giving full accounts of the developmental process behind each of their musicals, interspersed with deep-dive analyses of selected songs from their oeuvre. These analyses investigate the elements that make a Maltby/Shire number so compelling and distinctive.

Additionally, the book covers other well-known artistic figures who feature prominently in the Maltby/Shire story, including Sondheim, Tunick, Harold Prince, Francis Ford Coppola, Michael Stewart, Mike Ockrent, Susan Stroman, John Weidman, Craig Lucas, Adam Gopnik, Lynne Meadow, Victoria Clark, Ann Reinking, Thomas Z. Shepard, Jason Robert Brown,

Garth Drabinsky, and Arthur Laurents. Finally, the book explores the very nature of artistic collaboration: how songs actually get written, the mechanism of the give-and-take, and what enables some partnerships to last for decades. And the answer to the age-old question "Which comes first, the music or the lyrics?" turns out not to be quite so simple, at least for Maltby and Shire.

In terms of the book's overall structure, I take a primarily chronological approach to exploring the trajectory of Maltby and Shire's work as a team. Chapter 1 ("Origins") begins when the two young men meet as freshmen at Yale University in 1955 and covers the two musicals they wrote as students, *Cyrano* and *Grand Tour*, both of which received full productions at the Yale Dramat. The final chapter, "The Songwriters' Songwriters," includes an overview of Maltby/Shire projects currently in development, as both men extend their creative fertility into their mid-eighties, plus a final assessment of their place in the musical theater canon. Along the way, thorough consideration is given to all the shows they have written together, well known and otherwise.

Unsurprisingly, I give the most attention to the major musicals mentioned above: the two Broadway shows (*Baby* and *Big*) and the two off-Broadway revues (*Starting Here, Starting Now* and *Closer Than Ever*). Each of these four significant works has three chapters devoted to it: a background chapter describing the evolution of the show and the behind-the-scenes development process; a chapter that breaks down the show's musical, lyrical, and dramatic content, giving critical attention to individual songs and providing their theatrical contexts; and a third chapter that contains a more thorough analysis of one (usually) well-known standout number.

Other Maltby/Shire shows, though not covered quite as extensively, are still examined scrupulously, as each illuminates a distinctive development process and provides revealing anecdotes about the prominent musical theater figures who worked on them. Additionally, the lesser-known shows, although they never had Broadway productions, in many cases yielded songs that are well known due to their later inclusion in one of the aforementioned revues. The shows in this category include *How Do You Do, I Love You*; *Love Match*; and *The Sap of Life*, an obscure but significant Maltby/Shire musical that had an off-Broadway run in 1961 when the two men were barely out of college. Later musicals, including *Take Flight*, *Sousatzka*, and *Waterfall*, merit their own chapters. Much can be gleaned from both the troubled history of these shows and the brilliance of certain individual numbers. Thus, this book can be considered comprehensive in that it covers every completed Maltby/Shire musical (including the as-yet-unproduced *The Country Wife* and the still-in-development revue *About Time*), whether it ended up on Broadway or not, plus some noteworthy incomplete ones.

While most of this book is about Maltby and Shire as a collaborative songwriting team, both men are also highly accomplished separately. Shire has had an entire career as an Oscar- and Grammy-winning film and TV composer, and Maltby is a Tony-winning director. Thus, chapter 7 ("The First Thing They Give You Is Writing the Obits") is devoted to Shire's Hollywood career, and other individual chapters cover Maltby's work as a director on the Tony Award–winning *Ain't Misbehavin'* and *Fosse*, with additional discussion of his work as co-lyricist with Alain Boublil on the English translations of the international hit *Miss Saigon* and (less successfully) *The Pirate Queen*. Maltby's teaming up with composer Strouse for *Nick & Nora* and Shire's partnership with Gopnik on *Our Table* are also considered. Again, the flops are often as enlightening and fascinating as the successes—if not more so.

I am fortunate to have personal and professional relationships with both Richard and David, and they have been exceedingly generous in granting interview time for this book. I've quoted them extensively herein, and I'm certain the reader will find them both to be exceptionally engaging and witty raconteurs, as I have. In addition, the warmth of their own long-standing personal relationship emerged vividly when I interviewed the two men jointly; at times, I felt I was witnessing a polished vaudeville act. I hope at least some of this quality emerges on the printed page. In any case, Maltby's and Shire's illuminating observations about their own work, their writing process, and the collaborative nature of musical theater in general form an important part of this book.

In discussions of individual songs, the other significant component of this book, I provide my own critical analyses, supplemented by musical examples wherever I think they will be helpful. The chapters on specific numbers are enhanced by further insights from the songwriters themselves, giving readers the unusual opportunity to see in-depth commentary about these songs by the people who created them.

My song analyses are intended to be sufficiently rigorous that readers with musical backgrounds can be fully engaged but also easily comprehensible so those who don't read music will be drawn in as well. In almost all cases, the songs in question can be heard online if the reader doesn't happen to own cast recordings of the shows from which they come. Nearly anything can be found either on YouTube or on Spotify these days, including the UK cast recording of *Take Flight* (a welcome item in the absence of a New York production) and the original off-Broadway cast recording of *The Sap of Life*. For the handful of songs with no recordings publicly available (i.e., numbers from *Sousatzka* and *Waterfall*), I'm hopeful that my analytical comments will make their intended points without an available audio supplement.

Happily, Shire has graciously given me full access to his personal archive, which has been maintained and organized by the unfailingly helpful Deniz Cordell. This unusual privilege has enabled me to examine numerous Shire manuscripts, many of which offer rare insight into his compositional process, allowing us to see what happened from the time he first put pencil to paper to the emergence of the final version we know and love today. Several of Maltby's handwritten or typewritten first drafts provide the same invaluable opportunity.

As for the collaborative process itself—how the songs actually get written—Maltby and Shire are uncommonly eloquent in describing how they work together. Glimpses of this occur throughout the book amid discussions of individual songs. In addition, chapter 11 ("He's the Arbiter, Really") is largely devoted to the team's insights into the specific nature of their writing process. These excavations by an outstanding songwriting duo about how they manage the often inexplicable alchemy that results from combining music and lyrics are at the core of what I hope makes this book unique.

ORIGINS

Richard Eldridge Maltby, Jr. of Syosset, New York, and David Lee Shire of Buffalo, New York, met when both were freshmen at Yale University in 1955. They disliked each other immediately.

"I was a pretentious shit from Exeter," Maltby recalls amiably, "and David was this hick from Buffalo."[1]

"I thought he was a snob, he thought I was a hick," Shire confirms, in remarkably similar language.

Maltby joined the Yale Dramatic Association, known as the Dramat, right away when he arrived as a freshman. "I mean, where else was I going to go?" he asks rhetorically. "I picked Yale over Harvard because they had a theater and Harvard didn't."

Shire showed up at the Dramat later in the term, bringing with him a musical he had written. "No story, no lyrics, no plot," Shire explains. "Just the music." Shire sat down and played it through—the ballad, the comedy number, the beguine ("Every score has a beguine," he sagely told the Dramat members), the production numbers.

"We laughed at it," Maltby says. "A full musical with no book or lyrics!" Based on that encounter, Maltby dismissed Shire out of hand. "And that, by the way, is the definitive David Shire anecdote, as far as origins go," Maltby adds wryly.

But there was David, who wanted to be a composer, and Richard, who wanted to write a musical, and nobody else in sight for him to write songs with. "And so, I think reluctantly on both our parts, we started to work together," Maltby concludes. "And how amazing, I have said to myself, that it threw me together with a world-class composer."

Shire concurs that the pairing was fortuitous and then jokes, "Hey, if you had met Alan Menken instead, you'd be rich."

Closer Than Ever. Joshua Rosenblum, Oxford University Press. © Oxford University Press 2024.
DOI: 10.1093/oso/9780197758236.003.0001

First, they tried making a musical out of Budd Schulberg's 1941 novel *What Makes Sammy Run?*, which had been adapted as a live television drama in 1949 for the Philco Television Playhouse on NBC. They spent a fair amount of time on this, only to be informed that they needed the rights to the book.[2] After another false start, the pair decided it would be wiser to pick a public domain property and settled on *Cyrano de Bergerac*, the frequently adapted Edmond Rostand play. Along the way, they taught themselves how to write a musical.

Richard Maltby: Through all the time we were first writing show songs, I was meddling. I was, in fact, teaching David what a good song was, except that I didn't have any idea that I knew what it was. I had a stack of show albums, and I played them all the time. And what he did wasn't what the things I loved from cast albums did, so I would say, "No, David, it has to be *that* in order to do *this*." I was assessing the difference between a big show tune I loved from *Guys and Dolls* and what David was writing. I was learning it myself in the process of teaching him, and annoying him and driving him crazy. But it wasn't so much that I didn't like what he wrote—just that it didn't do what I thought it was supposed to do.

David Shire: Admittedly, I was totally music-oriented when I came. My father was a society orchestra leader and taught pop piano during the day. In those days, pop music *was* theater music, and hits came out of shows. So that's what I was listening to from the cradle all day long, hearing "All the Things You Are" and "Some Enchanted Evening," and I wasn't hearing lyrics, really, I was involved with "Oh, boy, I love that melody. I want to write melodies like that." And I was a cocktail pianist. I knew hundreds of those songs, so I thought, "I could do that—I'll write a Jerome Kern song, I'll write a Gershwin song." That was my frame of reference. [Richard's] frame of reference was actual drama and theater and the arc of a song, and how the arc of a whole show determined what a melody was. So he really taught me how to be conscious of all the elements I thought were secondary. At first, in the early days, I was annoyed because I just thought everything that dripped from my talented cocktail piano fingers was pure gold, and it took a while for me not to resent Richard saying, "No, that isn't 'All the Things You Are,' it's 'All the Things You Shouldn't Be'!"

RM: I guess the point I'm trying to make is I wasn't correcting him from some egotistical, Olympian I-know-and-you-don't. I was just responding to the fact that this wasn't what it wanted to be, and maybe it's because the melody should go up here. And suddenly, in that process, I was defining build and structure and release and emotional development. And then the words would follow in the same way, as David was learning it musically.

DS: I was learning how to make the music a handmaiden of the storytelling.

RM: And when it connected, suddenly, things started happening. Our first two years of working together at Yale, we didn't actually produce anything, but there was this process going on in which we were learning what a song was and what a show was. So that when we did get to *Cyrano*, we knew some things.

In their junior year, they completed their *Cyrano* score and prepared to mount it as a spring production at the Dramat, where Richard was now treasurer. There is actually a CD available of the production—the Yale cast recorded the show in 1958 as a limited pressing.[3] In 1999, the original tapes were digitally remastered, and the CD was released commercially on the Original Cast Records label. Though some of the numbers betray the newbie status of the fledgling songwriting team, quite a few of them, somewhat startlingly, sound like mature, fully formed Maltby/Shire songs. And one of them, "Autumn," is an enduring classic, largely thanks to Barbra Streisand's performance of it on her 1964 solo album, *People*.

Shire, who recently listened to the *Cyrano* recording for the first time in decades, was shocked by it. "I can look at it two ways," he says. "Either that we've advanced so little or that we really had then most of the tools that we have now. There are things in it that I really forgot I knew how to do back then. In some ways, I pretty much had the basic skills that I have traded on and developed for the rest of my career." Or to put it another way, he concludes, "There are some really good songs in there."

He's right. One particularly impressive example is a number near the beginning called "Had You but Wit," one of the first songs the pair wrote for the show. Those who know the *Cyrano* story will recognize this as the moment when Cyrano triumphs over his adversaries by proving to them that in making fun of his prominent proboscis, they are not being nearly clever enough, certainly nowhere near as clever as he himself would be. It's an ambitious undertaking—to write a song in which the primary character demonstrates that he can be wittier than anyone around him—but the young team delivered the goods amazingly well.

The number begins without even really beginning. "Sir, would you have us believe that you are devoid of imagination?" Cyrano prods, in a spoken line. "That you have no facility with the allegorical, the oratorical, that before the metaphorical your mind is as empty as a well?" He's still speaking, but starting on the third syllable of "alle*gor*ical," rhythmic chords start creeping in to emphasize the rhymes, and suddenly, we realize a musical number has started. It's a deft technique for transitioning from a scene into a song, a potentially awkward moment in any musical and one that can be handled in various ways, but this is a particularly smooth one.[4]

Maltby ends the introduction with the line "As you so readily admit / You have nary a whit of wit." Shire, in the meantime, keeps the accompaniment light and spare, the better to support the dense volley of lyrics, yet he also subtly manages to modulate his way through five different key areas before the main body of the song has even started.

"You might have said, 'What amazing composure / For one whose nose is indecent exposure,'" goes the first riposte. "You might have mentioned that you've heard a rumor / I wear this nose to promote a perfumer," goes a later one. In between verses, Shire cranks up the music, firing off iterations of a rhythmically agitated, three-note melodic motif that conjures genuine excitement over the growing incisiveness of Cyrano's verbal fusillades.

In the bridge, the orchestra switches to a fleet, heroic accompaniment of driving triplets in the woodwinds as Cyrano continues to run rings around his adversaries. When the A section returns, the writers introduce an enjoyably disruptive rhythmic variation, starting with the phrase "Had you but wit / Your comments might have seemed to be a / little ironic at / least be beyond the / chronic moronic / kind." Shire distributes the accents so that, starting with the word "little," it sounds like a $\genfrac{}{}{0pt}{}{6}{4}$ measure followed by two $\genfrac{}{}{0pt}{}{5}{8}$ measures. A glance at the manuscript, however, shows that the song actually stays in $\genfrac{}{}{0pt}{}{4}{4}$, even though the accents create the illusion of changing meters. Thus, Cyrano is dazzling his detractors not only with verbal intricacy but now with rhythmic intricacy as well.

Another song, "A Touch of Sweetness," which introduces the character of the baker Ragueneau, was a solo for the young Dick Cavett, who, quite amusingly, sounds very much like the adult Dick Cavett. "He was a talk show host in the cradle," Maltby observes. It sounds as if Cavett is doing his best Rex Harrison impression, speak-singing the song rather than hitting pitches. This is entirely plausible; *My Fair Lady* had had its out-of-town tryout just two years earlier at New Haven's fabled Shubert Theater. Cavett saw it, according to Maltby, although Shire did not.

"Richard was walking to the theater on opening night, and he came by and said, 'I have an extra ticket to *My Fair Lady*,'" Shire recalls. "I said, 'I have this paper to write, and that's the most boring title I've ever heard.' I pictured a period show with dainty little tunes. Richard saw history."

Also impossible to miss on the *Cyrano* recording are the whiz-bang, fully professional-sounding orchestrations. It turns out they are, in fact, the work of a professional orchestrator, Jay Brower.[5] Maltby met Brower during a summer at Tamiment, an entertainment resort in the Poconos with a strong focus on theater. Maltby was there as an assistant to the resident set designer, Fred Voepel. "At that time, what I really wanted to do was be a set designer," Maltby explains. "I mean, I couldn't draw, and I couldn't paint, but I talked a good game, and we had a lot of fun together."

Tamiment was a training ground for many future show-biz stars, including such luminaries as Danny Kaye, Imogene Coca, Jerome Robbins, and Neil Simon. An early version of *Once Upon a Mattress* was produced around the time Maltby was there as one of the resort's first original shows (although its eventual star, Carol Burnett, did not join the production until it moved to New York).

Brower was Tamiment's resident orchestrator at the time. Maltby asked Brower if he would orchestrate Maltby's new musical for the Yale Dramat. "And he said, 'Sure,'" Maltby recalls. "He came up, he lived at the Y for three weeks, and he orchestrated the show."

That cost money, which Maltby, as Dramat treasurer that year, cheerfully signed off on. In fact, expenses on the show were huge. As Maltby writes in the liner notes to the *Cyrano* CD:

> Did we realize that we had chosen a period with the most elaborate costumes in history? No. John Conklin, our classmate, later to be one of the world's great opera designers, designed a series of huge sets. We decided that this grand production should bring back the glory days of the early Dramatic Association, when they used to tour their productions to New York. The Alumni Association of Connecticut agreed to sponsor a performance at the Stratford Connecticut Shakespeare Festival, so while we were at it, we decided to do a performance in New York. We booked the Phoenix Theatre. Both were union theatres. We didn't know about unions. Or their costs. We spent a great deal of money on the production and found ourselves way over budget when we toured. At the end of the year the Dramat was nearly bankrupt.[6]

Unsurprisingly, Maltby was not re-elected as Dramat treasurer the following year. "The word 'self-serving' was bandied about," he observes dryly. But a second Maltby/Shire show was mounted that spring nonetheless. This show, *Grand Tour*, is represented on the CD with *Cyrano* by eight songs plus an orchestral prelude.

Grand Tour had a plot that vaguely echoed the Katharine Hepburn movie *Summertime* but not closely enough to require the young authors to secure the rights.[7] The story concerned an American schoolteacher traveling to Europe on a summer vacation. For the opening song, the teacher is given a big farewell by her fellow teachers and adoring students.

This peppy, Sousa-like number, "Bon Voyage," is a quodlibet. Or, as Maltby elegantly puts it in the song "One Step" from the 1977 revue *Starting Here, Starting Now*, it's "one of those songs with two parts where both of them go together." The classic example of this kind of number is "You're Just in Love" from Irving Berlin's *Call Me Madam*. Other great ones include "All for the Best" from *Godspell* and "Lida Rose"/"Will I Ever Tell You" from *The Music Man*. Among contemporary musicals, "Farmer Refuted" from *Hamilton* is a clever variation on the form.[8]

In "Bon Voyage," one young student is so excited about it that she can't help but burst out, after the first verse, "Wait, that's not all! Ready for part two! It's one of those songs where you have two parts and you put them both together!" Maltby's clear preference with quodlibets, even then, seemed to be that he wanted to announce them as such, inside the song itself.

Later in *Grand Tour* comes a winsome, winning song called "Could It Be?" in which the character Angelo sings of how he can hardly believe his great luck in becoming the object of Ellen's affections. It begins with a hesitant two-step feel, as Angelo tentatively explores the notion. ("Could it be? Could it be? Out of all this world she's really chosen me!") By the time he gets to the B section, and the lines "Yes, today, it could be," he is boldly singing octave leaps and major ninths in the melody, but the pacing remains deliberate. For the second verse, however, he launches into a high-speed cancan and triumphantly hits a high G♭ on the first word of the phrase "*She* loves me!" It's a thoroughly endearing number, and its success is considerably boosted by the superb performance of Bill Hinnant, who would go on eight years later to create the role of Snoopy in *You're a Good Man, Charlie Brown*.

Looking at the credits for *Cyrano* and *Grand Tour* is a highly entertaining exercise in spotting luminaries. Cavett is by no means the only one. Playing the minor role of Bellerose in *Cyrano* was a certain Bartlett Giamatti, future president of Yale and, after that, commissioner of Major League Baseball.

The role of Roxanne was played by a Yale School of Drama student named Toni Smith. "My first chance to have a crush on a leading lady," Shire reminisces. Smith, however, only had eyes for Giamatti, and they were married in 1960, right out of Yale. They had three children, including actors Paul and Marcus Giamatti. "I want to meet Paul Giamatti one day and tell him I'm not only responsible for his career, but that I'm responsible for his entire existence," Maltby quips.

John Badham, stage manager of *Grand Tour*, went on to become a successful director. Badham and Shire first worked together professionally in TV, with Shire scoring several of the "ABC Movies of the Week" that Badham directed. That led to Shire's being hired for Badham's gigantic breakthrough, *Saturday Night Fever*. The score is mostly famous for the Bee Gees songs, but Shire wrote several cues for the film that ended up on the soundtrack album, including the pulse-pounding Modest Mussorgsky adaptation "Night on Disco Mountain," the sizzling "Salsation," and the enduringly popular "Manhattan Skyline." The *Saturday Night Fever* recording was a huge runaway hit—at the time, the bestselling album in history—and is still the second bestselling soundtrack ever, after *The Bodyguard*. It had sold 40 million copies as of 2019. "That was my oil well," Shire says.

John Cunningham, who played the title role in *Cyrano*, has had an illustrious career, creating memorable roles in numerous Broadway plays and musicals, in addition to dozens of film and TV credits. Austin Pendleton, who appeared in both *Cyrano* and *Grand Tour*, went on to create the role of Motel in *Fiddler on the Roof* on Broadway and has since amassed numerous Broadway and off-Broadway directing credits, on top of nearly one hundred film and TV roles.

From the *Grand Tour* cast, Gretchen Cryer, who starred as Ellen MacDonald, and Nancy Currie (later Ford) went on to write the off-Broadway hit *I'm Getting My Act Together and Taking It on the Road*, in which Cryer also starred. Actor Sam Waterston was on the *Grand Tour* stage crew. Lighting designer Peter Hunt went on to direct *1776*, both the Broadway show and the film adaptation.

Among the chorus of children in *Grand Tour*'s opening number, "Bon Voyage," was twelve-year-old Lynne Meadow, whose mother, Virginia, was also in the cast. The younger Meadow grew up and attended the Yale School of Drama, then took over as the artistic director of Manhattan Theatre Club in 1972, where she has since produced and/or directed hundreds of productions and continues to forge a widely lauded career. A lot more on her later.

Shire started out as an English major—his father had advised him to major in something other than music so he'd have a career fallback—but in his senior year, he was fully immersed in writing *Grand Tour*, and he realized he wasn't going to have time to write a senior thesis in English. Seeking another option, he added music as a second major so that his thesis could be a musical composition. He had been taking music electives all along, such as theory, harmony, and orchestration, so he had enough of the necessary credits. As he explains, "I said to [my composition teacher] Quincy Porter, 'My senior thesis is going to be a musical,' and he kind of raised his eyebrows, and I said, 'You're really going to like it, there's a lot of Igor Stravinsky influence in it, and I think you'll pass me. I have no other choice.'"

Saying "there's a lot of Stravinsky influence" in *Grand Tour* was a bit of a stretch. Shire cites *Symphony in C*, a masterpiece of middle-period Stravinskian neoclassicism, as a particularly inspiring work. The piece begins with a driving series of eighth notes on the pitch B in ascending octaves, culminating with the melodic figure B-C-G in the second measure. Shire took those three pitches and used them as the melodic basis for several of the songs in *Grand Tour*. "You Can't Live Alone" uses the B-C-G pitch collection as its primary melodic cell, as indicated by the brackets in example 1.1. Other *Grand Tour* songs used permutations of this three-note pitch series, including "From Far Away," whose melody is based on the pitches C-B-G, and "All My Life," which begins with G-B-C.

Example 1.1. "You Can't Live Alone"

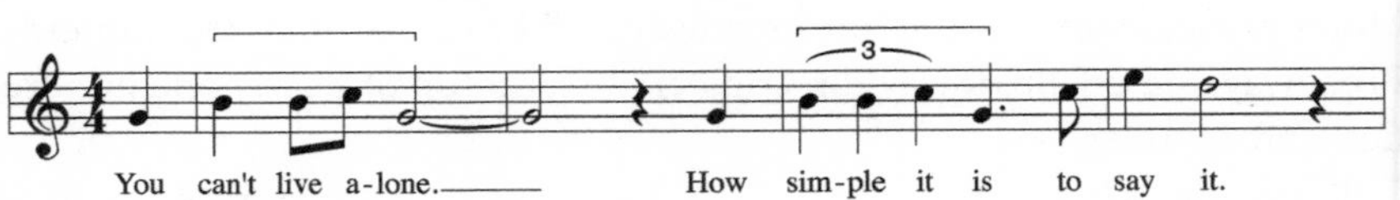

It seems fair to say this bit of pitch manipulation falls more in the category of compositional gamesmanship for one's own amusement than actual Stravinsky influence, although Shire stresses that Stravinsky's music—particularly from the Russian composer's neoclassical period—indeed had a primal impact on him. To hear a mature Shire work that shows genuinely Stravinskian characteristics, listen to the main title music from the 1977 TV movie *Raid on Entebbe*, which recalls Stravinsky's neoclassical masterpiece *Les noces* with its driving rhythms, pulse-pounding irregular accents, and a creative instrumentation that, like *Les noces*, includes four pianos and percussion.[9]

In any case, Porter was placated, one way or another. "He came to *Grand Tour*, and he was really surprised with how intelligent the music was," Shire relates, "and he said, 'Just write me the first movement of a piano sonatina, and I'll pass you.'"

Upon graduation from Yale in 1959, with two fully produced musicals under their belts, both Maltby and Shire opted for graduate school—Richard at Yale's School of Drama, and David at Brandeis University for further composition studies.

First, however, they spent a summer in Palm Springs, California. Among the New Yorkers who had come to New Haven to see *Grand Tour* was a woman named Selma Tamber, who worked for Saint Subber, a prominent theatrical producer.[10] Tamber introduced Maltby and Shire to her friend Larry Shayne, who was Henry Mancini's publisher. Shayne signed the fledgling songwriting team and offered them free use of his house in Palm Springs through the summer.

It wasn't as good as it sounded. "We thought we would go there and hang out with big celebrities in Palm Springs," Shire recalls, "but we got there, and nobody was there. Just people who couldn't afford to go somewhere else." They sweltered there for the summer in the three-digit heat (they successfully fried an egg on the pool deck), trying to write songs they thought might become hits but not getting very far. "We were so intent on writing a hit, and it was stupid because we should've been writing theater songs," Shire says.

At the end of the summer, after a long drive back east in Shire's family's Nash Rambler, Richard and David parted ways for graduate school. But they would be reunited sooner than they expected.

THE FAIR-HAIRED BOYS

THE SAP OF LIFE

By an amazing coincidence, both Maltby and Shire had fathers who were bandleaders (Richard Maltby, Sr. and Irving Shire). Unsurprisingly, they both learned important lessons from their dads that shaped their approaches to songwriting.

Shire, as mentioned, took several music courses at Yale, but when asked about the sophistication of his harmonic sensibility, he says, "I think that came from my father. The first music I learned was when he put me on his knee and showed me chords at the piano. He would tell me if a chord was vanilla or whether it needed more chromatic, altered notes. C7 was kind of boring, but C7♭9 was getting somewhere. And C7♭9♭5 was *really* something.[1] So harmony was the main thing that I concentrated on in music." (See figure 2.1.) Shire recalls that in his early piano lessons, he would tell his teacher, "I like things with chords."

By the time he was twelve or thirteen, however, Shire realized that to do what he wanted to do as a jazz pianist, he would need to have a lot more technique. He switched to someone he describes as "a serious piano teacher in Buffalo" and took lessons at Yale with Ellsworth Grumman, then a long-time distinguished member of the Yale School of Music faculty. He also put together jazz ensembles of his own, gigging around Buffalo with a group of friends in high school and forming the Shire-Fogg Quintet at Yale with trumpeter Dave Fogg. Shire eventually became a first-rate pianist.

Maltby's bandleader father influenced his son in equally pronounced, if less obvious, ways. Richard Maltby, Sr. came to New York from Chicago in 1945 to be a staff arranger at NBC and ABC, and he became a recording artist at RCA and Columbia Records. He had several hits and released dozens of albums.

Closer Than Ever. Joshua Rosenblum, Oxford University Press. © Oxford University Press 2024.
DOI: 10.1093/oso/9780197758236.003.0002

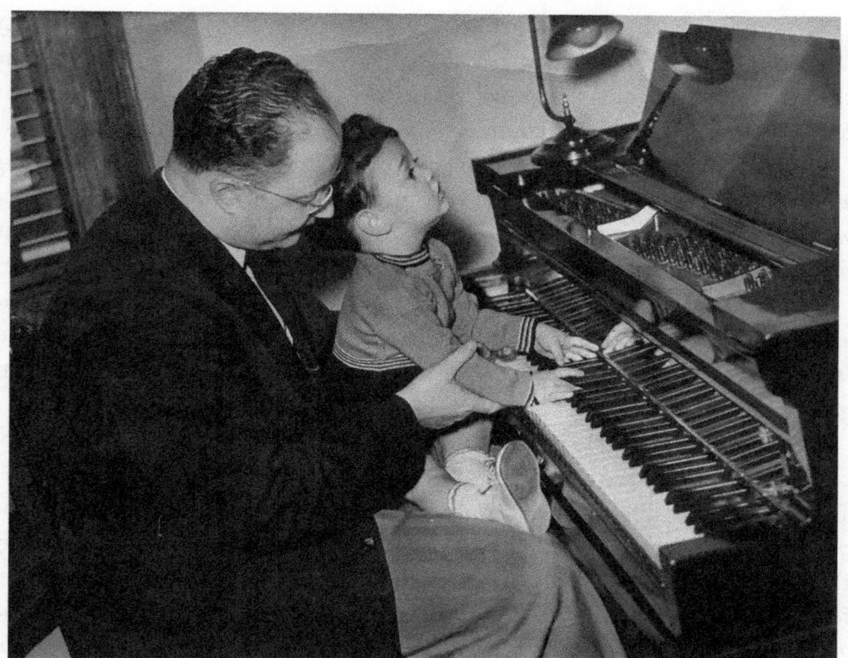

Figure 2.1. David Shire, age two, on the knee of his father, bandleader Irving Shire, presumably learning about altered chords and extended jazz harmonies.

"I had from my father a sense of structure and a really clear sense that the words had to follow the rhythm of the music," Maltby explains. "They couldn't be accented wrong or anything like that. Plus, a basic impulse that the lyrics had to sound like human speech—that was the main thing that I just had."

Maltby clarifies that attending his father's recording sessions of instrumental music influenced him as a budding lyricist:

> His genius was to do a two-and-a-half- or three-minute musical arrangement, and it was like a perfect little jigsaw puzzle, a balancing act of this theme followed by that counter-theme, and they come together at the end. He'd have an architecturally perfect structure in a three-minute musical arrangement for a band. I'd go to the session, and I got that through my skin—I just got structure in there. And somehow that related to the words doing the same thing. It was pure music, never singing, but the logic is exactly the same, and the rest I just sort of knew.[2]

One year, Maltby Sr. was the arranger for the Easter show at Radio City Music Hall. He brought young Richard (age about nine or ten) to see the changeovers that took place overnight; the last show came down at nine p.m., and there'd be a new, complete show onstage the next morning.

As Maltby remembers it, the Rockettes would rehearse onstage starting at five a.m., with a dress rehearsal at eight thirty. At nine thirty, the audience would come in for a few short subjects, followed by the movie and then the first performance of the stage show. "And they had changed it!" Maltby marvels. "They had written a new introductory scene, and it was onstage, in the show, two hours after the dress rehearsal! I didn't know you could do that. It completely blew my mind." The takeaway was that theater was a living organism, and shows could be rewritten on short notice.

Maltby's time at Yale provided many more chances to observe the process of how shows are rewritten when he served as an usher at the Shubert Theater. This enabled him not only to see all the shows for free but to be paid seven dollars a night. Broadway-bound shows would routinely play the Shubert for a week, often on their way to Boston or Philadelphia before landing in New York. During the time Maltby was ushering, *The Sound of Music*, *Fiorello!*, *A Raisin in the Sun*, and *Long Day's Journey into Night* all played at the house, in addition to the aforementioned *My Fair Lady*. Watching the same show night after night over the course of a week, Maltby got to see how it could be altered and fixed, scene by scene, song by song.

"[The shows] went out of town, and that's when all the work was done," he explains. "*My Fair Lady* had the 'Decorating Eliza Ballet,' 'Say a Prayer [for Me Tonight],' and 'Come to the Ball.' Three big numbers at the end of the first act that all disappeared and were replaced by one book scene. *Fiorello!* did not have 'Little Tin Box' in it."

Shire has an additional recollection regarding *Fiorello!*:

DS: You told me that when *Fiorello!* came in, it was kind of a disaster, but you said that each night, you saw the point that [director] George Abbott had worked up to. And he worked through the whole first act while it was in New Haven, and when they left, you said they had a hit first act and a second act which was not a hit. Then they went to Philly and finished rewrites, and it opened in New York and was a hit and won the Pulitzer Prize.

RM: I don't remember that.

DS: You told me that.

RM: I'm sure I did, and it was probably true.

Maltby went to graduate school at the Yale School of Drama essentially to finish the program he had begun as an undergraduate drama major.[3] (He was, in fact, Yale's *only* undergraduate drama major at the time.)[4] His curriculum had been equivalent to that of the graduate school's first-year program anyway—there were no actual undergraduate theater classes—so he would have been able to complete the graduate course of study in two years instead of three. He only lasted a term.

"They were forcing me to do not very much—'Give them time to write, they don't have enough time to write,'" Maltby recalls with a laugh. "As an undergraduate, I was designing scenery and doing the programs and organizing and casting and all that stuff, *and* writing. Now I just had to write plays, so of course I was bored."

Shire felt similarly out of place studying composition at Brandeis with Harold Shapero. Twelve-tone music, based on the system developed by Viennese composer Arnold Schoenberg, was the rage in classical music circles, and Shire didn't see how it was relevant to his interest in writing music for theater. As it would turn out, that compositional system would play a significant role in his later career as a film composer (see chapter 7), but for the time being, he, too, was ready to quit after one term. In Shire's words, "I went home for Christmas break that year and never went back."

They both wanted to move to New York City and get on with their careers writing musicals, but first they had to fulfill their military obligations. Enlisting for a six-month stint in the National Guard seemed like the best way (Maltby: "David and me in the Army is a hysterical movie all to itself"), and they were out before the end of the year. By October the following year, *The Sap of Life*, their first off-Broadway show, was up and running.

Maltby got the idea for *The Sap of Life* from John Cheever's debut novel, *The Wapshot Chronicle*—or, more accurately, from the back cover. "I read the back cover of the book and thought, that's a great plot for a musical, and I read the book, and it's not at all what the book is about," he recounts. "So I figured we wouldn't have to worry about getting rights if all I did was steal the back cover outline, which was not the book, somehow." As with *Grand Tour*, which had been loosely adapted from the movie *Summertime*, this proved to be true. Also appealing was the idea of doing a relatively small show—the team had recently seen *The Fantasticks*, whose legendary forty-two-year run began in 1960.

David and Richard managed to raise the $25,000 necessary for *The Sap of Life* by having backers' auditions. They first got the show on its feet at the Williamstown Theater Festival in Massachusetts in the summer of 1961, then opened it in New York a few months later on October 3, at One Sheridan

Square—an unusually quick path to an off-Broadway opening for two young writers. Already having put on *Cyrano* in New York as undergraduates provided them with some valuable industry cred. *The Sap of Life* employed several of Maltby and Shire's collaborators from the *Grand Tour* production back at Yale, including director Bill Francisco, Lewis Lloyd (one of the producers), and the ace design team of Peter Hunt (lights) and John Conklin (both sets and costumes).

The show opened to mixed reviews—no pans and no raves—although the *New York Times*'s Howard Taubman wrote, "The handling of the music is unusually ingenious and sophisticated," adding, "There are solo and group numbers of touching refinement and shining verve."[5]

The plot of *The Sap of Life* centers on Andrew Willowart, a young man who travels to the big city, aiming to gain life experience so he can add his own contribution to "The Willowart Family Song," a 157-verse-long history of the clan. Though he sets out with youthful optimism, Andrew inevitably encounters setbacks, such as an initial rejection by his dream girl and the obnoxious behavior of his boss and future father-in-law, a publisher. By the end, Andrew has learned the realities of life, largely from people who closely resemble the family he left behind.

When Taubman described the *Sap of Life* score as "ingenious and sophisticated," he was no doubt reacting to Shire's harmonic language, which is unusually rich and complex for a theater score, particularly in 1961. It's also likely that he was struck by the unusual instrumentation for two pianos and percussion. The percussion is mostly subtle—some added vibes, glock, xylophone or timpani, and a drum set on the bigger numbers—but the use of two keyboards provides dazzling torrents of music in several songs.[6] This is notably apparent in "A Charmed Life," which was later appropriated and subtly re-lyricized for *Starting Here, Starting Now* as "A New Life Coming."

The introduction to the song begins with brilliant downward piano cascades. This, as a note in the score says, is meant to be a musical representation of the Doppler effect, setting the stage for the opening lyric, which specifically refers to a train (example 2.1).

Example 2.1. "A Charmed Life"

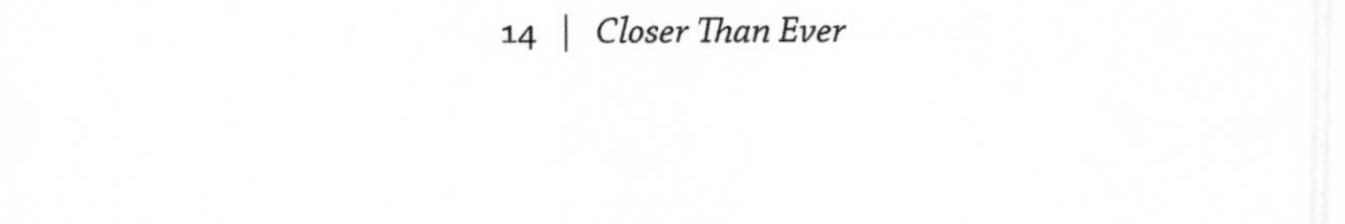

After the musical intro makes brief detours through $\frac{2}{4}$ and $\frac{9}{8}$ time, the verse begins, to a thundering, eighth-note-driven accompaniment in $\frac{6}{8}$ time that occasionally slips into $\frac{3}{4}$, creating a hemiola feel.[7] This shift in pulse first occurs on the phrase "charmed life" in the third bar of example 2.2; at that moment, the music lurches not only into that new rhythmic subdivision (evident in both the time signature and the left-hand grouping of the eighth notes) but into a new key area as well—C major, up a minor third from the home key of A major. This reinforces the feeling that we're on a rollicking journey with unlimited possibilities.

Example 2.2. "A Charmed Life"

There are plenty more rhythmic and tonal displacements to come: the third and fourth measures of example 2.3 are an unexpected transposition down a half step of the first two bars. Note that the slightly unsettling alternation between $\frac{6}{8}$ and $\frac{3}{4}$ time continues.

Example 2.3. "A Charmed Life"

I could - n't ig - nore if I tried
hear - in' those voi - ces out - side

In the section immediately following, strategically placed eighth-note rests on the downbeats of the first and third bars of example 2.4 throw the rhythm even more off-kilter than a standard hemiola does.

Example 2.4. "A Charmed Life"

Say___ in', boy,___ en - joy___ your joy - ride!

This is turning into quite a joy ride indeed, just as the lyric says. We get a further sense of the potentially exotic life barreling toward us as the verse concludes, "Bring my world to me!" The B minor seventh chord in the left hand that harmonizes the first two words slips down a half step in the third bar of example 2.5, becoming a B♭ minor seventh; the vocal melody, however, remains stubbornly on E, creating a pungent dissonance on "world" that lets us know the future, though exciting and unexpected, may also be fraught with peril.

Example 2.5. "A Charmed Life"

The Sap of Life also featured "She Loves Me Not," a beautiful number later resurrected for the 1989 revue *Closer Than Ever*. In this song, Shire shows off his skill with vocal counterpoint, as the number's unfulfilled love triangle spins out into a three-part fugue, with the voices layered in one at a time over the course of the three verses.

"Watching the Big Parade Go By," which also later found a place in *Starting Here, Starting Now*, is a great example of a song that begins decisively with a specific mood and context and by the end takes us somewhere else entirely. It starts in lively march tempo: $\frac{6}{8}$ time again, although not quite as relentlessly driving as "A Charmed Life," more like the festive feel of John Philip Sousa's "The Washington Post." Before the voice enters, there's a distant-sounding descant heard on the celeste—another deft use of hemiola—that hints at a certain wistful nostalgia.

As the verse begins, however, it sounds like the song's narrator couldn't be happier:

Beautiful balmy day,
Everyone's on display.
Marchin', marchin',
Struttin' a little and gettin' the glory 'n'
Here on the porch am I,
Watchin' the big parade go by.

He locates himself specifically in the scene, describing both the entertainers and his own unique perspective:

Look at the people go wild when
Cavalry three by three
Gives 'em a sight to see.
Doin' their drill,
Provin' their skill,
Thrillin' the fellow who's watchin' from up in a tree:
Me.

Later comes the humiliation:

Look at the people all turn and
Giggle and shout with glee
At the funniest sight you'd see.
Is it a clown
Whizzin' aroun'?
No, just some pitiful fool who fell out of a tree:
Me.

The way the embarrassed iteration of the word "Me" at the end of this verse echoes the narrator's joyful utterance of the same word at the end of the earlier one is almost unbearably sad. Shire, ever the musical dramatist, alters the harmony at the beginning of this verse, giving a harbinger of the impending grim turn of events by creating the dissonant juxtaposition of an A♭ chord over an A♮ in the bass, indicated by the brackets in example 2.6. In the previous iteration of this passage, this sonority was a perfectly cheerful major sixth chord.[8]

Example 2.6. "Watching the Big Parade Go By"

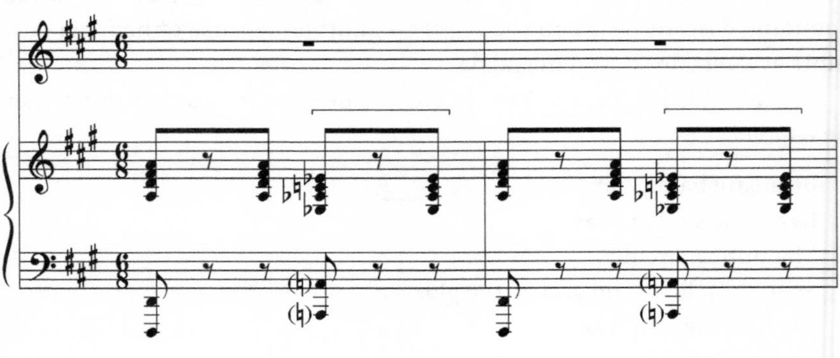

The parade is now gone; the narrator is "Hopin' to savor a faraway echo but hearin' the music die." In short, as the number concludes, there's "Always an empty sigh / Watchin' the big parade go by." The song, subtly devastating, has transitioned from contentedly cheerful to deeply melancholic. This is a perfect example of what Maltby means when he says a theater song needs to have an action.

One night early in the run, Stephen Sondheim came to see *The Sap of Life*. He came back several nights later with director/producer Harold Prince and then several nights after that with Jerome Robbins and Leonard Bernstein.[9] "They were all very impressed," Shire recalls. All of a sudden, he says, "We were the fair-haired boys."

"We were sort of picked up by that group," Maltby concurs. Around that time, they started going to dinner parties at Prince's home. At one such event, Barbara—Maltby's first wife—found herself pressed up against Paul Newman by the crowd that was jammed into the house. When the crowd eased up a moment later, Barbara remained pressed up against him. "She thought that was good enough for the rest of her life," Maltby says.

"Neither David nor I was from that kind of world," Maltby continues. "Steve grew up with Oscar Hammerstein next door and being friends with Mary Rodgers and Hal Prince right out of school. He worked in that world. It scared the shit out of me. I was never terribly comfortable there, but it was nice to be lionized."

After dinner, everybody would gather around the piano, and the composers in attendance would play recent songs. "'Travel' was kind of our big calling card," Maltby recalls. "We'd play 'Travel,' and Steve would play 'Pretty Little Picture' [from *Forum*]." Decades later, Sondheim would include "Travel" on his infamous list of "Songs I Wish I'd Written (At Least in Part)."[10]

The relationship with Sondheim would prove to be an important and lasting one.

BARBRA

Beginning in the fall of 1960, there was a buzz coming out of Bon Soir, a chic supper club in New York's Greenwich Village: a certain stylish young singer who performed there was going to be the next great recording artist. She was only nineteen years old, but if you were a composer—or a songwriting team—the word was that you should try to get a song to her. Her name was Barbra Streisand.

"She came out, and she sat on a stool," Maltby recalls. "She had a long skirt of men's suit material in wool and a satin blouse, which later became incredibly fashionable, but at the time, nobody had ever worn anything like that. And it wasn't staged at all. In those days, people did acts with dancing and everything else. She didn't play to the room, she didn't do any of the obvious things that a fledgling would do. She just sat there and sang these songs and talked. She was so sure of herself."

"She did things like 'Happy Days Are Here Again,' only as a ballad, which was really startling and wonderful," Shire adds. "And she did a lot of Harold Arlen. Right away, I thought, she's very compatible with the kind of music we write. She did offbeat things. It wasn't the standard cabaret act. It was totally fresh, and she was really weirdly wonderful, or wonderfully weird."

After the set, they went backstage to speak to her. "Bon Soir's dressing room was this infinitesimally narrow little room," Maltby remembers, "at the end of which was her clothing designer, this immensely large man, who filled it up basically wall-to-wall." At times, Streisand also shared this tiny room with comedian Phyllis Diller.

Many composers were going to Bon Soir to try to get an audience with Streisand, but Maltby and Shire had a secret weapon: Streisand's pianist, Peter Daniels, who loved Shire's music. "Peter was a really classy accompanist-pianist-arranger," Maltby says, "and he recognized how complex and harmonically interesting David's music was, so he kept putting the songs in front of Barbra." "Autumn" was one of them. Streisand gave it a spot on her

Closer Than Ever. Joshua Rosenblum, Oxford University Press. © Oxford University Press 2024.
DOI: 10.1093/oso/9780197758236.003.0003

album *People*, which came out in September 1964 and was the first Streisand record to hit number one on the Billboard 200.[1]

"Autumn," the first song the team wrote for *Cyrano*, their first completed musical, establishes its unique, melancholy mood with the first chord (example 3.1). The recurring melodic cell of a descending fourth (F to C), to which the word "autumn" is sung throughout the number, is harmonized with an A♭ dominant thirteenth chord—an unusual sonority in the home key of B♭ major, especially for the first chord of the piece. The chord's harmonic ambiguity gives the song a tonally undefined beginning, mirroring the emotionally unsettled state of the singer. In the second bar, Shire moves to a B♭ major seventh chord (with an added ninth), which establishes the home key and provides a more stable harmonization for the F-C melodic figure, but this is an unusual resolution for that opening A♭ chord.

Example 3.1. "Autumn"

As the song unfolds, the singer describes in aching terms that "although the breeze is still, I feel the chill of autumn." The sentiment is underlined by a series of plangent chords propelled by a bass line that descends by half step in bar 3 from A♭ down to F—a quiet swoon of emotion. Soon, at the end of the next phrase, the melody rises dramatically by step on the phrase "However green the hill, to me it still is autumn" (indicated by the bracket in example 3.2).

Example 3.2. "Autumn"

At the end of the soaring bridge ("I can feel the frost now"), we get symmetrical closure: a descending series of fifths in the vocal melody bookends the rising stepwise melody that earlier propelled us into the bridge (example 3.3).

Example 3.3. "Autumn"

This long musical sigh that stretches out over two measures effectively reflects the fading laughter of the lyrics. Why is this person so inconsolable? We don't find out until just after the bridge—fairly late into the song—when she informs us that "He left in autumn." Suddenly, it's clear: her heart has been broken. Thus, when we hear the bridge repeated a little later, although the words and music are the same, the song has deeper emotional meaning. The number, which remains a cabaret staple and an audition favorite, rarely fails to make a pronounced impact.

"People," the title song of the album on which "Autumn" appears, is from the Jule Styne/Bob Merrill musical *Funny Girl*, which had opened at the Winter Garden Theater in March 1964—six months prior to the release of the album—and propelled Streisand to Broadway stardom. A year into the run, Shire landed a job as pianist and assistant conductor for the show. Once again, he had Peter Daniels to thank for a career boost.

"I got the job in the pit because Peter [the show's original pit pianist] had a falling out with Barbra after their great collaboration," Shire remembers. "He fell in love with Lainie Kazan, Barbra's understudy." Kazan wanted to put together a nightclub act, and Daniels, eager to help her prepare it, took some of Streisand's arrangements and added them to Kazan's set. When Kazan performed them at a club in Queens, word got back to Streisand. "That was the end of Peter Daniels," Shire says, "and he turned the job over to me." (Kazan and Daniels got married in 1971.) In spite of the benefit to him personally, Shire regards the demise of the Streisand-Daniels relationship as unfortunate. "It was a shame, because most of the layouts for Barbra's distinctive early recordings were conceived with Peter."

Having a steady job playing on Broadway—he spent two years in the *Funny Girl* pit orchestra—was ideal for Shire during that period; it paid well and left most daylight hours free for composing. In addition, once he was playing and occasionally conducting Streisand's hit musical, Shire had contact with her nearly every day. "I went up to her dressing room one day after a matinee, and I played her some songs," he recalls. "She turned down the first two and then pointed to one on the pile on the piano and said, 'What's that?'" That song was "Starting Here, Starting Now." Shire had written it with Robert Goulet in mind, and he told Streisand that it was a man's song. Streisand nonetheless insisted on hearing it. "As soon as she heard it was intended for a man, she became interested," Shire notes.[2] "I was thinking of it as a bossa nova. I pictured [Goulet] doing it in Las Vegas. She turned it into a pop operatic number. So, strange things happen." It ended up as the closing track on *Color Me Barbra*, Streisand's seventh studio album, in 1966, as well as the dazzling finale to the TV special of the same name.

"And by the way," Shire observes, "for all the exposure that song has had, it's had practically no cover recordings." Singers Shire has approached about recording it inevitably say, "Oh, that's a Barbra song, we can't top that." "She has that way of killing the song even while she promotes it," he concludes somewhat wistfully.

Shire wrote both music and lyrics for the song "Starting Here, Starting Now," although he is careful to point out that Maltby contributed the line "For the greatest journey heaven can allow," toward the end of the song. "Reciprocal editing of and contribution to each other's work is a principal factor in the success of our collaboration," he emphasizes.

"What About Today?," for which Shire also composed both music and lyrics, is a terrific number with an inexorable build.[3] Streisand recorded it and used it as the title of her eleventh studio album in 1969.

As the song starts, the singer's emotions are very contained, as reflected by an almost one-note melody that only occasionally strays from B♭ during the song's A section (example 3.4).

Example 3.4. "What About Today?"

The tears I'm shed - ding now I hear will dry in time.
The fears I'm fear - ing now I hear will die in time.

Then it erupts. The rhythm of the accompaniment goes from smooth and legato to syncopated and driving, as the vocal line begins a stepwise ascent from E♭ to B♭, with each new downbeat landing on the next note of the scale over the course of five bars (example 3.5).

Example 3.5. "What About Today?"

This device of building excitement and/or sustaining tension through a stepwise melodic ascent is one of Shire's favorites.[4] We've just seen him put it to effective use in two very different songs, and we will continue to encounter it in subsequent analyses.

The bridge of "What About Today?" alternates stubbornly between B♭ and E♭. Despite the lack of melodic variety here, Shire generates considerable excitement with the driving groove, the punchy syncopated rhythm of the vocals, and the reharmonizations in the piano part (example 3.6).

Example 3.6. "What About Today?"

When we get to the fifth and sixth bars of the bridge, Shire quadruples the pace of oscillation between B♭ and E♭ in the melody, escalating the stakes further (example 3.7).

Example 3.7. "What About Today?"

Like "Starting Here, Starting Now," "What About Today?" was written with a different style in mind—Shire originally conceived it as a folk-rock ballad, possibly for Peter, Paul and Mary (he was, in fact, dating Mary Travers at the time). He also says it's probably the only song he's ever written to reflect a specific mood he was feeling. "I wrote it to get myself out of a depression," he explains. Did it work? "Yes, with the help of a psychoactive drug or two," he quips.[5]

Streisand's *What About Today?* album also included a relatively obscure song that Shire wrote (again, both music and lyrics) called "The Morning After"—obscure mostly because it was eclipsed a few years later by the Oscar-winning song of the same title by Al Kasha and Joel Hirschhorn from the 1972 film *The Poseidon Adventure*, subsequently made even more famous by Maureen McGovern's hit cover of the song. The Shire "Morning After" is well worth hearing, however. It was written as a response to the Detroit riot of 1968, which was brought on by the assassination of Dr. Martin Luther King, Jr. "They were burning down a city, and I wanted to write a protest song," Shire recalls. "It's the kind of thing I did in my spare time away from trying to think up ideas for musicals."

The song features an insinuating, syncopated two-bar ostinato figure that continues relentlessly throughout both verses but somehow does not become tiresome, as well as vivid imagery of a blackened sky, blood-reddened ground, and streets that are charred and dead. The chorus urges action, insisting that we not wait for the morning after, which will be too late. Streisand brings the full strength of her formidable artistry, giving credence to the idea that music can be a force for change.

Liz Callaway, who created the role of Lizzie in Maltby and Shire's 1983 Broadway musical *Baby*, rerecorded "The Morning After" in 2020, during the Covid-19 pandemic.[6] The arrangement Callaway uses (a track provided by Shire himself) isn't as souped-up as Streisand's glossy studio product, and her vocal performance, pure and mellifluous, is much more straightforward than Streisand's somewhat mannered delivery. In comparison with Streisand's rendition, Callaway's is almost self-effacing, prioritizing the message instead of the artist and letting the words land with a direct, powerful impact. Callaway's splendid new recording soberly demonstrates that Shire's 1968 protest song holds up amazingly (and alarmingly) well. The song's urgent advocacy of the need for change is, sadly, more relevant than ever, and it landed with particular potency in the immediate aftermath of the George Floyd murder and the Black Lives Matter movement.

Streisand also recorded "No More Songs for Me," which was released on her album *My Name Is Barbra, Two . . .* This song was also a Shire lyric, although Maltby again contributed a line when Shire was stuck. It's a slow, lovely waltz in F♯ minor, with a feel very similar to Shire's hit song "With You I'm Born Again," which has lyrics by Carol Connors. Of the five Maltby/Shire songs that Streisand recorded, three were given subsequent life in *Starting Here, Starting Now* ("Autumn," "What About Today?," and, of course, the title song). Callaway's reconsideration of "The Morning After" demonstrates its continuing relevance, and "No More Songs for Me" retains a pronounced poignancy and deserves renewed attention.

During the run of *Funny Girl*, in addition to trying to get more songs in front of Streisand, Shire wrote his glittering, three-movement solo *Sonata for Cocktail Piano*.[7] This intriguing, engaging work, composed in 1965 but not published until 1981, was the product of Shire's desire to "have a showpiece to play at parties when people said, 'Would you sit down and play something?' My experience was always that I'd sit down and play, and they'd start talking, and I'd become a background pianist. So I thought, when they hear *this*, they'll have to listen."

Shire's right about that—no one's attention would drift away while his *Sonata* was being performed. It's a dazzling showpiece with irresistible appeal. It brings to mind the jazz/classical crossover suites that Claude Bolling made a tremendous splash with starting in the mid-1970s, but it's worth noting that Bolling's groundbreaking *Suite for Flute and Jazz Piano* first topped the charts in 1975, whereas Shire wrote his *Sonata* ten years earlier. Apart from the autumnal *Peace Cantata* (discussed in chapter 30), written more than half a century later, the *Sonata for Cocktail Piano* remains Shire's only published concert piece not associated with a film, TV, or theater score.[8]

DEALING WITH STEVE

"You wake up in the morning, and there sits Stephen Sondheim. And anything you can think of, he's already thought of it. If you decide you want to go up this road, he's sitting in the middle of the road. If you decide you want to go up *that* road, he's sitting in the middle of that road, too." Thus spoke Maltby to a roomful of musical theater writers and performers at a Yale University master class in December 2007.

This isn't quite true anymore, but there was a long period of time when it certainly seemed that way. The hero worship of Sondheim in theater circles was perhaps most famously epitomized by a widely read *New York* magazine article by James Kaplan in the April 4, 1994, issue, titled "Is Stephen Sondheim God?"[1] The context for Kaplan's article was a press preview for the Sondheim/James Lapine musical *Passion* in a rehearsal studio on lower Broadway. Kaplan wrote, quite persuasively:

> A notoriously cool customer, [Sondheim] is equally fabled for the solitude of his personal life and for the mordant, magisterial precision he has brought to the Broadway show tune. He reinvented the form, daring to bring high art to the Great White Way, challenging the audience that stayed with him and scattering the rest quite mercilessly in his wake.
>
> Thus the awe in the room. For the writers, for the actors, Stephen Sondheim stands like a solitary colossus, pitilessly overlooking the arid landscape that is the modern musical theater: a desert of campy revivals; over-priced, whiz-bang, middlebrow extravaganzas; and forlorn postromantic experiments. . . . The engine of Sondheim's mystique is that to theater people—who worship sophistication; who live (or like to think they live) a kind of heightened existence, at once cynical and fervid, with a special language and an incestuous social network—he is a god.[2]

Closer Than Ever. Joshua Rosenblum, Oxford University Press. © Oxford University Press 2024.
DOI: 10.1093/oso/9780197758236.003.0004

Sondheim had a chance to publicly acknowledge this article sixteen years later, when Lapine asked him to come up with a new opening number for Act II of the 2010 Broadway revue *Sondheim on Sondheim*. The number, titled simply "God," was a sendup of Kaplan's take on Sondheim's own unique celebrity. The opening lyrics went like this:

God.
I mean the man's a god.
Wrote the score to *Sweeney Todd*,
With a nod
To de Sade—
Well, he's odd.
Well, he's God![3]

Of course, back in the early '60s, when Maltby and Shire first became friendly with him, Sondheim wasn't God yet. He'd had two huge successes as the lyricist of both *West Side Story* and *Gypsy*, but nobody regarded him as a composer. As Shire describes it, even after *A Funny Thing Happened on the Way to the Forum* (1962), the first Broadway show for which Sondheim contributed both music and lyrics, "People thought, 'He's a lyricist who's trying to be a composer,' when he always thought of himself as a composer who was writing his own lyrics."

The success of *Forum* actually involved considerable disappointment for Sondheim. Although the show won six Tony Awards, including for Best Musical, it was not even nominated in the Best Score category.[4] And as Meryle Secrest recounts in her impressively exhaustive biography *Stephen Sondheim: A Life*, none of his colleagues thanked Sondheim when they accepted their awards, not producer Hal Prince, director George Abbott, or co-librettists Larry Gelbart and Burt Shevelove. Secrest quotes Sondheim as saying, "Nobody mentioned me on the [Tony] program at all. As far as they were all concerned, my friends, my colleagues, I didn't exist. That's what really hurt." Flora Roberts, Sondheim's agent at the time, put it more bluntly: "Steve was so unhappy he wanted to kill himself."[5]

During that period and earlier, a mutual admiration society was forming between the Maltby/Shire team and Sondheim. "We used to spend a good deal of time together in the sixties," Maltby recalls. "We'd play our songs, and he'd play his songs."

"The first time I heard the score to *Forum* was when he sat at the piano and played it for us," Shire remembers. "I thought it was just wonderful." Shire continues, "He's very generous with other composers but very critical. He does not mince words by saying, 'I think that's pretty good.' He says, 'This doesn't work because of that.' Sometimes it's tough to hear that when you think you've taken him a masterpiece."

As Maltby recalls it, Sondheim and Shire mostly talked about music and left him out. But Maltby, too, was occasionally on the receiving end of Sondheim's critical eye:

> Every now and then, [Sondheim] would say, "I think that line could be more like that, could go into that world." And I would jot that down and go running home and try to write it. This happened numerous times, but I was never able to use a single suggestion that came from him. I really tried, and I thought it was because I just wasn't as good as he was. It was only years later I realized that our sensibilities are so different, his thought that a line could go *there* was something I didn't even understand. It was about that time that I realized I would never be able to out-Sondheim Sondheim.

Maltby cites the song "I'm a Little Bit Off"—originally written for an unfinished musical the writers refer to as "the John Reed show" (see chapter 6) and later resurrected for *Starting Here, Starting Now*—as a specific example of how he learned that lesson:

> "I'm a Little Bit Off" is a very intricately rhymed song as it is, and [the first version] had twice as many rhymes in it, so much so that it was almost impenetrable. I mean, you were so distracted by the elaborate wordplay that you couldn't understand what was going on. So I took half of the rhymes out to make it simpler to understand, and that was when I realized that although I would never be able to out-Steve Steve, there was only one thing that I was that he would never be, and that is he would never be me. He would never have the thoughts I have. That's all—no value or judgment attached to it. Just so long as I stayed with things I thought of, I'd be OK. And every writer has to go through that moment: what I have to offer is enough.

In light of this, it's instructive to compare the original "A Little Bit Off" lyrics to the final, revised version. The song, as seen in Maltby's original typewritten manuscript (figure 4.1), used to begin like this:

> I'm a little bit off
> I'm a little bit loose
> You've got me bedeviled, disheveled, diffuse
> I feel a little bit drunk
> Suddenly weak

I'm limp and unstable, unable to speak

Note the internal rhymes "bedeviled/disheveled" and "unstable/unable." These disappeared in the rewritten version:

I'm a little bit off,
I'm a little bit shot.
I am falling in love and I wish I were not.
I feel a little bit warm,
Suddenly weak.
I would like to say, "stop," but I find I can't speak.

Fewer internal rhymes, and possibly more clarity—at least in this opening verse. It's worth noting, however, that in another place, Maltby actually *added* an extra rhyming syllable in the song's final version: "I feel boozy and woozy and out of control" in the original became "I am boozy and woozy and *losing* control" in the rewrite. Apparently, the desire to out-Sondheim Sondheim is not so easily abandoned, despite Maltby's own statements on that subject.

MABEL
(sings)
I'M A LITTLE BIT OFF
I'M A LITTLE BIT LOOSE
YOU'VE GOT ME BEDEVILED, DISHEVELED, DIFFUSE
I FEEL A LITTLE BIT DRUNK
SUDDENLY WEAK
I'M LIMP AND UNSTABLE, UNABLE TO SPEAK
A BEAUTIFUL DAM I HAD BUILT IS ABOUT TO BREAK THROUGH
KNOWING IT'S GOING TO HAPPEN WITH YOU
SETS ME A LITTLE ON EDGE
A LITTLE ON FIRE
A LITTLE BIT OFF

(SHE is using the words, the flow of the song, to keep herself away from REED, whose onslaught is inexorable.)

YOU'RE A LITTLE TOO FAST
I'M A LITTLE NON-PLUSSED
I'VE LOST REASON AND RHYME, I NEED TIME TO ADJUST
FOR YOU'RE A LITTLE TOO CLOSE
AND I'M TOO UPSET
WE WANT TO GET WET, BUT NOT YET, OH NOT YET
I WANT AN EXPLOSION SO GREAT THIS DULL WORLD WILL BE GONE
LET'S KEEP THE RELEASE COMING ON
AND THEN IN ONE BLAST
I'LL GO TEARFULLY, CHEERFULLY OFF.

Figure 4.1. "I'm a Little Bit Off," original typewritten draft

Sondheim may have been critical, but he also clearly admired Maltby and Shire's work. (He had, after all, returned to see *The Sap of Life* two additional times, with different eminent friends in tow.) "He really appreciates what David does," Maltby maintains. Maltby even claims there are certain passages in Sondheim where one can hear chord progressions he borrowed from Shire.[6] Shire demurs on this topic: "I don't know if he was ever directly influenced by me."

In general, Shire's and Sondheim's respective harmonic languages, though they share the qualities of musical sophistication and originality, are largely distinct. As for Sondheim's influence on Shire's work, Shire says, "I had all his scores, and I used to play through them, and sometimes my first attempts were clearly too close to Steve. But when I let myself speak, it sounded like Maltby and Shire." Even though, as Broadway composer Scott Frankel once quipped, "Anytime you use anything more complicated than a seventh chord, people accuse you of imitating Sondheim,"[7] the fact is that Shire was fully formed as a composer with a distinctive voice before he had a chance to be musically influenced by Sondheim. According to Maltby, "Steve was not writing things that we even would have been imitating until the seventies, starting with *Company* [1970]." By that time, Maltby and Shire had already written five musicals together, not including the unfinished or abandoned ones.

The influence question, however, runs deeper than merely the possible appropriation of particular chord progressions. Sondheim's expansion of traditional song-form structures—to the point where a single number could encompass an extended multipart musical scene—resulted in such wonders as "A Weekend in the Country" from *A Little Night Music*, "Waiting for the Girls Upstairs" from *Follies*, and the "Putting It Together" sequence from *Sunday in the Park with George*. Most impressive of all, however, and essentially in a category by itself, is "Please Hello" from *Pacific Overtures*.

The song introduces, in succession, five separate "admirals," each of a different nationality, all of whom are eager to establish formal trading arrangements with Japan in the show's mid-nineteenth-century setting, now that the Americans have made inroads. Sondheim casts each admiral in a distinctive, culturally appropriate, and instantly recognizable musical style that humorously and effectively pegs each one to his country of origin: the American sings in the style of a rousing Sousa march in $\frac{6}{8}$ time; the Englishman sings a Gilbert and Sullivan parody (hewing closely to the structure and meter of "The Major General's Song" from *The Pirates of Penzance*). The Dutchman's music, perhaps less recognizable but equally distinctive, resembles the idiom of a Dutch "clog dance," a cheerful number in $\frac{3}{4}$ time. (His lyrics mention the chocolate, tulips, and wooden shoes that will be traded, in case the musical reference isn't enough of a signifier.) The Russian's verse is a somber, slightly menacing two-step, reminiscent of the halting, then accelerating pace of Reinhold Glière's "Russian Sailor's Dance." Finally, the Frenchman sings a bright ditty that recalls the ubiquitous cancan from Jacques Offenbach's *Orpheus in the Underworld*.

Merely listing these stylistic references doesn't begin to do justice to the singular brilliance of "Please Hello"; every verse is packed with Sondheimian wit, dense internal rhyming, and sharp, humorous characterization, not to mention plenty of compositional originality that somehow coexists with the entertaining musical pastiche. And over the course of the number, the admirals sing in various combinations with one another (and with Abe, the clearly unenthusiastic shogun), then all at once in counterpoint before joining in unison for the concluding verse, sung to the Frenchman's invigorating tune. It's an astonishing and unforgettable sequence. As we will see in subsequent chapters, "Please Hello" has been an enduring, if not always conscious, model for Maltby and Shire, in standout numbers from both *Baby* ("The Ladies Singin' Their Song") and *Take Flight* ("Back of the Line").

Those shows, however, were far off in the future when Sondheim called on Shire in 1970 during one particular hour of need. In Shire's words:

> I did the Donna McKechnie dance number in *Company*,[8] and that was because Wally Harper, who did the rest of the dance music, when it came to that one, they felt it didn't sound like it was part of Steve's score, so they called me in, just as I was about to get married two days later to Talia [Shire, his first wife].[9] I said, "But I'm about to get married and go on a honeymoon." He says, "Well, you'll have your honeymoon in Boston! You'll be at the Ritz! It'll just be wonderful." So I dragged Talia to Boston, and she got bronchitis right away and was in our hotel room, sneezing and coughing and feeling terrible for several days while I was locked up with Jonathan Tunick and [choreographer] Michael Bennett, writing this piece which was all based on Steve's themes, but we turned it into something like a concert piece that had real compositional integrity. It did sound like Steve, so Steve knew how influenced I was by him, but I was kind of surprised to hear that it went the other way, too.

As a side note, Shire claims Prince and Sondheim told him that he (Shire) was one of the models for Bobby in *Company*. According to *The Sondheim Encyclopedia*, librettist George Furth used actor Warren Beatty as an inspiration when he envisioned the role of Bobby.[10] This does not preclude the possibility that the show's creators also thought of Shire as the show developed.

DS: When I came up there [to Boston], they said, "It's kind of ironic you're coming up here as a married man, because you were one of our models for Bobby." I was the guy in my late twenties, early thirties that Judy and Hal were always trying to fix up with a friend. Judy fixed me up with Mary Travers. I was also fixed up once with Gloria Steinem, but I never seemed to get involved. They thought it was really amazing that [someone they thought of as] a Bobby came up there and was married.

Joshua Rosenblum: Who said that you were a model for Bobby?

DS: Either Steve or Hal; somebody definitely said it because I've always been very proud of that. No one knows it, but it's an interesting story. I also heard from somebody else that Steve said it.

RM: Now I'm insulted! They never tried to fix me up with anybody!

One year in the late '70s, Maltby—on Sondheim's recommendation—taught a musical theater writing class at New York University, as part of the playwriting program. It was the first-ever musical comedy class at the university. The students went up to Maltby's apartment, sat on the floor, and had two-hour sessions.

In the '80s, NYU instituted a full course of study devoted to musical theater, which endures today as the Tisch Graduate Musical Theater Writing Program. It was a two-year cycle, and the first class graduated in 1983. "Arthur Laurents set up the curriculum and taught it for the first cycle," Maltby explains. By year three, when it was time to start the second series, Laurents was overwhelmed by the job and asked Maltby if he wanted to split the program. Maltby agreed. "Then, a month into the beginning of that series, [Laurents] had a big fight with whoever was the head of the program and quit," Maltby says. "So suddenly, I was teaching the whole program. I didn't know the curriculum—I didn't know anything about it at all."

Maltby did, however, notice that all the students were trying to write like Sondheim. "Everybody was imitating Steve's vamps, imitating Steve's line readings, his melody structures," he recounts. "There's less of that going on now, but at that time, anybody who was anybody as a young writer was imitating Steve. So I decided to have one class period that was called 'Dealing with Steve.' I actually taught a whole class on it."

The primary lesson for the students was the same one Maltby had learned for himself with "I'm a Little Bit Off." As he put it to the class, in language similar to his own epiphany, "There's only one thing that you are that Steve is not, and that is you. And if you follow your own instincts for what is structure, your own vision of what makes it interesting, it will be unique."

The irony of it is that Sondheim co-opted even that very theme of artistic individuality, in a lyric from the song "Move On," the penultimate number of *Sunday in the Park with George*. "'Anything you do, let it come from you, then it will be new,'" Maltby quotes. "That's in *Sunday*. So eventually, he even wrote *that* as well!"

Back in the early '60s, Sondheim had helped kickstart Maltby and Shire's career by getting them a New York publisher and a New York agent. At the time, the team was signed with Larry Shayne, Henry Mancini's publisher, who had let them stay in his Palm Springs home postgraduation during the long hot summer of 1959. The LA-based Shayne, however, had no connection with New York theater. Sondheim, accordingly, introduced Maltby and Shire to Flora Roberts, his powerful agent, and to Chappell & Co. (now Warner Chappell Music), his publisher. They signed with both.

Ironically, signing with a New York publisher is what first enabled Maltby and Shire to get a song placed in a Hollywood movie.

"That was a time when the film companies would call Chappell, who had all the writers, and say, 'We're making a movie. It's gonna star these people, and it's about this, and we're looking for songs,'" Maltby recounts. In this case, the film was a Universal picture called *I'd Rather Be Rich,* starring Robert Goulet, Sandra Dee, and Andy Williams, and the studio wanted a title song. The team wrote one, and Universal used it. Maltby and Shire subsequently had the startling experience of walking into a movie theater in August 1964 to see the film and watching Goulet and Williams perform their song on-screen over the opening credits.[11] The appealingly swinging number sets a perfect, breezy, insouciant tone for the romantic comedy. (For good measure, Dee sashays across the screen in the first fifteen seconds as the instrumental intro plays.)

A seemingly unrelated aspect of Maltby's creative life also has unexpected Sondheimian influence. ("All roads lead to Stephen Sondheim," he reiterates.) Maltby is revered among crossword mavens for the cryptic puzzles he has been creating for *Harper's* magazine since 1976. This, too, was indirectly the result of a Sondheim referral. "Steve introduced cryptic puzzles to America," Maltby explains. "The British ones. They're very esoteric. Nobody knew what they were."

Cryptics have long appeared as a feature in *The Times* of London, although Sondheim first discovered them in a now-defunct weekly British magazine called *The Listener*. Sondheim and Leonard Bernstein used to love trying to complete them competitively.[12] When *New York* magazine started publishing in April 1968, Sondheim created a cryptic for the first issue, along with a long article that explained what they were and how to solve them. For the rest of the year, Sondheim provided a cryptic puzzle for nearly every weekly issue of *New York*. By 1969, it was getting to be too relentless, and he cut it back to every third week. Sondheim recruited his friend Mary Ann Madden to create word games that would fill in the missing weeks. (Madden continued to challenge readers with her highly popular *New York* Magazine Competition until she retired in 2000.) Then, when the original Broadway production of *Company* went into rehearsal, Sondheim felt he needed to stop doing the cryptics altogether.

"By then, I was addicted to the puzzles," Maltby recounts, "and I said to Steve, 'I can't imagine that they aren't gonna appear. Could I take over doing them?,' because I'd done a couple of guest puzzles for him, and he said sure, so I went in and met [*New York* cofounder and editor] Clay Felker, who didn't know what to make of me, but he said sure, so I started doing them."[13]

Maltby created cryptics for *New York* magazine for several years but then stopped. "Even one every three weeks was a lot," he recalls. Then, in 1976, *Harper's* magazine editor Lewis Lapham asked him if he would contribute cryptics for that publication. Since *Harper's* is a monthly, it was a slightly less demanding schedule, and Maltby signed on. He continues to make cryptics for *Harper's* to this day. On that subject, Shire quips, "If Richard had never gotten so involved with turning out those cryptic puzzles, I think we might have written another half dozen shows."

The close relationship with Sondheim endured to the end of his life, along with a certain amount of awe. This was reflected as recently as 2019. Maltby and Shire had the opportunity to revisit *The Sap of Life* when students at Virginia Tech University put on a concert version of the show. Maltby recalls it like this:

> After the show was done in Virginia, I thought, good Lord. This show was [originally] done in 1961, right? It must have been breathtaking. Nobody was writing this kind of music. I mean, show music was Jule Styne, Frank Loesser and Rodgers and Hammerstein. No one was writing with this sort of flashiness.
>
> So I wrote Steve a note saying I recently had the occasion to listen to [*The Sap of Life*], and I thought the writing had three or four nice lyrics in it, like "Watching the Big Parade Go By," but mostly it's sort of filler and not terribly good. But I thought the score was breathtaking, and I asked [Sondheim] if that was what his reaction was. I said it must

have been just astonishing to hear that score in 1961. Was that why he kept coming back? He wrote back, "You're right. I was knocked out by David's score, but I left the theater murmuring the lyrics." And he quoted one: "'While plucking the plums from the tree, flip a few pits back to me'—a line which occurs to me about once a week," he said, And I thought, Steve Sondheim remembers a lyric from *The Sap of Life* sixty years later?

Sondheim passed away on November 26, 2021, at the age of ninety-one, amid an outpouring of grief that, at least in New York City, seemed unparalleled in recent memory. Among other tributes, hordes of Broadway denizens, including the full casts of the currently running shows, turned out in Times Square for a special performance of the song "Sunday" from *Sunday in the Park with George* in a pre-matinee gathering on November 28.

Adulatory encomiums poured in from all quarters; the reverential Sondheim obit in the *New York Times* began above the fold on the front page. Although he hadn't had a new work on Broadway since *Passion* in 1994, Sondheim's lifetime body of work and undisputed status as a giant of the art form spoke for themselves.[14] At the time of his death, *Company* was enjoying a hugely successful revival (with Katrina Lenk starring in the gender-reversed leading role of Bobbie), and *Assassins* was in the middle of a well-received run off-Broadway. Six months later, a revival of *Into the Woods* would open on Broadway for a limited run and prove to be a smash hit that was repeatedly extended. By 2023, successful revivals of *Sweeney Todd* and *Merrily We Roll Along* were running as well.

If Sondheim's work seemed more appreciated than ever at the time of his death, his influence on the young generation of musical theater writers has waned. He no longer seems so firmly planted in the middle of the road, as Maltby once described him. "Back then, he bestrode the world like a colossus," Maltby reflects. "Nowadays they probably all want to write like Lin-Manuel [Miranda]."

Upon Sondheim's passing, music critic Tim Page noted that the last time New Yorkers had mourned collectively to such a degree was for John Lennon in 1980.[15] Maltby's response: "John Lennon lived in New York, but Steve *was* New York."

I HAVE A RICH WIFE

LOVE MATCH

After the off-Broadway run of *The Sap of Life* in 1961, Maltby and Shire turned their attention to writing a musical based on the 1946 book *The River* by English author Rumer Godden. Loosely based on Godden's childhood in India, the book had also been made into a prestigious movie by Jean Renoir. Henry Guettel, then head of Music Theater of Lincoln Center, was starting a new initiative to present the work of young musical theater writers. He was interested in Maltby and Shire's adaptation of *The River* and wanted it to be one of the first shows for his new program. The team, however, did not have the rights yet, so they contacted Godden, who came to New York to hear the score.

"She was sort of against it, but then she heard the songs and thought they were really quite interesting," Maltby recounts. "Then she decided that the book needed to be better." Godden eventually said they could have the rights if they got an English writer for the book instead of Maltby. For a time, it seemed like Peter Shaffer was interested. Maltby and Shire had met Shaffer through Stephen Sondheim, who was close to Shaffer's brother Anthony, author of the play and film *Sleuth*.[1] According to Shire, they went to England to play the score for Shaffer, and he seemed interested. In the end, however, he declined.

As Shire recalls, "It was either his schedule, or I suspect he decided he just didn't want to do it." The word from Lincoln Center was that unless they could get a writer of Shaffer's stature to work on the show, they couldn't move forward with it. "I didn't know another writer of the stature of Peter Shaffer, and so therefore the show did not get written," Maltby concludes. "It would've changed our lives if we had done it."

"It was a major disappointment," Shire concurs.

Closer Than Ever. Joshua Rosenblum, Oxford University Press. © Oxford University Press 2024.
DOI: 10.1093/oso/9780197758236.003.0005

The team happened into their next project unexpectedly, via Michael Stewart, the renowned librettist. By the mid-1960s, Stewart had already been represented on Broadway by *Bye Bye Birdie*, *Carnival!*, and *Hello, Dolly!* (Still to come for him were the books to the musicals *Mack and Mabel*, *I Love My Wife*, *Barnum*, and *42nd Street*). Around this time, he had the idea for a show about a woman searching for a husband who finds a man through a computer dating program. Stewart had taken the concept first to Sondheim, who declined the offer but referred Stewart to Maltby and Shire. As it happened, the team had requested a meeting with Stewart to discuss a project of their own, a show called *You're What's Happening, Baby* ("Terrible title," Maltby laments). The numbers were all sung about or sung to the main character—a young woman trying to maneuver her way through New York—who never speaks herself. Many colleagues were encouraging; Jule Styne was interested in producing it. He had sent Maltby and Shire to LA to meet Peter Stone as a potential book writer, but Stone passed on it.[2] Stewart passed on it as well but asked the songwriters if they were interested in his computer dating concept. Thus, the three ended up working together on what became *How Do You Do, I Love You*.

Computer dating in the 1960s? It sounds way ahead of its time. "She got a job at an insurance company," Maltby explains, "which had a gigantic computer—one of those early ones that filled an entire room—and it had a big database of unmarried men. It was second-rate *Bells Are Ringing* kind of scriptwriting." The songwriters had an original concept, however: this would be the first musical to use rock and roll or contemporary pop as its primary musical language.

"This was the mid-sixties," Maltby elaborates. "There were musicals that had rock songs or pop songs, but they were always treated like a foreign country. Like we'd go to a club and hear a rock song. So we thought, wouldn't it be interesting if rock music were the natural vocabulary of the characters?"

Under the aegis of producers Lee Guber and Shelly Gross, *How Do You Do, I Love You* (*HDYDILY*) received performances at the Shady Grove (Maryland), Painters Mill (Maryland), Valley Forge (Pennsylvania), and Westbury (Long Island, New York) Music Fairs—venues known then as "music tents"—in October and November 1967. It's interesting to note that *Hair*, usually considered the first rock musical, debuted at exactly the same time off-Broadway at Joseph Papp's Public Theater, on October 17, 1967. (*Hair*'s transfer to Broadway took place in April 1968.) As a point of reference, *Jesus Christ Superstar*, innovatively billed as a "rock opera," wouldn't appear until 1970.

HDYDILY starred Phyllis Newman, who had won a Tony Award in 1961 for her performance in *Subways Are for Sleeping* (beating out Barbra Streisand in *I Can Get It for You Wholesale*). Newman, who would go on to rack up numerous Broadway and television roles and found the Phyllis Newman Women's Health Initiative in 1995, was married to fabled lyricist, librettist, and screenwriter Adolph Green for forty-two years until his death in 2002. Shire remembers that Green would attend rehearsals and sit in the house. "He was usually asleep," Shire reminisces, "but still—there was Adolph Green at our rehearsals!"

The *HDYDILY* company also included Loni Ackerman, who would go on to become one of the three original cast members of *Starting Here, Starting Now*.

There's no cast album of *HDYDILY*, but five songs from a bootleg recording of one of the Westbury performances can be heard on YouTube. The show's go-go, pop/rock sound seems, paradoxically, both outmoded and fresh today. The sexist assumption, however—that a woman's primary goal is to find a husband—was awkward even then, according to Maltby. "It was the same as all those forties and fifties premises that the only thing that matters for a woman is that she gets married, and the songs kind of bear that out. I don't think anybody would even understand it today."

Nonetheless, three songs from *HDYDILY* were successfully resurrected for *Starting Here, Starting Now*, including "Just Across the River." The song, which opens with the lyric "There's a big wide nuptial world just waiting for me," was rewritten for all three characters in the revue version, and one entire verse goes to the man ("And a partnership with a wife, yes I start the trip of my life"). With two genders searching for partners instead of one, the sexism issue is bypassed.

The musical style of the *Starting Here, Starting Now* adaptation of the song is slightly different as well. The original "Just Across the River" has a cheerful, quasi-Motown groove, with electric guitar, early synthesizer sounds (like rock organ), aggressive backbeats, and "yeah, yeah" girl-group backup vocals. There's also a rip-roaring dance break. By contrast, the *Starting Here, Starting Now* version is a decidedly '70s update—more sedate and contemplative, at least to start out, with a light bossa nova pulse as opposed to the rowdier '60's beat. The vocal arrangements, however, become more elaborate and overlap more intricately as the song proceeds, with the excitement building commensurately. And as a bonus, the man sings the melody from the title song, "Starting Here, Starting Now," toward the end as the women are holding the final note—a deft bit of counterpoint that adds some continuity to the show. (That, obviously, was not part of the number in *HDYDILY*.) It's a remarkably infectious song in both the original version and its update.

Also extracted from *HDYDILY* for *Starting Here, Starting Now* was "One Step," an equally irresistible number about moving gradually toward self-confidence that ends with a kick-line feel and ideally includes a top hat and cane in the last verse. As adapted for *Starting Here, Starting Now*, it memorably turns into (as described in chapter 1) "one of those songs with two parts where both of them go together"—that is, a quodlibet.

"I was with Ethel Martin, the choreographer," Maltby recalls, "and I had this idea that it needed some other thing to turn it into something more, and she said, 'Well, just do it,' and out came that patter."

Strictly speaking, "One Step" is a bit of a cheat in terms of the musical legerdemain involved with a standard quodlibet. The second part isn't really a melody—it's spoken patter, starting with the line "It was one of those days I spend in a haze, I mean, I was just moping around." So we don't really get the subsequent gratification of two melodies interweaving in counterpoint, as we do in, say, "Lounging at the Waldorf" from *Ain't Misbehavin'* (more on that one later), since only one of them is an actual melody. But this is nitpicking—the second-verse patter is loads of fun, and it's definitely a moment of peak entertainment when the two parts come together as promised, in the last verse.

Even in its original version in *HDYDILY* with only the first part—no patter section, no climactic juxtaposition of the two verses—"One Step" was still a standout number. That turned out to be a problem. The authors recall it like this:

RM: So we learned some things. "One Step" was a big showstopper, sort of our "Hello, Dolly!" number. We had written it for a secondary character. Never write a showstopper for a secondary character when your star is waiting in the wings and has to walk into their applause. Phyllis Newman was a nice person, but she could not bear walking into the applause of someone else's number.

DS: She was lovely—so sweet and easy to work with. The only time I remember she really bristled was when she said, "Listen, guys, never ever do that again. Never have the star walk in—"

RM: David, she did more than bristle. She exploded. She called Mike Stewart—it really got to her. Performers have this dark place where they sometimes go to, where their deep ambition suddenly gets unmasked or put under a microscope, and she couldn't stand it. Mike came out and said, "There was, like, foam coming out of her mouth."

DS: I didn't see that.

RM: No, I don't think you did.

DS: But we stayed good friends after that forever.

"One Step" also contains the notably charming triple rhyme "When did / My world become splendid? / Unhappiness ended / the moment I flew."

"Pleased with Myself," the third song adapted for use in *Starting Here, Starting Now*, begins with a catchy honky-tonk beat in the piano. As a lyric a bit later in the song puts it, "Somewhere God's rhythm section's startin' to go." This number is not among the *HDYDILY* excerpts available on YouTube, but in the bridge, you can hear the "My Guy"-esque Motown groove that would have made the song right at home as part of the *HDYDILY* score. "Don't it make you wanna sing and dance and shout and bounce right off of the walls?" the last verse asks. This is a very bold statement to make in the middle of your own song. The words, of course, refer to what it feels like to fall in love, but if a lyricist says something like that in a number, it's essential to deliver the goods musically. A quick listen to (or revisit of) this song on the *Starting Here, Starting Now* original cast recording will confirm how thoroughly it does just that.

Despite the slew of fun songs, the *HDYDILY* reviews were not good. Maltby recalls it this way:

> Talk about our prototypical moment. We opened in Gaithersburg, Maryland [at the Shady Grove Music Fair]. It was a small town, and there was a local newspaper. It was the only newspaper that was going to have a review, and we knew the paper came out about a week after we opened. We were looking through it, and we couldn't find the review anywhere, and David said, "Oh, here it is!" and the headline was "Goodbye, I Hate You." And I thought, you know what, this is kind of good, because if the first professional review you ever get is "Goodbye, I Hate You," and you get up the next day and go back to work, they can never hurt you again.

Even so, the show attracted a fair amount of attention. It turned out to be a very good showcase for orchestrator Jonathan Tunick, for whom *HDYDILY* was an early professional credit. Tunick's brassy, driving, coloristically inventive, and thoroughly idiomatic arrangements for the show appealed to both Burt Bacharach (who hired him for *Promises, Promises*) and Sondheim, each of whom came to see the production. As Shire puts it:

> I remember one night, [Sondheim] called, and he was making the decision about who was going to orchestrate *Company*, and he said it was between Don Walker and Jonathan. "Should I take a chance with Jonathan?" he wanted to know. Don Walker had orchestrated *Anyone Can Whistle*, which I was one of the rehearsal pianists on. I lived through

that whole show. And I was present when numbers were given to Don, so I saw what was happening, and to cut to the chase, Don, as much as I thought he was a fabulous orchestrator—his orchestrations for [Frank Loesser's] *The Most Happy Fella* are as good as it gets—but he did what I think almost any orchestrator would have done with Steve's music at the time, because it looked so thin. It was different from other Broadway music. He [Walker] did not appreciate the transparency, and so he thickened everything. He doubled lots of things. With *Anyone Can Whistle*, a lot of it doesn't sound as much like Steve's music as when Jonathan or Michael Starobin orchestrates it. My music is similar to Steve's in that sense, and since I had worked with Jonathan, I knew he could take pianistic music and make it sound orchestral. So I said go with Jonathan, and that began their whole relationship.

Shire concludes, with typical modesty, "That someday may register as my biggest contribution to musical theater history."

Maltby's take: "We got all excited that Hal Prince and Stephen Sondheim came down to see our show, and they hired Jonathan Tunick. David Merrick and Burt Bacharach came down to see our show, and *they* hired Jonathan Tunick and Artie Rubinstein, our musical director.[3] We thought maybe Merrick was out there because he was interested in the show. Turned out he was not."

HDYDILY may have ended in disappointment, but Maltby and Shire's next project seemed like a shoo-in for Broadway. They were approached by Ivor David Balding,[4] a theater producer who had founded his own off-Broadway company and had produced a Broadway play called *A Hand Is on the Gate* by actor Roscoe Lee Browne. Balding was producing a musical about Queen Victoria and Prince Albert and how they met when they were young. Much of the show was written, but Balding wasn't happy with the score. Maltby and Shire were asked to come in and write a few additional numbers, for about a thousand dollars per song.

"At the time, it seemed like we had hit the f***ing jackpot," Shire marvels. The show was called *Love Match*, and from all appearances, it was financed and headed for a New York production. "So," Shire continues, "we thought, we'll get a few numbers in a Broadway show, and that will help push us along."

They wrote a couple of songs; the producers loved what they heard and asked for more. Before too long, Maltby and Shire were asked to take over the writing of the entire score. "So even though it was a subject we would never choose in our wildest dreams, we thought, well, it's a Broadway show, and

Patricia Routledge, who was an English star, was playing the lead, and Larry Guittard was Albert, so we thought, OK, we'll do it, we can make something of this."[5] Neither the producers nor the songwriters were deterred by the fact that Broadway composer Charles Strouse was concurrently writing another show on the same subject, which was scheduled for a Broadway opening at about the same time.[6]

Love Match had a book by Christian Hamilton, a playwright and university drama teacher who had submitted the work to Balding as a play. It was Balding's idea to make it into a musical. "I think [Hamilton] kind of semi-reluctantly agreed that, OK, we'll make it a musical and stick some songs in it and at least get it on," Shire speculates. But it wasn't a happy collaborative marriage. Shire relates one particularly memorable moment:

> At one point, they asked us to write a new number, and we agreed that it would be a good idea, and as we were leaving the meeting, Richard said to Christian Hamilton, "You know, you'll have to revise the scene to lead into this number because it won't quite fit into the setup that's in the existing scene," and he said, "No, I don't have to." And Richard said, "What do you mean?" He said, "I don't have to." And Richard said, "Well, why not?" and he said, "Because I have a rich wife."[7]

This, of course, is an extreme example of poor collaboration, but it serves to underline the potential pitfalls in any creative working relationship. "Musicals fail when not everybody is writing the same show, so to speak," Shire explains. "They may not even realize they have different ideas about it, because musicals are so complicated. It's such a collaborative medium that unless everybody's on the same page, eventually there's going to be dissension, and then the show doesn't work."

Integrating the book scenes and the songs is an exquisite balancing act in any musical. The scenes need to set up the songs without making them redundant. The songs need to further the action and develop the characters; if they don't tell us anything new, they will land with a thud. This means that if a song is added to a scene, it might require that the scene be trimmed, reconceived, or even eliminated. It's also possible that it's the wrong song for the moment, but either way, the relationship between the book and the score of a musical is a delicate one that needs careful nurturing from all the creative participants. Since it's a musical and not a "bookical," as one colleague used to quip, priority is usually given to making the songs work.

On the other hand, Maltby is also on record as saying that the scene is always more important than the song (see chapter 27), implying that if the scene changes, the song that follows should be rewritten. Either way, a flourishing and functional relationship among the members of the artistic team is essential, as Maltby and Shire would continue to discover in their partnerships with other directors and librettists.

Love Match opened in Phoenix, Arizona, in an old movie theater, "with an audience of kind of rural cowboy types—this was fifty-some years ago," Shire remembers. The next move was to LA and the Ahmanson Theater. "We opened there, and we were kind of a big deal," he continues. "It was a very lavish show because it took place in the beginning of the Victorian Era." There were some good reviews and some bad reviews. "It needed work," Shire admits, "but it was very savable."

Out-of-town tryouts are a chance for the creative team to work on the show, to fix it, to rewrite where necessary, and, as the term implies, to try the changes out in front of an audience every night, thus getting instant feedback on what's working and what isn't. It can be a difficult, frustrating process—most notably summarized by Larry Gelbart's famous quip: "If Hitler's still alive, I hope he's out of town with a musical." But the daunting challenges are seriously compounded if the director leaves the country.

Love Match's director was an Irishman named Noel Willman, who had started out as an actor but achieved great success as the director of *A Man for All Seasons* on Broadway, for which he won a Tony Award in 1962. During the six-week run of *Love Match*, he had another directing engagement in England that he had previously booked, and as a result, he was not present for that crucial period in *Love Match*'s development. In Willman's absence, Danny Daniels, the show's choreographer, took over as director. Daniels, who already had three Tony nominations as a performer, had also been the choreographer of, among others, the original Broadway production of *Annie Get Your Gun*. (He would go on to have four Tony nominations as a choreographer, finally winning for *The Tap Dance Kid* in 1984.) In Shire's view, Daniels understood the show much better than Willman did. Daniels, for his part, felt that he was in charge once Willman departed. "But then Noel Willman came back and said, 'Well, it's my show,'" Shire explains.

Daniels ultimately left the show, requiring that the three ballets he had created for the production (all "dazzling," in Maltby's view) had to be restaged. It was another example of how musicals fail unless everyone on the creative team is on the same page.

"I think we might have been able to save it if, say, Hal Prince had come in to help us," Shire reflects. "And I think he would have at least looked at it if we had been in Boston or New Haven and not LA." In the absence of guidance like that, however, the show closed at the Ahmanson.

In the course of working on *Love Match*, Maltby and Shire found that not only could directors and book writers of musicals fail to integrate the songs into the scenes properly, but they could also misinterpret the musical numbers entirely. As Maltby has observed, "I think that we write totally accessible, absolutely obvious songs that anybody can get, but I'm surprised when I find other people dealing with the songs, other directors or other performers, how much they miss the point."

According to Shire, "[Our songs] are very easy to misunderstand, because often they have the surface music, they have a pastiche thing where they might sound Jerry Herman-ish on top, but really, the number ironically plays off against that. We found early on that directors would often treat only what's on the surface and miss the subtext. Our songs tend to be as much subtextual as textual."

A case in point from *Love Match*, and an eye-opener for Maltby in terms of how easily he felt their songs could be misinterpreted, was "I Think I May Want to Remember Today," which was later successfully resurrected for *Starting Here, Starting Now*.

In the original scene, Queen Victoria has finally allowed Prince Albert to come to England and meet her, since their marriage has been prearranged. However, she doesn't particularly want to meet him, because she likes being queen and doesn't really care to share the throne with a German guy she doesn't know, so she's been holding him off. But—surprise! When they actually meet, she sees that he is dashing and attractive. Nonetheless, their meeting remains quite formal—this is the Victorian era, after all—so they talk for a while, and he departs, leaving her standing there, showing no emotion whatsoever. Then the music starts, with an agitated, propulsive piano ostinato. This driving figure would seem to indicate that Victoria's emotions are roiling; however, the lyrics are formal and contained:

We have met and I think I can safely assume
That I've had a quite adequate look.
So if you will excuse me I'll go to my room
And write this all down in my book.

The music is pulsing inside her, but she doesn't know what it means. The words are the stiff language of a monarch who believes that showing one's feelings is unseemly. As Maltby sums it up, "The drama of it is she is *not* going to express what has just happened to her. That is the action of the song."

However, in the original staging of the number, as Maltby describes it, "She comes in, all kind of agitated with a fan, 'Oh my God, oh my God, oh my God.' No drama, no surprise." Performed like this, there's nowhere for the song to go. And this is how it was staged by choreographer Danny Daniels—the one who better understood the show, according to Shire.

Toward the end of the first verse, Victoria sings, "For ohhhhh—," holding out a long high note for eight bars, as her emotions threaten to break through her regal reserve. However, she tamps them back down with the title refrain, "I think I may want to remember today." She *thinks* she *may* want to remember today. Nothing impulsive, mind you, just an offhand possibility.

By the time she gets to the bridge, her observations become somewhat more explicit:

Did you see his shoulders?
Broad as the masthead on ships.
Like a pair of boulders,
Tapering down to his hips.

This is rather anatomical, shall we say, for a woman whose name is synonymous with adjectives such as strait-laced, stuffy, and even sexless. She does her best, once again, to keep a lid on it, especially when it comes time to speak to him:

When we met as children,
He was skin and bone.
Oh, Albert . . .
My, how you've grown!

"My, how you've grown" is something your doting auntie might say, not the words of someone whose pulse is quickening uncontrollably. And the music sets us up for that punchline: after "Oh, Albert," the vocal line is silent for two bars while the piano hammers out six accented, dissonant chords—what is she going to say? "My, how you've grown," with its obvious understatement and sly innuendo, lands all the better after we had to wait for it for a few measures.

In the third verse, she makes one last attempt to keep it reserved and proper:

As a matter of course, I should like to confess
That I hear a remarkable sound.
To be perfectly honest, I think it's no less
Than my heart that is starting to pound.

And at this point, she gives up completely, and instead of singing "Ohhhh," she literally calls out his name four times, as the piano accompaniment surges underneath the vocal line, finally revealing her true feelings.

Thus, the song is actually about the woman trying *not* to show her feelings and losing out by the end to the tidal wave of her attraction. It is, in fact, a prime example of a "head versus heart" number, a Maltby/Shire specialty about which more will be said later. In any case, it's easy for someone—either a performer or a director—who hasn't fully digested both the text and the subtext of the number to get it wrong.

"Richard took up directing literally so that he could direct his own shows," Shire observes.

"Or, at the very least, to ensure that the songs would not be misdirected," Maltby adds.

HOW BAD COULD I BE?

Love Match was followed by another disappointment, an even greater one for Maltby personally. It was referred to by the creative team as "the John Reed show."

John Reed was an American journalist and communist activist who made his name as a war correspondent during World War I and covered the October Revolution in Petrograd in 1917. When he died in Moscow three years later, he was buried at the Kremlin Wall, one of only a handful of Americans given that honor. He is probably best remembered today as the subject of the 1981 Warren Beatty movie *Reds*. More than a decade before *Reds*, however, Hal Prince was planning to direct a musical about Reed.

"It was this really interesting idea," Maltby says. "It was fabulous. It was all about the radical scene in New York before 1913, before we went into the First World War, the incredible explosion of art and everything that was taking place in Greenwich Village. It seemed really wonderful."

The idea for the John Reed show[1] came from Edward Winter, an actor who starred in the original Broadway production of *Promises, Promises* and went on to further prominence as Colonel Samuel Flagg on the TV show *M*A*S*H*. Prince was completely on board with the idea, having been greatly impressed by a stage adaptation of Reed's book *Ten Days That Shook the World* that he had seen in Moscow. Maltby and Shire wrote four or five songs for the project and played them for Prince, who was demonstrably enthusiastic. Prince felt, however, that Winter wasn't an experienced enough writer to pull it off and brought in Allan Knee, who later went on to write *The Man Who Was Peter Pan*, the 1998 play on which the movie *Finding Neverland* was based.[2] As Maltby remembers it:

> Allan brought in a very weirdly structured show in which he skipped all the connecting pieces and everything. I'm sure it was really good,

Closer Than Ever. Joshua Rosenblum, Oxford University Press. © Oxford University Press 2024.
DOI: 10.1093/oso/9780197758236.003.0006

but it terrified me. I thought, "What the hell is this? I don't understand this at all." I wrote a big letter about how I didn't know what was going on, and on the basis of that letter, Hal dropped the show. And the subtext of it was—and I think Hal maybe even said this to David—that he wondered whether I was good enough for it.[3] And that was the darkest time of my life, because Hal Prince turned me down, and that's the only person I wanted to work with.

At around the same time, Shire was starting to get leads on work in film and TV. Equally discouraged by the prospects of the New York theater scene, he had sought out the advice of Billy Goldenberg after *Love Match* closed in LA.

"Billy was a friend from the theater," Shire explains. "He and I and Marvin Hamlisch were the top audition and rehearsal pianists in New York. Billy had come out to LA and had been working there a year and had become the fair-haired boy at Universal through television movies of the week and TV series. So we had dinner one night, and I said, 'I'm really disgusted with prospects in New York,' and he said, 'Well, why don't I introduce you to some people in the music department at Universal, and I think you'll be able to get work there.'"

So Shire went into the movies. Maltby went into therapy. "There was nothing else to do," he says.

Maltby's experience in therapy turned out to be pivotal professionally. "What the therapy revealed eventually, over years, was that what I really was sitting on was being a director," he relates.

He had never particularly wanted to be a lyricist. One summer, his father built him a marionette theater. "The puppets didn't really do anything," he recalls. "They sort of dangled in the middle of the stage, but the scenery moved like crazy."[4] Maltby started writing shows to go with his scenery and then started writing lyrics to go with the shows that went with the scenery.

In high school, at Phillips Exeter Academy, he wanted to design the sets for musicals, but that meant creating a musical to design. He found fellow students to write the book and compose the score, but, as he puts it, "I had to write lyrics because nobody else wanted to."[5] It was the same when he got to Yale.

After he moved to New York, the reality set in. "David and I were now a songwriting team, and we had a publisher, and I was standing in my apartment, and I said, 'I'm a lyricist. I don't want to be a lyricist. Lyricists sit at home and try to fix those two bad lines while everybody else is having fun in the rehearsal room.' You're just the lowest man on the totem pole. I really did feel that I was trapped."

Realizing that directing was what he wanted to do was a revelation. "I had always had trouble with directors," Maltby reflects. "Whenever a director misunderstood the songs that we wrote, I would always think it was my fault. I never ever thought that it was *their* fault." Or, from a slightly different perspective: "Whenever I found myself in opposition to a person of authority, I always stepped back. It had to do with my father—I had this idea that if I unleashed myself, I'd destroy him. It wasn't true, but you know, these things are psychologically true, not realistically true."

Maltby stresses that he and his bandleader father always had a great relationship. "Deliriously wonderful," as he puts it. But at one point, in college or shortly thereafter, when Maltby Sr. realized he had a lyricist in the family, they decided to collaborate. And when Maltby Jr. criticized something his father had written, as he had gotten accustomed to doing with Shire, "[My dad] got very nervous and very testy," Maltby recalls. "I got the sense that he was vulnerable in that area. There was a fragility that I couldn't deal with, and so to spare him, I wouldn't go there. I wouldn't criticize him." This reluctance to criticize authority figures became a pattern that would repeat itself throughout Maltby's creative life:

> One way to save [my father] was to remain the wunderkind. So long as I'm the talented kid, I'm OK, but whenever I was called upon to take charge over somebody else, particularly somebody who was older, I fell apart. And if that person was a director, I would become a good soldier—I'd do whatever I was told. And that was not very healthy. But I realized that I had a real problem being on a show in which someone else was creating the show. So having finally defined that, I set out to become a director.

All well and good, but the path ahead was not clear. "So by now I'm, like, thirty. How do I start? I have no training. I didn't go to school. I didn't study directing, I don't know anything. And then I thought, 'On the other hand, how bad could I be? Could I be worse than anyone I'd ever worked with? Piece of cake!'"

Maltby proceeded to create an on-the-job training program for himself to learn how to direct. He started with nightclub acts and one-man shows, including one starring Murray Horwitz called "An Evening with Sholom Aleichem." (Horwitz, a jazz buff, later had the idea of doing a show about Fats Waller, which eventually turned into *Ain't Misbehavin'*.) Maltby also made plans to stage a revival of the 1959 Broadway musical *Juno*, in his own revised version. This sent him to the Long Wharf Theatre in New Haven to see its production of *Juno and the Paycock*, the Sean O'Casey play on which the musical *Juno* (with music and lyrics by Marc Blitzstein) is based. The Long Wharf production starred Geraldine Fitzgerald, whom Maltby met afterward. He mentioned his plans for *Juno*, the musical, and Fitzgerald said she'd love to be in it. Long Wharf said it would produce the show, but Arvin Brown, the theater's longtime artistic director, wanted to direct it himself. Maltby agreed, figuring he could attend rehearsals as author of the revised *Juno* and learn by watching Brown, a far more experienced director.

In the meantime, Fitzgerald had been asked to do a nightclub act at Reno Sweeney's, a then-popular Greenwich Village cabaret spot. Maltby went with Fitzgerald for a session with her vocal coach to hear some of her repertoire. As he recounts it:

> I sat in this chair, and she started to sing, and out came the most hideous sound I'd ever heard. I mean, her eyes sort of glazed over, and out came this croak. I thought, "Oh my God. I've committed a whole musical to somebody who cannot sing at all." She was going to play Juno. She finishes the first song, and I don't know what I'm going to respond to, but her teacher says, "Oh, that's wonderful, Geraldine! You're doing so much better," and I'm in freak-out land here. All I could think to say was, "Sing another!" I did that for an hour, and it was one song after another, uglier and uglier, and I was just dying because I'd just committed myself to this.

Finally, at the end of the session, Fitzgerald sang the "Pirate Jenny" number from the Bertolt Brecht/Kurt Weill show *The Threepenny Opera*, a role she had performed. And because she had played the part, the character came through. As Maltby explains it, "You don't necessarily have to sing well to deliver the number. It can be a thrilling performance if you're playing the character. As she sang it, her voice kind of trued, because she wasn't thinking about singing. She just delivered the song, and her pitch improved, and I thought, 'She's an actress.'"

Maltby decided that the way forward with the nightclub act was to construct a character for each one of Fitzgerald's numbers—a whole play to precede each song, for which the song would become an extension. "And in fact, it really worked," Maltby marvels. We'd construct the play, and we'd never do it—she would just become that character and then do the song. And she ended up having a nice little career in cabaret. She toured all over the place and over time got better and better as a singer—never any good, but the evenings were just thrilling."

Working with Maltby on her club act was enough for Fitzgerald to decide that he was her director of choice. When she signed on to star in Eugene

O'Neill's *Long Day's Journey into Night* at the Walnut Street Theatre in Philadelphia, she insisted that Maltby be brought in to direct the play.

Jim Freydberg was managing director of the Walnut Street Theatre at the time. Freydberg, who would go on to play an important role in Maltby and Shire's history as lead producer on both *Baby* and *Big*, remembers that *Long Day's Journey* production as part of an important transition for his theater.

"We were changing from being a stock company to being a LORT theater," Freydberg explains.[6] The LORT (League of Resident Theaters) contracts between theater owners and the Actors' Equity Association stipulate higher fees and better working conditions for actors; usually, this means a member theater will be able to attract higher-quality performers and raise their own prestige. Freydberg felt that having Fitzgerald star in a play would be a great coup for Walnut Street at that point. "Geraldine Fitzgerald was this fabulous actress. So here she was coming in saying she wanted to do this piece here, and she had been working with a young guy on reinterpreting *Long Day's Journey*, making it shorter. She presented him as somebody she had been working with, and she wanted him to direct it, but she really couldn't say any directorial stuff he had done," Freydberg says.

"In truth, *she* wanted to direct it, but she couldn't do that, so she sort of wanted me to be the surrogate," Maltby relates candidly. "I thought that was just fine, because I didn't know what to do." He had never directed a straight play, let alone a behemoth like this one. "If there was ever a straight play that is the antithesis of a musical, it is *Long Day's Journey into Night*," Maltby quips. "It is three hours of not-a-musical."

Freydberg and Douglas Seale, the theater's artistic director, met with Maltby and signed him on to the project. Maltby ended up staying at Freydberg's house for the duration. As Maltby recalls it, "I was in such a panic—I didn't really know what I was doing—I said, 'Jim, I've got to talk to somebody, and you're the choice. So I'm gonna just tell you everything that is worrying me when I don't know what I'm gonna do.' It turns out that was a life-changing experience for Jim, because he had never been brought into a director's thought processes like that, and it was really valuable to me, too."

Maltby says that the turning point for himself as director on *Long Day's Journey* was one pivotal scene between the two brothers. The elder, Jamie, is a drunken ne'er-do-well but also charming and lovable. Family relations are deeply fraught. As Maltby describes it, "Edmund has just gone through a big long scene with his father, which has produced horrible truths" and a long scene with his morphine-addicted mother as well. Edmund is also in poor health and is about to receive a diagnosis of tuberculosis. Maltby was working on the scene with his two actors, Philip Kerr (Jamie) and John Glover (Edmund), and found he was getting nowhere:

> We rehearsed it one night and it was just sort of deadly. I really didn't know what to do. Jamie comes home, and all Edmund wants is to have his fun-loving brother there. But Jamie decides he needs to do something good for his younger brother, and the thing he thought he could do [for Edmund] was to cure him of his admiration for Jamie, so he says, "You shouldn't trust me because I'm actually jealous of you. I will hurt you. Don't trust me," and that's the last thing the brother wants to hear.
>
> So I said, "OK, Edmund, what do you want?" And he said, "I want my brother," and I said, "Well, what do you want, Jamie?" and he said, "I want to warn him never to trust me." I said, "Edmund, what would you do if you heard that?" He said, "I wouldn't want to stay and listen. I would want to get out of the room." And I said to Jamie, "What would happen if he tried to get out?" He said, "I wouldn't let him leave." I said, "OK, now play the scene." And as soon as Edmund started to figure out what was going on and didn't want to hear any more, he started to leave. Jamie, who was drunk, tried to pull him back, and it became almost a wrestling match. It was electrifyingly true—it was a perfectly blocked, staged scene. And when it was finished, I said, "OK, that's it. We're not gonna do it again. I want you to recreate the immediacy of this version. The only thing I would say for next time is when you wrestle and you fall to the floor, do it in front of the sofa instead of behind it, because we can't see you. But everything else, do it exactly." And they did, and it was electrifying, and to me, everything I learned about directing I learned in that moment.

Maltby concludes, "That's the premise, which is that directing is not telling somebody what to do, which is what people seem to think. It isn't. It's giving them a *direction*—giving a goal to go toward. If that's clear, the scene comes alive because of the brilliance and the intelligence of the actors."

"The production was brilliant. It was really good," Freydberg affirms. "And Geraldine was amazing." The reviews were amazing as well. It turned out it had been worth taking a risk on Maltby as director. "I actually found him to be an extraordinary talent," Freydberg emphasizes.

To this day, even though he has now been nominated four times for and once awarded a Best Direction Tony, Maltby is still diffident about his own prowess as a director. Replying recently to an amateur director who had contacted him, asking if he could shadow Maltby on a project, Maltby wrote, in part:

> I'm not sure what you'd get out of being around me directing. I don't actually know anything. I never studied directing, nor did I work assisting anyone great. The only greatness I've encountered was being around Nick Hytner.[7] And even then I didn't know what brilliance I was in the presence of. I can only say that the process of directing, to me, is the process of finding out what the goal is and getting everyone to understand and go there with you.
>
> When they are on the right track, that's when they start making their own brilliant discoveries and contributions—those amazing, unexpected things that you can just take credit for. Directing is figuring [out] what the story is and getting everyone to be their own part of it. It's especially true of new musicals—because no one knows what the final show will be—everyone has a slightly different vision, and you have figure it out. To that extent the director has to "write" the musical. Not the lines or the music, but the entity. That's what's terrifying and thrilling and creative. When you're knee deep in the unknown. My guess is you already know how to do this—you may just not think that it's enough. But actually it is the only thing that matters. And that's true even if you are working with kids.
>
> Well—I do go on. But I am excited for your school.
>
> Love,
> Richard

THE FIRST THING THEY GIVE YOU IS WRITING THE OBITS

True to his word, Billy Goldenberg took Shire to meet Stanley Wilson, the influential and innovative head of music at Universal Studios. Wilson employed, early in their careers, such luminaries as John Williams, Elmer Bernstein, Dave Grusin, Henry Mancini, Lalo Schifrin, and Bernard Herrmann.[1] But beyond that, Wilson had a reputation for bringing cultural diversity to television and film music. As Shire puts it, "He was really terrific at getting a lot of composers who weren't necessarily film composers—jazz composers like Quincy Jones.[2] He gave them starts doing scores because he believed that if you were a good composer and if you were doing music for one medium, you could do it well for another and get some fresh thought in it."

Shire already had a demo reel with some TV work. He had been a rehearsal pianist on *Evening Primrose*, Stephen Sondheim's 1966 written-for-television musical. The director was Paul Bogart. As Shire describes it, "[Bogart] asked me to write some incidental connectives and things, and we really hit it off together, so when he got this big CBS movie of the week called *The Final War of Olly Winter*, about a black soldier in Vietnam and his relationship with a Vietnamese girl, he asked me to do the score."

Shire was slightly trepidatious about the assignment, not knowing anything about the music of Southeast Asia, but he did his research, consulted with a percussionist who collected world instruments, and wrote an economical score for harp, percussion, and a shakuhachi-like flute. The movie turned out to be a big success, and Bogart hired Shire to score two more TV movies over the next couple of years. Thus, he was able to demonstrate to Wilson that he could handle TV and film work. Wilson put Shire to work right away—a week later, he was scoring an episode of *The Virginian*.

"I always compared it to when you're starting in journalism and you get a job at a newspaper and you're really excited, and the first thing they give you

Closer Than Ever. Joshua Rosenblum, Oxford University Press. © Oxford University Press 2024.
DOI: 10.1093/oso/9780197758236.003.0007

is writing the obits," Shire says. "This was the equivalent of that. The series theme had been written by somebody else, and the show was an old favorite, in its fifth or sixth season. But suddenly, I had a real gig, and we spotted the episode, and in two weeks, I was supposed to write a half an hour of music for an orchestra that hadn't even been hired yet." Soon he was scoring a new episode every three or four weeks.

Writing for a twenty-five-piece Hollywood orchestra was different from writing chamber-sized scores for *CBS Playhouse*. Shire had basic orchestration skills from his music courses at Yale but not a lot of practical experience. He learned quickly in the trenches of his early studio sessions and was soon a masterful orchestrator, but the pressure took its toll. "That's when I started dry-heaving from stage fright before going to work many mornings, which went on for years," Shire relates. "I was always fearful that I would fail, that I wouldn't be able to come up with something good enough in time. I even had dreams that I would show up for a date and get up to conduct, but there would be no music on the stands."

Shire did six episodes of *The Virginian*. Soon he moved into scoring his own series, *McCloud*, starring Dennis Weaver, for which he wrote the theme and scored the first season of episodes. Extending the newspaper analogy, Shire compares this to moving from writing obits into doing small feature articles. "And then," he continues, "that kind of stuff led to bad movies, and bad movies led to better movies."

Shire's first feature film for Universal was the not especially memorable 1971 comedy western *One More Train to Rob*, starring George Peppard and Diana Muldaur. In addition to Shire's score, two Maltby/Shire songs made it into the film, including the sweetly nostalgic waltz "Take a Look Around" and "Havin' Myself a Fine Time," sung over the opening credits.[3] The latter nods to the country-western idiom but features characteristic Shirean originality—a syncopated, quietly driving groove in the bass and a chorus whose second half features a melody that rises dramatically by half step.

During these early years making his way up the Hollywood food chain, Shire met a girl named Talia Coppola.

Before this, he had been going out with an actress but was only mildly interested in her. "She gave a party for all her single uninvolved girlfriends because she wanted me to meet other girls so I'd stop asking her out all the time," he deadpans. One of those other girls was Talia. Shire was attracted to her but didn't want to be hasty, so he took out her roommate, a screenwriter named Brenda Perla, "in order to be able to check out Talia" when he went over to their house. "Finally, I started taking her out, and we hit it off and eventually got married," he concludes. They tied the knot in 1970. Then, a few years later, Talia's brother, director Francis Ford Coppola, hired Shire to score his new film *The Conversation*.[4] Shire says, "That really broke it open for me."

Shire had heard Coppola talk about *The Conversation* before he signed on to compose the music. The film tells the story of Harry Caul, a surveillance expert, who is hired to surreptitiously record the conversations of a couple, only to inadvertently uncover a possible murder plot. Coppola, who also wrote the script, had wanted to make the movie for years but was only given the green light after the success of the first *Godfather* movie.[5] When it came time to discuss the music, Coppola told Shire he didn't want a big orchestral score; his concept was for solo piano. "My heart sank," Shire says, "because I had been doing television with smaller orchestras and chamber scores, and I was thinking, 'Oh, boy, I've finally got a big high-profile picture with a major director, and I'm gonna get a big-budget-size orchestra.'"

Coppola, however, felt that the best scores were the ones that give the picture a dimension that is not already on the screen. "He said, 'I'm showing you everything on the surface about Harry Caul, but I want the score to be telling us what's going on inside of him,'" Shire recollects. Caul (played by Gene Hackman) is very private; we don't know much about him except that he's a closet jazz musician, and when he goes home, he takes out his tenor sax and plays along with old recordings. Coppola told Shire to write five short piano pieces, two or three minutes each, to go with specific titles, none of which was an actual scene in the movie. The idea was for Shire to get his creative juices flowing. "He gave me these ridiculous titles like 'Harry Caul Picks up His Laundry,' 'Harry Caul Visits His Grandmother,'" Shire remembers. "In my mind, I'm saying he's nuts, but I thought, well, he's Francis Coppola, and he must know what he's doing."

Shire fulfilled the assignment and brought the piano pieces back for Coppola. When he played the third one, Coppola said, "That's the theme for *The Conversation*." Much of the rest of the score consists of variations on that theme. Because of this unusual preproduction process with the score, Coppola was able to have the film's cast members listen to some of Shire's music prior to filming their scenes so they could absorb the mood of the music. This contrasts with the normal procedure for scoring a film, wherein work on the music isn't begun until the picture is finished.

Shire describes the *Conversation* theme as essentially bipolar. He composed the piece mostly through improvisation, so he didn't notice until later that the left hand, as he puts it, is "faux Chopin nocturne," of which he had played several when he was studying classical piano. The right hand, by contrast, is decidedly jazzy, outlining the contours of a blues scale (example 7.1).

Example 7.1. The Conversation.

"What I realized," he relates, "is this is the two sides of Harry: the right hand was a musical analogue of Harry's private self, and the left hand was the rigidly self-controlled audio technician he shows to the world. The right hand is Dionysian and the left hand Apollonian. That's kind of pretentious, but you get the idea, because those are the two big influences on me: jazz and classical piano." The net effect is reminiscent of Erik Satie in the way it combines melancholy and wit. Then, later in the theme, Shire adds major seconds to the right hand, evoking Thelonious Monk as well. In any case, the piano cues from *The Conversation* are exquisite pieces and would make a wonderful concert suite for solo pianists with creative programming impulses.[6]

The Conversation had a hugely positive critical reception. It won the top prize at the Cannes Film Festival in 1974 and received Oscar nominations for Best Picture, Best Original Screenplay (both for Coppola), and Best Sound (Walter Murch and Art Rochester). Regarding the film, Shire says:

> I was just trying to get the work done, but the movie has become more of a cult thing. At the time, it was squeezed between the first two *Godfather* films—I figured it was so low-profile in comparison that I thought, "Well, it's just a piano score, it's not going to get me any more work." It turns out that I have gotten more work because of that score than from any other single thing I've ever written. I've been asked to do a lot of piano scores or piano-based scores, and people talk about [*The Conversation*] a lot. At the time, it was largely unnoticed, but as the years have gone on, that and *Pelham* seem to have become my two signature scores.

Shire is referring to *The Taking of Pelham One Two Three*, another now-classic film with a breakthrough score. *Pelham*, also released in 1974, is a gritty, urban thriller that revolves around a subway train that has been hijacked by a group of thugs who demand that a $1 million ransom be paid within an hour. Shire's score has been described as "one of the best and most inventive thriller scores of the 1970s,"[7] "a mix of jagged big-band jazz and edgy modernism,"[8] "a stroke of genius,"[9] and "the most badass soundtrack ever recorded."[10]

The unique quality of Shire's *Pelham* score (and the outsize reactions to it) is linked to his novel use of the twelve-tone method of composition. This system, also known as dodecaphony or serialism, was developed in the 1920s by Austrian composer Arnold Schoenberg as a way of organizing atonal music. This, Schoenberg felt, was a historic necessity, because he believed that the composition of tonal music, as it had been practiced since J. S. Bach, had nearly run its course. The fundamental unit of the twelve-tone method is the tone row, a specific ordering of the twelve notes of the chromatic scale, in which each pitch is used once and only once sequentially before it can be used again in the next cycle of the row. The row, which is comparable to the diatonic (or major) scale as the organizing principle of tonal music, can then be manipulated in various ways to supply the musical content of the piece: it can be used forward, backward (retrograde), with its intervals inverted (upside-down, as it were), or inverted *and* backward (retrograde inversion). It can be transposed to start on any pitch, and it can be used horizontally (to create melodies) or vertically (to create chords). The point was to make sure that, in contrast to tonal music, no single pitch would be more prominent than any other. Schoenberg believed that the twelve-tone technique would ensure the supremacy of German music for the next one hundred years. That turned out to be quite incorrect. As one colleague wryly puts it, "At the end of the twentieth century, Schoenberg was sent to bed without supper." As early as 1983, in fact, the New York Philharmonic was giving concerts focused around the theme "The New Romanticism," reflecting the loosening of dodecaphonic music's grip on contemporary classical composition.

For several decades in the middle of the last century, however, twelve-tone composition was almost synonymous with "modern" or "avant-garde" music (a term that sounds quaint today). It was the predominant method of composition taught in university music departments, but it was largely rejected by mainstream audiences, who found atonal music, if not completely off-putting, then challenging to acclimate their ears to.

When Shire was studying composition as a graduate student at Brandeis in the fall of 1959, he felt like a misfit. "Everybody else was writing this really complicated Webernian, Schoenbergian, proto-electronic, proto-everything, and I just wanted to upgrade my chops for writing musicals," he recalls. Arthur Berger, then dean of the graduate composition department, was a hardcore serialist ("the type of composer whose works weren't being played at school dances," Shire quips) and a representative of the kind of music Shire had no interest in composing.

Much later, in Hollywood, Shire attended an informal composition seminar with Paul Glass (no relation to Philip). Glass was primarily a classical composer who also had a track record in film and was equally comfortable in multiple idioms. Glass first introduced Shire to the idea that the twelve-tone method was flexible. As Shire describes it, "In one of our discussions, I was putting down serial music.[11] I said, 'How do you write this stuff?' because a lot of his scores were super-complex serial things, and he said, 'You know, serial music does not have to be atonal.'" The twelve-tone method can be applied in a wide variety of ways and has resulted in some memorable music. As an example, Glass cited Alban Berg's Violin Concerto (1935), an early-twentieth-century masterpiece that is built on a row that mostly consists of a sequence of thirds, the building blocks of triads. The first three notes of Berg's row (G-B♭-D), in fact, constitute a G minor chord, and the third, fourth, and fifth spell out D major. As a result, large sections of the piece sound predominantly tonal.[12] The takeaway was that a tone row can be manipulated to adapt to a wide range of styles and purposes while providing the unity and coherence Schoenberg was seeking in a compositional tool.

Shire remembered this when it came time to tackle the score to *Pelham*:

> I knew that it was New York and it was jazz, but for the first couple of weeks I worked on the score, all that came out of my fingers was bad Lalo Schifrin—I mean, bad imitations of Schifrin and all of the jazz scores that I had heard. Everything sounded derivative and clichéd, and I got to the point, I think after working maybe three or four weeks, where I was almost ready to give up the project. And then I had an epiphany. I remembered [my discussion with Glass], and I thought, "If I create a row that has a basic jazz sound in it by using the most common jazz intervals, maybe something fresh will start happening." So I wrote that row and found that I could rather easily do a whole bunch of things with it that naturally sounded like the fresh jazz material I had been searching for.

Shire's tone row for *Pelham* consists of intervals characteristic of progressive jazz: major sevenths, minor thirds, and their inversions (minor seconds and major sixths), as indicated in example 7.2.

Example 7.2. Tone row for The Taking of Pelham One Two Three, with intervals

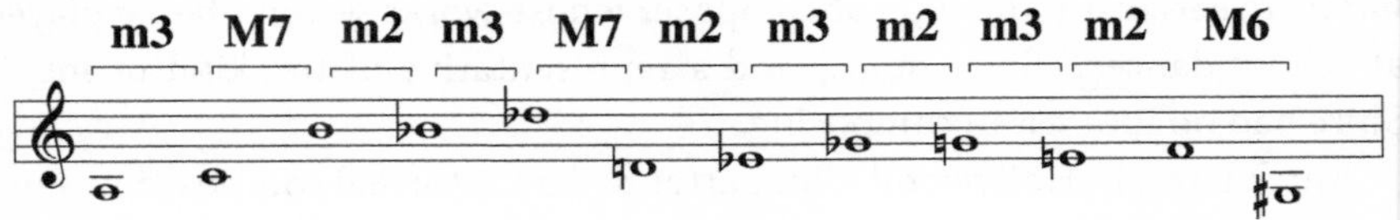

Next, he wrote out a matrix of all forty-eight permutations, according to standard twelve-tone procedure (see figure 7.1). "I put them up on the piano and started improvising," he says, "just using permutations of that particular row, and it started sounding exactly like the jazz I wanted. It was like suddenly finding the mother lode, and from then on, it was fun. And it's the only time I've had an experience like that, where the lights suddenly went on and I did a whole thing I'd never done before."

Prior to experimenting with twelve-tone composition, Shire says his approach whenever a scoring assignment required something dissonant was essentially random. "I was just hunting and pecking," he reflects. "But this way, I had something that I could control that no matter what I did, it sounded like progressive jazz."

The pitch content, however, is only part of what gives the *Pelham* score such a blockbuster quality. The syncopated, driving, three-note bass figure (B♭–B♭–D♭) of the main theme and the blistering multiethnic percussion that underlies the angular, tone-row-derived melodic figures in the brass are what provide the relentless, pulse-pounding energy. The music, in a genre described as "crime jazz" by one musicologist,[13] immediately conjures the dangerous yet thrilling essence of New York City in the mid-'70s, an era of urban decay and graffiti-laden subways. In short, it's unforgettable.

These two standout scores—*The Conversation* and *Pelham One Two Three*—inaugurated a successful string of 1970s movie hits for Shire that include *The Hindenburg* (1975),[14] *Farewell, My Lovely* (1975), *All the President's Men* (1976), *Raid on Entebbe* (1977), *Saturday Night Fever* (1977), *The Promise* (1979), and *Norma Rae* (1979), which yielded the Oscar-winning song "It Goes Like It Goes," with lyrics by Norman Gimbel.

The year 1979 also saw the release of *Fast Break*, with a score by Shire that included a memorably languorous piano solo underscoring a romantic scene. When the soundtrack album was released, Motown Records wanted another song for it, so it hired Carol Connors, a co-lyricist on "Gonna Fly

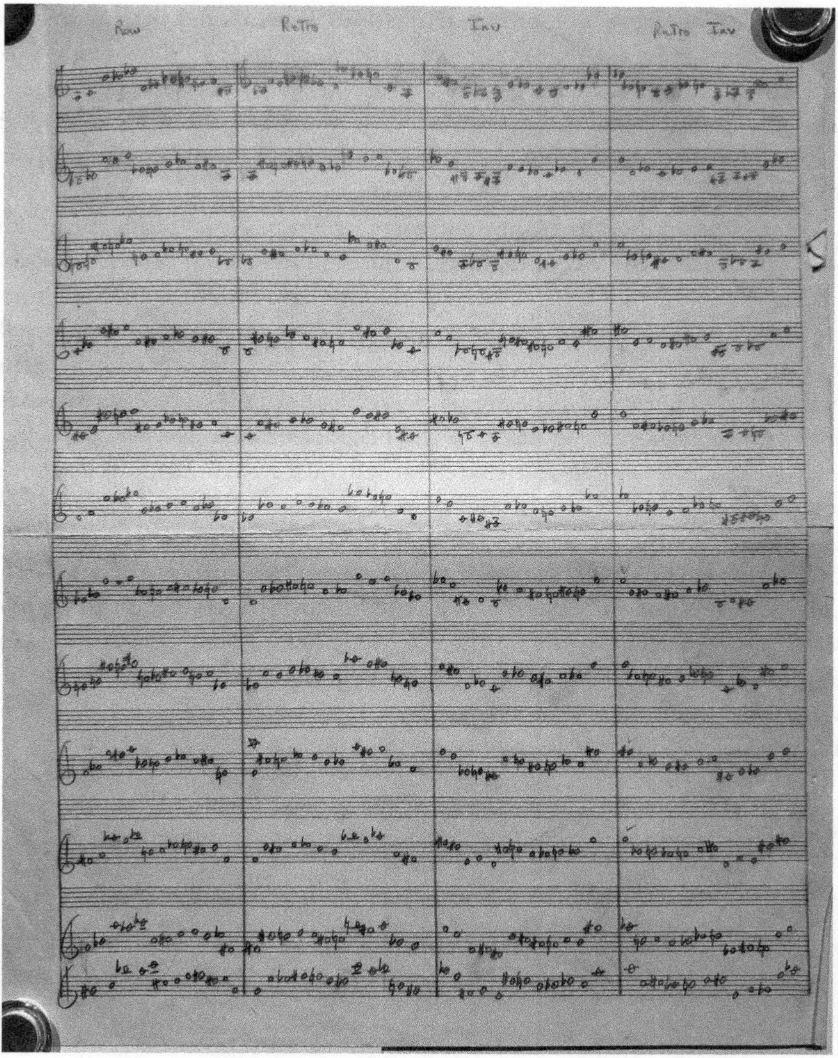

Figure 7.1. Tone row permutation table for The Taking of Pelham One Two Three (manuscript)

Now" from *Rocky*, to write lyrics for Shire's aforementioned piano solo. *Fast Break*'s theme song, a disco number called "Go for It" (also with lyrics by Connors), was supposed to be the hit release from the album, but when it was issued as a single, it went largely unnoticed. Connors's lyricization of Shire's piano melody, however, resulted in a song called "With You I'm Born Again." Although originally the B-side of the "Go for It" single, "With You I'm

Born Again," as sung by Motown artists Billy Preston and Syreeta Wright, became a runaway hit that reached number four on the Billboard Hot 100 and stayed on the charts for twenty-one weeks, with enough sales to qualify as a gold record.[15] Shire says that he never imagined the song, a leisurely paced minor-key waltz, would become a hit and that people who know it are often surprised to find out that he wrote it.

A few scattered Maltby/Shire numbers would make it into feature films over the subsequent years, thanks to Shire's film-scoring career.[16] Notable among these is "Only When I Laugh," the title track to the 1981 Neil Simon movie of the same name, which Shire scored. The song shifts unexpectedly (and enjoyably) from a straight eighth-note feel in the verses to swaggering swing in the choruses as the singer describes her only partial victory over post-breakup blues. In addition to the original Brenda Lee version, which was released as a single and charted briefly after the movie's release, the song has also been covered by Maureen McGovern and Shirley Bassey.

Additionally, the 2001 comedy *These Old Broads*, co-written by Carrie Fisher and starring her mother, Debbie Reynolds, as well as Shirley MacLaine, Joan Collins, and Elizabeth Taylor, was not scored by Shire but did include two Maltby/Shire songs written for the film: "Boy Crazy," sung over the opening credits, and "What a Life." The latter is winningly performed by Reynolds, MacLaine, and Collins as a triumphant comeback number toward the end of the film.

LYNNE

"She's the one who brought us back together," Maltby says.

He's talking about Lynne Meadow, the longtime artistic director of New York's award-winning Manhattan Theatre Club, who, at age twelve, had appeared in the children's chorus of Maltby and Shire's *Grand Tour* at the Yale Dramat in 1959. That experience changed Meadow's life. Consequently, she would play a crucial role in resurrecting their collaboration seventeen years later, after a period in the '70s during which the two men were living on opposite coasts and hadn't written anything together in years.

Meadow grew up in New Haven—a townie, as she puts it. Town-gown relations between Yale and the city of New Haven have been notoriously fraught for centuries; the university has been regarded variously with envy, admiration, resentment, pride, and even outright hostility by New Haven residents. For Meadow, however, Yale was the shining city on the hill.

"It's hard to describe the love a townie has for Yalies," she says, articulating one prevalent, though by no means universally held, viewpoint. "When you're in junior high school, a Yale undergrad is an amazing thing to behold. They're like grown-ups—they're smart and funny. It was the fifties, and the guys wore loafers with no socks. So sexy! As far as I was concerned, there was nothing better than a Yale undergraduate."[1] As a *Grand Tour* cast member, Meadow would suddenly find herself surrounded by them, including Richard Maltby and David Shire.

She found her way into the *Grand Tour* company via director Bill Francisco. When Meadow was ten, she was cast in a play at New Haven's Jewish Community Center called *Guest in the House*. Francisco, then a graduate student at the Yale School of Drama, was the director. Meadow played a neurotic child ("Probably not that far off," she quips) and had the time of her life. Next up at the JCC was a musical, co-written, in fact, by Meadow's mother, Virginia. Francisco directed that as well.[2] The following year, when

Closer Than Ever. Joshua Rosenblum, Oxford University Press. © Oxford University Press 2024.
DOI: 10.1093/oso/9780197758236.003.0008

Francisco was directing *Grand Tour* at the Yale Dramat, he needed a chorus of children for the opening number, so Lynne was a natural choice. He also cast Virginia in a small role, so both Meadows were in the show.

Meadow had grown up seeing shows at the Dramat. "My mom was passionate about theater," she says. "She would take me to see everything that was done there. We didn't live in New York. The Yale Dramat was about as good as it got." And it seemed awfully good. Naturally, Meadow saw the Maltby/Shire *Cyrano* when it played there in 1958. "I was a kid full of wonder," she admits, "but I think I had a certain acumen, and I knew those guys were really talented."

Meadow recalls watching *Cyrano* from the balcony. "There was a song in it called 'Autumn,'" she relates. "And the leaves were falling, and I was ten, so I was very impressionable, but I turned to my mother and said, 'You know, there's one really great song in the show,' and she said, 'What's that?' and I said, '"Autumn." That really is the best song in the show.'"

Beyond the excitement of performing in *Grand Tour* at the Dramat, Meadow was transfixed by watching Francisco direct the show. She recalls in particular his approach to fixing one of the production numbers during tech rehearsal:

> A boat lands, it's a big production number, and she [Ellen, the leading role played by Gretchen Cryer] arrives, and there are all these townspeople, so Bill stands up and says, "Wait, wait, wait," and he goes down the aisle, goes onstage, talks to each different group of people. So I had watched what it looked like before he went onstage, and I remember him walking offstage, sitting down in the house, and I watched what happened after he spoke to everybody, individually and quietly, and it was transformed. And I said, "That's what I want to do." I saw him, without making a lot of noise, just going there and completely changing what was there, and I saw how he made it so much better. There was a lifeless picture on the stage, and suddenly there was life, and it was inhabited, and people knew what they were doing, and who they were, and it was so thrilling, and I was twelve years old, but I thought, "That's for me."

Something about Francisco vitalized everyone around him. "He really was a galvanizing force, and there was an incredibly talented group of people who rallied around him," Meadow affirms. The overall level of expertise, as Meadow views it, was a function of Francisco. "He was a great director," she emphasizes. "There was just so much talent around. Peter Hunt was a great lighting designer. John Conklin was a fabulous set designer. And Gretchen

Cryer was absolutely charming in the lead. I was like a little Sherlock Holmes, walking around just fascinated by what seemed to me to be such excellence." This became, in a sense, the essence of Meadow's credo as director and producer. She elaborates:

> Maybe it happens all the time, but I can only describe what happened to me. I felt in the presence of great talent. I felt it around David Shire and Richard Maltby, and I felt it around Bill Francisco. I have the feeling that Richard and David were so ahead of their own time—they were so much more advanced, to write that musical at that time. They just represented to me people who had a gift and a vision and somehow told me it's possible to do that when you're grown up, because to me they were grown up.
>
> It really was some kind of primal lesson in excellence, and in getting the very best people you can get together to make something happen. It sounds very simple, but it has been my aesthetic. I've always been fascinated by how people influence each other in the most positive ways. The theater and what we do is so collaborative—and we can be so guided and helped and inspired by the people who are around.
>
> So that was *Grand Tour*. That was my arrival. I owe to them close to fifty years of Manhattan Theatre Club's history. My proudest thing is the sheer amount of talent that has occupied the space that I created. And I was influenced by Richard Maltby, David Shire, and Bill Francisco to create the best.[3]

Meadow went off to college at Bryn Mawr in 1964 (Yale would not start admitting women as undergraduates until 1969) and then, after finishing her studies there, was admitted to the Yale School of Drama's graduate program in directing.

She didn't get in the first time around. "I couldn't believe it," she says, recalling her disappointment. "It was all I ever wanted. It was like 'All I ever wanted was the music and the mirror.'" Meadow got on a train from Bryn Mawr to New Haven and asked to meet with the dean. "I said, and this was before women's lib and before we were gathering in groups and [raising] consciousness, and I said to him, 'I just don't understand why I wasn't accepted.' I had written an essay and everything. It was a little pretentious, but they all were. And he said it was really competitive, there were only five places, and very naively I asked him, 'Did you take any women?' And he said no. And he added, 'We haven't had that much luck with the women.' I'll never forget the words."

That summer, Meadow wrote a long letter explaining why she felt that, as a woman, she would direct something differently from the way a man would direct it but that she would do an equally good job. She sent the letter off to Yale at the end of the summer; a week later, she got a call saying she had been admitted. She had been first alternate on the waiting list, and someone had dropped out. It wasn't clear if her storming the dean's office or her subsequent letter made the difference, but it didn't matter—her dream had come true.

Meadow arrived at the Yale School of Drama in the fall of 1968. It came as no surprise that there weren't many other female directors around. In fact, in Meadow's second year at the drama school, she was the only woman in all three years of the directing program.

She spent the summer after her first year of graduate school at the Williamstown Theater Festival as an assistant to Nikos Psacharopoulos, a Yale Drama faculty member and the festival's founder.[4] When Meadow got her MFA in 1971 and moved to New York to start her directing career, everyone told her she had to begin as a stage manager or as some established director's assistant. Psacharopoulos said that was wrong, that she had to direct, but there weren't a lot of opportunities.

Before too much time passed, however, she was quite unexpectedly offered the leadership of the Manhattan Theatre Club (MTC), a then-obscure group that was deep in debt and about to go out of business. She was twenty-five. Meadow took over the teetering organization as artistic director starting with the 1972–1973 season and eventually turned it into the powerhouse theater company it has been known as for decades.

In 1976, Meadow created a cabaret space as part of MTC. She had already been working with Maltby for a few years—he had directed some spring benefits for the company and had even acted in one play. Looking for material for the new cabaret, Meadow said to an associate at MTC, "There are these guys, and they wrote musicals, and I'm sure they have a body of work that we could make into an evening."

Maltby and Shire weren't in touch much at this point, a period they half-jokingly refer to as "the divorce."

"Yes, it was a divorce, but it wasn't one in which we decided we wouldn't work together anymore," Maltby says. "There was no rancor, but we didn't talk much."

Shire says it was the natural result of their string of theatrical disappointments. "It just kind of happened that we weren't working on anything together, we didn't have any projects that were coming to us, and we were just tired of writing things that didn't get on."

Nonetheless, Meadow called Maltby and asked him to send her all the material he had. "I said, 'I know you [and David] are not really dealing with

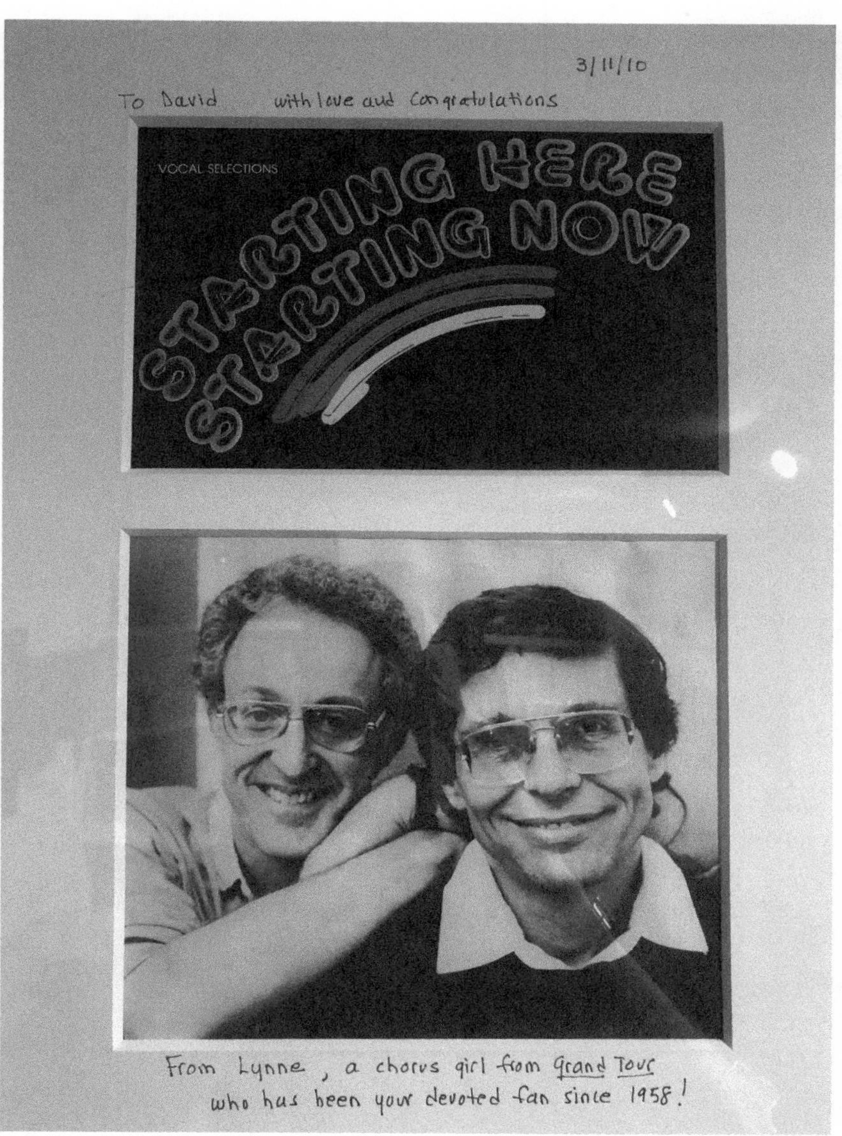
3/11/10
To David with love and Congratulations
VOCAL SELECTIONS
STARTING HERE
STARTING NOW
From Lynne, a chorus girl from Grand Tour
who has been your devoted fan since 1958!

Figure 8.1. Framed gift from Lynne Meadow to David Shire, incorporating the artwork and photo of the authors from the Starting Here, Starting Now published vocal selections.

each other, but I want to listen to what you've got and see if we can put together a show."

Maltby dug up a bunch of recordings. Meadow listened—it was the '70s, so it was all on cassette tapes. "I thought, there is definitely a show here, and Richard can really put it together." She played some of the songs for her MTC colleague. "He said, 'Are you out of your mind? What is this? What is this material?' I said, 'You just have to trust me. These guys are great. They've always been great. They're great.' And I asked Richard to direct."

STARTING HERE, STARTING NOW

Lynne Meadow knew that Maltby could direct the show she was proposing. She had gone down to Philly to see the production of *The Glass Menagerie* with Geraldine Fitzgerald that Maltby had directed. Maltby, for his part, was initially not entirely thrilled by the idea of making a show out of his and Shire's trunk songs.

"My first reaction was that all of the songs were losers," he states frankly. "They were all connected with shows that hadn't worked. I wasn't even sure I liked a lot of them, because they were all attached to failures." At the same time, however, he was looking for a chance to direct his own material—that was the primary reason he had moved into directing in the first place. "I was in the process of saying yes to anything that came along, and so I said, 'Sure, why not?'"

Shire, for his part, was even more pessimistic about the project. "Why do you want to take all these songs that never went anywhere and make an evening of them? I think it's a terrible idea," he recalls thinking. "But Richard said, 'No, no, no, let me put something together.'"

So Shire sent Maltby a trove of their material. "At least once, I picked up sheet music and literally blew dust off it," Maltby remembers with amusement. But as he looked through what they had, it started to fall together.

"What I discovered was that the songs really were good," he relates candidly. "When the show doesn't work, you tend to flush everything down the toilet. Not only were they good, but they could really stand alone. They had a voice, which was ours." In a video from the Masterworks Broadway series, he elaborates further on the experience of revisiting the material that eventually became *Starting Here, Starting Now*:

> When I started putting this show together, I realized, "Oh, these songs are subtle. You really do have to be a person inhabiting the songs. You can't just sing it as if it's a Cole Porter tune. They are character

Closer Than Ever. Joshua Rosenblum, Oxford University Press. © Oxford University Press 2024.
DOI: 10.1093/oso/9780197758236.003.0009

songs—you have to have the character inside of it in order for it to come alive. And when you do, they come alive in a way that's not like other songs. So it was a big rediscovery of our own craft, really. We were . . . surprised by the fact that these were good, just because they'd been associated with shows that hadn't succeeded.[1]

In assembling the song list for *Starting Here, Starting Now (SHSN)*, Maltby pulled numbers from *The Sap of Life*, including "Watching the Big Parade Go By" and "A Charmed Life," the latter rewritten as "A New Life Coming." In addition, *SHSN*'s opening number, "The Word Is Love," is adapted from *The Sap of Life*'s Act II finale (see figure 9.1). *How Do You Do, I Love You* yielded "Just Across the River," "One Step," and "Pleased with Myself," as discussed previously. From *Love Match* came, in addition to "I Think I May Want to Remember Today," the melodically sumptuous "I Hear Bells," and the exuberant, genuinely stirring "Today Is the First Day of the Rest of My Life." "I Don't Believe It" also came from *Love Match*, although Maltby rewrote most of the lyrics to create the glimpses of modern marriage that are now the subject of the song. From *Cyrano* came "Autumn," which the ten-year-old Meadow had pegged as the musical's best song, but ironically, nothing was used from *Grand Tour*, the show Meadow appeared in that changed her life.

The score to *The River*, the abandoned Rumer Godden project, supplied both "Song of Me" and "Travel." The latter, as mentioned in chapter 2, is included on Stephen Sondheim's intriguing list of "Songs I Wish I'd Written (At Least in Part)." "Travel" seems like an unusual number for Sondheim to single out, from all the distinctive songs in the Maltby/Shire canon. It doesn't have the musical or lyrical sophistication that many of their numbers do, although it is certainly upbeat and immediately appealing. "I guess he heard something in it that he felt was really honest and fresh," Shire muses.

"I'm a Little Bit Off" (discussed in chapter 4) was salvaged from the abandoned John Reed show. *You're What's Happening, Baby*, the show the team had proposed to Michael Stewart in the '60s, yielded "We Can Talk to Each Other," "A Girl You Should Know," and "The Girl of the Minute."[2]

"The Girl of the Minute," which indeed has a running time of approximately sixty seconds, was first repurposed for the revue *New Faces of 1968* and constituted Maltby and Shire's first Broadway credit. In the number, the singer heaps praise on some current "it" girl, but the clock is ticking for her:

You're the girl of the minute, as timely as now
And in every conceivable way,
Your face seems to capture this instant in time.
You're the young pulsing heart of today.

So be grateful, enjoy it, as long as it lasts.
Let everyone fill up your cup.
You're the heartbreaking, breathtaking girl of the minute
And your minute's . . . up.

Figure 9.1. Manuscript of "Finale—Act II" from The Sap of Life

In Andy Warhol's world, everyone would get fifteen minutes of fame. Maltby and Shire's girl only gets one.

This startling ditty is followed immediately by "A Girl You Should Know," an increasingly rhapsodic waltz with a sinuous, rising chromatic figure in the accompaniment that suggests rich, unplumbed depths. In this number, the former "Girl of the Minute" pleads to be recognized as a unique and special human being, possessed of many wonderful qualities that you might miss if you judge her too quickly.

"Crossword Puzzle" first appeared in *Graham Crackers*, a 1963 revue that played at Upstairs at the Downstairs, a now-shuttered NYC nightclub. Created and directed by Ronny Graham, the show contained several Maltby/Shire songs. When it came time to locate the sheet music for "Crossword Puzzle" so that it could be used in *SHSN*, nobody could find it. It finally turned out that Maltby's sister had a copy of the song—Shire's original manuscript, complete with coffee stains.

"Crossword Puzzle," like "I Think I May Want to Remember Today," is a classic Maltby/Shire "head versus heart" number, meaning the person singing it is grappling with the conflict between what they know intellectually and what they feel emotionally. As Maltby puts it, "With *Starting Here, Starting Now*, I discovered that essentially, they're almost always the same song, in a curious sort of way. They're always about cerebral people being defeated, or made human, by their feelings. Who do you suppose *that* could be about?"

In a perfect illustration of this syndrome, the woman singing "Crossword Puzzle" is clearly "as bright as a girl can be," as she immodestly describes herself. She can easily get the right answers to difficult clues like "hartebeest" and "Afghani nomad," but she can't figure out why her boyfriend left her.[3] As she stumbles through more clues with increasing frustration, it gradually dawns on her that it may have been because he was tired of having his nose rubbed in her superior puzzle-solving ability. ("If I weren't so dumb, I'd be spending this Sunday in a church, hearing wedding chimes," she concludes ruefully.) As we will see, this conflict between the intellect and the emotions is a recurring theme in the Maltby/Shire canon and lies at the core of many of their best songs, including "I Don't Remember Christmas," "The Bear, the Tiger, the Hamster and the Mole," "What Am I Doin'?," "One of the Good Guys," "Patterns," and others.

SHSN also includes some standalone numbers (i.e., not written for a specific show), such as "What About Today?" (discussed in chapter 3) and "Barbara," which was written for Maltby's first wife for their first anniversary.[4] The closing sequence consists of "Song of Me," followed by "Today Is the First Day of the Rest of My Life," which segues directly into the fusillade of notes that is the Doppler-effect-inspired opening of "A New Life Coming." The pairing of these latter two numbers forms an irresistible doubleheader of pure, open-hearted optimism about the life that is yet to come.

As the contents of the show began to come into focus, Maltby called three actor friends—Loni Ackerman, Margery Cohen, and Michael Tucci—and asked if they wanted to be in it. ("I was petrified," Maltby recalls.) To his amazement, they all said yes. Then came the hard part: creating a show out of a disparate collection of unrelated songs. As Maltby describes it:

> When we started, I had no idea what it was. We played through things I thought would work, and after two weeks, they had learned the songs, and now it was time to get it on its feet. I did not have a clue what to do. The opening was that rising figure where the vocals come in, "The word is love, I am in love." That was written for *Sap of Life*. It also sets the tone—the story begins when you suddenly realize you're in love. They sang that and went into "Starting Here, Starting Now." And I didn't know what to do, so I said, do it again. And then again. It happened about six times. I'm waiting for lightning to strike, and it didn't. So the seventh time through, to help out, Michael Tucci went over to one of the girls and sang that part to her. And I thought, why didn't he go to the other one? Oh—I have a triangle here! That's a story. Maybe a guy who thinks he can pull off a relationship with two girls. Oh, they found out about each other. Oh, now they're dumping me. So I put together seven songs telling that little story about a guy trying to play off two women. There was no connective dialogue; the sequence of songs told the plot. It's a little playlet that lasts halfway through the first act. Inadvertently, I had taken a collection of songs and made a story out of it. [Now] it's a device I use all the time.

Or, putting it slightly differently: "By accident, I invented the bookless book musical."

Shire, meanwhile, stayed in LA, keeping the project at arm's length. But when Maltby said he thought he had something, Shire flew to New York to hear it.

"[Richard] had said, let me put something together, and if you think it's embarrassing or something you don't want out in the real world, we'll just scrap it," Shire recounts. "So I came back, and I was just bowled over. I was practically in tears. I thought, this does not sound like an anthology of failure, this sounds like something wonderful in its own right. I felt he had rescued stuff that I was all ready to forget about. And that started the whole streak that got us back together."

Now that Shire was on board, he did his part, composing musical connective tissue where Maltby said it was needed, linking one song to the next. Maltby recalls that Shire did all of them in about an hour. "Yes, and then I flew back to LA where I could make a living," Shire quips.

SHSN opened for a limited three-week engagement at MTC in the fall of 1976. (The show's original title was *An Evening of Theater Songs by Maltby and Shire*.) As William H. Evans put it in the original liner notes to the cast recording, "On opening night . . . Maltby and Shire experienced for the first time a full evening of their own material that was an unqualified success. In a single moment, it seemed, they had arrived fully formed. It was ironic that it took a full-fledged 'retrospective' to mark what was undeniably a beginning."[5]

Plans were quickly made for a transfer to an open-ended run; the show moved in March 1977 to the Barbarann Theater Restaurant (now Swing 46 Jazz and Supper Club), an off-Broadway cabaret venue. Ackerman and Cohen from the original cast continued on with the production when it moved; Tucci did not. "Michael was a charming performer, but he really wasn't a singer. Margery and Loni really were, so when we moved, we had to get a real singer, and in came George Lee Andrews, who was a golden boy," Maltby explains.[6] Robert Preston was brought in as pianist and musical director, replacing Tom Babbitt, who was unavailable for the transfer.

Four songs were added for the move off-Broadway. In the original MTC production, most of the numbers coalesced around the theme of young love, which provided a pleasing sense of unity. "We were younger then," Shire observes. "Those were the things we wrote. But when we moved, the comment was that the show didn't have an edge." The added numbers—"I Don't Remember Christmas," "Flair," "I Don't Believe It," and "I'm Going to Make You Beautiful"—provided that missing element. The first two of these were written specifically for the show when it transferred; the last one was originally part of *You're What's Happening, Baby*.

"I Don't Believe It," a revision of the original song of that title from *Love Match*, is a refreshingly cynical number set to a rollicking waltz. In the updated version, the rotating married couples try a little too hard to convince the audience how happy they are, while the observing commentators express their skepticism. The vocal line moves in slithering half-step intervals and has a fragmented declamation ("I . . . I don't . . . I don't believe . . . I don't believe it one bit")—the antithesis, one might say, of a traditionally romantic melody. It also has this memorable observation:

All I can hear is the
Drone of her phrases

And while she's extolling her joy,
Why is he eyeing that boy?

When the show reopened, it received what Maltby describes as "a nice, pleasant, sort of pat-on-the-back review" from the *New York Times*—not bad but not enough to keep the show running. The write-up from the *Daily News* was less excited than the one from the *Times*. Which left the *Post*. As Maltby recalls:

> In those days, the *Post* was an afternoon paper. I remember coming into my apartment at noon, saying to David, "The *New York Post* has to start by saying, 'Wow, wow, wow, what wonderful songs,' and 'Wow, wow, wow, what a wonderful show.' If it doesn't say that, we'll close in a week." And Martin Gottfried's review started, "Wow, wow, wow, what a wonderful show,"[7] and it was that kind of turn-everything-around review. It kept us running for a while.[8]

Still, it was hand-to-mouth in terms of the show's weekly operating budget. "We never knew from week to week whether anyone was going to come, but we managed to sort of break even," Maltby recounts. In the meantime, Betty Lee Hunt, the show's press agent, had been working on Walter Kerr to come and review the show.[9] Kerr, as the *Times*'s chief theater critic, normally did not review off-Broadway productions, but Hunt thought she had him to the point where he was going to show up. That might have worked out well if Maltby hadn't fired her. This was about four months in.

"At that time," he explains, "one of our producers had had a nervous breakdown, the other had disappeared, so I was sort of producing it [myself] and getting all sorts of pressure to get a different press agent, that we needed different press." He did not realize Hunt had made this connection with Kerr. "I went to replace [Hunt], and she then said, 'Well, in that case, I'll just call up Walter Kerr and tell him not to come.' So he never did come. That would have changed the world. But it didn't." The show ended up running for 120 performances.

Fortunately, there was a cast recording, produced by Jay David Saks, a now-retired, notably successful record producer with a long career in both the musical theater and classical worlds, including the live Metropolitan Opera broadcasts on both radio and, later, HD. At the time, Saks was a protégé of legendary record producer Thomas Z. Shepard at RCA. Shepard, who has won twelve Grammys and has a sterling catalogue of Broadway, classical, and opera recordings to his credit, had been in Shire's composition class back at Yale with Quincy Porter. Shire was a senior at the time; Shepard was a first-year graduate student.

"There were three of us," Shire recalls. "Me, Tom, and some percussionist who wanted to be a composer." For his part, Shepard remembers only Shire in the class—"because he's the one I was so fiercely jealous of," he quips.[10]

Shepard took in Maltby and Shire's senior-year production of *Grand Tour*. "I was so knocked out by it," he remembers. "David was fantastic. These guys, they seemed to be born adults. It was incredible." Shepard crossed paths again with Shire during the recording session for *Company*, which Shepard produced and for which Shire had written the "Tick-Tock" dance music. By 1977, when *SHSN* had its debut, Shepard was division vice president of RCA Red Seal, and he wanted the show recorded.

The *SHSN* original cast recording, released in 1977, received a Grammy nomination for Best Cast Show Album, as the category was then called, but lost out to the megahit musical *Annie*. As reviewer David Wolf effused about the *SHSN* recording:

> Few cast recordings are as good as this one. . . . These actable showpieces are the best ever written by the team, and this assemblage is just about the best songwriter anthology ever created. . . . With so much imitative musical theater writing out there, the best thing about these songs is that each of them is a fresh and original piece of work.[11]

Maltby says of the recording:

> It was a real risk to take this show that was just done in a nightclub, really, and give it a full recording. Same thing happened several years later when we did *Closer Than Ever*, which we actually had orchestrated for the album. Those albums went out into the world, and the shows are done all the time, all over the place. People come to us who have just gotten out of college, saying, "Oh my God, we did a production of it, and these songs changed my life." And that's thrilling. And that only happened because the shows were recorded, and stunningly.

"I DON'T REMEMBER CHRISTMAS"

"I Don't Remember Christmas," one of the songs written specifically for *Starting Here, Starting Now*'s off-Broadway transfer, is a perfect example of what is sometimes called a liar's song. This is exactly what it sounds like: it's a number in which the singer is saying the opposite of what's true. Sometimes the singer knows he or she is lying, in which case that person is essentially a huckster, selling a bill of goods. A great example of this is Billy Flynn's "All I Care about Is Love" from John Kander and Fred Ebb's *Chicago*. Flynn doesn't care about love; all he cares about is the money he's going to make as a defense attorney in his high-profile, show-business murder cases. "My Girlfriend, Who Lives in Canada" from *Avenue Q* also falls into this category. Rod doesn't really have a girlfriend named Alberta up in Vancouver—he's gay (and closeted). And of course, Harold Hill's "Ya Got Trouble" from Meredith Willson's *The Music Man* is one big huckster number that describes the spreading danger of youthful corruption and offers a solution (a boys' band) that Hill has no intention of providing to this nonexistent problem.

Sometimes a liar's song claims to be about one thing but is actually about another. "The Tennis Song" from *City of Angels* leads the pack in this category. On the surface, it's about a game on a court involving rackets, but it's actually all about sex, featuring one innuendo after another.

But perhaps the most intriguing subgenre in this category is the type of number in which singers are lying to themselves. In other words, they're deep in denial. Most liar's songs are enjoyable because we in the audience know something the other people onstage don't know. "I Don't Remember Christmas" has a particular kind of appeal because, as the song progresses, we become aware of something that the singer himself doesn't even know (or isn't willing to acknowledge).

The instrumental intro to the song is a bass line only, and the accompaniment stays like this, without any chords or filled-in harmonies, for the entire first verse. This unusually sparse texture sets us up in an atmosphere of quiet

Closer Than Ever. Joshua Rosenblum, Oxford University Press. © Oxford University Press 2024.
DOI: 10.1093/oso/9780197758236.003.0010

reflection and (purportedly) forthright expression. The singer doesn't start out in denial; he's merely making observations. In fact, he sounds somewhat relieved: "I was standing in the bedroom when it suddenly came clear / That at last I don't remember that at one time you were here." The melody is relatively low in the male range, and it follows a simple sequence of up a step/down a third, almost as if he's murmuring to himself (example 10.1).

Example 10.1. "I Don't Remember Christmas"

I was stand - ing in the bed - room when it sud - den - ly came clear

— that at last I don't re - mem - ber that at one time you were here.

Next, the melody stops sequencing down and returns to the initial melody note of E. This is the beginning of a long, steady, tension-building stepwise climb upward for the next nine bars. As the melody slowly rises, the situation starts to get real, with vivid, specific imagery, starting with "your robe behind the door" (example 10.2). We've already seen that creating tension via a slowly rising stepwise melody is a favorite device of Shire's ("Autumn," "What About Today?"), and we'll continue to see other examples.

Example 10.2. "I Don't Remember Christmas"

The line continues to build to the chorus and the emotional (as well as melodic) climax of the song so far: starting on a bracing D major seventh chord, he begins reciting all the things he claims *not* to remember. Summer, fall, December—as for that last one, he says it's possible it "never happened after all," and the pounding syncopation on those last three syllables ("after all"), doubled by the piano, drives the point home (example 10.3).

Example 10.3. "I Don't Remember Christmas"

The list ends with "I don't remember Christmas, and I don't remember you." The song's title takes the penultimate spot in the chorus, but the final four words are the crux of the matter, and this is where the denial first emerges: of course, he remembers her. Although the song may have started with the comforting thought that he is over the painful memories, once his thoughts begin cascading, the unsettling recollections come raging back. And as soon as the lie of "I don't remember you" is stated, the piano comes pounding in with the instrumental interlude, barging in immediately after the final "you" (example 10.4).

Example 10.4. "I Don't Remember Christmas"

This is a purely musical representation of his effort to annihilate the tormenting feelings that are just starting to re-emerge. The first chord is notated in one edition as an A minor ninth with an added eleventh, but it's actually just a dissonant four-note cluster in the right hand. Then, when the chord changes and the bass note becomes B♭ in the third bar of example 10.4, it's even more dissonant and jarring. To a pianist hammering it out at the prescribed forte dynamic, it almost feels like committing an act of violence: her memory, now bubbling back to the surface, has to be physically eradicated.

In the second verse, the litany of lies accelerates: "Later on to my astonishment I did not feel a tug / When I walked into the living room and saw that sheepskin rug." Clearly, a tug is *exactly* what he is feeling now, to say the least, and the syncopated, still-pounding piano part emphasizes it. Regardless of where the song started, his feelings are taking an unanticipated turn. This verse ends with a deft reference to a well-known song from the musical theater canon: "It was good to know I could grow unaccustomed to your face," complete with the arresting internal "know"/"grow" rhyme.

The second chorus maintains the "I don't remember" theme, but the torrent of new detail reminds us just how vividly he *does* remember her, despite his eloquent protests to the contrary. The reference to yet another time of year ("Did I think that you were springtime?") tells us not only that he associates that period with her—as he did summer, fall, and December in the first chorus—but also that he might have thought she *was* springtime. And though he claims that it has "all vanished in the blue," the words and the music increasingly tell us otherwise.

In the bridge, the texture relaxes: the pounding jazz/samba rhythm and chord clusters give way to a legato feel in the piano and a more sustained vocal line. He is referencing his rational side, the one that says, "If she wants to leave you, well, let her." The *sostenuto* melody stays on a single note (E) for all but the last of the nine syllables in that line. Obviously, he's on a more even keel mentally when he tries to reason with himself like that—this is the "practical voice" in his head (example 10.5).

Example 10.5. "I Don't Remember Christmas"

"If she wants to leave you,— well, let her,"—

— says— a prac - ti— cal voice in— my head.

But matters quickly devolve from that short-lived state of mental equilibrium. Starting with the line "Any sensible man would forget her," the melody (and the right hand of the piano part) switches to broad, half-note triplets, while the bass continues playing quarter notes, four to a bar. This means that rhythmically, we have a disorienting three-against-four feel, which implies that the hoped-for rational approach is breaking down, and his thoughts are starting to swirl uncontrollably again. He's reduced to helplessly repeating the phrase "forget her" two more times, sequencing up (and escalating the tension) with each reiteration, and ending on a sustained D while the hammering triplets in the piano carry us into the next section.

It's abundantly clear at this point that "I Don't Remember Christmas" is another "head versus heart" number, as described in chapter 9 in reference to "Crossword Puzzle," in which the intellect battles the emotions; the singer understands rationally that he needs to forget his ex, but he's overpowered by his unshakable obsession.

We're expecting a final chorus now, but Shire cleverly varies the melody slightly, so that instead of the original, it's a series of downwardly spiraling fifths (example 10.6). With this melodic variation, it's almost as if the singer is reduced to helplessly intoning a rote melody at this point, oscillating in an almost sing-song fashion across the perfect fifth intervals, futilely trying to convince himself of what he knows not to be true: that "Thanksgiving never happened and Bermuda is a blur." With an especially pronounced lack of self-knowledge, he claims that he's "not the type to waste time over things that never were," whereas the fact is, he has by now wasted plenty of time, and if these are "things that never were," he somehow manages to recall them in unusually precise detail.

Example 10.6. "I Don't Remember Christmas"

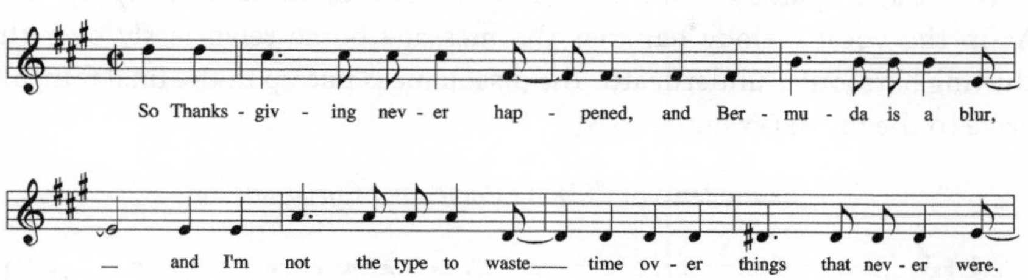
So Thanks - giv - ing nev - er hap - pened, and Ber - mu - da is a blur,
— and I'm not the type to waste— time ov - er things that nev - er were.

Next, Shire plants us firmly back in the second half of the verse, with the same stepwise melodic ascent (example 10.3) that carried us with considerable momentum into the previous choruses. And the lyric is revealing: "Were you really my obsession 'til our ship of pleasure sank?" Yes—obviously she was, and still is. The final chorus provides more imagery and becomes even more intimate: "I don't remember crying, and I can't recall your touch." It's extraordinary, really—we get a nearly blow-by-blow recounting of the entire relationship by way of someone who is denying that any of it even took place.

The coup de grâce is a sixteen-bar coda that continues to pile up details while the harmony keeps us in suspense, driven by a bass line that cycles through a pattern of B-C♯-D-C♯, but with a striking harmonic variation on the third chord in the sequence (D minor seventh the first time and D major seventh the second, as indicated in example 10.7).

Example 10.7. "I Don't Remember Christmas"

As the syncopated rhythm plunges ever forward, the obsessively repeated As in the vocal melody hammer the message home relentlessly over the shifting harmonies underneath. The dissonances pile up in the final four-bar drive to the finish (example 10.8).

Example 10.8. "I Don't Remember Christmas"

The final "I don't remember you" ends on the syncopated and-of-four beat, the last eighth note of the measure, as it did in its previous iterations. However, this time, there's no piano to come charging in as it did before; as a result, the off-the-beat ending, in the absence of any subsequent downbeat, hangs suspended in midair, leaving the audience breathless at the abrupt finish.

Thus, Maltby and Shire's quintessential liar's song ends with the impact of a sledgehammer.

"I Don't Remember Christmas," like "I Think I May Want to Remember Today" (discussed in chapter 5), is a good example of a number that can be easily misinterpreted or misdirected. As Shire explains it, "Singers go at it whole hog, right from the beginning, with anger. It's more of a suppressed ironic feeling. He has to start it from a kind of surfacy, happy-go-lucky thing and then get angrier and angrier as the number builds and builds and finally explodes at the end." Once again, it's easy for a singer to leave himself nowhere to go unless he considers both text and subtext.

George Lee Andrews, who sang "I Don't Remember Christmas" in the original production of *Starting Here, Starting Now*, can be seen on YouTube in a terrific performance of the number from 2013.[1] He remains positively amiable until the exhortation in the second chorus, "Come on, tell me, I forget!," at which point you can see a flash of anger and the growing conflict within, which continues to snowball through the end of the number.

Andrews on "I Don't Remember Christmas":

> I considered it a gift when they turned up with it at rehearsal, and of course still feel that way today. It's wonderful to be associated with such a great piece. Using it for auditions, it has propelled me into many a great job. Not many songs have that kind of succinct power. It's one of my very favorite songs to sing, and always delivers. And, of course, having that great [original cast] recording is huge. People have been captivated by it for many years.[2]

Maltby and Shire on "I Don't Remember Christmas":

RM: This is one of the few songs that started with a lyric, at least the first two A sections.

DS: You've done that often, Richard, more than you'd like to admit. I can think of other songs where you gave me the first couple of lines.

RM: I seldom give him an entirely complete lyric that he stays with.

JR: Did you have an idea about what you wanted it to sound like?

RM: I had this idea that it was going to be this pop song—it's just going to tell the story about discovering that all the things that reminded this person of the other person were gone, and he could deal with it. I described the character and the story to David, and he with his left brain went off and wrote that story in music. And when he brought in the music, which was that driving rhythm, I was rather appalled, because I thought, "Where's that pop song?" It wasn't what I expected, or even wanted, but it was a full dramatic, theatrical expression of what I had actually described, in fact much more rooted in the person than I foresaw. This is one of the examples of songs where if you play the music alone, you can hear the story in it. Right in the music. Hearing that, I went back, threw out whatever pop song ideas I had, and wrote the words—which I would say are the words that were already in the music waiting to be found.

DS: I don't remember Christmas, and I don't remember writing this song! It was just one of those gifts from the creative gods that come along every so often to compensate for the struggle it takes to wrest so many other songs from them. I think I don't remember writing it because it came so easily, especially with my jazz background, which doesn't frequently get an opportunity to cut loose like this.

RM: He can't recall writing it because he was channeling the character and hearing him tell his story. That image, by the way, is something that actually happened to me. I literally closed the door, and the robe that used to be hanging on the door wasn't there. And because somehow the robe on the door was the thing, you know, the connection, when it wasn't there, first it was painful, and then—hey, it's not there, oh my goodness! I've actually gotten over this. I can go through the rest of the house. That sheepskin rug, all those things, they're not there. Aren't I lucky!

DS: Of course, he's lying.

RM: Basically, it was an emotional journey the guy wants to forget, but in the course of this thing, it comes back to him. The song has an action, which is what makes it a theater song. We didn't intend it as such, but it had a dramatic structure, a dramatic progress, and so it was very much like a monologue. More like a monologue than a song, and goodbye to its pop-song-ness.

DS: It's happened many times. Every time we've attempted to write a pop song and played it for a record producer, they say, "Well, you know, that's a great song, but it really is a theater song," and I can't tell you how many times that happened until we finally realized, this was what our métier was.

11
HE'S THE ARBITER, REALLY

The "head versus heart" conflict is a dynamic that is often at the root of the songwriting process itself for Maltby and Shire. In that context, one could think of it as "intellect versus instinct."

"I intellectualize a lot when I'm trying to write something," Shire muses, "but as Richard has seen many times, it's only when I get disgusted, and I can't find anything, that I let my left brain relax and suddenly under my fingers pops out something worthwhile."

Maltby goes even further. "I think it is actually the essence of David Shire as a songwriter. He fundamentally wants to be an intellectual. He wants his brain to control what he's doing. I mean, his smarts are his calling. That's what got him into Yale, that's what he's proudest of. He was Phi Beta Kappa! I sure as hell wasn't. However, when writing, the only time anything really thrilling ever happened was when he locked into the other side or did something completely instinctive. I found early on that if I described something in an intellectual way, nothing happened. But if we talked about the character and the circumstance, somehow that connected, and he would go off and out came this great thing. The melody would suddenly go to some unexpected place, like in the bridge of 'I Don't Remember Christmas'—the emotion that has been buried inside the singer starts spilling out, and he doesn't want it to, but it's there."

This is not to say that surrendering to one's natural creative instincts makes the process easy. "I don't want to give you the impression that I just turn off the left brain and suddenly it's all there," Shire hastens to add. "More often than not, it's a second, third, or fourth attempt that finally cracks it, and not right away. Sometimes it takes a week or two to stew. But I finally just let the emotion translate through the fingers, and that's a process I still don't quite understand. It feels, when it happens, like I didn't do anything, so why am I getting praise for it? I'm not being falsely humble when I say

Closer Than Ever. Joshua Rosenblum, Oxford University Press. © Oxford University Press 2024.
DOI: 10.1093/oso/9780197758236.003.0011

that I feel some compositional goodies are really gifts from the gods, and I'm just a vessel."

For Shire, the right brain is like "the quiet student in the back row who has the correct answer and keeps shyly raising her hand but can't get recognized until all the show-off know-it-alls in the front row have had their overrationalized say."

In terms of the back-and-forth process between the two collaborators, the dynamic they established as fledgling songwriters at Yale has largely remained in place over the course of more than six decades.

DS: I have a lot of false starts, and Richard has thrown away many more things of mine than he has accepted. He's the arbiter, really. He deals with me like a good director deals with an actor. He doesn't say, "That should be happy, and that should be sad, and do this, do that." There's always a reason for it, and I tend most of the time—maybe all of the time—to go with him. He claims that the reason we've lasted sixty-five years is basically because neither one of us has ever said, "It has to be my way."

RM: If we disagree, if I have an idea I really like and David doesn't like it, we try to figure it out. Either I convince him it's a good idea, or he convinces me that it isn't. And if after that, one of us can't convince the other, the answer is always that neither position is serving the dramatic moment, and we discard both positions. Invariably, we end up with a better idea than either of us had.

As far as the answer to the age-old question of which comes first, the music or the lyrics, the answer for Maltby and Shire is . . . the idea.

DS: The truth is, every song is kind of an ad hoc situation. There's a different mix of our abilities. Richard has written some lyrics which I have set almost exactly.

RM: Yes, but not very many. When I have to do lyrics first, I tend to write very ordinary rhythms, like doggerel. Mostly, we have a discussion about what the song is. Sometimes I write a little bit, sometimes I write more, but nothing really happens until somehow David goes off and it connects in some sort of way.

DS: You know when it's right or wrong.

RM: But we would also spend a good deal of time, at least early on, on the melody itself, before I ever started working. All without the words—we were working on the premise that when the music was right, the words were in the music. If we shaped the melody *this* way, by the time we got to the end, the whole story we had set out to do had been written, just in the music, and then it was just a matter of filling it in with words. I don't know if anyone else works that way.

DS: Here's another basic fact about our collaboration: Richard, who never learned an instrument and doesn't write music, is one of the most astute musical minds that I know—I mean, his feeling for the details of music. His ear. There are some melodies where I've brought in something that was half right and half wrong, and his comments are quite specific. Once we were working on a song for *The Sap of Life*, and he said, "That isn't what you played yesterday. You went from this chord straight to that chord." And I said, "No, I didn't! There's no way this chord leads to that one." As it happened, we had taped that session, and he played it back, and it went from one chord straight to the other, just like he said, and I said, "Oh my God, how did I do that?" There are many moments like that.

RM: But when David lets himself go in his creative sense, strange quirky structures and rhythms appear to him. And they produce verbal rhythms that I wouldn't ever think of. That quirkiness forces me to find language that will make the rhythms work, and that makes me say different, more conversational, more interesting things. I usually play the melody over and over in my head until the melody itself sings the words to me. Like in *Baby* [Maltby sings from the song "Romance" from *Baby*]: "On the ninth, eleventh, thirteenth, fifteenth, and seventeenth / When there's magic in the air / It's nice to know that we would share / a rendezvous." That wouldn't have happened if it had been lyrics first.

There can be other hazards in writing lyrics first.

RM: Occasionally, I will write what I think is a David Shire lyric—a lyric for a David Shire melody. Absolutely without exception, when I give it to David, he'll say, "What am I supposed to do with this?" And I'll sing some kind of dummy melody that I thought would be comparable to what David would write, and he'll go, "Huh? That doesn't make any sense at all!"

DS: But Richard always says, "Forget what I wrote. Take what it's saying, and go off and write your own thing." He's very non-possessive about his work as it develops. He has a sense of where the song is going, and if I question his lyric, even if it's something he worked hard on, he immediately says, "Forget this. Just use it as a model."

RM: Yeah, you should go to what inspires you.

DS: In those cases, I like to say, "It's an embarrassment of Richards."

RM: I do absolutely realize that when he comes back with a melody that really is good, that means I then have to write the whole damn thing over again.

DS: Like many composers, there is an element of me that wants to show off my technique or my originality, or what I think is my originality. So there will often be too many notes, or a chord or a progression that I've really worked over to make it very technically correct, and the answer is not to do that. Richard clears out the underbrush and makes an honest man of me—or makes me appear to be less self-aggrandizing. And he also trusts me when I say, "I don't quite understand that line," or "It isn't quite clear what you mean," or "That's a little ambiguous." I try to be as hard on the lyrics as he is on the music. We constantly edit each other's work.

RM: I've only come to realize this later on that David is fundamentally a playwright, and he doesn't even know it. That is to say, he thinks composing is about composing, and that's what's important to him, but he doesn't write anything unless he understands the character of the scene, and once he understands that, then he can compose.

The notion of songwriting as playwriting is a key concept for both writers.

RM: I mean, that's what it is, when all is said and done. The older I get, the more I realize there's nothing going on except playwriting—in the score, in the lyrics, in anything. And the reason why Steve Sondheim is Steve Sondheim is not mainly because he's clever or even because he's a great lyricist or a great composer—it's that he is always a great playwright. I mean, his sensitivity for what is going on in the scene, in the dramatic moment, is exceptional, and in many cases, you wouldn't know that something was happening in the show if it weren't happening in the song.

DS: It's true. Musical theater songwriting is about playwriting. It's not the same with pop songs. People often ask the difference, but a typical pop song goes from A to B dramatically, and a good theater song goes from A to at least K or L. Pop songs tend to repeat the same thing over and over again in different ways, or they're about just one thing. I tend to write songs that go someplace, so they come out as good material for Richard to fit that dramatic playwriting aspect to it. He really is as much responsible for making me look like a musical playwright as anything, because if I were working with a pop lyricist, it wouldn't happen.

This reflexive tendency to give each other a large share of the credit is something that comes up repeatedly in conversation. As for who is responsible for the overall structure of "The Bear, the Tiger, the Hamster and the Mole" (see chapter 19):

RM: I wish I remembered the sequence of inventing the song, who thought up what, but I have an idea the shape was David's entirely, based only on the arc of the thought process building to the title I had given him.

Conversely:

DS: I can't even remember where the lyric came first or where the music took the lead. But I'm sure Richard had a big hand in the overall structure and such.

These two contrasting views are typical of the esteem in which the songwriting partners hold each other and of their tendency to give each other credit. It's also an indication of why their collaboration has been so successful for so long. One might say it's a great model for relationships of any type—not just creative ones.

Kevin Stites, a veteran Broadway conductor who has worked with the team on numerous projects, observes, "Richard cares more about the music than David does, and David cares more about the lyrics than Richard does. Richard will defend the music before he defends the lyrics. And vice versa. I think that's why their relationship is so healthy."

Shire refers back to "Autumn," which has endured as one of their most popular numbers, to give an example of how Maltby helped shape the melody before any lyrics were even written.

DS: Richard kept rejecting melody after melody that I thought was just wonderful. I had already taken something of a distaste to his criticism. Finally, I just got disgusted, and I went home and kind of in anger, I came up with that melody. And I played it for him, and he said, "Ah, that's a melody."

RM: The one change that I made was in the bridge, where he had a lot of extra notes. [He sings, to demonstrate, as transcribed in example 11.1a].

Example 11.1a. "Autumn" (original draft version of the bridge melody, as recalled by Maltby)

Maltby continues: "I said, 'Why don't we just have a whole note there?' So I did muck around a little bit. I couldn't completely take the spurs off."

This resulted in the more economical, more vocally sympathetic, and more affecting revised version that has endured (example 11.1b).

Example 11.1b. "Autumn" (final version of the bridge melody)

Maltby, in other words, identified certain melody notes as excessive even before any lyrics were written.

After Maltby sings what he recalls of the first draft, Shire chimes in, as if on cue, with an example of what the lyricization might have been of the original, not nearly as good, version: "'There's a touch and a nip of frost now / And all my thoughts of somewhere summer spring seem lost now.' Don't you think that would have been better?" he deadpans.

Deniz Cordell, a Maltby/Shire associate who has worked for the team variously as pianist, musical director, arranger, archivist, and general facilitator, says that the dynamic between the two has mellowed somewhat but remains fundamentally unchanged. "It's still basically, David will write, Richard will critique, and then they'll both go back and do more writing," Cordell says.[1] He affirms that Maltby is still the final arbiter, just as he was in 1957. In terms of the level of pique when a potential piece of music is rejected, Cordell says, "On the rare occasions when a bit of dander flies, it's a creative argument. It's never personal, and it doesn't get heated.

"Richard still prefers working when there's at least something of a melody in place," Cordell continues. "He doesn't always like it when David just sets a lyric. They've done that once or twice in recent memory. But even then, if it's something David sets, Richard will rewrite the lyric so it conforms better. Or sometimes David will set the lyric, and Richard will say, 'No, David! That wasn't the finished lyric! I didn't want you to set it exactly!'"

Shire also had a trick early in their collaboration when he felt Maltby was taking too long to come up with lyrics to one of his melodies.

"Richard used to take so long to write lyrics because he felt he had to make the first line absolutely perfect before he could go to the next one," Shire relates. "He just angsted over it. But he loved to rewrite. When I wrote a rough lyric, he'd improve it immediately. So, as a ruse to get him going, I'd write a quick rough draft of something, and then he'd rewrite it because then he wouldn't have to spend so much time on it." This, in Shire's view, was like an ongoing advanced master class in lyric writing and is a large part of how he developed his own lyric-writing skills for the songs he wrote alone.

12

REMEMBER THAT FATS WALLER IDEA?

AIN'T MISBEHAVIN'

After the success of *Starting Here, Starting Now*, there was renewed impetus for the reunited team to continue writing musicals together. At the same time, both were finding great success in their respective independent careers but not without some setbacks.

For Maltby, the setback took the form of a play called *Chez Nous*, by British playwright Peter Nichols. Nichols's play, as Richard Eder put it in his pan of the show in the *New York Times*, centered around "the mild and cerebral sexual entanglements of two English couples who don't much like each other but vacation together, nonetheless, in the south of France."[1] Lynne Meadow hired Maltby to direct the show at Manhattan Theatre Club, and it didn't go well. "I directed it really badly," Maltby recalls, "and I thought it was a humiliating mistake."

Meadow remembers that "Richard was struggling, the company knew he was struggling, and he knew he was struggling. I had worked with a number of these people [in the cast] before. I said, 'Richard, why don't I just come in with you and see if we can figure it out, because everybody's a little lost?' and he said OK." Meadow says this isn't unusual for her in her role as artistic director of MTC. "One of the things I've done for many years is come in and work with directors, give my opinions, and help solve problems, make recommendations, just say it's great, or give extensive notes. This was a very difficult play to do, and I'd directed a fair number of English plays. I wanted to make it as painless as possible."

In hindsight, Maltby has a little more perspective on the experience. "I couldn't make sense of the story. I tried to construct the backstory from elements that were mentioned in the script, and I couldn't get them to make sense. Turns out it wasn't me. They didn't make sense. It was the play."

Closer Than Ever. Joshua Rosenblum, Oxford University Press. © Oxford University Press 2024.
DOI: 10.1093/oso/9780197758236.003.0012

At the time, however, it was painful. "He felt bad, and I knew he felt bad. I cared about him tremendously as my friend, as an artist, as someone whom I've adored since I was twelve," Meadow emphasizes. "I have a closeness to him and to David that's very deep."

Meadow knew what Maltby needed was to work again. "I said, 'Come on, you're terrific. This was what it was. We did this—now you gotta get back on the horse.' I said, 'Remember that Fats Waller idea you were talking about? We need a show in February. I'm desperate.' And he said, 'OK.'"

Maltby recalls the conversation in almost identical terms. "She said that in, like, October or maybe even November [1977]. The trajectory of the show after that was just astonishing."

"I thought it was a cool idea," Meadow continues, "but little did I know it would be so groundbreaking and that he was the perfect person to put it together. I remember casting it and meeting talent, meeting Nell [Carter] in a pair of overalls. The experience was really fantastic."

"That Fats Waller idea," of course, turned out to be *Ain't Misbehavin'*, the exuberant, trailblazing, widely lauded show that in 1978 became the first revue in Broadway's history to win the Tony Award for Best Musical and also scored Maltby a Tony win for Best Director of a Musical.

The idea originated with Maltby's friend Murray Horwitz, who, after seeing *Starting Here, Starting Now*, told Maltby that his next project should be a similar type of show using Waller songs. Maltby, not particularly enthusiastic and not then a great fan of jazz, nonetheless agreed to go to Murray's apartment and listen to his Waller collection. Maltby recalls his reaction upon hearing the music:

> I went crazy because [Waller] was so witty. It wasn't the jokes—what absolutely knocked me over was the piano music. He would play, and you could feel him playing with the audience the whole time. He was teasing them and caressing them and saying, "I'm gonna give you this note. You like that one? I'll give you another one. You want this? I'll give you this. Notice the little hand up here doin' that." He wasn't saying those words, but that's what the music was doing, and I thought, well, why not? If a company of performers on the stage could play with the audience, tease the audience the way Waller did, you'd have something that belongs onstage. And that was the first perception I had that actually held all the way through [the production].
>
> First day of rehearsal, I showed a lot of movies—every movie that had Fats Waller in it. And I told the cast to just look at these films. And I said, I didn't know what you would see in Waller, and they didn't have

> to tell me, but find yourself in him and use that. Then, the second day, we started, with these great singers, these great songs, the Waller persona, and I thought, something's going to explode here.[2]

Maltby attributes a large part of the show's success to the cast. "The shape of the show came because of who came in," he explains. "Five incredibly talented people. I would not have conceived any of the parts for any of them until they were there. Who could imagine Nell Carter? Who could imagine Armelia McQueen, Ken Page, or, for God's sake, André De Shields? Or who could imagine Charlayne Woodard, who joined us when we went to Broadway? The show built off them, and they became the parts."[3]

Carter, who won both Drama Desk and Tony Awards for her performance, apparently took Maltby's injunction about adapting the teasing Waller persona particularly to heart. As Maltby recounts it:

> Nell Carter was, you know, a superstar. The show is going on OK, and then Nell walked in with "Honeysuckle Rose" and started singing "Every honeybee fills with jealousy," and she started hitting those high notes, and then the audience went crazy—I mean, they could feel the walls coming down like they'd never heard anything like it, and at that moment, we were sailing. She had an instinct to get the audience. She would say something mean to them, and then she would say something nice. She would say, "Oh, honey, you're the only person I've ever wanted." She would just toy with you all the time. You never quite know what's going on, but her brain is so full of stuff—she just had an instinct to do that. And you dare not look anywhere else, because you're gonna miss something.

The cast had gone into rehearsal on January 1 for performances at the MTC cabaret space in February. They closed as scheduled on March 1. At the beginning of April, they began rehearsals for the Broadway production, which opened on May 9.

"By June 1st, we had won every award a musical can win in New York, except the Pulitzer Prize," Maltby recalls, "including an Obie because we had also opened off-Broadway. I don't think any show ever moved as fast as that."

Ain't Misbehavin' spawned five touring companies within the first two years—four in the United States and one in England. In 1988, ten years after the show's original debut, the show was revived on Broadway, this time at the Ambassador Theatre. The entire original cast as well as pianist and musical director Luther Henderson returned in the roles they had created, along with Henderson's electrifying orchestrations, Arthur Faria's dazzling choreography, and Maltby as director. This time out, the show won the Tony for Best Revival of a Musical.

"I had no idea it was ever going to be anything more than a little nightclub act," Maltby concludes.

Among the many knockout Waller songs from *Ain't Misbehavin'* is "Lounging at the Waldorf," which originated as an instrumental number with three swinging melodies that go together in counterpoint. Maltby took the piece, wrote lyrics for it, and turned it into a quodlibet, or, in this case, one of those songs with *three* parts where all of them go together. In its final form, the first melody is sung wordlessly in two-part harmony on "ooh" while another performer (Page) seemingly ad-libs spoken remarks as if he's greeting pretentious friends. Then Carter sings the first verse, Page reappears for the second verse, and finally, in a grand bit of serendipity, all three melodies are heard together (although the first one is still wordless).

"I guess it comes from being the son of an arranger," Maltby reflects, "but I just love multiple levels. I was basically just setting [Waller's] band arrangement. I love the way the parts talk to each other."

The song is a Black person's cheerful sendup of pompous upper-class white folk, and Page's ad libs are based on Waller's subtly scathing spoken interjections on his original recording of the number.

"The music had the story in it, and I just put in the words that were already there," Maltby concludes. The result is one of the musical theater canon's great quodlibets.

Around the same time, Shire had his own disappointing setback that led to a triumph. Francis Coppola had hired him once again, this time to compose the score for his film *Apocalypse Now*. In Shire's words:

> It's been well documented that Francis was going crazy down in the Philippines. Lots of drugs, the set was blown away by a monsoon. Footage would come my way, but intermittently. When I was asked to do *Norma Rae*, I thought I could easily do that and handle whatever came back from the Philippines. But the third element of the perfect storm was that Talia and I were separated, heading for divorce. Francis called and said, "I hear you're working on another movie." He was angry, and he fired me. It was a big blow to lose that.[4]

The loss of the *Apocalypse* assignment gave Shire plenty of time to work on the score for *Norma Rae*, which included the song "It Goes Like It Goes," sung by Jennifer Warnes on the movie soundtrack, with lyrics by Normal Gimbel. The same year, Shire also scored *The Promise*, which yielded the song "I'll Never Say Goodbye," sung by Melissa Manchester, with lyrics by Alan and Marilyn Bergman.[5] In a highly unusual turn of events, both of Shire's songs were nominated for an Academy Award in 1979. "It Goes Like It Goes" won.

"I really thought I would lose," Shire insists. "I thought half my friends would vote for each. Also, I was up against Marvin Hamlisch [for "Through the Eyes of Love," with lyrics by Carole Bayer Sager, from *Ice Castles*] and Kermit the Frog [for "Rainbow Connection" from *The Muppet Movie*, written by Kenny Ascher and Paul Williams]. How can you win under those conditions?"[6]

"It Goes Like It Goes" was the second attempt at a song for *Norma Rae*. The film's producers wanted country music star Waylon Jennings to sing the number, so Shire and Gimbel wrote what Shire says was "a very undistinguished song" for him. Jennings, however, came to a screening of the picture and decided he didn't want to do the song, without even having heard it. "So then there was a real scramble to find someone who was as chartable as [Jennings] was," Shire remembers. The producers settled on Warnes, who was indeed on the charts around that time with her hit single "I Know a Heartache When I See One."

But a new song had to be written. For starters, now that a female singer was on board, the number could be written in first person instead of third, which meant the song could now express Norma's thoughts directly. "Also," Shire observes dryly, "we could write a song that had a range of more than five notes."

Shire had been hired to score the whole movie, which included the song or any rewrites of the song, but Gimbel, who had been brought in from the outside, was under no such agreement and felt he should be paid again for writing a second song. "I think he had an argument there," Shire admits, "but I didn't feel I should get another fee." Gimbel was furious at Shire for not backing him up. "He wrote that lyric and had it delivered to me via messenger with a note that said, 'Don't change a syllable of this, I'm going off on a ski trip.' He didn't talk to me for the whole next year."

When the song was nominated, Shire thought Gimbel would resume speaking to him, but all communication remained through their agents. Even during the Academy Awards ceremony itself, Gimbel continued to stew. As Shire relates it:

> The night of the Oscars, the Bergmans were sitting on one side and Norman was sitting on the other, and he still wasn't talking to me. They called our names, we went up there, we gave our acceptance speeches.

Then they hustle you off the stage and into an elevator to go up to the press room, and there was silence for a moment as the elevator went up, and then Norman turned to me and said, "Well, I guess I'm gonna have to talk to you now."

Shire's discarded score for *Apocalypse Now* can actually be heard today, on a La-La Land Records release from 2017.[7] Arts journalist and film music aficionado Tim Greiving found cassette recordings of the music cues while going through Shire's archives and felt the score needed to be heard. The process was somewhat arduous, but Shire, characteristically, finds the humor in it.

"There was a yearlong saga trying to get the rights. We got permission from Francis and the studio, and we were able to find the master recordings. The funniest thing was when I called Francis—we patched things up not long after *Apocalypse Now*, and Talia and I had a reasonably friendly divorce—I called him up to say, 'Somebody wants to put out my score, any objection to that?' There was a long silence. Then he said, 'What score?' "

13 AT THE END OF THE SONG, EVERYONE'S PREGNANT!

While Shire was still married to Talia (they divorced in 1980) and before the *Apocalypse Now* falling-out, he occasionally made trips to Napa Valley with Francis Coppola. Coppola, commonly regarded as one of the all-time great film directors, was born into a musical household. His father was Carmine Coppola, composer and, for a time, principal flutist of the NBC Symphony under Arturo Toscanini. Francis's uncle, Carmine's brother, was Anton Coppola, an opera conductor and composer. Francis had studied the tuba as a child and won a music scholarship to the New York Military Academy. At Hofstra University, he studied to be a theater director, writing and directing musicals and graduating with a degree in theater arts. As Shire puts it, "He's very into music."

During one drive to Napa, Shire mentioned that it was difficult to find topics for new musicals and that he and Maltby were stalled on something to write about. Shire and Coppola discussed the fact that big, spectacle-oriented musicals were taking over Broadway. As Shire recalls, "[Coppola] said, 'Why don't you write a small musical about something that may have happened to you? What's the most emotional experience you've had in the last couple of years?' And I said, 'Being present at the birth of my first son, Matthew.' And he went [Shire claps his hands together loudly]."

Shire took the idea back to Maltby, who hated it. "I thought, 'He's in California, he's gone bonkers. What does he know anymore?'" Maltby recalls dryly.[1] "He was imagining a diaper musical," Shire muses. "But then he went off for a while, and he had this stroke of insight where he realized that it wasn't about the baby, it was about the couples and what happens to them over that period of time. The baby was just the McGuffin."

Closer Than Ever. Joshua Rosenblum, Oxford University Press. © Oxford University Press 2024.
DOI: 10.1093/oso/9780197758236.003.0013

Maltby agrees and elaborates:

> There had been in the seventies a bunch of movies like *Georgy Girl* and *Darling* that were part of the British new wave, and they were all about the new sexual freedom. Relationships were kind of fluid—you could sort of be together and sort of not. But they all had one idiosyncrasy that I thought was really funny, which was that in the last twenty minutes of the movie, the heroine always got pregnant. And I suddenly thought, oh, wait, that's not just an oddity. The fact is, if you're going to tell a story about relationships that are fluid, that's fine. But a baby is reality. The moment you have a baby, you have to stop and say, wait a minute, what am I to the other person? What are we together? And then I thought, if the show could do that, tell how babies change relationships, then that would be something good to put on the stage. That's what I think was the whole genesis of the show. The show covers a nine-month time span from conception to birth. In the course of that, [the couples] go through these incredible soul-searching experiences. I think it resonated with a lot of people.

Maltby was counting on veteran Broadway producer Emanuel Azenberg, who had brought *Ain't Misbehavin'* to Broadway in 1979, to do the same for *Baby*. Azenberg, however, eventually decided against it and pulled out of the project, so Maltby went to Jim Freydberg, who was now in New York. Freydberg already had a major Broadway producing credit with Athol Fugard's play *"Master Harold" . . . and the Boys*, but he had never produced a Broadway musical. Nonetheless, Freydberg was by this time a devout Maltby/Shire fan—he had brought *Starting Here, Starting Now* to Walnut Street's black-box space and later to San Francisco—and he was eager to get to work on *Baby*. "I owe my life to Jim," Maltby states unequivocally.

Freydberg pleaded with Bernie Jacobs of the Shubert Organization for a theater, and Jacobs made the Barrymore Theatre available. But raising money for *Baby* was slow and difficult. "We had a really hard time getting it on," Maltby recalls. He feels it would have been easier to get backers on board if the show had had a big Broadway director attached, "but Jim insisted on it being me."[2]

Freydberg says it wasn't a big issue. "I never present things that way," he insists. "I never let it come up. 'This is our director, he happens to be our writer, that's the way we're going.' If they don't want to do it, they don't have to."[3] Freydberg had reason to be confident that the right person could be both writer—or, in this case, lyricist—and director, based on his experience with *"Master Harold."* "I had an association with Athol Fugard way before he was on Broadway. And I knew that he was also a director." In Maltby's case, Freydberg had known him as a director first from *Long Day's Journey into Night* at the Walnut Street Theatre in Philadelphia.

Freydberg also helped Maltby and Shire find Sybille Pearson, their librettist for the show. Pearson had submitted her play *Sally and Marsha* to Freydberg, who thought it contained particularly good writing for the female characters. Freydberg suggested that she meet with the songwriters about *Baby*, and they all hit it off. At that point, however, Lynne Meadow had committed to directing *Sally and Marsha* at Manhattan Theatre Club, in a production starring Bernadette Peters and Christine Baranski. Pearson felt she couldn't take on writing the book for *Baby* until *Sally and Marsha* was mounted. Maltby and Shire were willing to wait six months for Pearson to be available.

Before the team settled on Pearson, several other writers had been involved to one degree or another as librettists, including Susan Yankowitz, Tina Howe, and Ted Tally, now best known for his film adaptation of the Thomas Harris novel *The Silence of the Lambs*.[4] There was also a brief flirtation with Jules Feiffer. "[He] listened to the score, and we talked," Maltby recounts, "and he said, 'You have to understand that I have just written a play at the end of which a couple throws the baby out the window, and I consider that a happy ending.'" The team did not move forward with Feiffer.

They also approached Neil Simon at one point. "We read an article where he said that he got a lot of writing done while he was waiting in the dentist's office to have his teeth fixed," Shire remembers. "So we called him and asked him if he'd be interested in writing the book [to *Baby*] because we'd read that about him, and he said, 'My teeth have all been fixed.'"

When a draft of the show was completed with Pearson, *Baby* had a workshop production. The show ultimately revolved around three couples, but originally there was an additional principal character, a single woman trying to decide whether to have a baby or not. In the workshop draft, this character sang the Maltby/Shire classic "The Bear, the Tiger, the Hamster and the Mole." However, the feeling was that once that character performed that number, the audience knew everything about her there was to know, and there was no further use for her in the show.

In Maltby's words, "When we took her out, I had kind of a breakdown over it. I had created in my head an architecture that included that character, and if you took that out, everything just seemed to fall apart, and I didn't know how to start. When I confessed that to Sybille, she said, 'Well, OK. Let's just start at the beginning. What's the first thing that would happen? What's the next thing that would happen?' And we slowly did that, and pretty soon we went through the whole show and obviated that part."

Much work, however, lay ahead, as the writers and cast members headed into rehearsal for the Broadway production ("with just enough money to get the show open," as Maltby recalls). On the first day, the cast read through the script. Freydberg came to the writers after the read-through and said he found it unpleasant. "He said, 'It seems to be saying that if you have a baby, it ruins your life,'" Maltby recounts. "This was after we had already done a whole lot of work on it."

This was certainly not what they intended for the show to say. "We wanted to show that [having a baby] changes your relationships," Maltby reiterates. "It makes you confront what's missing and the darkest fears you have about yourself, which eventually get addressed in a marriage. So it's about marriage, really. We realized that it would take a really substantial restructuring of the whole show to correct that."

This was a daunting discovery to make mere weeks before a show starts Broadway previews, but there was nothing to do except get to work. Maltby describes the ensuing process:

> We started reconstructing the whole show in the four-week rehearsal period, but it was kind of extraordinary. We would bring in the new scene, and then we would do it. Songs got dropped, songs got written. The end of the show was originally "I Wouldn't Go Back,"[5] which we replaced with the birth sequence—David just came up with that piece of music one day. "Easier to Love" was written in rehearsal. Even through two weeks of previews, we were changing things every night. Not just changing a line here and there but reorganizing a whole scene. It changed enormously, right in front of our eyes. The same thing had happened with *Ain't Misbehavin'* years earlier. It was the same sense of building the show on its feet in front of us.

Even songs that were kept were changed. For Maltby, the most illuminating example was "What Could Be Better?," a number near the beginning of the show for Lizzie and Danny, the youngest of the three couples, sophomores in college who have just moved in together. The surprise news of Lizzie's pregnancy forces them to make some important decisions.

In the original draft, Lizzie and Danny decide in the scene preceding the song that they will have the baby but not get married; then they sing the number. But with the scene having already resolved the important issues, the song seemed to be marking time. "I thought it was very long," Maltby says. He realized that for the sequence to have a dramatic action, they had to withhold something until the end of the song. Thus, this exchange of dialogue, which had originally preceded the number, was placed inside the song, spoken over musical underscoring, just before the final verse:

Lizzie: So?
Danny: Yes!
Lizzie: Yes!
Both: We're going to have a baby!
Lizzie: And not get married!
[Danny looks shocked.]

In this revised version, it takes almost the entire song to reach this conclusion. Suddenly, the song had a dramatic storyline and didn't seem long at all.[6] As Maltby sums it up, "If songwriting is playwriting, then the song has to go somewhere. The trick is withholding something until the end."

Having realized that this crucial placement of a pivotal dramatic moment had saved the number, Maltby then went through and did the same thing with nearly every song in the show. The opening number, "We Start Today," shows the three couples all going about their business. Lizzie and Danny are moving in together; Pam and Nick, a basketball coach and a college professor, are trying to conceive a child; Arlene and Alan, newly empty nesters, are getting used to each other again now that their children are off to college. "And then," Maltby explains, "having established that life is just going on for these people, the end of the number is the three different couples getting this news [that the wives are pregnant] all at once. That's the last moment of the song—we're going to throw a baby in, too. So that's definitely an action. At the end of the song, everyone's pregnant!"

Maltby added a deft directorial flourish right at this point: the women receive the big life-altering news without anyone saying anything. It comes at the end of a quatrain of characteristically Maltby-esque concision and economy:

Lizzie: Oh, I guess it's just the flu.
Arlene: Guess I have a checkup due.
Pam: Yes, I'm late, don't ask me how.
Nurse: Yes, the doctor will see you now.

In three lines of just seven syllables each, we get a status report on why each woman needs a medical appointment that day, and on the fourth line, we are catapulted right into the doctor's office. Then, at the moment of truth, all three women face front, dumbstruck. We don't need a lyric to tell us what information they've just received, and the women themselves don't need to say anything, either.[7] Then, shortly after this wonderfully wordless reveal (and right before the number's final button), the couples get to verbalize their astonishment: "A baby?!," each pair exclaims in turn. Lizzie and Danny are stunned, Pam and Nick are overjoyed, and Arlene and Alan, who already have three grown children, are (at least for now) horrified.

The best part is that the audience knows all along that conception has taken place, well before the couples get the news. During the show's prologue, a biology teacher intones, "In a way, it's a truly romantic story. Somewhere, unseen, sperm meets egg. The great miracle occurs. And no one knows that it has happened."[8] But now—crucially for the drama—the audience knows, before the opening number has even started.[9] This makes the pregnancy-reveal moment at the end of "We Start Today" even better, as the audience gets to enjoy seeing the characters' shock at discovering what they, the audience, already know. Once again, the placement of crucial dramatic material at the end of the number gives the song an action and enhances its theatricality exponentially.

Shire's manuscript for "We Start Today" indicates the melody for the bridge (example 13.1a). We can see by comparison that he altered the rhythm of the melody for the final version of the song (example 13.1b) so that instead of straight quarter notes, the rhythm is syncopated, giving it a jazzier, more propulsive and exciting feel.

Example 13.1a. "We Start Today," manuscript.

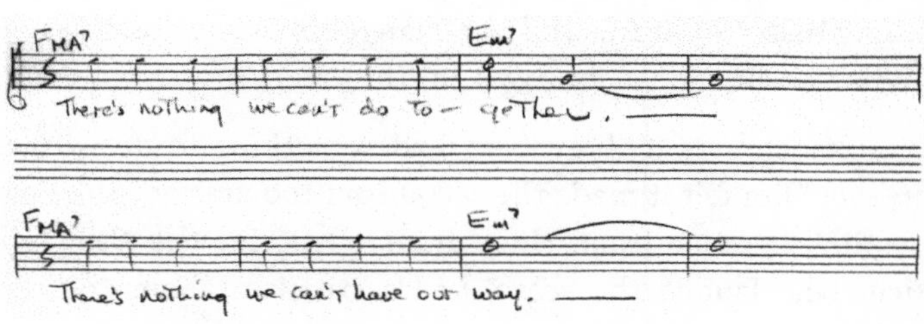

Example 13.1b. "We Start Today," final version.

The song "Patterns," a big, reflective solo number for Arlene (Beth Fowler in the Broadway production), appears on the cast recording but was cut from the show in previews.[10] In the song, a visibly pregnant Arlene expresses her uneasiness over the familiar patterns of impending motherhood that she feels herself falling into. Toward the end of the emotionally fraught number, Arlene sings these lines:

> And I must change or else I'll break apart,
> Or break away,
> And end up having to start . . . again.

Librettist Pearson found this objectionable. To Pearson, the change Arlene was saying she had to make in order to break out of those oppressive patterns was that she had to end her pregnancy. This sense was compounded by the recurring video of the developing embryo that had been projected during the prologue and was then brought back periodically during scene transitions, including the one just prior to "Patterns." In Maltby's recollection:

> We were following the fetal development with the video, and [Sybille] found it offensive that we should see the fetus developing and then this woman comes out and sings about how maybe she should have an abortion. It takes a bit of doing to make the leap that that's what [the character Arlene] is talking about, but some women, I guess, read it that way, and because of that, and because Sybille felt really strongly about it, we decided we had to cut the song and put in a reprise of something instead.[11] It was the last change we made, and it was a mistake. What we should've done was cut the video.

As Shire remembers it, Freydberg had something to do with the song being cut, too. "Jim felt it made the second act too dreary," Shire says. "And it's interesting, because [then chief drama critic for the *New York Times*] Frank Rich, who lauded the score, had a criticism about the second act being weaker because the women were not fully realized. We attributed it to 'Patterns' being missing. If that had been in, it would've given a three-dimensionality to Arlene's character. Without it, you don't see her conflicted feelings about always doing the same thing."

On the other hand, Rich's review gave credence to Coppola's instinct that the team would do well to focus on a small, personal story rather than create a more fashionable Broadway spectacle. "At a time when nearly every Broadway musical, good and bad, aims for the big kill with gargantuan pyrotechnics, here is a modestly scaled entertainment that woos us with such basic commodities as warm feelings, an exuberant cast and a lovely score," Rich opined in the opening paragraph of his write-up.[12]

Continuing his praise of the team's work, Rich wrote:

> Mr. Shire writes with sophistication over a range that embraces rock, jazz and the best of Broadway schmaltz. His music receives its full due from Jonathan Tunick's lithe, endlessly varied orchestrations and from a sizable onstage band conducted by Peter Howard. Mr. Maltby's lyrics are not just smart and funny, but often ingenious—as befits a lyricist who has a sideline inventing intricate crossword puzzles for Harper's magazine.

Interestingly, Rich found the projected film of embryonic development effective, even though it was cut in subsequent productions and in the licensed version of the show. "[Maltby] does a dexterous job of interweaving projected film animation into the action. As the mothers push toward D-day, we follow their intrauterine development to ultimately touching effect." Rich concluded:

> If the virtues of *Baby* can't override all its hitches, so be it. In achievement, this show is a throwback to the early 1960s—the last era when Broadway regularly produced some casual-spirited musicals that were not instantly categorizable as blockbusters or fiascos. Those musicals—like, say, *Do Re Mi* or *110 in the Shade*—weren't built for the ages but could brighten a theater season or two: they were ingratiatingly professional, had both lulls and peaks, and inspired you to run to the record store as soon as the original cast album came out. So it is with *Baby*, and wouldn't it be cheering if such a show could find a home on the do-or-die Broadway of today?

The *Times* review and the other generally positive notices enabled *Baby* to run for 241 performances, almost eight months. Perhaps unfairly, theater critic Ken Mandelbaum chose to include the show in his book *Not Since Carrie: Forty Years of Broadway Musical Flops*, observing that in spite of *Baby*'s "outstanding score, one of the best heard on Broadway in the eighties," the show was a "starless nonspectacle, requiring much stronger reviews for survival than it received; the reviews made the show sound clinical and unappetizing, and gave little indication of its humor and warmth."[13]

Baby was nominated for seven Tony Awards, including Best Musical, Best Book of a Musical, Best Original Score, Best Featured Actor (Todd Graff as Danny), Best Featured Actress (Liz Callaway as Lizzie), Best Direction (Maltby), and Best Choreography (Wayne Cilento).

It was a competitive year for musicals at the Tonys. *La Cage aux Folles* won out over *Baby*, *The Tap Dance Kid*, and *Sunday in the Park with George* for Best Musical. In addition, to the surprise of many, Jerry Herman's score for *La Cage* edged out Stephen Sondheim's *Sunday in the Park* in the Best Score category.[14] Pearson and Maltby also lost out to *La Cage* in their categories—to Harvey Fierstein (book) and Arthur Laurents (director), respectively. Callaway lost in the Best Featured Actress category to Lila Kedrova for her performance in *Zorba*. Although none of that year's Tonys went to *Baby*, both Martin Vidnovic (Nick) and Catherine Cox (Pam) won Drama Desk Awards, for Outstanding Featured Actor and Actress in a Musical, respectively, and Graff won a Theatre World Award.

Callaway never formally auditioned for *Baby*. In 1981, when she was in rehearsal for Sondheim's *Merrily We Roll Along*, her first Broadway show, she was called in to audition for the leading role in a new Ed Kleban musical called *Gallery*, whose songs were inspired by famous paintings. Maltby was directing the show. Callaway knew she already had a great job as a cast member of the new Sondheim musical, but she went to the audition on her lunch break one day just for the experience. "After I sang, Richard said, 'You're just right for this show I'm writing about this pregnant college student,'" Callaway recalls.[15]

In a 2021 podcast featuring the songwriters and most of the original *Baby* cast, Maltby showed that he still remembered Callaway's audition vividly, even forty years later:

> [You came in wearing] work overalls and sneakers, planted your feet, and then you started to sing "Be a Lion" [from *The Wiz*], and it was heaven on earth. About halfway through it, as the melody went up, I was sitting next to [musical director] Bill Elliot. I just grabbed him by the knee as that voice just went and went. "She doesn't have a break! She goes from low register to top register, and there is no break!" It was the most thrilling sound ever—I never heard anything like it.[16]

Callaway was offered the leading role in *Gallery* but opted to stay with *Merrily*. (Director Hal Prince sweetened the pot for her by offering to move her from her position as female swing to an onstage ensemble member as well as understudy for Mary, the female lead.) This proved to be a wise choice: *Gallery* had a workshop but was never produced.

Maltby later brought Shire to hear Callaway in a Frank Loesser revue; Shire was equally impressed. "I told them, 'If you guys ever need to hear your songs sung, I would be so happy to help you out,'" Callaway says. "I said it completely sincerely. Now that I look back . . . God, that was a ballsy thing to say!"

The team took her up on it. Callaway started going to Maltby's apartment and singing through songs from *Baby*. As she recalls: "After the fourth or fifth session, this guy came, and they introduced him as the producer of their show [Freydberg], and I said, 'Is this an audition?' and David said, 'Well, you've been auditioning all along.' And I just thought I was being helpful!"[17] She says, "I knew all the songs were really special. Doing *Baby* spoiled me for other things because I thought, 'Oh, this is what it's always like. Everything's going to be this good.' But no, it was really a one-in-a-million show, and a one-in-a-million role for me."

Baby had profound ramifications in Callaway's life, not only for career-related reasons, as in her first major role in a Broadway show and her permanent association with an iconic song ("The Story Goes On"), but also because that's how she met her husband, theater director and producer Dan Foster.

"This guy named Dan went to the first preview, and he liked what he saw onstage, and then he pursued me during the run of the show," Callaway relates. "He would leave me little notes." Fellow cast member Cox, who created the role of Pam, convinced Callaway to at least go on a date with Foster. "I finally went out with him two weeks before we closed to say, 'You're a nice guy, but I don't want to date you.' We closed three restaurants that night, and we moved in together two weeks later."[18]

14 BABY

Most people, including Maltby and Shire themselves, cite "The Story Goes On" as the standout song from *Baby*, and we will examine this number in chapter 15. More impressive from both a conceptual and a compositional standpoint, however, is "The Ladies Singin' Their Song," in which Lizzie is accosted by a succession of five women who insist on telling her their own pregnancy adventures.

When Lizzie sings her verses, it's to the beat of a great Shire swing tune (example 14.1). The first measure of the piano part lays out the primary accompanimental figure for the song's recurring verse. It is worth noting that this bar (which repeats largely unaltered for the first six measures) contains a microcosm of the entire number: the first beat is a B♭ major chord, while the third beat, containing the blues note D♭ (doubling the vocal line), implies B♭ minor, even though the root of the chord is missing. Thus, this fundamental building block of the song, alternating as it does between major and minor, embodies both the joys and the frustrations of pregnancy—the elation of gestating a new life and the annoyance of the intrusive gawkers.

Example 14.1. "The Ladies Singin' Their Song"

I go walk-in' and at once they're stalk-in' me, the la-dies sing-in' their song.

In terms of its expansive structure and the succession of colorful characters who all sing in different styles, this song, as briefly mentioned in

Closer Than Ever. Joshua Rosenblum, Oxford University Press. © Oxford University Press 2024.
DOI: 10.1093/oso/9780197758236.003.0014

chapter 4, owes a conceptual debt to Stephen Sondheim's "Please Hello" from *Pacific Overtures*. The first woman Lizzie encounters sings to a classical-style accompaniment with rolling triplets ("The way you look I'd say that it's your first, my dear"). The next woman's verse has a twangy, country-western feel, and the stage directions in the score confirm that "She looks and sounds something like Loretta Lynn." She croons about having babies "The natural way-y-y-y." After a recitative-like eight-bar intro accompanied by a gypsy-style solo violin, the third and fourth women sing a tango duet ("There is no moment in life that's rougher / But when you're through you'll be that much tougher"). The fifth woman sings for only four bars, but it's enough to make a big impact: her first note is a loud, sustained D♯ on the word "Pain!" She then proceeds to sing in a style that parodies grand opera, with a broad, arching melody that takes the vocalist up to a high A♯, closer to the range of a classical soprano than a contemporary musical theater female singer (although Kim Criswell on the original cast recording somehow manages to belt the whole thing). Finally, they all sing together in a sumptuous, harmonically adventurous chorale near the end.

Although Maltby conjured all five colorful ladies and their various stories himself, the idea for the number came from playwright Tina Howe. According to Maltby, "Tina didn't eventually want to write a musical, but she was the one talking about how you're walking around when you're pregnant, and everyone wants to touch you, and they come up to tell you their stories, and you turn around and there are those ladies singin' their song. She gave us that exact phrase." More than that, Maltby says, Howe was the one who pointed out how rarely those feelings are expressed:

> She was the one who articulated the idea that childbirth is a thing that's inexpressible. No one, not your best friends, not your mother, not your husband, can understand the unique feelings *you* experienced. Other women will respond by telling you what *they* felt. Your husband will listen lovingly but won't really understand. So you give up trying to share it, and for the rest of your life, you have this unexpressed longing inside —which comes out when you see another pregnant woman and you can't resist doing something clumsy and ridiculous like asking to touch. How else to explain this curious desire of women to touch the bellies of pregnant strangers? That was inspired by Tina.

In the song, that notion of inexpressibility is addressed in the aforementioned a cappella chorale that precedes the last verse (example 14.2). This serendipitous, harmonically rich passage is full of surprises, like the move from an E♭ major chord with an added second (the downbeat of the third bar) to the remote key area of A minor (the third beat of the last bar) in the short span of a measure and a half. The passing chord, on the downbeat of the last bar, is a striking instance of quartal harmony—a chord built on a stack of fourths instead of the thirds that are the normal building blocks of triads. These unusual chromatics are a perfect fit for a passage that describes the difficulty of putting certain feelings into words.

Example 14.2. "The Ladies Singin' Their Song"

"The Ladies Singin' Their Song" contains plenty of storytelling action—explicitly so. But even as Lizzie describes being accosted by the succession of five women who insist on telling her their own pregnancy adventures, she has one line toward the end indicating that she, too, traverses her own dramatic arc over the course of the song: "But we both know that soon they'll number me in the throng." In other words, Lizzie will—not too long from now—become one of those annoying people unleashing her personal narrative on perfect strangers. All told, it's a magnificently imaginative number and a worthy companion piece to "Please Hello," its influential Sondheimian predecessor. In chapter 24, we'll see how "Back of the Line" from *Take Flight* adheres even more closely to the "Please Hello" model.

Maltby and Shire on "The Ladies Singin' Their Song":

DS: Richard will often give me a first line or a title. The phrase "the ladies singin' their song" has this rhythm, and once you get that, it ignites other things.

RM: We had the title and the premise. Then David came up with that music.

DS: All I really wrote first was the thirty-two-bar song for Lizzie, and then Richard just directed me through the other sections—"This is the emotional feeling of this section, this woman is this kind of woman"—and then we worked through them one at a time. I never came up with the idea of having the chorale at the end. All the really dramatic ideas came from Richard, and as I got them, I wrote each of the sections. It's a much more complicated process than which comes first, music or lyrics.

Further discussion of "The Ladies Singin' Their Song" with the authors led to this amusing exchange:

DS: (misremembering the lyrics) "The first kid was brought by a stork. The second one you couldn't pry out with a fork."
RM: "Stork"!? There's no "stork"!
DS: No, you're right, it was "cork"!
RM: It's "cork"! "My first kid kind of popped out like a cork. My next you couldn't pry out with a fork."[1]
DS: "Stork"! That's what I would've written, and you would've corrected it.
RM: "There is no moment in life that's rougher, but when you're through, you'll be that much tougher."
DS: A lot of wisdom in that song. Richard, you were at the top of your game.
RM: (without false modesty) I know, I know.

"And What If We Had Loved Like That?," which comes in the eleven-o'clock-number slot, is a powerful song with a lingering, unexpected impact. It starts out, seemingly, as a solid affirmation of Alan and Arlene's marriage, as Alan (James Congdon in the Broadway production) sings:

You and me,
The perfect pair.
No one questioned it;
Who would dare?

But later, leading into the chorus, a series of seven pickup eighth notes (indicated by the brackets in example 14.3) propels the melody toward the downbeat as the very serious heart of the matter begins to unfold.

Example 14.3. "And What If We Had Loved Like That?"

And now I'm ask-ing if I loved you.
What does it mat-ter that I loved you?

Whatever it was they had, Alan goes on to sing, "It wasn't enough / To get us the whole way through." This is a shock for an audience that is expecting a testimony to this couple's abiding love at this point in the show. At the climax of the chorus (example 14.4), the pickup figure with seven downward-racing eighth notes doubles in intensity, occurring in every bar, three measures in a row, instead of in every other bar as in the previous example.

Example 14.4. "And What If We Had Loved Like That?"

Some peo - ple dare to risk the flak And nev - er hold the feel - ings
back. And what if we had loved like that, You and I?

This creates an urgent series of melodic cascades as an emotionally overcome Alan is left wondering what it would have been like to have experienced the kind of passionate relationship he can only envy in other people. It is a deeply human moment and sobering to think that this is his takeaway from two decades of marriage.

Arlene's verse follows, expressing similar sentiments, but her chorus is followed by a third and final chorus, in which the couple (significantly) sings together, both in alternating, call-and-response-type counterpoint and in harmony, as if to say, "No, our marriage hasn't been perfect, but we're still together, and for a good reason."

"Easier to Love," a second-act song written during previews, shows Alan undergoing his own development. He starts out making observations about how it's easier to love a child than it is to love your wife, because your child loves you unconditionally, and your wife sees through you.

> Children tell you everything
> And give you their whole heart.
> Your wife tells you everything
> And blows your day apart.

And later:

> Anything a child needs, a kiss can make all right.
> Your wife needs your life.
> Children want to hear the same story every night—
> Try that on your wife.

The song has a lighthearted, almost joking tone, and it is further distanced by the impersonal, casual use of second-person pronouns ("you," "your"). By the end of the song, however, the sobering truth behind the lyrics hits home, and Alan has shifted to the more intimate use of the first person:

> That's why from the day they got here,
> My kids were by far

Easier to love,
So much easier to love.

As Maltby puts it, the idea that he'd rather have another child than deal with his wife "is not just a joke—it's literally true, and it's the story of their marriage." (The extended held note on Alan's last "So" gives emphasis to the moment he has this realization.) The song's evolution in tone stands as a good example of the old saw that most things said in jest have an element of truth.

"Easier to Love" also has unusual status in the show (and in the Maltby/Shire canon as a whole) in that Maltby wrote both the lyrics and the first draft of the music. A discussion about how the number came to be written went like this:

RM: We didn't know quite what to do [for that spot in the show]—it hit me just as I was waking up one morning, and I wrote the whole lyric in just fifteen minutes.

DS: And also the first draft of the music.

RM: Yeah, it came with the shape of the music.

DS: More than the shape. I just had to clean up the harmonies.

RM: I heard it in my head. [sings the opening melody]

JR: It didn't come from David?

RM: It came in basic shape from me, with the lyric, and then David did his magic stuff to it.

DS: I didn't have to do any magic. It was just finding what the natural harmony was. He had most of the melody.

JR: Does that happen often, that you have a lyric and you have a preliminary melody in your head?

RM: Yeah, almost always I have something, and what's difficult is that the melody I have in my head doesn't always translate itself into anything else. I get annoyed when David responds to the words and not to the music that was underlying them. He takes the words and does something else with them.

JR: But in that case, he basically took what you had.

RM: Well, at that point in rehearsal, we needed to get this in immediately.

At this moment in the discussion, the author points out the relationship between the main melody from "Easier to Love" and the keyboard introduction to "We Start Today" (example 14.5). Example 14.6 is the first line of "Easier to Love," transposed for comparison purposes.

Example 14.5. "We Start Today"

Example 14.6. "Easier to Love"

Chil-dren tell you ev - 'ry thing and give you their whole heart.

This side-by-side comparison makes it clear that apart from the B♮s in the first bar of "Easier to Love" replacing the corresponding B♭s in "We Start Today," the first eleven notes of the melodies are identical. After this similarity was pointed out, the dialogue continued:

> **DS:** Well, I thought it was a great melody that I couldn't do any better with.
> **JR:** That's because it was based on something you had already composed.
> **DS:** No, it wasn't, really.
> **RM:** Well, it *is*, David! [Maltby demonstrates, singing the melodic figure.]

It thus turns out that, unbeknownst to the writers, the vocal melody that Maltby came up with for "Easier to Love" is, in fact, the same as the keyboard intro Shire had already written for "We Start Today," a discovery made almost forty years after the fact.

The title song, "Baby, Baby, Baby," is set to a steady pop beat with a sinuous, recurring melodic figure on alto sax that features the oscillating interval of a minor third, indicated by the bracket in example 14.7.

Example 14.7. "Baby, Baby, Baby"

This catchy little riff turns into the vocal melody for the hook phrase of the title, with a slight rhythmic displacement so that the Gs (instead of the B♭s) fall on the strong beats (example 14.8).

Example 14.8. "Baby, Baby, Baby"

The three men croon to the fetuses inside their partners' wombs, and everyone speculates about what the adored babies' lives will be like. In between all the fun and loving speculation, however, we get more character backstory from Pam. Since she and Nick are the only couple who have actively been trying to conceive a child, this is a particularly meaningful moment.

As Pam starts her verse, it sounds as if she is introducing new musical material, but her melody is based on the same oscillating interval of a minor third that we've already heard in both the "Baby, baby, baby" melody and the introductory sax figure (example 14.9).

Example 14.9. "Baby, Baby, Baby"

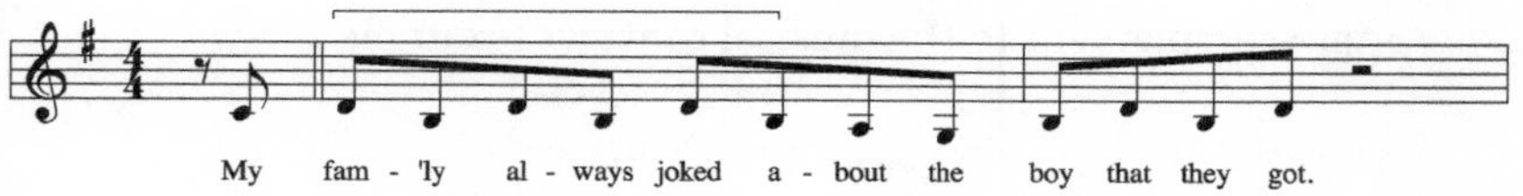

The last line of Pam's verse clearly resembles the opening sax solo (example 14.7)—now in the key of C. The rhythm of the melody and the last five notes (as indicated by the brackets) are the same, while the first four notes sound like an improvised variation (example 14.10).

Example 14.10. "Baby, Baby, Baby"

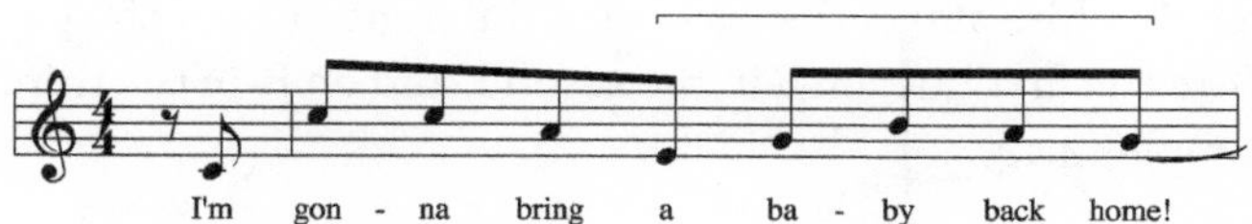

Then the figure occurs again, two bars later, in a version almost identical to the original sax instrumental (example 14.11).

Example 14.11. "Baby, Baby, Baby"

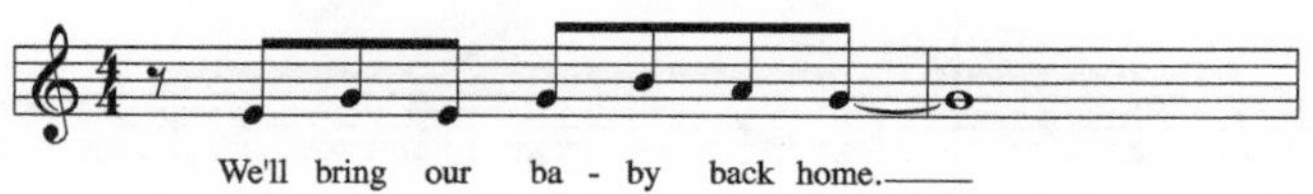

The title song isn't the only number in *Baby* that is built around a single melodic cell; the song "Patterns" is, appropriately, largely derived from a three-note pattern, indicated by the brackets in example 14.12.

Example 14.12. "Patterns"

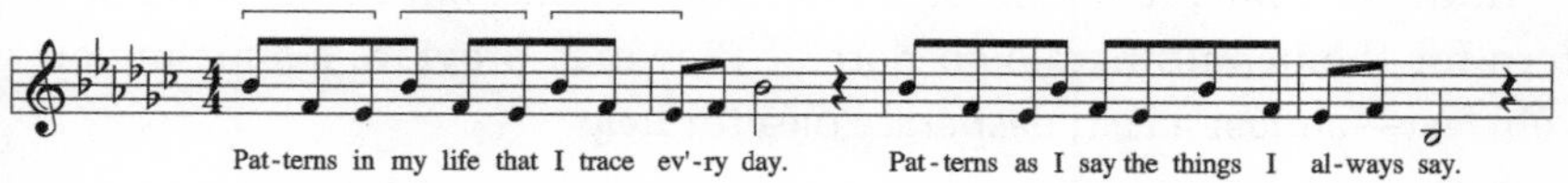

In the first phrase of the vocal line, the three-note set B♭-F-E♭ is repeated three times in a row and then shifts into reverse for the last two notes, concluding the melody with F-B♭. The second phrase also concludes with F-B♭, but this time with the closure of a falling perfect fifth instead of a rising perfect fourth. The repetition of the melodic pattern emphasizes Arlene's sense that her life is stuck in a rut, a feeling that the melancholy key of E♭ minor readily confirms. This four-bar phrase, itself full of repeats, is repeated in the next four bars.

The bridge provides some welcome change, giving the melody a chance to soar instead of cycle, with sustained half notes on C♭ breaking out of the melodic rut of B♭-F-E♭. Maltby's lyric—"And yet today I am not the same"—is an appropriate complement to the musical contrast (example 14.13).

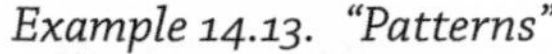

Example 14.13. "Patterns"

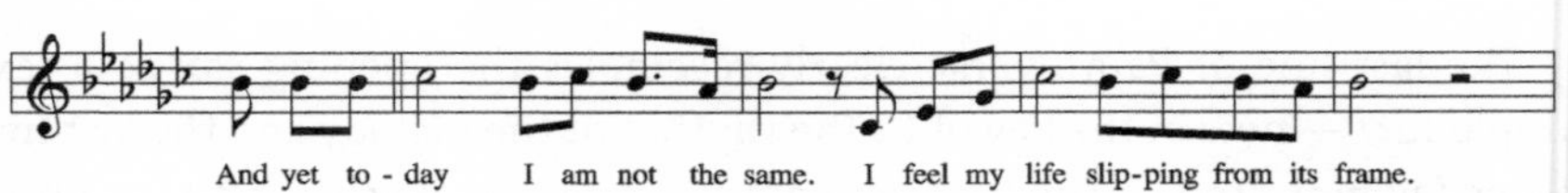
And yet to - day I am not the same. I feel my life slip-ping from its frame.

In the last verse, Arlene is stuck again in her rut but even more so. The melodic cell of B♭-F-E♭ now cycles five times instead of three. As an added creative touch, Shire starts the cycle on a different note of the pattern each time: on B♭ in the first line, on F in the second, and on E♭ in the third and final line of example 14.14.

Example 14.14. "Patterns"

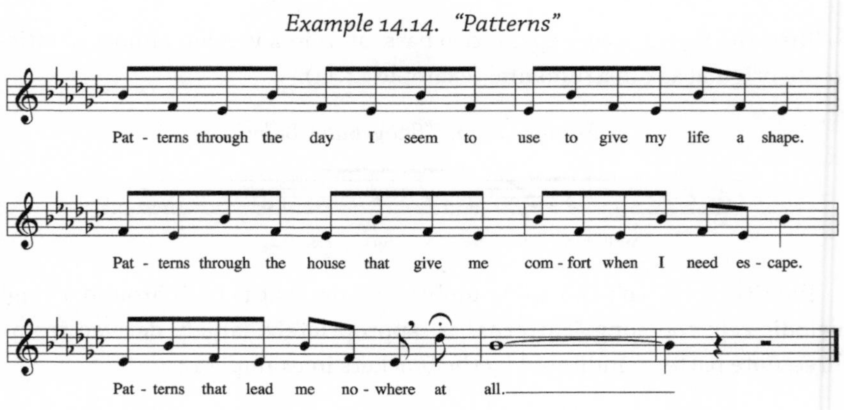
Pat - terns through the day I seem to use to give my life a shape.
Pat - terns through the house that give me com - fort when I need es - cape.
Pat - terns that lead me no - where at all.

In the last line, it should be noted, Shire breaks out of the melodic pattern for the penultimate high note of D♭, which provides a startling bit of contrast—almost a last, desperate plea for help.

"THE STORY GOES ON"

Maltby and Shire consider "The Story Goes On," the number that brings the curtain down on Act I of *Baby*, the most definitive song of their collaboration. It comes as a surprise, then, that the basic melody was originally written as a pop song and had nothing to do with *Baby*.

"I'm actually embarrassed about this," Shire admits. "This was when I was mostly in California scoring movies, and I was trying to find a lyricist to write a pop hit with. I met with this woman who had written some movie songs, and I can't even remember her name, but one of the things I brought her was the basic melody of 'The Story Goes On.' But nothing ever happened to it. She never wrote a lyric to it." Sometime after that, Shire was back in New York, and he played the melody for Maltby. "Richard heard it and said, 'If you ever give this melody to anyone else, we're finished,'" Shire remembers. "So it wasn't written for the scene [in *Baby*] at all."

This is a rare occurrence for two songwriters who are known for numbers that are carefully crafted for specific characters and dramatic situations. Nevertheless, the song makes a powerful impact in the show. As the team worked on turning Shire's melody into the number that became "The Story Goes On," Maltby suggested adding the rhythmic ostinato figure in the bass that implies the sound of a heartbeat (example 15.1).

Example 15.1. "The Story Goes On"

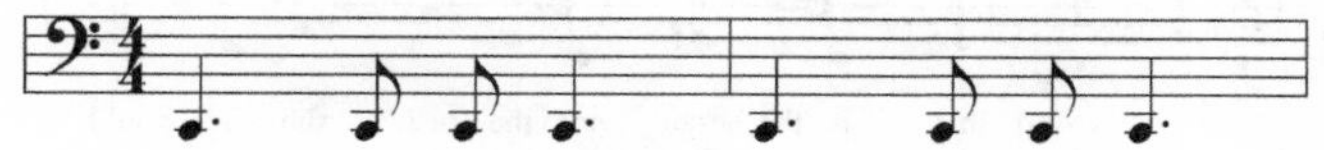

Shire came up with the evocative right-hand figure with the triplet sixteenths that comes in two bars later (example 15.2). "It's a musical metaphor for the birth of a fertilized egg," he explains. "It's just something I wanted to express—the coming to life, the quickening."

Closer Than Ever. Joshua Rosenblum, Oxford University Press. © Oxford University Press 2024.
DOI: 10.1093/oso/9780197758236.003.0015

Example 15.2. "The Story Goes On"

It's also, as it turns out, the "story goes on" motif of the song; when Lizzie sings those lyrics the first time (example 15.3), it's the same E-D-C-D melody that is outlined by the "quickening" figure in the previous example (example 15.2).

Example 15.3. "The Story Goes On"

The song makes its impact in part because it's about the realization that there are things in life larger than ourselves—and in this case, much larger. Lizzie makes that point right away in the opening lines:

So this is the tale my mother told me.
That tale that was much too dull to hold me.

Lizzie is singing about something important she heard from her own mother—something she wasn't mature enough to realize at the time was even worth listening to. Now, however, it merits its own song. And it's not just a story—it's a surge and a rush. These vivid words are emphasized by the propulsive sixteenth-note pickups and rising melodic line in the music (example 15.4).

Example 15.4. "The Story Goes On"

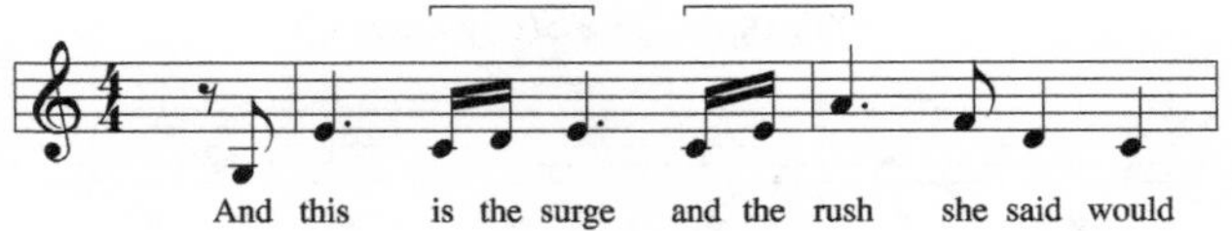

The second A section begins:

Oh, I was young. I forgot that things outlive me.
My goal was the kick that life would give me.

Again comes the realization that the important things are those that are larger than oneself. And the use of the word "kick" carries the additional meaning of the physical experience pregnant women have that reminds them they are carrying a developing life inside them.

The bridge is the crux of the song:

And all these things I feel and more,
My mother's mother felt, and hers before.
A chain of life begun upon the shore
Of some dark sea
Has reached to me.

With these lines, Lizzie identifies her own place as part of the biological cycle of the entire human race. That recursive phrase "and hers before," carried to its logical conclusion, ties Lizzie all the way back to antiquity and makes her part of a story so vast we can barely comprehend it.

The music plays an equal role in buttressing this sense of something continuously evolving; as the bridge begins, so does a long, rising melody that carries us all the way to the end of this section and beyond (example 15.5). The melodic journey starts on D with the pickup quarter note on the word "And," then begins its slow, upward movement, rising to E and continuing through F, G, A, and up to B, over the course of seven bars (indicated by asterisks in example 15.5). This deliberately paced, stepwise melodic ascent, sustaining the musical and dramatic tension through the entire bridge, is a favorite technique of Shire's, as we have previously seen.

Example 15.5. "The Story Goes On"

At the end of eight bars—the standard length of the bridge of a song—we reflexively expect this section to end, on the phrase "some dark sea." The songwriters, however, prolong the phrase by two additional bars ("Has reached to me"), thus extending the tension and confirming the sense of a long, continuously unfolding process (example 15.6). The melodic B is sustained through four consecutive measures in example 15.6 and undergoes some deft reharmonizations. The last of these bars (measure 34) makes a particularly crunchy impact, with the D♭ in the bass replacing the G from the previous bar as the root of the dominant seventh chord.[1] It's worth noting that Shire has also brought back the "quickening of life" motif with its triplet sixteenths over the course of these four bars.

Example 15.6. "The Story Goes On"

The next section prolongs the tension further: instead of arriving at a cadence in the home key of C, Shire gives us a suspended chord on the downbeat (on the word "now") that, instead of resolving, propels the music ahead (example 15.7).

Example 15.7. "The Story Goes On"

This suspension works remarkably well hand in hand with the words, which spell out the idea of prolongation:

> And now I can see the chain extending.
> My child is next in a line that has no ending.
> And here am I, full of life, that her child will feel
> When I'm long gone.

We're now looking ahead, after looking back to antiquity; Lizzie is talking not just about her own child but that child's child—and of course, by extension, a long line of descendants yet to be born. The importance of the continuing chain is hammered home by the emphatic triplets on the phrase "her child will feel," as well as another dramatically rising stepwise figure, this time driven by doubled eighth notes in the right hand of the piano part in the second and third measures of example 15.8.

Example 15.8. "The Story Goes On"

This section, too, avoids resolution when we expect it. The chord on the word "thus" at the beginning of example 15.9 is a C chord, but it has the dominant G in the bass instead of the root note C, so it doesn't sound like an arrival. And, in fact, it isn't—we get another two-bar extension that postpones the cadence until the third bar of example 15.9.

Example 15.9. "The Story Goes On"

But even here, when we get an actual cadence in the home key and it sounds as if the phrase is complete in the third bar of example 15.9 (at the end of the lyric "And thus it is our story goes on"), we get yet another extension. The story goes on, to be sure, *and* "on and on and on," for another eight bars. Shire makes sure this doesn't get repetitious by doubling the pace in the third bar of example 15.10.

Example 15.10. "The Story Goes On"

Clearly, the musical design of the song is a process of building, prolonging, and extending.

Next comes the actual, physical kick from the fetus that Lizzie feels—represented in the music by the low tremolo in the bass and the accented, rising quarter notes that follow (example 15.11).

Example 15.11. "The Story Goes On"

Now Lizzie sings the bridge again, but she's transformed. There are small adjustments in the lyrics (identified in italics below) that drive the message home even more acutely: "A chain of life begun upon the shore of some dark sea has reached to me" is expanded as "A chain of life begun upon the shore of some *primordial* sea has *stretched through time to* reach to me." The added syllables create additional urgency, both semantically and rhythmically.

A repeat of the post-bridge, altered A section ("And now I can feel the chain extending") contains an exciting alteration of the melody from its previous iteration (seen in example 15.8), on the phrase "when I'm long gone," taking Lizzie up to an E (the highest note of the song up to this point), as seen in example 15.12.

Example 15.12. "The Story Goes On"

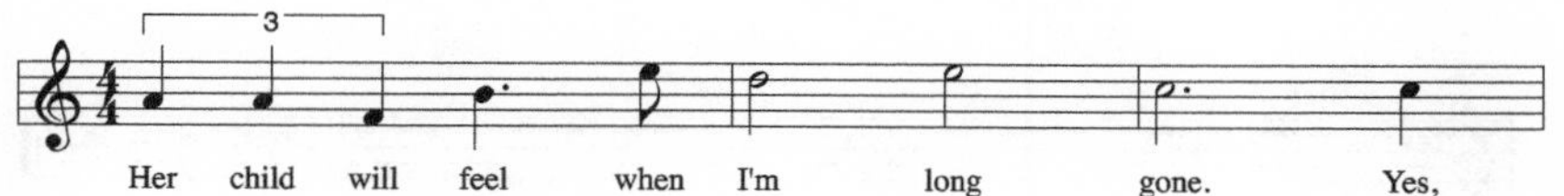

A comparison of examples 15.8 and 15.12 will show how Shire raises the stakes melodically as the song drives toward its conclusion.

A coda follows, with surging music and new lyrics:

Yes, all that was, is part of me,
As I am part of what's to be.
And thus it is our story goes on.

As before, the story goes "on and on and on," this time with the melody rising all the way to an F and the "quickening" motif restored to the accompaniment, but now fortissimo, with a triumphantly repeating rising eighth-note figure in the horn line (here the accented notes in the left hand of the piano part) and an exuberant, long, sustained C in the vocal melody at the end, as seen in example 15.13.

Example 15.13. "The Story Goes On"

On and on and

on and on and on

ff

molto rall.

It's hard to imagine a song that more effectively depicts one's own awe at being part of something almost incomprehensibly vast.

Liz Callaway on "The Story Goes On":

I knew it was an incredible song when I first heard it. I must've been twenty-one.

Funny thing about it, I was so young when I did *Baby*, before I had my own child. Then I had my child, and it's like, "Oh, it has a whole new meaning." And then, when I lost my mom, it had another new meaning to me. And during the pandemic, thinking about what our ancestors went through, all these different challenges in the world—that's what we've done through the years. So I still sing it at all my concerts, although I do it a half step lower now! But a really great song stands the test of time and means different things over the years, and that's definitely an example of a great song.

It is indeed extraordinary to hear Callaway sing this song now. Both her interpretation and her vocal timbre have ripened and become beautifully burnished with age. Every word sinks in with authentic, lived-in substance and a new depth of understanding she couldn't possibly have mustered when she first played the role in 1983. The song almost serves as a Rorschach test for the fullness of life experience brought to bear by whoever is singing it.

Maltby and Shire on "The Story Goes On":

DS: Can you believe "The Story Goes On" was a trunk melody that I'd written for a pop lyricist out in California, and Richard turned it into "The Story Goes On"? The sophistication of that lyric and what it's describing is just amazing. He made it sound like I set a perfect lyric that he wrote.

RM: My goal is if you took the music away, would you say exactly the same thing, and the answer has to be yes. I want the language to be exactly the language a character would use if it weren't sung, weren't a lyric, and weren't rhymed. "So this is the tale my mother told me, the tale that was much too dull to hold me. And this is the surge and the rush she said would show our story goes on." That's a paragraph. You'd say it exactly the same way if you weren't singing.

JR: You get away with repeating a big chunk of it—the lyrics to the bridge, and then the section after that.

DS: It's very interesting, because that's the only time I can remember where Richard has repeated a lyric almost verbatim. But it's not all the same if the actress plays it right. Richard's direction to Liz was that the first time Lizzie sings those words, she's a pretentious college student, her whole mien is as a sophomore, she's just using language. And then, in the transition, the baby kicks for the first time, and after that musical buildup, when she says those words again, she's really understanding them. She now has felt them, rather than describing them from the outside in.

RM: Yes, but that should be the premise of any duplicated lyric in a show. The second time you sing it, you have to come to a new understanding of what you have just said.

DS: Yes, but this was an actual motivation for her understanding it, which was the most exciting part of the song—the baby kicking for the first time.

RM: What a strange opening line. I thought about it so much and ended up keeping it, but it seemed like a strange way to start a song.

JR: It's great because she's saying, "I didn't get it then, and I couldn't, but now I get it." And that's what you just said about reinterpreting the bridge the second time. It means something different.

RM: David and I just love to write songs about emotions that nobody's ever written before. It's hard to find them.

JR: As two men, I assume you had to do some research by talking to women about being pregnant.

RM: You don't have to go very far afield to find somebody.

JR: Did Sybille have anything to do with the content of this song?

RM: I think it was written before she even came on the show.

DS: We both had lived with women who were pregnant for nine months.

JR: This vast chain back to antiquity is part of what people find so moving.

RM: The key to that—one of the tricks of lyric writing—is to find the locution that cuts syllables. Normal sentences have extra beats in them, and lyrics have to be tighter. So you have to find a natural locution that starts in the present and gets back to primordial times. There's a certain amount of process to go through.

JR: "Find the locution that cuts syllables." That's kind of a whole course in lyric writing right there.

RM: It really is. In this case, it's four syllables—"and hers before." That's how you can cram information into something. It's my proudest achievement as a lyricist.

DS: What's interesting is sometimes when I've seen Richard struggling to cut out a syllable that just won't get out of there, I've offered many times, I've said, I'll give you another note [in the melody], and he refuses. He says that alters the melody.

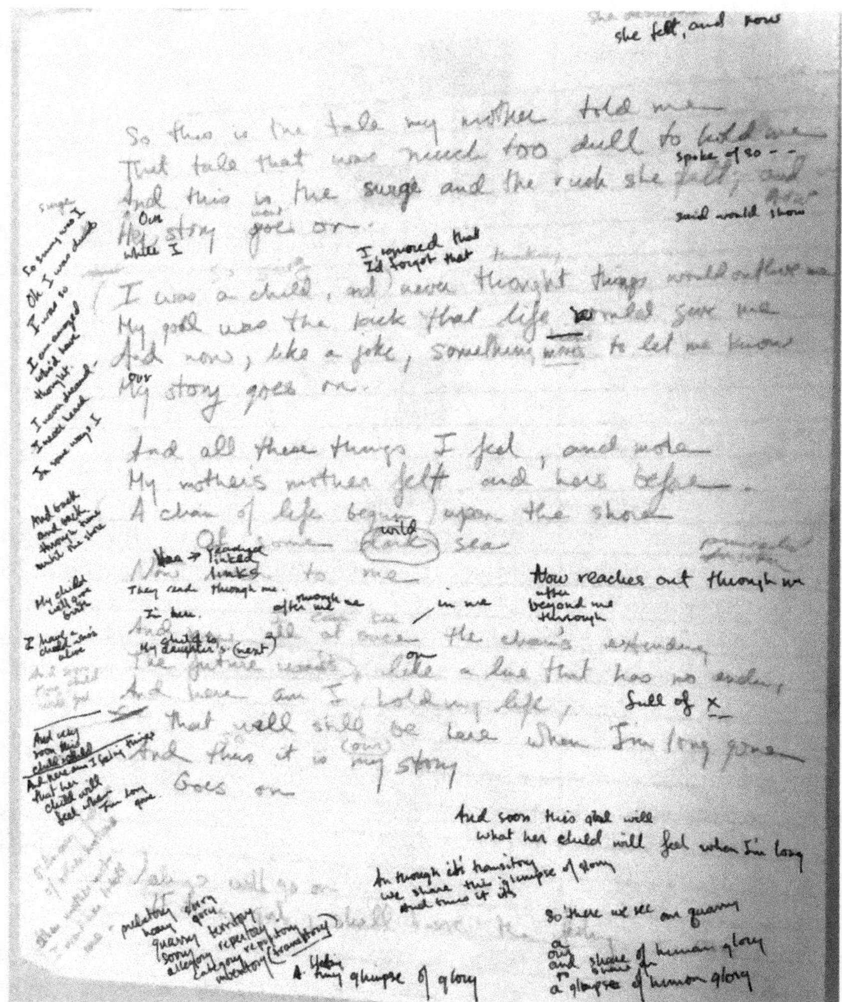

So this is the tale my mother told me
That tale that was much too dull to hold me
And this is the surge and the rush she felt, and
Her story goes on.

I was a child, and never thought things would
My goal was the luck that life would give me
And now, like a joke, something to let me know
My story goes on.

And all these things I feel, and more
My mother's mother felt and knew before.
A chain of life begun upon the shore
Of some dark sea
Now links to me.
And all at once the chain's extending
The future waits, like a line that has no ending,
And here am I holding life,
That will still be here when I'm long gone
And thus it is my story
Goes on

Figure 15.1. "The Story Goes On," draft lyrics (manuscript)

JR: Most lyricists would say, add another melody note, but Richard clearly respects the melody and makes it his job to cut a syllable.

DS: In fact, it works the other way, too, because when Richard finds ways of cutting syllables, I have to cut notes. And sometimes there are notes I want to keep, or thought I wanted to keep, but they invariably are better without the notes Richard wanted to cut.

FRENCH IS A LANGUAGE THAT DOESN'T SCAN

• • •

MISS SAIGON

Maltby had made the necessary but painful decision to cut "The Bear, the Tiger, the Hamster and the Mole" from *Baby*, but he and Shire both felt strongly that the song should have a future life. In 1984, about a year after *Baby* closed, Maltby began gathering ideas, lyric fragments, and character sketches/anecdotes inspired by friends and acquaintances into a collection he called the "Urban File." Shire began collecting musical ideas as well, with the notion that at some point, these incomplete elements might be combined into a set of companion pieces for "The Bear, the Tiger." In the meantime, the writers kept busy in their respective independent careers. For Maltby, this involved solidifying an important alliance with producer Cameron Mackintosh and composer Andrew Lloyd Webber.

Tyler Gatchell and Peter Neufeld had been the general management team for *Starting Here, Starting Now*. By 1984, their company, Gatchell & Neufeld Ltd., had an impressive Broadway track record, including the hit musical *Cats*, and an association with Lloyd Webber that extended all the way back to the original New York production of *Jesus Christ Superstar* in 1971. When Lloyd Webber was looking for new lyricists, Gatchell told the composer that he should meet Maltby, and, as Maltby puts it, "I was summoned to England." Maltby was supposedly under consideration to write the lyrics for Lloyd Webber's *Aspects of Love*,[1] but in the course of their meeting, the subject turned to *Song and Dance*, another Lloyd Webber musical, with lyrics by Don Black, which had just closed on the West End in March 1984.

Song and Dance was in two parts. The "Song" part (Act I) was a solo song cycle Lloyd Webber and Black had written for Marti Webb, the English singer

Closer Than Ever. Joshua Rosenblum, Oxford University Press. © Oxford University Press 2024.
DOI: 10.1093/oso/9780197758236.003.0016

and actress who succeeded Elaine Paige in the title role of the original West End production of *Evita.* The cycle, originally titled *Tell Me on a Sunday,* was premiered at Lloyd Webber's Sydmonton Festival and later released as a concept album. The "Dance" portion of the show (Act II) was a plotless ballet, choreographed to *Variations,* a piece the composer had written for his brother, cellist Julian Lloyd Webber, based on Niccolò Paganini's Caprice No. 24 in A minor. It was Mackintosh's idea to combine the two works as a single show, billing it as "a concert for the theater." *Song and Dance* ran on the West End for nearly two years.

Mackintosh and Lloyd Webber were toying with the idea of bringing *Song and Dance* to Broadway but were concerned that the two separate, unrelated parts wouldn't play well for American audiences. Maltby recalls:

> Andrew showed me a video of the show. It was literally a collection of songs and a dance piece. He said, "It needs somebody who can find a way to put the two pieces together into one story. Someone who's not only a writer but also a director, like . . . well, like *you,* Richard!" And so I went back, and I came up with a plot for the two pieces, which they thought was very clever, and that's how I suddenly found myself doing that.

Plans for the Broadway transfer proceeded, and Maltby was hired to direct the production and to adapt the show for an American audience, giving unity and coherence to the two acts. *Song and Dance* opened in New York at the Royale Theatre in September 1985 and ran for 474 performances, about a year and two months. Bernadette Peters, the solo performer in Act I (the "Song" part of *Song and Dance*), won the 1986 Tony and Drama Desk Awards for her role. Maltby received a Tony nomination for Best Director of a Musical and, for his contributions as co-lyricist, shared a Best Score nomination with Lloyd Webber and Black.

Mackintosh's follow-up to *Song and Dance* was the gigantic international hit *Les Misérables,* which debuted on the West End in October 1985 and opened on Broadway in March 1987. The original version of the show, the work of composer Claude-Michel Schönberg and lyricist Alain Boublil, had been written in French and received its premiere at the Palais des Sports (now the Dôme de Paris) in 1980.[2] When Mackintosh wanted to bring an English-language version of *Les Misérables* to the West End, he enlisted the British journalist and lyricist Herbert Kretzmer, who at the time was best known for his English lyrics to songs by French singer-songwriter Charles Aznavour.

After the huge success of *Les Misérables,* Schönberg and Boublil followed up with *Miss Saigon,* an adaptation of the *Madame Butterfly* story set amid the backdrop of war-torn Vietnam. Mackintosh felt that a show dealing with the Vietnam War needed an American point of view to supplement the European perspective of the French composer-and-lyricist team. The producer offered Maltby the job of creating the English version of *Miss Saigon* with Boublil and provided a recording of the score with the French lyrics.

"It was [Schönberg] playing piano and singing in French for two hours. I didn't know what the hell it was," Maltby recalls. In addition, films, TV shows, and books about Vietnam were almost universally failing to find audiences around this time. Doubtful about the commercial prospects for a musical on a topic that was still raw for many Americans, Maltby turned it down. He had also seen *Les Misérables* in its original French version at Palais des Sports when he was putting together a company of *Ain't Misbehavin'* in Paris. His takeaway was that although the show had some nice melodies (some of them now quite famous), "These French guys don't understand the musical at all."[3]

Not too long after he turned down the *Miss Saigon* job, Maltby saw *Les Misérables* in London in its new English incarnation. "Now I understood what it was," he says. "Suddenly, I could hear what they were doing with recitative and everything." The show, according to Boublil, had also changed considerably during its evolution from French into English.

Also, in the interim, Oliver Stone's film *Platoon* (1986) opened and was a big success. This contributed to Maltby's decision that maybe the world was now ready to accept a musical theater piece about the Vietnam War. At this point, it had been about a year since he first heard the tape of Schönberg singing the score in French. He called Mackintosh and asked if the job was still open; Mackintosh told him it was. ("I was waiting for *you*, Richard," the producer said, according to Maltby.) A meeting was arranged in New York for Maltby, Schönberg, and Boublil. As Boublil remembers it:

> We had several meetings. I found out how much of an opera fan he [Maltby] was. I realized what *Madame Butterfly* meant for him and how much he knew about the history of Puccini and the masters of the art form, and he was bowled over, I think, by the sense of structure Claude-Michel and I had and the way I structure the book. That is what led to the lyrics, rather than just writing songs and then trying to make them fit into the book. The approach was so close to what he wanted and admired that it was an obvious match.[4]

On *Les Misérables*, Kretzmer had been the sole author of the English lyrics.[5] "It was not a collaboration," Boublil explains. "[Kretzmer] was the only adapter in English, with my blessing. I collaborated in accepting, agreeing, and giving the ideas." On *Miss Saigon*, however, Boublil was a full partner in creating the English version. "With Richard, we spent days, weeks, months, in the room together. It was my first experience co-writing in English, and now I write in English on my own," he says.

Mackintosh wanted Boublil to be involved in writing the English lyrics for *Miss Saigon*. "He thought I had reached a level of mastering the language which allowed me to be part of the writing team," Boublil says. "He knew I could not and was not going to write it on my own, and he wanted me to meet Richard Maltby and see if we could collaborate. Richard graciously thought that it was a good idea." Maltby and Boublil still speak in effusive terms about each other. "We really worked well together, and I admire him enormously," Maltby enthuses. "I loved the collaboration," Boublil concurs.

Boublil, at that time the coauthor of the most successful musical on the planet, freely admits that he became Maltby's pupil in certain ways when they started working together. One of the main challenges had to do with the role of accents in their respective languages.

"French is an uninflected language," Maltby explains, and he demonstrates it by rattling off a string of quasi-French nonsense syllables in a monotone. This means you can set it however you want, with little attention to which syllables fall on strong beats—nearly any syllable can fit anywhere.

It's quite different in English. As Boublil puts it, providing the perspective of a nonnative English speaker, "French is a language that doesn't scan. In English, you don't realize that you are *ac*-centing *ev*-ery *word* you're *say*-ing." This means it's crucial that strong beats in the music contain only syllables that are accented in normal speech. This principle is obvious to English-language songwriters—or at least, to the good ones—but it was something Boublil had no prior experience with. "I didn't realize how much [the scansion and the accenting] would affect the way you write in English," he elaborates. "And so, little by little, I got used to that, and I tried to comply when he'd say, 'Alain, that doesn't work. Not because what you are saying is wrong, but because it doesn't scan.' Richard has been my master on this."

Boublil and Maltby had a long series of work sessions, usually at some elegant retreat, such as one of Boublil's favorite hotels in Brittany. Although Schönberg wasn't around for these sessions, the three of them were, as Boublil puts it, "in permanent collaboration."[6] He says, "Claude-Michel knew everything we were doing anytime there were ten minutes of the show written."

To start out, Boublil would do a literal translation of the original French lyrics. As Maltby puts it, however, "I didn't care about the French. It didn't matter, because Alain would tell me what the song was about, and I would usually say something like, 'But the character is doing this.' We would dramatize the scene in ways that were significantly different from the French version."

In Boublil's view, the final version of *Miss Saigon* is very similar to the original French one. Maltby's take is slightly different. "The songs in French tended to be lyrics without story content," he says, citing the song "The Last Night of the World." "The solo saxophone was there in the original, but in English, the idea is, 'If we go to America together, I can show you this and this, and I can save you.' So the lyrics may have been similar, but the specific content was often different."

Miss Saigon, like *Les Misérables*, was a huge hit when it opened on the West End in 1989. Prior to its Broadway opening, the show ran into considerable controversy: the decision to cast Jonathan Pryce, the white actor who had created the role of the Engineer—a Eurasian character—was met with pushback from Actors' Equity Association, whose leadership felt that casting Pryce and making him up to appear Asian were an affront to Asian actors.[7] Additionally, many felt that the show stereotyped and overly sexualized the Asian women in the cast, who appeared as strippers and hookers in two scenes. In spite of these controversies, the Broadway production ran for just less than ten years. The show has since been revived in both London and New York.

Maltby's involvement on Schönberg and Boublil's *The Pirate Queen* was entirely different. Although he received a coauthor credit on both the book and the lyrics, he was not part of the original writing team. He had turned down an offer to work on *Martin Guerre*, the Schönberg/Boublil musical that opened on the West End in July 1996 and toured in both the United Kingdom and the United States but never made it to Broadway ("I thought it was a story that had no place to go," Maltby declares candidly). Having passed on *Martin Guerre*, Maltby was not surprised when he wasn't asked to join the *Pirate Queen* creative team.

"I thought they had given up on me," he says. John Dempsey, who had written book and lyrics for the musical adaptation of *The Witches of Eastwick* (produced on the West End by Mackintosh in 2000), was brought on board instead and created the English libretto for *The Pirate Queen* with Boublil.

Still a good friend of the creators, Maltby went to see *The Pirate Queen* in Chicago, where reviews were mostly negative. What he saw was "a big huge production, and big lumbering sets that bogged everything down." He also felt that a lot of the songs had exactly the same kind of rhythm, repeating the pattern of a short upbeat followed by a long sustained note, symbolizing royalty in a faux-Baroque style.

"I think Claude-Michel got suckered into the idea that these were kings and queens, so he had to write pageant-y kinds of music," Maltby speculates. "There must've been six or seven songs that had that rhythm—ba *dummmmm*, ba *dummmmm*, ba *dummmmm*."

Maltby was fairly certain he knew how to fix the production, so he wrote a four-page memo to Boublil, who came to New York and invited Maltby to meet in his hotel room. As Maltby recalls, Boublil got right to the point: "He said, 'How much, Richard?' and I said, 'Huh?' And he said, 'How much do you want to come in and take over writing the show?' It was kind of great, actually, a cut-to-the-chase kind of moment." Ultimately, Maltby was paid $100,000 to work with Boublil to revise both the story and the lyrics. Unlike with *Saigon*, it didn't turn out so well.

On paper, *The Pirate Queen* had looked like another sure-fire hit. It was billed as "From the creators of *Les Misérables* and the producers of *Riverdance*." How could it miss? The musicians in the pit orchestra were told they could expect a ten-year run, at least.[8] Instead, the show, which opened on Broadway in April 2007, closed ignominiously after thirty-two previews and eighty-five performances. Maltby was dismayed, having been paid so much to fix the show and having failed. As he recounts:

> There was a three-month gap between Chicago and rehearsals in New York. I went to London, and we wrote a whole script. We really did fix the story. Rehearsals went well. However, when we got into the theater after the rehearsals, suddenly, the scenery was there, and those big lumbering sets were there, and I felt like the whole show was like Silly Putty, going right back into its original shape. We'd changed the lines and changed the drama, but it didn't matter whether it was good playwriting or bad playwriting, because it still just sat there. And I was really shocked and quite embarrassed because I had sold them a bill of goods about fixing the story. We did fix the story, but it didn't fix the show. It just got swallowed by the physical production.

Maltby also never addressed the issue of the repetitive royalty-associated rhythmic patterns in the music. "We did not do much work with the score, and that was another failing of mine," he says. "I never took it on as an issue—it just was not my relationship with Claude-Michel. I don't think I even said anything to Alain. And thinking back on it, if I had called them in and said, 'All these songs have this same rhythm, and it's boring,' I think they would've addressed it. But I was too circumspect about it, and somehow I didn't think it was my job."

Boublil says that the problem with *The Pirate Queen* is that it was never intended as a Broadway show. "It was written to be done under a tent in Ireland," he explains. "It was supposed to be a show that people go and see like what they call an immersive experience today." According to Boublil, Moya Doherty and John McColgan, the producers of the hugely successful *Riverdance*, decided *The Pirate Queen* had Broadway potential. "They opted, and we were weak enough to agree, that it would become a regular Broadway musical. But I think the subject doesn't lead to a regular musical," he concludes.

In this light, Boublil says Maltby probably couldn't have done much to save *The Pirate Queen*. "Richard thought the show could be improved by some suggestions he had," he muses. "I thought some of them were right; some others I thought wouldn't change too much. At the end, because we trusted his impulse, we made some of the changes, not all. But the show was already what it was, and nothing could change the nature of it, and in fact, none of his suggestions changed its fate."

17

ONE OF THE FINEST SCORES OF THE YEAR

In 1987, Lynne Meadow once again was the catalyst for what turned out to be a major entry in the Maltby/Shire canon. This time, though, she just asked if the team could contribute one song to a planned evening of sketches that director John Tillinger was putting together at Manhattan Theatre Club. The show would be centered on urban themes. A song on an urban theme? Maltby had an entire Urban File (see chapter 16). In the end, Maltby and Shire contributed six out of the seven songs that appeared in what was eventually titled *Urban Blight*. (The seventh was by Ed Kleban, best known as the lyricist of *A Chorus Line*.) Shire points out that it was like both *Love Match* and the revue *Graham Crackers*, "where we went in to audition one song and ended up writing most of the show."

Urban Blight ultimately contained twenty-two scenes and sketches by a starry assemblage of writers that included Christopher Durang, Jules Feiffer, A. R. Gurney, Jr., Tina Howe, David Mamet, Terrence McNally, Arthur Miller, Shel Silverstein, Ted Tally, Wendy Wasserstein, August Wilson, and George C. Wolfe. Due partly to the daunting logistics of coordinating so many moving parts (Meadow called it "an act of madness"),[1] the originally scheduled opening on May 18, 1988, had to be postponed a month until June 19, and as a result, the show could only run for twelve performances.

It was enough, however, to attract positive critical attention and audience enthusiasm. In the *New York Times*, both Patricia Leigh Brown's feature article just prior to the opening and Frank Rich's review the following day singled out the song "Miss Byrd," with Rich declaring that Nancy Giles "turns it into an old-time showstopper."[2] Rich went on to observe, "Without ever leaving her swivel office chair, Ms. Giles dances about the stage in a sizzling comic frenzy, with her Miss Byrd at times bringing back memories of the

Closer Than Ever. Joshua Rosenblum, Oxford University Press. © Oxford University Press 2024.
DOI: 10.1093/oso/9780197758236.003.0017

young Barbra Streisand's early Broadway turn as Miss Marmelstein [in *I Can Get It for you Wholesale*]."

The song "Miss Byrd" is unquestionably memorable, and yet, ironically, the character, who works in the real estate agent's office of an apartment building, begins by declaring how unmemorable she is (example 17.1).

Example 17.1. "Miss Byrd"

The sign says I'm Miss Byrd,
And that's my name.

I'm one of those peo - ple who all look the same.

This is not what most songs do (although "Mr. Cellophane" from the Kander and Ebb musical *Chicago* comes to mind as another example). There is, however, a certain tension between her self-described unnoticeability ("I'm one of those people who all look the same") and the bouncing, even funky groove that is propelling the song. In the next verse, we find out why:

I sit here at my desk
And no one knows
Not twenty minutes ago
I was not wearing clothes.

Miss Byrd, it turns out, is having a torrid affair with the building's super. ("He says I'm super, too," she gushes later.) Nice little scheme she has going there! Without Maltby's having to spell it out, we get the clear picture that Miss Byrd is pretending to leave the office to show the basement apartments to potential buyers but is actually using one of them as a love nest.

At this point, we are captivated by the contrast between the outward appearance and the secret life of this now-intriguing person. In addition, the boisterous beat of the music now makes sense: this unprepossessing woman's life is pretty wild.

Leading into the first chorus, it starts to get even more fun:

If it's true a bird makes music
When her heart takes wing,
This bird is singing,
Miss Byrd is singing.

Maltby gets to use the metaphor of a bird making music and have it simultaneously work as a pun on the character's name. Even better, the name Miss Byrd sounds (deliberately) somewhat prim and schoolmarmish, but on the flip side, a bird that is bursting into song is a symbol of joy, and Maltby turns the former into the latter with those four deft lines. Shire does his part by opening out the vocal line, which has hitherto been primarily syncopated and composed of relatively rapid-fire eighth notes. Now, on the phrase "This bird is singing," the melody takes flight, with a broad sustained note on (appropriately enough) the syllable "sing" (example 17.2).

Example 17.2. "Miss Byrd"

This bird is sing - ing.___ Miss Byrd is sing - ing,

Singing about singing, especially to such a great, soaring melody, is always gratifying for the listener. We also get to enjoy the felicitous inner rhyme that comes from the juxtaposition of the metaphorical "*This* bird" with the flesh-and-blood character "*Miss* Byrd."

The run of *Urban Blight* was brief, and the songs were not the focal point, but it was enough to interest playwright/director Steven Scott Smith, Maltby's assistant, in the contents of the Urban File. Smith proposed to Maltby and Shire the idea of adapting some of the Urban File songs into a cabaret evening, along with other unknown Maltby/Shire numbers from previous musicals. The resulting show, titled *Next Time, Now!*,[3] debuted in January 1989 at Eighty-Eights, a Greenwich Village nightclub. The cast included Brent Barrett, Michael Brian, and Lynne Wintersteller, with musical director and arranger Patrick Brady at the piano. The show immediately attracted notice. *New York Times* critic Stephen Holden, who would turn out to be an ongoing champion of the piece, wrote of this first outing:

> The finest songs of Richard Maltby Jr. and David Shire, the collaborative team best known for the 1977 cabaret revue "Starting Here, Starting Now" and the 1983 Broadway show "Baby," communicate something rarely found in theater music nowadays: a rich sweeping sense of lives being lived and people changing over time. . . . Both in style and subject matter, Mr. Maltby's lyrics and Mr. Shire's music have taken directions suggested by Stephen Sondheim's "Company" and developed an urban contemporary style as smooth as it is sophisticated. Mr. Shire's experience as a composer of film music has given his theater songs a cosmopolitan gloss that confidently

embraces rock and folk echoes without compromising its complexity. Mr. Maltby's most ambitious lyrics match Sondheim's in seriousness but bring a warmer and more easygoing perspective to grown-up relationships.[4]

Holden concluded: "At the very least, 'Next Time, Now!' deserves a good recording."

This, plus the enthusiastic sold-out crowds the show had been attracting, was enough to convince the team that the show merited further development. *Next Time, Now!* ran an hour; the expanded version, titled *Closer Than Ever*, would be a full evening with an intermission. Additional songs were added from the Urban File, and new ones were written. In fact, Holden's observations in his review influenced the team in terms of what kinds of songs they would add to the show.

"[Holden] talked about how the songs were all about life lived over time," Maltby says. Unlike many of the numbers in *Starting Here, Starting Now*, they were not about young love—quite to the contrary. "They were about things that happen after you've gone through some experiences, and time has expanded your knowledge of what life is. So we actually wrote some more songs that were about that. One of them was 'The March of Time.' It was specifically on that theme [of growing into mature adulthood], and it was absolutely in response to Holden's observation."

"The March of Time" now seems like one of the quintessential numbers from the *Closer Than Ever* score. It gives a unique perspective on what it feels like to realize that one is no longer young. Numerous songs have been written about growing older, but they typically have a wistful, bittersweet quality. "The March of Time," however, is set to a rousing, near-manic march tempo—like "Seventy-Six Trombones" or "The Washington Post March"—with a precarious edge of panicky helplessness masked by forced cheerfulness. Aging, in this song, is like being swept along by a runaway train; it's scary, but it's also fun in its way. After a misleadingly slow introductory verse, we hear the distant approach of mortality:

And in my ear I hear a sound like distant drumming.
At first I think it's something in the plumbing.
But no, it's something I can't stop from coming.

Then, once the march tempo kicks in, Maltby turns it into a clever list song, including this stanza in the second verse:

I wasn't ready for tuitions
Or finding boyfriends for my mom
Or friends who flip their lids

Or adolescent kids
Who've never heard of Vietnam.

Toward the end, there are notes of decided optimism as well:

I wasn't ready to keep moving
I wasn't ready for the dawn
Or learning pain can fade
Recoveries get made
No matter what, your life goes on.

These positive aspects make the point that aging, though inevitably a mixed bag, can also be the source of deeper and more richly satisfying experiences than youth offers.

The team, now supported by producers Michael Gill, Daryl Roth, and Janet Brenner (Maltby's second wife), decided to do a tryout of the reconceived show at the Williamstown Theatre Festival in Massachusetts, the same locale where, twenty-eight years earlier, they had done a tryout of *The Sap of Life*, their first off-Broadway show. Marcia Milgrom Dodge came on board as choreographer, and Maltby took over the direction of the show, with Smith given the credit "Conceived and Co-Directed by." The cast was expanded to include a second woman—the ebullient and clarion-voiced Sally Mayes. The resonant baritone Richard Muenz replaced Brian from the original cast at Eighty-Eights. Barrett and Wintersteller retained their spots.

The reconceived show needed a closing number. Playwright and record producer Bill Rosenfeld writes in the liner notes to the *Closer Than Ever* original cast recording:

> It occurred to the authors that the themes of time passing and relationships altering are depicted as things "lost," but they are also gains. Adversity can cement a relationship as well as destroy it, and the closeness that follows is often the most startling emotion that life can produce. Soon the finale had its title, and so did the show.[5]

As the song's lyric concludes:

We still have our stormy days.
Even the worst can't shake us.
If all we have come through could not break us,
What's ahead can only make us
Stronger than ever,
Clearer than ever,
I'm closer than ever to you.

These are not sentiments that the characters in *Starting Here, Starting Now* would have been able to express or even understand. These people are grown-ups who, reflecting the experience of the now-middle-aged authors, have taken some of life's hard knocks and emerged with richly textured experiences to show for it.

There are no through lines for the characters in *Closer Than Ever*. With *Starting Here, Starting Now*, Maltby had turned the first several numbers into an implied story about three people in a love triangle. "Once we get past that, it's just a collection of songs," he clarifies. "But by then, you've established the forward motion of a story, and you just fit everything else into it."

Closer Than Ever was different. Maltby explains:

> We played around with [through lines for the characters] for a very brief period of time, but no information from one song could be carried into another one. The woman singing "The Bear, the Tiger" is not the same as the woman singing "Patterns," even though it's the same actress. There's no emotional information from the first song that enhances the second. So, in fact, I made sure that at the end of the first number going into the second, we specifically stopped being who we were in the opening and became somebody else. You just do it—you do it with no connection to the person who was there before.

Yet the show still manages to come off as a coherent evening because of the common theme of people dealing with life at a certain age. Shire adds that if a play is like a novel, *Closer Than Ever* is like a collection of short stories. "They're not connected in any way—they're different stories—but they have the common point of view of that particular writer."

Another unifying factor for the show is that there is musical continuity whenever the four cast members appear as a group in ensemble numbers; they come together every now and then, starting with the opening number, "Doors." "The song 'Doors' is a group of people expressing how just when you get your life together, then *pling*! You get thrown into something new," Maltby says. "It's like life is just a series of doors opening and closing on you. And a collection of people say that collectively. Then, at the end of the first act, they're suddenly back to being the people they were at the very beginning. It's never spelled out, but the audience feels it."

To underscore this, the end of the first act features the recurrence of some of the musical material from the beginning, namely the opening lines from "Doors" that begin the show: "Well, whaddaya know / In front of me now is an open door." Those lines, though they function seamlessly as the intro to "Doors," originated as the beginning of the song "I Wouldn't Go Back," the outtake from *Baby* that serves as the Act I finale of *Closer Than Ever*. Thus, when we get to the invigorating opening of "I Wouldn't Go Back," it's effectively a musical reprise.

"That was one of those lucky accidents," Maltby says when he's reminded of this. "'Doors' was a completely separate idea." Taking the phrase "Well, whaddaya know? / In front of me now is an open door" from the song "I Wouldn't Go Back" and sticking it in as the intro to a separate song that happened to be called "Doors" was a felicitous opportunity to create continuity and give the show more unity.

In a similar manner, "Next Time" has a musical intro that consists of three lines of text set to the melody from the verse of "Doors," in a slow, out-of-tempo setting:

She's at your door, are your eyes deceiving you?
Your life takes off, and there's no retrieving you.
Then there's the door that shuts as she's leaving you.
Doors.

The "Doors" melody then reappears at the end of "Next Time" to form a transition into "I Wouldn't Go Back." It begins in a bright instrumental version, underscoring the last held "now" of the song; then the cast joins in on the line "Every day another door," and "I Wouldn't Go Back" races out of the gate to close Act I.

Finally, at the end of the show, as an intro to the title song, we get a full new stanza set to the "Doors" chorus music:

Well, what do you know, a door locked tight
Opens at last and shows some light.
Once more a door you've tried and tried
Gives, and you're on the other side.

All this skillful transplanting and reuse of musical phrases (often with new lyrics by Maltby) among the group numbers is the work of musical director and arranger Brady. His inspired and singular contributions in this category go a long way toward creating additional continuity and coherence for the show.

Brady also gets credit for the seamless merging of "It's Never That Easy" and "I've Been Here Before," a pairing that appears in the show's penultimate slot. Woman 1 sings the first of these two songs, which is followed by a piano transition that changes both the feel and the key but still seems fully integrated. Woman 2 proceeds to sing "I've Been Here Before," and then, in a musically and dramatically gratifying final section, the two songs interweave with each other, as Woman 2 goes back for a repeat of the bridge of "I've Been Here Before," and Woman 1 picks up with the final line of her verse ("I know it's never that easy. Believe me, it isn't at all") and proceeds from there.

A perfect juxtaposition of the two numbers in their original forms, in the manner of a quodlibet, is not actually possible, since they weren't written to go together and don't follow the same harmonic progression. Brady, however, by carefully selecting and shuffling phrases from "I've Been Here Before" and subtly altering the melodic lines so they fit the harmonies of "It's Never That Easy," creates the illusion that this is exactly what you're hearing. It sounds as if the songs were composed to dovetail like this, but they were, in fact, created for two different musicals, written almost a quarter of a century apart: "It's Never That Easy" comes from *The River*, the aborted Rumer Godden adaptation, while "I've Been Here Before" is from *Village Bells*, a project with playwright Bill C. Davis that also yielded "What Am I Doin'?" (discussed in chapter 18). The result of the merging is a thrilling duet for two female singers supporting each other through their respective romantic challenges—a relatively sparse subgenre.

Closer Than Ever opened in New York at the Cherry Lane Theatre on November 6, 1989. There were some flat-out rave reviews—the kind that sound as if the creative team might have written them themselves. David Patrick Stearns of *USA Today* wrote that "Maltby and Shire are one of the great song-writing teams, and possibly the funniest. *Closer Than Ever* is the most satisfying and humanizing new musical this season."[6] Michael Kuchwara of the Associated Press called the show "One of the finest scores of the year. *Closer Than Ever* is an exhilarating musical revue that reaffirms one's belief that the American musical theatre isn't dead yet."[7] Howard Kissel wrote in the *New York Daily News* that "There is more genuine drama in each Maltby and Shire song than in the entirety of most of the bloated spectacles that now pass for Broadway musicals."[8]

Those are the kinds of reviews that creative types dream about. But Laurie Winer's pan in the *New York Times* was a setback. Winer dismissed the show as "a gallery of contemporary people struggling with the usual dilemmas . . . only too willing to share their dreams and woes, however banal."[9] (Maltby refers to it as "that terrible review from that terrible woman who lasted only three months at the *Times* and then got fired.")[10]

"The afterlife of the show has implied that it was really a hit," Shire observes. "It wasn't a hit. It ran nine months." Whether or not the show was a hit seems to be a debatable point—nine months (312 performances) is a respectable run for an off-Broadway show, and references routinely cite the show as a hit, a critical success, or both. In any case, as with *Starting Here,*

Starting Now, the original cast recording—once again produced by Jay David Saks for RCA Victor—gave the show a prolonged life well beyond its original production. This time, the label was even willing to pay for orchestrating the show. Broadway orchestrator Michael Starobin expanded the original piano and bass combo to create a rousing, often electrifying orchestration that includes drums, guitar, synthesizer, woodwind doubler, French horn, and cello.

When the album was released, Holden wrote another love letter in the *Times*, a fourteen-paragraph deep dive that explored the material in admiring detail and which he concluded with the eminently blurb-able statement that *Closer Than Ever* is "one of the half-dozen finest American theater scores of the last decade." Typical of the review was this paragraph's analysis of the song "Life Story":

> "Life Story" combines an amiable Billy Joel-style tunefulness with a lyric that suggests a colloquialized echo of one of Stephen Sondheim's monologues. In the song Mr. Shire builds an elaborate musical structure that transcends cliches while still keeping a fluent, easygoing tone. Throughout, Mr. Maltby and Mr. Shire succeed in combining some of the best of two worlds—the elegant craftsmanship of a theater tradition that runs from Gilbert and Sullivan to Sondheim and the openhearted spirit of contemporary folk-pop.[11]

Holden also singled out a quality that in some ways made the recording a more profound experience than even the live theatrical performance:

> When performed on the stage by Brent Barrett, Sally Mayes, Richard Muenz and Lynne Wintersteller, four good-looking 30ish actors with superb singing voices, "Closer Than Ever" fizzes with youthful exuberance. Portraying assorted angst-ridden urbanites between 35 to 55 reflecting on their lives, they imbue everything with a spirited playfulness.
>
> On the recording, the deeper, bittersweet qualities of this chipper early-1960's-style revue seep to the surface. Without the performers' faces, their voices seem more mature. And enlarged by Mr. Starobin's exquisite chamber orchestrations, the show's 25 songs mesh into an often wrenching conceptual album about the satisfactions, regrets and anxieties felt by people who have reached an age when it is too late to start over.[12]

As a result of the recording, the show had a powerful impact, particularly among a young generation of musical theater lovers. Joel Fram, a Broadway and West End conductor and musical director most recently seen conducting the hugely successful Broadway revival of Sondheim's *Merrily We Roll Along*, recalls being an assistant musical director during a season of summer stock at the Candlewood Playhouse in New Fairfield, Connecticut, in 1991 and essentially turning the post-show cabaret into a performance of *Closer Than Ever*.

"I was half responsible, and the cast was half responsible," Fram recalls. "I would say, 'Let's do this song, this song, and this song,' and then, of course, someone would come up and say, 'I want to do "Miss Byrd,"' and someone else would say, 'Wouldn't it be great if we did "Fathers of Fathers" as well?' And by the time I got my songs in and they got their songs in, we were essentially doing the whole show."[13] The exceptionally well-plugged-in Fram says the *Closer Than Ever* fever that swept the Candlewood Playhouse that season was representative of what was going on at other summer theaters.

Prominent among *Closer Than Ever*'s first generation of fans was Jason Robert Brown, the Tony- winning composer and lyricist of *Parade*, *The Last Five Years*, and *The Bridges of Madison County*, among others. Brown cites *Closer Than Ever* as an enormous influence on his own work, specifically on *Songs for a New World*, his first produced show, which ran off-Broadway at the WPA Theatre in 1995. In a blog post on the subject, Brown writes about seeing *Closer Than Ever* during its initial run in 1989:

> I remember so much about the experience, from the enormous charm of the Cherry Lane Theatre to Patrick Brady's extraordinary playing, the astonishing vocal arrangements, Sally Mayes's total star presence, even the staging of most of the songs. I'd never seen anything like it before, and I was enthralled.
>
> Once I arrived in NY, I determined to create something exactly like Richard and David had done. Four characters, a piano and an onstage band, a non-narrative but thematically arranged revue—I even became a pianist at Eighty-Eight's in the West Village because I knew that's where the first performances of *Closer Than Ever* had taken place.[14]

Brown actually ran into Maltby around that time, at a copy shop in Greenwich Village, where they both lived.[15] Brown arranged to drop off a cassette of the revue he had written ("so clearly modeled on [*Closer Than Ever*]"). "Richard then called me and invited me over to a lovely lunch in his backyard, where he essentially said it was unlikely that my show would ever get produced, but I seemed talented and I should keep writing," Brown continues good-naturedly. *Songs for a New World* opened three years later, launching Brown's successful career as a leading musical theater writer. Maltby was in the opening-night audience, happy to have been proven wrong.

The young generation of composers, musical theater buffs, and college students in acting programs who fell in love with the songs from *Closer Than Ever* when the show first emerged would have a chance to encounter the show with an illuminating new perspective, having aged a few decades themselves, when the York Theatre Company mounted an off-Broadway revival and issued a new cast recording in 2012.[16]

18 CLOSER THAN EVER

"Doors," the opening number to *Closer Than Ever*, is followed by "She Loves Me Not," the alluring and poignant three-part fugue from *The Sap of Life*. For the *Closer Than Ever* adaptation, Maltby added a sly change of pronouns.

In *The Sap of Life*'s original context, Horatio is in love with Hazel, who is in love with Andrew, who is in love with Ruthanne. As Maltby puts it, "It was a cycle, but it wasn't a circuit." Thus, in the third and final verse of the *Closer Than Ever* version, when the second man enters, he glances over not at the woman but at the first man and laments, "*He* loves me not," thus closing the loop.

"If the third verse is a gay man, that makes it a circle of unrequited love. It also makes it a surprise," Maltby explains. "And it was a gift to the eighty percent of our audience which was gay," Shire adds. "In fact, if we hadn't done that, we might've gotten criticism for making it purely heterosexual."

"What Am I Doin'?" is an exceptionally memorable tale—both comic and disturbing—of the extreme lengths to which one can be driven by obsessive love. It's from a project the team worked on with Bill C. Davis, author of the play *Mass Appeal*. The show, titled *Village Bells*, was inspired by Davis's real-life experience working as an intern at a facility for emotionally disturbed young people. The show was never produced, but it yielded two songs for *Closer Than Ever.* (The other was "I've Been Here Before," discussed in chapter 17.) In "What Am I Doin'?," the singer finds himself climbing onto the roof of the house where the young woman who has cut off their relationship lives, and sitting there in the rain:

What am I doin' up on a roof?
What am I doin' out in the rain?
What kind of feelings make a man blind?
What am I doin' out of my mind
With love?

Closer Than Ever. Joshua Rosenblum, Oxford University Press. © Oxford University Press 2024.
DOI: 10.1093/oso/9780197758236.003.0018

Not much changes in the second chorus, except for the fact that both of their fathers are now on-site, observing the insanity. ("And her father and my father are down on the lawn, and they're shouting . . .") It's the same lyrics but from the fathers' point of view: "What is *he* doin' up on a roof," and so on. "The humiliation has to be global," Maltby says. "Not just that he felt bad—he was a laughingstock in front of both families. 'What does this wacko kid want? She doesn't love you!' "

The singer eventually realizes how insane his behavior is when the verse of the song returns:

I decided that I'd learned my lesson.
I rejoined all the sensible men.
Now no matter how tempting the woman
I won't ever go crazy again.

There's an obvious parallel between this moment and the bridge of "I Don't Remember Christmas":

"If she wants to leave you, well, let her,"
Says a practical voice in my head.
Any sensible man would forget her,
Forget her, forget her![1]

"They're both saying, 'I'm not going to humiliate myself ever again, I don't feel that anymore,' " Maltby elaborates. "A lot of writers have *their* song which they write over and over again. That's mine." Shire concurs: "Many of our songs have that same arc."

Then, leading into the final chorus of "What Am I Doin'?," which features cascading descriptions of more obsessive behavior, the singer delivers a final kicker:

I think back to that night I felt tingles,
Holding tight not to slide down the shingles,
Feeling feelings I'll never forget,
And I wish I was saying,
"What am I doin' up on a roof?" (etc.)

That single, subtle phrase—"And I *wish* I was saying"—is the most shocking part of the song. After his avowed declaration that he will henceforth cling to sanity at all costs, he admits that he wishes he were back on the roof in the rain! In the end, at least to this person, it's better to feel *something* than to feel numb. Better to go crazy and humiliate yourself than to cut yourself off from your feelings.

"I Wouldn't Go Back," which brings the curtain down on Act I, features a galvanizing, syncopated rock beat; fresh, unexpected harmonies; an exciting, upwardly sequencing melody on the words "But here I am, amazed to find that I can turn and walk right through the door"; and an exuberant, life-affirming message. This song was the original final number of *Baby*, until it was replaced with the "Birth/Finale" sequence, a skillfully woven reprise/transformation of "We Start Today" and "The Story Goes On" that is sung as we witness the actual birth of Lizzie and Danny's baby. As discussed in chapter 17, "I Wouldn't Go Back" makes a terrific curtain number for Act I of *Closer Than Ever*, but one wonders why it was cut from *Baby*. Maltby explains:

> ["I Wouldn't Go Back"] was a big winner in all of our backers' auditions [for *Baby*]. It was exciting in rehearsal, but in previews, it was like we weren't getting to the point. All the characters just stood there and sang in their position for three minutes, and it didn't move the story, and that was when we hit upon the idea of the birth moment. That quote from the script, "For nine months, the womb has been the baby's universe. Now the time has come to leave this safe place and journey into the unknown." That's from right out of a textbook, and I thought, that's basically the story of the show. You move from a safe place out into the cold and hostile world, and that's when life starts, and everybody in the show did the same thing, so that the birth of the baby was this whole beginning for everyone. And David came in and played that whole build, the birth moment, in one piece. It really made the ending, both the birth of the baby and the rebirth of these three couples. I think it was magical.

That meant "I Wouldn't Go Back" went into the trunk, waiting to be resurrected by Steven Scott Smith and merged with "Next Time" by Patrick Brady for a perfect Act 1 finale to *Closer Than Ever*.

"Back on Base," which features both music and lyrics by Shire, was written when the composer realized that everyone onstage had a number except Robert Renino, the bass player. Musical director Brady sang from the piano in the duet number "There" with Sally Mayes and also joined in with Richard Muenz and Brent Barrett in "Fathers of Fathers," one of the outtakes from *Baby*, but Renino had no comparable moment in the spotlight. The bass player doesn't sing in "Back on Base," but he is the prominent object of the singer's affection, and the number is primarily bass-focused. For the entire first verse, in fact, Mayes is accompanied only by solo bass. (The piano joins in very lightly on the second verse and proceeds to add some delectable jazz fills.)

The song is full of base/bass puns. As the singer puts it in the first stanza, to swinging, walking bass accompaniment:

My scattered life had no foundation,
Couldn't seem to find my space.
Then all at once came inspiration,
Now I'm back on base.

There's plenty of naughty innuendo, too, specifically related to the low range of the instrument in question:

When his fingers touch my strings,
I tingle to my teeth
I seem to sing the wildest things
When he is underneath.

And:

He's got eyes for something tall
So maybe I should go.
Then once more my defenses fall
When he gets down below oh oh oh . . .

It's not always easy for her to get his full attention; music is a demanding mistress. But she makes it clear that it's worth sticking around.

DS: The bass player didn't have anything to do in the show except play bass, so that gave me the idea.

RM: He also said, "I think we should write a song for a bass player—and here it is!" If there was some idea that we were gonna work together on it, it was gone already.

DS: You were very averse to having them put it in the show at first.

RM: Well, "Back on Base" is not really a story song. It isn't really a dramatizable story like that.

DS: It's not your kind of story song, but I had a story for it.

RM: It is not consistent with the kind of story songs that are in the rest of the show, as you can hear in the London version, where, for stupid reasons, they never got to "Three Friends" and they never got to "The March of Time," and the second act now consists of only the story songs, and that stands out as not being the same kind of story song as the other songs. You didn't notice so much when the other material was there.

DS: Nobody's counting and saying, "That's not a story song, that doesn't belong." I think of "Back on Base" as a story. I had a character in mind of a woman who is trying to get a man to pay attention to her and doing everything she can to do it, so in my mind it's a story song.

RM: I know that's true, I'm just saying that relative to the rest of the show, it is not the same kind of story song. And it is not a character song, really.

DS: I respectfully disagree.

Over the course of more than a dozen joint interviews about their sixty-seven years of collaboration, the song "Back on Base" seems to be Maltby and Shire's single biggest bone of contention. Actress Didi Conn, Shire's second (and current) wife, says it's the only time she's ever confronted Maltby about anything. "I went up to him, and I said, 'You have to leave that song in!'" she recalls. "He was going to cut it!"[2]

Regardless of whether it's a story song according to Maltby's exacting definition, it's a marvelous number; it showcases Shire's jazz background and focuses on the unique relationship between a singer and the sometimes overlooked instrumentalist who accompanies her. Certainly, Mayes and Renino are pleased it ended up in the show—in a fairy-tale ending, they wound up getting married and continue to live happily together.

"If I Sing," probably the most moving number in the show, is about Shire's father. Particularly if you come from a family of musicians, it's nearly impossible to listen to this song without tearing up. In the words of the chorus:

If I sing, you are the music.
If I fly, you're why I'm good.
If my hands can find some magic,
You're the one who said they could.

Maltby and Shire had decided to write a song about the fact that both of their fathers were bandleaders and what they as songwriters owed their fathers. "We might have even had a title, might have had the line 'If I sing, you are the music,'" Maltby says. "Then I went to England to open *Miss Saigon*, and shortly afterward, David sent me that amazing melody. I did not tinker. We did not change a note."

Shire points out that "If I Sing" is a "recursive" song—a song that references itself. He elaborates:

> We had started on the song, but we didn't know where it was going. When Richard went to England, I went to Buffalo to visit my father. The second stanza of that song says exactly what happened during the visit. I said, "Dad, this is the song we're trying to write about our fathers," and I played him the melody. He told me at that time that his fingers were starting to get numb and that he couldn't play anymore. But when he

heard the music, he smiled. So I came back and told Richard about that, and Richard immediately said, "The song is about *your* father!"

Here are the second-verse lyrics that were a result of Shire's visit to see his ailing father:

My dad grew old.
His hands were numb.
And now he cannot play.
I came to visit.
He sat and asked me,
"How can it be this way?"
I couldn't find an answer.
I played this tune for him instead.
My father sat there smiling,
For he knew what it said.

Thus, the act of playing the unfinished song for the person who inspired it became part of the content of the song itself.

Shire concludes the story: "My father got to see *Closer Than Ever* just in time. We carried him into the Cherry Lane Theatre in a wheelchair, and he sat in the back. Then he died soon after that. It's a very personal song."

A manuscript page with an early sketch of the melody for the verse differs significantly from what we know as the final version (example 18.1a). Looking at the final version of this passage (transposed for comparison purposes), we can see that Shire's rewrite gave the melody in the second system of example 18.1a more of an upwardly yearning quality, making it a better representation of a son striving to emulate his father (example 18.1b).

Example 18.1a. "If I Sing," original version (manuscript)

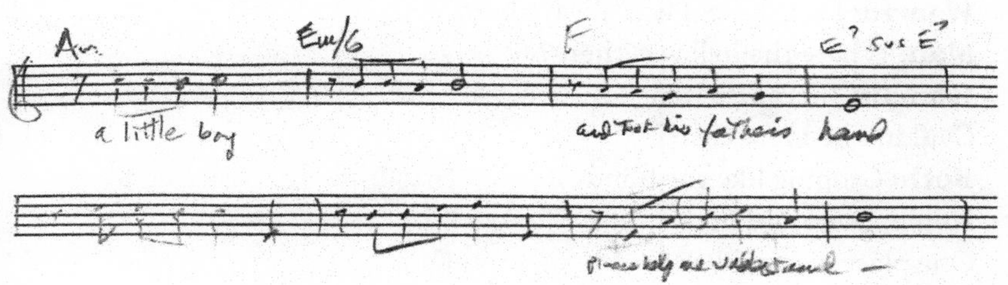

Example 18.1b. "If I Sing," final version

Another personal song, though much lighter in tone, is "There," which has a fun but deceptive swinging cabaret bounce that conceals the pain contained in the description of a marriage that failed. Why does the relationship fall apart? Because, as the opening lyric puts it succinctly:

There.
He was never there.
Every time we talked,
I'd look in his eyes,
And his mind was
Where?

Maltby says the original inspiration for the song came from his first wife, Barbara. "However," he adds candidly, "it's the lifelong complaint of anyone I've ever been involved with."

The song lightheartedly cycles through a plethora of puns on the ambiguous, single-word title; at one point, we get four "theres" in a row:

Still, the fault's not mine.
Quoting Gertrude Stein,
"There was just no
There there."
[and then, consoling:]
There, there.

Later, the deconstruction of both "there" and the relationship becomes positively existential:

Man: Think of my dismay, finding she had moved
By the time I got there.
She was over there.
Woman: I was here. I was always here.
Man: Where the hell was there?
Woman: There was here,
Couldn't be more clear.
Both: Groping like the blind
Hoping we could find
One place we could share.[3]

Regarding the staging of the number, with the woman on the piano, torch-song-style, singing directly to the pianist, Maltby observes:

I staged it completely wrong, because David wrote this sort of cocktail piano music, and I thought, "Well, it's like a lounge song, so I had her on the piano, lying down, singing to her accompanist, who was Patrick Brady, and that's the way I thought the song should be done because of the music. And then, when we went to, I think, a production at the Pasadena Playhouse, the pianist didn't sing, so I thought, "I guess I'll have to give it to the guy in the show." And then suddenly, they were sitting side by side in a marriage counselor's office, and that's suddenly, oh, my God, *that's* the song. What on earth was I thinking?

The marriage counselor's office concept for the staging may have gotten closer to the essence of the song in the lyricist's opinion, but the number is very entertaining when it's done by the woman on top of the piano to the pianist. In that version, it also makes a nice parallel to "Back on Base," which is also about a woman who feels insufficiently attended to by a man who is currently playing a musical instrument.

"Fandango" also came out of a real-life Maltby marital experience. His second wife, Janet Brenner, was one of the producers on *Closer Than Ever*, working to bring it back to New York in its expanded form while her husband and his collaborator were working furiously to get the show finished. Once again, an upbeat, tuneful musical setting belies the tensions that lurk beneath: the number is in rollicking $\frac{6}{8}$ time, with alternating duplet and triplet subdivisions[4] and sliding inner voices in the harmonies, as if the whole thing were a game spinning slightly out of control. And the game in question is, how can I persuade my spouse to take care of the baby while I do the work that I have to do? Or, as the end of each verse memorably puts it, ". . . if maybe / You'd take the baby." Maltby's recollection of the real-life incident that precipitated the song is both hilarious and painfully relatable for any couple who has ever juggled careers and kids:

> We had just had Jordan, and Janet had to go to an ad meeting or something, and I had to stay and work with David, and she said, "Oh, well, can you just not work on it and take the baby while I go off to my meeting?" and I'm thinking, I'm really excited that Janet is really excited about being a producer and that she's not just staying at home and being a mother. She's going to be fulfilled and everything—but not now! And while it's getting real, your ad meeting does *not* match up to my need to write something now for the show, for *your* show! But I didn't say that. I said, "I know that this is important to you and I wanna help, but can't you, like, you know, give a little bit?" And so the two of us are lying through our teeth trying to wheedle the other one into doing it. The basic premise of "restarting your career, which I can't support enough, makes your work as important as mine!" Except it

isn't. Suddenly, we played out that thing, and David and I wrote that song in just a matter of a couple of days, and it went in the show.

Apart from "If I Sing," the most personal song for Shire in the show is "Another Wedding Song," which he wrote to be performed at his wedding to Conn in 1982. It was the second marriage for both Shire and Conn, and the song references this in a manner that is both affectionate and witty, with lines like "You're so much more than merely first / You are the first to be second." When the discussion turned to this song, the following exchange ensued:

DS: "Another Wedding Song" was a song I wrote for me and Didi to sing at our wedding, and it just happened to be in the trunk, and I thought it would be a nice lead-in to the song that followed it.[5]

JR: You managed to come up with those three great rhymes for "second": "beckoned," "reckoned," and "fecund"—the most unexpected one.

RM: You stole those! He stole them from me!

DS: I did?

RM: Yes, you did!

DS: What do you mean?

RM: I had all of those rhymes in another song, I don't remember what it was. You apologized for it!

DS: Did I? I don't remember.

RM: You told me I used those rhymes.

DS: But you know what, I don't think there were any other rhymes. I was forced to use them. That was one of those gifts you were talking about, where you need the third rhyme and oh, my God, it's the perfect word.

RM: Yeah, I mean in a song about a marriage, "fecund" really works well. If it was a song about a baseball player who was on second base, you'd have a bit of a hard time putting fecund in there.

JR: What was your song where you used those rhymes?

RM: I don't remember right at the moment. It might have been from some industrial show I wrote. But you're welcome to them.

DS: Well anyway, we influence each other.

"One of the Good Guys" came right out of the Urban File. It's based, in fact, on Maltby's college roommate, with whom he had also gone to Exeter. "I thought, here's a guy who makes all the right choices," Maltby relates. "He's faithful, he doesn't play around, he doesn't do any of those awful things. But the world does not reward him. The world does not send him special points because he does it; as a matter of fact, the world does the opposite. The world rewards the Donald Trump shitheads and gives them everything in the world, and the good guys get nothing, and I thought it would be interesting to write that."

In the song, a happily married man reflects on the time many years ago when he had the opportunity to have an affair but at the moment of truth decided it was the wrong thing to do and declined to follow through: "But I stopped and said 'no.' 'Cause that isn't me / I'm one of the good guys / One of the smart ones / Whose virtue survives." The verse ends with the lines "That's the part that's sweet / That only the good guys know."

At this point, it almost seems as if the song is over. The music reaches a cadence, and the actor starts to head offstage; then another chord—an unresolved dominant hanging momentarily in the air—stops him. "That's not the end, as you suspected," he sings. This flatters the audience—they *did* think it was the end, and the moment always gets a laugh. ("When it's just right, the audience would even start to applaud," Shire says.) That is followed by the lines "Time flipped some pages / I'm now forty-four." This is another great example of Maltby's remarkable ability to telescope time with a minimal number of syllables. It's reminiscent of "Blink and twenty years have gone" from "We Start Today" and the four-syllable "and hers before" from "The Story Goes On."

The song continues. Sometimes as he lies in bed, he tells us, he has memories of the almost-affair and wonders if his life is "second best" because he missed out on this opportunity. Shire's evocative music comes swirling back to remind us what it was like for the man, there on a beach in Hawaii. But once again, he decides he did the right thing. The ending is an elegant, concise, and ultimately painful conclusion:

It's not which road you take,
Which life you pick to live in.
Whichever choice you make
The longing is a given.
And that's what brings the ache
That only the good guys know.

As Maltby summarizes it, "If you do it, you'll regret it; if you don't do it, you'll regret it. Either way, you're screwed. But a shithead would not have this dilemma—only a good guy knows this. We don't dignify those people. We don't write songs about them."

Shire says this is one of his two or three favorites of all of Maltby's lyrics: "It's just so perfect. It says exactly what it needs to say. There may be other songs about people like that, but they don't have the deeply felt and nuanced lyrics that song has." Record producer Tom Shepard also singles out this number when asked to name a favorite Maltby/Shire song.[6]

"THE BEAR, THE TIGER, THE HAMSTER AND THE MOLE"

"The Bear, the Tiger, the Hamster and the Mole," cut from the musical *Baby* but resurrected for *Closer Than Ever*, is probably the quintessential Maltby/Shire "head versus heart" conflict number, a by-now-familiar recurring theme.

Right out of the gate, in the syncopated, driving piano introduction, we can clearly hear the cognitive dissonance that the struggle between intellect and emotions is creating in this poor woman (example 19.1).

Example 19.1. "The Bear, the Tiger, the Hamster and the Mole"

Finally, after six bars of this, she yells "Stop!," literally ordering the clangorous, battling thoughts in her head to cease. But nothing is settled yet: when the music resumes, after a startlingly empty two bars, the right-hand chords are literally unresolved—suspended fourths alternating back and forth over the course of four measures. The left hand of the piano, meanwhile, keeps resolutely coming back to an A♭ on each downbeat, regardless of what chords are in the right hand—much like, say, a relationship that is stuck in a rut (example 19.2).

Closer Than Ever. Joshua Rosenblum, Oxford University Press. © Oxford University Press 2024.
DOI: 10.1093/oso/9780197758236.003.0019

Example 19.2. "The Bear, the Tiger, the Hamster and the Mole"

When the bass finally moves up to an E♭ (at the end of the first full bar of example 19.3), it is now the root of what is almost a conventional E♭ dominant seventh chord, except for one altered note: the A♮, replacing a normal B♭, transforms the chord into a more ominous-sounding cluster, which is a perfect coloring for the last word of the phrase "'Til relationships don't stand a *chance*."

Example 19.3. "The Bear, the Tiger, the Hamster and the Mole"

Shortly, the song switches gears, with the revelation that "I, thank God, am a scientist" (example 19.4). We go out of tempo, as both the vocal melody and the authoritative-sounding right-hand chords move upward by step on each downbeat (even as the bass stays grounded resolutely on B♭), creating a series of spiky altered dominant chords that peak on the word "real" before launching into the body of the song.[1]

Example 19.4. "The Bear, the Tiger, the Hamster and the Mole"

Now Shire provides an entirely different rhythmic feel; it's moderate, steady, and controlled, as opposed to the aggressive, driving beginning. In other words, it's exactly what seems appropriate for a scientist who is giving an interesting and informative lecture about animal mating habits (example 19.5). The head, in other words, takes over from the heart.

Example 19.5. "The Bear, the Tiger, the Hamster and the Mole"

The musical language is slightly different, too, with its emphasis on the interval of the fourth, as opposed to more common thirds, the regular building blocks of major and minor triads. A rising fourth is the opening interval of example 19.5, and the fourth is also the emphasized interval heard in the right hand before each eighth-note rest in this recurring four-bar piano figure. (The only exception is the sixth before the rest in the third measure of the example.) The preponderance of fourths is a signal that we are making a subtle shift from the normal subject of conversation (humans) to a slightly different one (animals).

In the first verse, the scientist lays out her case that female animals are much more sensible in how they deal with males than are their human counterparts:

Like a soul possessed
I have studied and assessed

The creatures of this earth.
And from moose to eel,
What my studies most reveal
Is the male's inflated worth.
For in most of the animal kingdom,
The ladies only rarely need men.
Their dealings are straight:
They meet them to mate
And never see them again.

Men! Who needs 'em? That's the clear message. But it's far more effective—and revealing of her character—when it's laid out in technical language and supported with examples from observation and research.

Note that in the pre-chorus,[2] starting on "For in most of the animal kingdom" (example 19.6), Shire creates a rising half-step line in the middle voice of the piano—the stems-down notes in the right hand, indicated by the asterisks. This device, sometimes called a "thumb line," is an effective way to sustain forward motion: as the line gradually rises from B♭ to E♭, the harmony shifts subtly, building the tension to the last three phrases that drive home the punchline ("Their dealings are straight / they meet them to mate / and never see them again").

Example 19.6. "The Bear, the Tiger, the Hamster and the Mole"

Now comes the first chorus, and the title of the song (example 19.7). The revered animals from her studies are introduced triumphantly with hammered-out power triads and strong rising intervals of first an octave and then a fifth in the vocal melody on "The bear" and "tiger." These animals are the heroes of her story, not the infuriating, unreliable men. In fact, the male role for these species lasts only for the duration of (in a memorable Maltbian phrase) "one mindless spasm."

Example 19.7. "The Bear, the Tiger, the Hamster and the Mole"

The bear, the ti - ger, the

ham - ster and the mole,

At the end of the chorus comes another clever method of propelling the song forward. The scientist starts to repeat the animals of the title—"That's marriage for the tiger, bear, and hamster"—but by the time she gets to the mole, she's on to the next section. The mole, in other words, doesn't end the first chorus; she is the subject of the launch into the second verse, which provides further pertinent scientific observations about both the mole and the boa constrictor. This is clever enjambment that enhances the song's momentum.

A new quartet of animals (they just keep coming) opens the second chorus, on the same celebratory note (example 19.8). As before, they come with an accompanying takedown of men in general: "Those females know that motherhood is not a male concern." In the subsequent pre-chorus, the battle of the sexes verges alarmingly close to murder:

Now I make no brief for the mantis
Who decapitates her mate during sex
But I do like the auk
Who mates with a "*squawk*,"
And then throws rocks at her "ex."

OK, we don't want to actually bite anyone's head off, but a few well aimed projectiles? Not necessarily a bad thing.

Example 19.8. "The Bear, the Tiger, the Hamster and the Mole"

The ray,— the rhi - no, the pen-guin and the tern—

The third chorus restores certain maligned words to their proper context in the animal kingdom:

The bitch, the vixen, the queen bee and the shrew,
What men have done to those fine words we never can undo.

And at the end of that chorus, the songwriters provide the same clever enjambment that we saw at the end of the first chorus, along with a pun that catapults the song into its contrasting, wonderfully lyrical bridge:

Let's redefine the shrew, the bitch and vixen,
And be like the seagull . . .

Transforming the "bee" of "queen bee" into the homonym "be" allows the word to soar melodically on a long-held note, very evocative of the seagull whose imagery it is introducing.

With this joyfully airborne bridge, our scientist has achieved what sounds like true liberation, amid a great Shirean melodic blossoming. Her identification with the wonders of the animal kingdom elicits the song's most transcendent passage. This section, however, soon crashes back to human reality. How wonderful to "cruise like the caribous if we choose," as opposed to confronting those perennially vexing human men. Here the rhymes start piling up as she once again contemplates the frustrations of her dating life:

And not have to wait for those sly little winks
From some man who envies the sex life of minks.

And not have to guess if he's one of the finks,
Or whether he drinks,
Or whether he stinks,
Or what he thinks
Of me.

As the stage direction in the sheet music puts it, "She realizes she has revealed more of herself than she intended; she composes herself." The heart, in other words, has unexpectedly intruded into the realm of the head, where it is not welcome. So it's back to science and the language, both musical and verbal, of the verse:

Now, of course, if fate
Should put upon my plate
That quintessential male
I would stick like glue
Yes, I would be as true
As any beaver, owl or whale.

Under the right circumstances, she will contemplate a permanent romantic partner, but she's still most comfortable describing it in the context of the animal kingdom.

The final chorus brings our last quartet of exemplary animals: "The hare, the condor, the guppy, and the bream." The second half of this chorus has a particularly stirring lyricization from Maltby: "Come march toward the future on my scientific team." Ah, the joys of intellectual discovery! At the end of the song, the scientist triumphantly aligns herself with those admirably independent, happily single members of the animal kingdom:

For now that you've seen and can compare,
Why anyone with the will to dare
Can follow the tiger and the bear
And hamster and mole
And me!

Including herself with these exemplars from the song's title tells us she will be just fine, whether she ends up with a husband or not.

Probably.

The drive to the finish is a classic Shire coda/extension, powered by a relentless descending bass, starting in the left hand of the second bar of example 19.9 (indicated by the asterisk), that thunders its way relentlessly from E♭ down by step to low F, before resting on a prolonged dominant B♭ at the beginning of the third system. The following two measures build grippingly, once again featuring chords built on stacks of fourths, and ending decisively in triumphant E♭ major in the last bar of the example.

Example 19.9. "The Bear, the Tiger, the Hamster and the Mole"

The attentive listener will note that somehow Maltby and Shire have managed to sneak a detailed (and fully accurate) discourse on animal reproductive rituals into a vivid and rousing character song that brilliantly excavates the struggle between the brain and the emotions, while traversing a journey from a near-meltdown to an exhilarating affirmation of female self-actualization. There's a case to be made that this, even more than "The Story Goes On," is the single defining song of their entire oeuvre.

Maltby and Shire on "The Bear, the Tiger, the Hamster and the Mole":

RM: The switch at the end of the bridge when she says ". . . and not have to wait for the sly little winks . . . and not have to guess . . . what he thinks of me"—it shows that the reason she doesn't want to get married is that she doesn't want to put herself in that circumstance of dating and waiting around for some guy to find her not enough. But in the next verse she says, "Now, of course, *if* fate should put upon my plate that quintessential male," she admits, yes, she really does want the man. But if it doesn't happen, then she'll envy the oyster. And then a nice little pun came there, "who lives a happy life on the shelf," because oysters live on shelves! And the oyster really does release sperm, and she "fertilizes herself." And because oysters live on shelves, and the woman is on the shelf, too, it's a great pun, and there's no other rhyme for "shelf" and "self," other than "elf."

DS: You get gifts like that if you're good and say your prayers.

RM: I say that to young writers: you do get presents if your heart is pure. The more you go toward the truth, the more you will find rhymes you didn't think you'd get. Another example of it is in "Romance" [from *Baby*]. David had written "DA da dum / da DA da dum," and I had to do the turning point of the song in it, and it was about fertilizing the egg, for which there is only one good rhyme, which is "keg." Or "powder keg." So it's "Why else would he make *hu*-man hearts a *pow*-der keg / To get one lousy sperm to reach an egg," but it came because I was following the reality of the physical process that involves these words, and suddenly, there was a whole other possibility. I would never have come up with those lines by themselves, but by being honest about what was going on, the vocabulary expands. As a writer, if you really dig into the character, as opposed to, say, the generalities of pop songs, the contour of the music guides you. It sends you away from standard prosody, and it will bring you different words. The truth will take you into a vocabulary you might not have come up with on your own.

JR: The truth will set you free.

RM: Yes, it literally is true.

JR: Did writing this song take a lot of research?

RM: I had one book, something like "They Love and Fight" or "They Fight and Die."

DS: "They Kill While They Love."

RM: "They Fight and Kill."[3]

JR: There's a lot of skill in placing the perfect punchline at the end of each verse.

RM: And then topping it. Each one is slightly more complex. There's the first one ["Their dealings are straight, they meet them to mate, and never see them again"]. The second was the boa constrictor who "stores it for years to use whenever she wants"—more complex and funnier. And then we needed a topper, which was the oyster who "fertilizes herself." You have to build them so that, yes, you keep outdoing yourself.

IT SHOULD HAVE BEEN CALLED *SMALL*

The fertility issues addressed in *Baby* were familiar to Shire; he and his first wife Talia had had their own such struggles, although they became the parents of Matthew (now screenwriter Matt Shire) in 1975. According to Didi Conn, to whom Shire has been married since 1984, a similar set of challenges for herself and Shire led indirectly to the idea of adapting the movie *Big* as a Broadway show.

"We were on this fertility trip, and I'd had an insemination by a doctor, and I had my legs up for, like, hours," Conn relates candidly. "So I watched [the movie] *Big* about five times in this hotel that we were in, and I thought, 'Gee, this would make a good musical.' "[1] That was in 1989.

The story of *Big* the musical has been documented by author and journalist Barbara Isenberg, whose 1996 book *Making It Big* is an entertaining and meticulous chronicle of the show's journey from Conn's brainstorm all the way through the Broadway run of the show, including obtaining the rights, finding producers, assembling the artistic team, the writing process, auditions, rehearsals, the out-of-town tryout in Detroit, rewrites, Broadway opening night, the 1996 Tony Awards, and beyond.[2]

"She wrote it because she thought she was going to have the next *Chorus Line* backstory, but instead, she had the profile of a flop," Shire observes.

"There's nothing in the book that's not accurate, but it's not the full story," Maltby adds.

The writers wanted Susan Stroman to direct the show. Stroman, now one of Broadway's most celebrated director/choreographers, was at the time already a notably successful choreographer, with two Tony Awards to her name. One of those was for *Crazy for You*, a 1992 hit show largely based on the 1930 George and Ira Gershwin musical *Girl Crazy*, with a new book by Ken Ludwig and additional songs incorporated from other Gershwin shows. *Crazy for You* had been directed by Mike Ockrent, who, prior to that show, had scored another huge Broadway hit in 1986 with *Me and My Girl*, a revised

Closer Than Ever. Joshua Rosenblum, Oxford University Press. © Oxford University Press 2024.
DOI: 10.1093/oso/9780197758236.003.0020

version of a show that originally had a successful run on London's West End in 1937. When Stroman showed up to meet with Maltby and Shire about *Big*, she brought Ockrent with her.

As Shire puts it, "Mike Ockrent was like Beyoncé. He'd done these two big hit musicals." Maltby adds, "What we didn't know was that they were engaged and about to get married."

Nobody wants to say anything negative about the universally beloved Ockrent, who died tragically of leukemia in 1999 at the young age of fifty-three. "Mike Ockrent is the sweetest man in the world," Maltby affirms, referring to Ockrent in the present tense, which reflects the closeness he felt. "He's a really wonderful collaborator and a great person to talk to. And he's a wonderful, compelling director, so you follow him." But Maltby knew right away that Ockrent was the wrong person to direct *Big*, at least the way he and Shire had conceived the show:

> We were expecting just Susan, and Susan came in with Mike, and I had this blink moment—it's one of Malcolm Gladwell's things. Basically, you're confronted with a circumstance, and *blink*, you see the whole thing in an instant. My blink moment—and it was utterly clear—was that he had done these two shows based on songs that were standards, and nothing he learned from those two shows would apply to *Big*. Everything he thought he knew—those things would not work. He would tinker with comedy scenes, and he was very good at it. He did that with *Crazy for You* and with *Me and My Girl*, and they were wonderful. But if the song is "Embraceable You," you can't kill it. You can tinker with the scene, but "Embraceable You" is still there. It doesn't rely on the scene that comes before it. But if you have written a song specifically for a scene or a character, then tinkering like that doesn't work.

Later Maltby adds, "I then spent the next two years in all of my behavior being embarrassed for that blink moment. I didn't want to admit I had that thought. I personally thought that was a terrible thought to have had."

Interestingly, Stroman has no recollection of being sought out to direct *Big* herself. "I don't think so," she replies when asked about this. "They came to me and Mike as a team. Mike and I had hits with *Crazy for You* and *A Christmas Carol* as a team, so they came to us together."[3]

There had been some discussion about the possibility of having Maltby as the director of *Big* as well as the lyricist. The consensus was, however, that it would be useful to have another voice in the room, an opinion shared by Jim Freydberg, once again serving as lead producer on a Maltby/Shire musical. As *Big* librettist John Weidman puts it, "I think we were trying to solve a lot of writing problems continuously from the moment we started working on the show, and if Richard's focus had been split between writing and directing, he would have been less available to focus on the writing part."[4]

Big the movie, written by Gary Ross and Anne Spielberg and directed by Penny Marshall, was a critical and commercial hit in 1988, catapulting Tom Hanks to star status and grossing $151 million worldwide. The story concerns twelve-year-old Josh Baskin, who, while trying to impress an older girl, is told he is too short for a carnival ride. Frustrated and embarrassed, he puts a coin into an antique fortune-teller machine ("Zoltar") and makes a wish to become "big." His wish is granted: when he wakes up the next morning, he's in a fully grown adult body (Hanks).

Fleeing from his panicked mother, Josh acquires a job at the MacMillan Toy Company, whose owner is impressed with Josh's youthful enthusiasm and remarkable knowledge of currently popular toys. Josh attracts the attention of Susan Lawrence (Elizabeth Perkins), a fellow MacMillan executive, and a romance develops. Josh, however, becomes overwhelmed by the responsibility of his adult relationships. With the help of his friend Billy, he hunts down the Zoltar machine and makes a wish to become a kid again. After an emotional goodbye to Susan, Josh reunites with his friends and family, now content to grow older at the normal pace.

For his part, Shire didn't realize until later that the shows Ockrent had done were all revivals and adaptations. "He had never shepherded a new musical," Shire reflects, "and he really didn't understand certain things about how our score and the book related, and he cut songs that he didn't realize had a necessary place in the story arc."

Before he continues, Shire stresses yet again that he and Maltby don't want to sound as if they're coming down hard on the late, much-revered Ockrent. "He and Susan were trying to make a terrific hit show, which we had never had, and the feeling was, 'We know how to make a hit, so let us present you with your first Broadway triumph.'"

Having said that, Shire relates that, for him, the biggest casualty of Ockrent's "rules" was the song "Little Susan Lawrence." This was a number for the character Susan herself, in her scene with grown-up Josh in his loft. After Josh falls asleep, she takes this moment to reflect on her girlhood self. While the show was still out of town in Detroit, Josh and Susan already had a few numbers together in this scene—"Let's Not Move Too Fast,"[5] "Do You Wanna Play Games?" and "Stars, Stars, Stars"[6]—and Ockrent felt there could not be a ballad after three other songs in the same scene. Thus, "Little Susan Lawrence" was cut.

Shire reflects, "That song was the heart of her character. [Ockrent] really didn't understand why we were so disturbed by having it cut and why we felt it was so essential. It's the moment you realize she isn't a cold-hearted business bitch but a real human being." Without the song, the writers felt, Susan Lawrence didn't become a sympathetic character until her Act II number, "Dancing All the Time." And by then, it was too late.

Another Ockrent rule—that you can't introduce a big new song right before the end of the show—resulted in the loss of "We're Gonna Be Fine," a number for Josh and Susan that allows them to grieve for their relationship that was never to be—to acknowledge the joy it briefly brought them before they both, by necessity, have to resume their previous lives.

Those weren't the only instances of what the writers saw as key songs getting cut. Maltby explains:

> One after another, songs we wrote for a scene would get . . . they didn't so much get cut as they got obviated. The scene would change—he would change the comedy scene—and pretty soon, whatever the song was supposed to accomplish would no longer need to be accomplished, so it would go away, and then we'd have to write something else. And the replacement songs, sometimes two or three for the same spot, got progressively worse and worse.

Stroman concurs about the creative process in general, but politely disagrees about the results:

> As you work with any creative team, you have to make sure the scene flows into the song, and out of the song the scene continues, so it does have to be of a piece, and that happens a lot, where all of a sudden, you come up with another idea, and something is sacrificed, either the scene or the song. But I love the score. I don't feel like they wrote anything that wasn't wonderful.

Shire, in return, emphasizes how highly he and Maltby thought of Stroman's contribution to the show. "Her dance sequences were thrilling as pure choreography and yet always fulfilled their obligation to tell the part of the story arc that they were supposed to," he elaborates. "This kind of talent is not found as often as one would like among musical theater choreographers, a surprising number of whom too often deliver a number that is choreographically exciting and wonderfully inventive but doesn't take care of its dramatic, storytelling obligations. Susan is one of the happiest of exceptions." Shire places Stroman in the ranks of history's great director/choreographers, such as Jerome Robbins, Gower Champion, Bob Fosse, and, more recently, Casey Nicholaw.

All in all, Maltby and Shire wrote fifty-seven songs for *Big* before the show opened on Broadway. In truth, they didn't always mind seeing numbers get cut. As Maltby puts it, "The thing about a song is, you write it, you love it, you put it in the show. Suddenly, the song becomes not appropriate for the scene, and then you loathe it, you cannot wait to get that horrible turd out of the scene, just because it stopped doing what you wanted it to do."

But apart from songs being endlessly swapped in and out of the show, the production was beset with additional, even more fundamental difficulties. One of them was the underlying issue of scale.

For Maltby, Shire, and librettist Weidman, the appeal of the project came from the purity of the plot at its center. As Shire explains, "We had been attracted to the material—John especially—because it was an intimate story at heart about a boy who wanted to be an adult too fast."

According to Maltby, part of *Big*'s broad appeal was that it tapped into something universal. "Human beings really want to skip the teenage years, like, 'Can we just get over it and get to adulthood?' And the point of the story is, 'No, you can't. You have to go through it, because that's how you become a person.' " Weidman, whose credits as librettist include three musicals with Stephen Sondheim (*Pacific Overtures*, *Assassins*, *Road Show*) said of *Big*, "It's one of the nine elemental human stories."[7] Or, per producer Freydberg, "It's a story with a heart. Every boy wishes he were an adult, and every man wishes he could go back to being a child."[8]

This focus on the intimacy of the story stayed with the writers all the way through the show's development, even as the production got bigger and bigger. Shire recalls showing up in Detroit at the beginning of the show's out-of-town tryout run. "When we walked in, we realized we had been writing a show called *Small and Intimate*, and [Ockrent] was directing a show called *Big and Lavish*."

Freydberg agreed years later, saying, "It should have been called *Small*."

Stroman, for her part, recalls, "I probably wasn't in that loop. I actually always thought it was going to be a big Broadway musical. I wasn't in the room for [any discussion of] an intimate musical called *Big*. I missed that room," she concludes good-naturedly.

Stroman agrees that the emotions about recovering childhood are small, private feelings. However, she is quick to point out, the story of *Big* takes place in big locations: in New York City, in FAO Schwarz, at carnivals. "And in order to tell the story," she continues, "it needed two sets of actors. It needed enough children to have the joy of children being children, and it also had to have a whole group of successful, corporate adults. So right there you have a big cast."

Weidman concurs that the scale of the show was not necessarily the fundamental issue. "I honestly feel that the problems were dramatic storytelling problems," he says. "If we'd had the story working right, the show could have been done at Madison Square Garden for $20 million, or in a high school auditorium for $20."[9]

The subject of FAO Schwarz brings up another fundamental challenge faced by *Big* the musical: the show risked alienating people who felt that not only was the show leveraging a much-loved property (the movie) into an outsize spectacle, but it was also cynically benefiting from the presence of the famous toy store as an inappropriate corporate partner.

To a certain degree, this was unavoidable. The movie's most iconic scene takes place inside the well-known toy emporium, where the newly "big" Josh meets MacMillan Toy Company owner George MacMillan (Robert Loggia) for the first time. If viewers remember only one scene from the film, it's usually the one with Hanks and Loggia playing duets on the Walking Piano, a large foot-operated electronic keyboard. The team knew that this scene in the store had to be recreated in the musical—audiences would expect to see it. Accordingly, a certain relationship with the company became inevitable. As Isenberg describes it, FAO Schwarz agreed to provide props and toy-store design expertise and to develop new products with the musical's marketing team. Additionally, they would sell tickets to the show in their Fifth Avenue store and host the opening-night party there.[10] Eventually, FAO Schwarz would become a corporate investor and one of the show's producers.

The writers thought this was a terrible idea. Maltby went to Freydberg and begged him not to take money from the toy conglomerate. Shire recalls, "They offered us something like a million dollars. Jim said he didn't need the money. They had already raised enough. And Richard said, 'Don't take it, because it's gonna put a bad vibe on the show,' but [Freydberg] went ahead and took the money, and that really cost us. I think it was one of the reasons the show got this very negative attention, like, oh, this is just a publicity piece for FAO Schwarz."

There were consequences to the store's involvement, as unavoidable as it may have been. *Variety* magazine blasted the Detroit tryout for the perceived corporatization of the musical:

> The script's blatant celebration of FAO Schwarz—a major backer—goes well beyond artistic necessity. "Is this some kind of store or what?" exclaims one character. "There is even a sale going on in the mezzanine!" adds another sycophantic lyric. And an awful, unnecessary coda occurs in the store at Christmas, even though the obvious dramatic

climax—Josh's return to childhood and mother—has already taken place in another location.[11]

John Eyler, president and CEO of FAO Schwarz at the time and the production's point person, was shocked by this harsh criticism, pointing out, correctly, that the store was part of the concept for the show's set, plot, and choreography long before the company itself was involved. "Any criticism that we commercialized the show was inaccurate and misinformed," he declared.[12] Or, as Freydberg put it in a *New York Times* article prior to the show's Broadway opening, "You see FAO Schwarz in one scene and at the curtain call. If this is exploitation, I'll eat the set."[13] In Shire's words, "We never consulted with them; they had zero artistic input."

Librettist Weidman puts it this way: "When you look at the group of people creating the show—Maltby, Shire, me, Stroman, Ockrent—this is not a cynical group of Broadway artists who are only interested in producing a hit, never mind what the content is. But the show had that cloud over it. And I think a lot of the reaction was based on that, and it was congruent with the fact that in some ways, it could feel like it was overproduced. But I think for a lot of people, I hope, the Broadway production still delivered the emotional story that was the whole reason for the show to be there in the first place."

Stroman points out that this controversy would have been ridiculous by today's standards, when a show can have dozens of producers above the title, including the names of numerous faceless corporations. At the time, as she puts it, "The politics of Broadway didn't help us out. I'm so deep in the art of it all that sometimes I don't realize what's happening politically, which is probably a good thing. We were all in it together, creating this very special story about time and realizing how precious it is. So then, when we came up for air after we opened, it was, like, 'What? What's going on? Why are people upset? We're doing a show about toys in a toy store!' I'm not quite sure what people were upset about."

To a degree, the show never recovered from the perception that it was a calculatedly commercial enterprise, in spite of Vincent Canby's largely positive *New York Times* review of the Broadway production. Canby even explicitly dismissed the criticisms that had been leveled at the show out of town:

> You don't have to worry about those horror stories you heard when the production was trying out in Detroit: about problems with the book, about musical numbers being pulled out, rewritten or replaced, and even about the blatant promotion of FAO Schwarz, Fifth Avenue, the toy store that's one of the show's producers and one of its principal settings.[14]

In Canby's view, the show was a "bright, shiny, larger-than-life toy of a show." *Big* the musical, he wrote, "has been fabricated with Broadway savvy and verve, though for all its professionalism it seldom seems to push too hard." He went on to praise the performances of Daniel Jenkins, who played the role of grown-up Josh with his own brand of endearing charm; Patrick Levis as Young Josh; Brett Tabisel, who played Billy, Young Josh's best friend; and Stroman's "corps of extraordinary young dancers," particularly Lizzy Mack, who also doubled as Cynthia Benson, Young Josh's crush. Canby concluded his review by observing of the show, "It worked as a movie. It works as a show."[15]

As Maltby notes, in New York theater at that time, a positive review in the *Times* was normally enough to balance out negative reviews elsewhere. "It didn't happen with *Big*," he says. "The Canby review just did not carry a whole lot of weight."

Part of this was due to the unlucky timing of *Big* opening the day before *Rent*.

Rent is a gritty, urban musical with a groundbreaking rock-and-roll score by Jonathan Larson. Loosely adapted from Giacomo Puccini's *La Bohème*, *Rent* showcases an appealing crew of impoverished young East Village bohemians in the shadow of the AIDS crisis—a group of people not normally given voice in musicals. In 1996, this felt both contemporary and urgent. Not only that, but the show had already achieved the status of legend by the time it opened on Broadway, in no small part because Larson, who wrote the show's book, music, and lyrics, had died suddenly the night before the show's off-Broadway premiere at New York Theatre Workshop three months earlier. *Rent* went on to win not only four Tony Awards (including Best Musical) but also the Pulitzer Prize for Drama as well, and it ran for more than twelve years on Broadway.

Theater critics usually don't see Broadway shows on opening nights; they see one of several "press previews" in the days leading up to the opening. Thus, many in the press had already seen *Rent* before they saw *Big*. For that matter, most of them had seen *Rent* back in January during its off-Broadway run.

Big was still out of town in Detroit when *Rent* opened off-Broadway. "Jonathan had died, and it was all over the news, and everybody was proclaiming that this was the second coming, or the first coming, and we all looked at each other and thought, 'Well, there it goes,'" Shire recalls. And when the shows had their Broadway openings back-to-back, "We were like the tired old Broadway musical, whereas *Rent* was the wave of the future."

Big was nominated for five Tony Awards, including Best Book of a Musical (Weidman), Best Original Score (Maltby and Shire), Best Leading Actress in a musical (Crista Moore as Susan Lawrence), Best Featured Actor in a Musical (Brett Tabisel), and Best Choreography (Stroman); it did not, however, win in any category. And the absence of even a nomination in the Best Musical category was considered a slap in the face (a "gigantic blow," according to Freydberg).[16] The show ran for six months, but by the time it closed, it had lost its entire $10.3 million investment in "one of the biggest financial disasters in Broadway history" up to that point.[17]

Conn, whose brainstorm ultimately brought the show into existence, is quick to object when anyone refers to *Big* as a flop. "It got standing ovations every night, and people had a really good time," she avers. "It was just a difficult process. You know, in our business, luck is a big part of it, and at that time, there had been a glut of musicals based on movies, and it was just one too many, and they all had to comment about it. It was also at that time the highest budget for any Broadway show, so unfortunately, that's what got the attention rather than the content. It's a shame."[18]

In the show's post-Broadway afterlife, Maltby and Shire ended up with something closer to the show they thought they had written. Eric Schaeffer, cofounder and, for more than thirty years, artistic director of the Signature Theatre in Arlington, Virginia, directed the national touring production of *Big* in 1998 and worked with the writers to retool the show.

"We'd get to a scene," Maltby says, "and we'd talk about it, and one of us would say, 'Well, we wrote a song about that to cover that moment,' and we'd play it, and he'd say, 'Well, that's better, why don't we use that?' And that happened about seven times."

"We basically put up a brand-new musical," Schaeffer said at the time. "It's totally reconceived. It's totally redesigned."[19] The result, Maltby says, is that "we found the beating heart of the story again."

"We're Gonna Be Fine," the eleven o'clock farewell ballad for Susan and Josh, went back into the show. So did "Little Susan Lawrence." "Let's Not Move Too Fast," which had been cut before Broadway, was also restored, so the scene in Josh's apartment once again had four entire songs, in defiance of the Ockrent doctrine.

Arguably, the national tour was the success that the Broadway production had not been. "One critic who panned the Broadway production came and saw our opening in Wilmington and said in his review of *that*, 'This is wonderful. Why were all those songs cut?'" Shire recalls ruefully.

Weidman says it wasn't quite that simple. "We caught a break with the first national tour. Whoever the stringer was for *Variety* liked it a lot in

Wilmington. But it then marched around the country and got just as many not good reviews as good reviews. So the tour could have easily opened up with a not very good review, and that would have put the whole conversation in a different place."

In 2000, Alvin Klein of the *New York Times* reviewed a production of the rewritten version at the Gateway Playhouse on Long Island, writing:

> "Big" cannot be cavalierly dismissed as a failed musical that was no match for a blockbuster movie. It is satisfyingly good—and it was shortchanged. The music of David Shire, the lyrics of Richard Maltby Jr., the book by John Weidman and the choreography by Susan Stroman extol all the values of the grand tradition of musicals. The characters are very dear and complex. It is hard to sit still when the dances take over. You can sing the songs. The words explore the interior child—his own and the man's.[20]

Notices like these would seem to support the Maltby/Shire viewpoint that the reconstituted touring version was finally the show they'd wanted all along, although, according to Weidman, the process of revision continued up to and including the 2019 production on London's West End (more to follow about this in chapter 22).

Big returned to New York in 2014 as part of the York Theatre Company's Musicals in Mufti series. "At the York, we could honestly see it in its most stripped-down form, and we used that as a basis for a rethink of what the show could be going forward," Weidman says. "We kept chipping away at it in a variety of different ways to make it better."

Big had its UK premiere in 2016 at Theatre Royal Plymouth, which led to the 2019 West End production at London's Dominion Theatre. The UK original cast recording (from the Plymouth production) includes many of the aforementioned songs originally cut from the show. This is largely the version that is now licensed for stock, regional, and university productions.

21 BIG

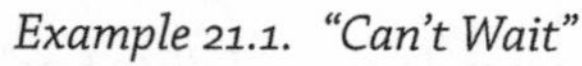

Big opens with what sounds as if it's going to be a classic Broadway overture. We really only hear one song, however—a grand, instrumental version of "I Want to Know"—before the orchestra, after a brief upbeat transition, segues into "Can't Wait," the show's opening number. Now we're in contemporary territory, with an electric-bass-driven, "Funkytown"-style disco beat and sonic artifacts that sound like hip-hop samples and video game music. We're also thrown right into Young Josh's central dilemma, his crush on an older girl:

How come I couldn't cross my own street?
Why was I scared to get to my door?
Just 'cause I knew that I'd have to meet
Cynthia Benson?

The name "Cynthia Benson" is set to a memorable melodic fragment consisting of three quarter-note triplets and two straight quarters (example 21.1). The phrase recurs later in the show as an instrumental theme, emphasizing the presence of Cynthia in Josh's mind.

Example 21.1. "Can't Wait"

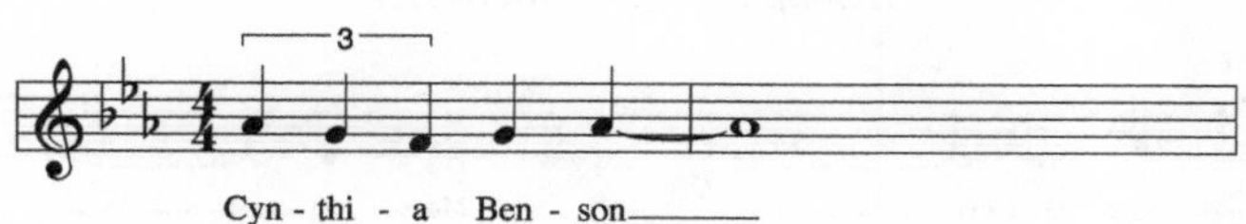

By the time Young Josh gets to the song's chorus, the number has settled comfortably into a more familiar theater-pop-rock idiom, a genre that Shire had previously mined successfully in *Baby*:[1]

I wish mom wouldn't bug me
I wish I'd start to grow.
I wish mom wouldn't hug me
In front of kids I know.

Closer Than Ever. Joshua Rosenblum, Oxford University Press. © Oxford University Press 2024.
DOI: 10.1093/oso/9780197758236.003.0021

The song continues to alternate comfortably between these two genres. Shire, in general, is quite adept at juggling, combining, and synthesizing different styles (here with an impressive assist from Doug Besterman's blazing orchestrations). In addition to the ones previously mentioned, *Big* leaps adroitly among a slew of musical idioms, including big band jazz ("Coffee, Black"), pseudo-classical ("The Real Thing"), Motown rock ("Cross the Line"), swing ballad ("Dancing All the Time"), rap ("It's Time"), romantic waltz ("Stars, Stars, Stars"), burlesque ("Say Good Morning to Mom"), and others. Few of the reviews recognized the score for this versatility.

In "Talk to Her," where Josh actually encounters his heartthrob, the music starts with a kinetic, sixteenth-note-driven accompaniment that propels the action, as Josh's pal Billy urges his smitten friend to at least try engaging Cynthia in conversation. Billy's melodic line (example 21.2) appropriates the quarter-note triplet motif from example 21.1's "Cynthia Benson" theme:

Example 21.2. "Talk to Her"

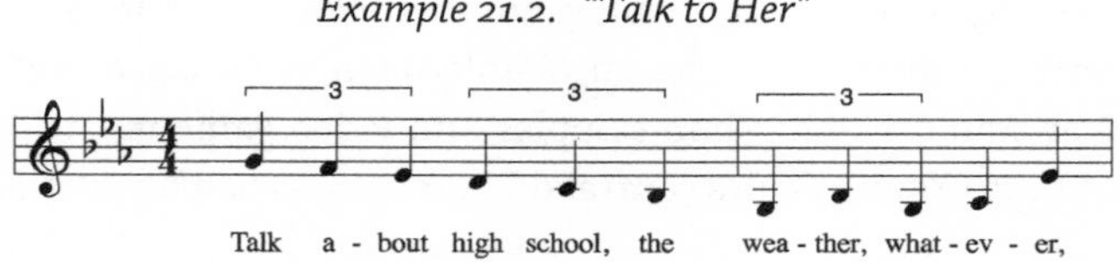

After an extended, imaginative carnival sequence by dance music arranger David Krane that takes us into the realm of calypso and beyond, Cynthia appears, and Josh, coached by Billy, tries halting efforts to make conversation. Maltby gives the "Talk to Her" melody different lyrics ("Close your eyes / Move up close"), and Shire alternates them with the "Cynthia Benson" melodic motif, as indicated by the brackets in the second and fourth bars of example 21.3, allowing the music to swell romantically as the moment of truth approaches.

Example 21.3. "Talk to Her"

Josh finally works up his courage to offer to accompany Cynthia on the carnival ride, only to be crushed by the appearance of her boyfriend and two short, devastating lines: "This is Derek. He drives." This is followed by mock funeral cortège music ("Why does disaster follow me?"), complete with interspersed trumpet fanfares that underline the epic nature of Josh's personal catastrophe. Then, adding humiliation to injury, he's told he's not tall enough to go on the ride anyway. This is followed by the fateful Zoltar encounter.

Next up, on the UK cast recording only, is another of the numbers that was a casualty of the pre-Broadway tryout in Detroit—a terrific song for Mrs. Baskin, Josh's mother (Barbara Walsh in the Broadway production), called "Say Good Morning to Mom." The music has a grinding, stripper-like feel that recalls "Hey, Big Spender" from *Sweet Charity*. The song, however, playing against its spicy groove, is really about domestic drudgery, as Mrs. Baskin goes through the morning routine of making breakfast and getting her son up in time for school. (She is, at least for the moment, unaware that he now inhabits a thirty-year-old man's body.) The number gives us a humorous and relatable insight into what daily life is like for Mrs. Baskin ("The coffee, the O.J., the oatmeal, the grits / The prune juice, the peaches, the pits") and involves the audience in her character so that her emotional Act II song, "Stop, Time," which laments how quickly children grow up, lands with even more poignancy.

Mike Ockrent, however, felt that it was wrong to have Josh wake up and experience his shocking transformation but not sing anything and instead to give the whole musical moment to Mrs. Baskin, a secondary character.

"This observation was not crazy," Maltby admits. As a result, he and Shire wrote "This Isn't Me" for Josh, and the song went into the show for the Broadway production. "I was embarrassed by the number at the time," Maltby says, "but 'This Isn't Me' actually manages to compress all the storytelling into one number." Sometime later, when Alex Gemignani (son of Paul Gemignani, *Big*'s musical director) sang the song at a benefit, Maltby concluded that it was a good number. Still, without "Say Good Morning to Mom" to enable the audience to identify early with Mrs. Baskin, "Stop, Time" doesn't have quite the same impact when she sings it in Act II.

The phrase "Say good morning to mom" is memorably set to a downward-sliding minor scale in triplets, with a prominent flatted second (E♭ instead of E♮, in the key of D minor) on the penultimate word "to," which gives the phrase an added wry zing, particularly as set against the C♯ in the bass (example 21.4).

Example 21.4. "Say Good Morning to Mom"

We also get an especially deft trick rhyme from Maltby in the bridge:

Another morning in the everyday *continuum*.
Another mess of clothes and junk.
If moms won kewpie dolls for genius, kid, I'd *win you 'em*,
'Cause if I was blind
I bet I could find
Pajamas behind
Or over or under the bunk.

The "continuum"/"win you 'em" trick rhyme reminds us that the desire to out-Sondheim Sondheim isn't easily suppressed. (Not to mention the triple internal rhyme of "blind," "find," and "behind.")

"Say Good Morning to Mom" was cut out of town in Detroit and then restored for the national tour, but whether it should or shouldn't be in the show remained the subject of debate. The song was removed again for the York Theatre Company's 2014 run and replaced by "This Isn't Me," as it had been on Broadway. John Weidman, Maltby, and Shire all agreed that it should stay that way for the UK production, but, according to Weidman, the producer had made a commitment to Jessica Martin, the actress playing Mrs. Baskin, that she would have a certain amount of solo material, so the song was reinstated yet again.

"But my memory of the discussions about it is that the story just needs to start," Weidman says. "It's a good number, but we're kind of treading water to give Mom a chance to sing a really good Maltby/Shire song. We'd be better off if the kid wakes up, freaks out, and we just go from there."[2]

A lot of work went into finding the right song for Susan Lawrence's first entrance, when Josh meets her on-site at the MacMillan Toys office. In fact, Shire is on record with a great quote about this struggle: "If you put Richard and me in a room with a piano and three monkeys with a typewriter for the age of the universe, it's just possible that we might come up with the right first number for Susan Lawrence before the monkeys type *Hamlet*."[3]

For Broadway, that number ended up being "Here We Go Again." For the tour, "My Secretary's in Love," which was one of the earliest songs the team wrote for the Susan Lawrence character, was restored and can be heard on the original UK cast recording. This latter number is fairly faithful to the corresponding scene in the movie, where the audience meets Susan for the first time and she's complaining about her secretary, who, as Maltby puts it, "is all goo-goo-eyed about getting married, and as far as Susan is concerned, marriage talk has no place in an office, particularly the office of a woman focused only on her career, so forget about it." As for "Here We Go Again," the eventual replacement, Maltby was never thrilled with it. In fact, it was such a throwaway that he barely remembers it: "When I looked back at the album and saw that it was a song called 'Here We Go Again,' I thought, 'What is that? We wrote a song called "Here We Go Again," and it opened in New York?' I just had no memory of writing it."

The song isn't bad at all, but it does have a certain predictably well-crafted feel to it, just as Maltby implies. It follows a traditional A-A-B-A structure (although the bridge is interestingly extended each time), and the song's title phrase appears reliably at the end of each quatrain in the verses, including at the very end of the number, to wrap it up tidily. The song is a vehicle for Susan to tell us about herself in an essentially straightforward manner—no subtext to speak of and no action, either, at least not in the sense of the best Maltby/Shire numbers.

"My Secretary's in Love" is much better. It's Susan's wit's-end description of how hard it is to get her secretary to concentrate on work instead of her upcoming wedding. It tells us a lot about the secretary, but it tells us even more about Susan, in the way one gains considerable insight into a person from whatever they complain about most vehemently.

My secretary's in love,
And the wedding's set for June,
And the color scheme is either baby blue or pink or gray
Or maybe multi-colored like a lovely spring bouquet.
Oh, we can't decide but we discuss it seven hours a day.
My secretary's in love.

On the UK recording, Diana Vickers as Susan imitates her secretary in a nasty singsong little girl's voice, beginning with the line about the color scheme. It's wickedly funny, but it also pegs Susan right away as a grown-up mean girl. Her secretary should indeed manage to stay professional, even in the run-up to her wedding, but there's no need to be quite this vicious about it. One could argue, in fact, that Susan's exaggerated meanness tells us something about what she really wants—to get married herself—and that it's her jealousy coming through. In that sense, it's another example of a Maltby/Shire song that is not what it appears to be; it comes off like a comedy number, but it's a revealing outburst that gives instant insight into Susan's character.

The repeated iterations of the hook "My secretary's in love" at the end of each verse include the word "love" being held on a long, belted D. We're used to hearing that word sustained in the upper register in musical theater numbers, usually as an expression of joy; the comic twist here is that it's being sung with exasperation and ridicule. Susan's percolating irritation is amusingly heightened between phrases by a recurring, downwardly cascading figure, a musical representation of her secretary's incessant chattering. It's a rip-roaring number, with a zany, rollicking orchestration to match. Why was it cut in the run-up to Broadway? According to Maltby:

> Well, it isn't overtly on the plot, so Mike questioned it. It actually *is* on the plot, but it's subtle. It obliquely introduced a character who was focused on her career to the exclusion of anything that might touch her heart, a character who was off-base and needed to be saved. But this was subtext, and we authors were very susceptible to the idea that the song might have to go. Trouble is, all the replacement songs sucked. They had no subtlety or wit. Your leading lady needs an introductory song. Here it is. Boring.

We learn more about Susan from the earnestly insincere "Let's Not Move Too Fast," which she sings at the door of Josh's loft apartment. (This is another number that was cut before the Broadway opening and reinstated for the tour.) Susan is playing her version of the dating game, not realizing that her date is essentially a twelve-year-old. She sings, to an uncomprehending Josh:

> Let's not move too fast.
> Let's proceed real slow.
> It's quite clear
> What's happening here.
> I think that we both know.

Josh has no idea what she's talking about, and the audience is in on the joke. It keeps getting better:

> There's no need to rush.
> We both know the score.

We can read
Where this may lead.
We've both been here before.

That last one is a laugh line, especially when Josh responds, "We have?" It's clear that none of Susan's well-practiced feminine wiles is having any effect. In fact, the result is the opposite of what she intends.

Maltby says this is the song he missed more than any of the others when it was cut. He explains:

> This is the game you play in order to sleep with a guy on the first night and you don't say that's what you're doing. You say, "Well, maybe I'll come up for just a drink"—you pretend that you're not doing what you're actually doing. The trouble was, Josh didn't know the rules of the game, so when she says, "Oh, I think I should just go home," he says, "Oh, OK, goodbye, I'll see you tomorrow," and closes the door. So the joke was to put that into a song, and I must say that when we restored that, it helped an enormous amount.

"Cross the Line" was the Act I finale on Broadway and was retained for the tour and UK productions. It was not, however, in place until after the Detroit tryout; the team wrote it during the move-in to the Shubert Theatre for the Broadway production. They had the idea for the title but weren't sure what the song should be. The inspiration came from Susan Stroman, who, when asked to name a song that had the right beat for her to create a dance, mentioned Billy Joel's "Tell Her about It." Shire responded, "Oh, I can do that," and wrote the number. The cast learned the song, and Stroman created and rehearsed the dance while the show was in tech rehearsals.

"Cross the Line" is very catchy, in both verse and chorus. The song starts out in A major, with a toe-tapping syncopation in the bass that's doubled in the vocal melody. The verse ends on an E dominant seventh chord, implying a natural move back to the home key of A, but Shire instead modulates unexpectedly to F♯ major for the bridge, driving home the theme of "crossing the line" with a border-crashing move into a new tonal area.

The springboard for the number is George MacMillan's insistence that his executives generate fresh ideas for a new Christmas toy by trying to relate better to their children. Josh suggests dancing, and the number unfolds, with Josh and the kids leading the way and the grown-up execs participating only under the threat of being fired by MacMillan ("Take your pick, Paul—you can dance on this line or the unemployment line").

In the last section of the song, after the big dance break, Susan plants a prolonged kiss on Josh's lips, ostensibly to congratulate him for the success of the evening, and it has a transformative effect. He sings to the melody of the verse but with a dreamier, more subdued orchestration:

That was a kiss, golly she kissed me,
Out of the blue, suddenly kissed me.
What do I make of this, where is she coming from?
All I know is this wasn't a kiss from mom.
Is tonight the night when I cross the line?
Is tonight the night that something happens?
I feel wild, I feel goosed,
I feel scared, I feel juiced,
I feel bounced like a ball,
What I don't feel is small.
I feel where I belong.
I feel strong, most of all,
I feel tall!
I feel grown!
I feel "Big!"

So in addition to serving as a spectacular Act I closing dance number, the sequence has a clear action: just as the grown-ups and the kids cross the line in being able to relate to each other better, Josh crosses the line as he steps toward the reality of an adult romantic relationship.

"It's Time" is the Act II opener on both the Broadway and the UK recordings. The number starts with a reprise of the music from "Can't Wait," the opening number, with different lyrics but the same disco beat. After a verse, it transitions into rap. On Broadway, "It's Time" was the big number for Brett Tabisel as Josh's friend Billy. In the song, Billy, feeling rejected by grown-up Josh, corrals his gang of friends for a group hangout at the mall. As Maltby put it while they were writing the song, "What you're listening to is two people who said they will never have rap music in this show finally coming to terms with the fact that it's the language of 13-year-olds in the '90s."[4]

Writing a rap number, or at least a pseudo-rap number, was a risky proposition for "two white Jewish boys," as Shire describes himself and Maltby.[5] "We knew that." At one point, Billy has the couplet "Nothing's worse crap / Than a little white Polish boy from Jersey talkin' rap."

"That's a John Weidman line," Maltby cheerfully admits. "He wrote it in a scene, and I just stole it. I called him up and said, 'That's no longer your line,' and he said, 'There you go, that's fair.'" Shire mentions that "Richard has famously said on a number of occasions, when accused of taking someone else's idea and expressing it as his own, 'Nobody has an idea until I have it.'" (Maltby clarifies: "What I actually say is, 'It's not a good idea until I've had it.'")

A meta, self-aware line like the one mentioned above from Billy's rap would seem to inoculate the writers from any criticism about politically incorrect appropriation of the genre. Unfortunately, not all the critics got the message; the *Variety* review of the New York production carped that "for all its dabbling in rap and hip-hop and all its invocations of pop culture icons, [the show] is laughably out of date where kids are concerned."[6] On the other hand, it's probably one of the moments that earned young Tabisel his Tony and Drama Desk nominations and his Theater World Award.

"Stop, Time," Mrs. Baskin's moving second act number, was a high point for the show in Walsh's powerful rendering, even though Walsh and the writers felt the impact was diminished without the Act I setup of "Say Good Morning to Mom." Nonetheless, even Chris Jones in his mostly critical *Variety* review of the Detroit tryout named "Stop, Time" the show's best song.[7] The number begins as Billy is sitting in a mall with Mrs. Baskin on Josh's birthday (his party would have taken place at the mall), reassuring her that the absent Josh will indeed come home. The song is about how fast children grow up, a bittersweet experience for their parents. Or, as Maltby puts it:

> Parents spend their entire life saying goodbye. You'll never see that three-year-old again. You'll have a four-year-old, and you'll never see that four-year-old again. You'll have a five-year-old, and that five-year-old is wonderful and thrilling, but you'll never see that kid again, and you spend your entire life saying goodbye to something that you love enormously.

The song starts with a lyric that immediately elicits powerful emotions:

> Two months old, he looks up at you.
> How his smile melts your heart,
> You want to say,
> "Stop, time."

The bridge delivers an elegant summary of the simultaneous joy and sorrow that come from watching a beloved child grow up:

> Nobody warns you of this parent's paradox.
> You want your kid to change and grow.
> But when he does, another child you've just begun to know
> Leaves forever.

The arresting phrase "parent's paradox" provides characteristic concision and also seems to jump out of the song with its punchy consonants. Contrariwise, the second and third lines both end with wonderfully open "oh" vowels that are ideal for sustained singing, and the word "forever" is lyrical and supremely evocative. The beginning of the following stanza—"Birthdays fly, seven, eight, nine, ten"—is another great example of economical time compression, a Maltby specialty.

"Dancing All the Time" is another song that was directly inspired by Stroman. Maltby and Shire were working with her and Ockrent in London, trying to find the right second act song for Susan Lawrence. Speculating that the number could be about the character's childhood, they asked Stroman what her own experiences as a teen were like, and she said, "Oh, I was dancing all the time." As Shire put it then, "It was worth flying to London just to hear her say that."[8] They completed the song in twenty-four hours.

"Dancing All the Time" has a light, infectious bounce to it, exactly the feel one might like to imagine characterized a happy, bygone era. The title phrase, the number's hook, has an interesting placement. Usually, a song's hook goes either at the beginning or at the end of a stanza, in order to give it the most prominent, memorable position possible. In this case, however, the hook is casually tossed off in the middle:

I was running all the time,
I was dancing all the time.
I had all the time in the world.

That phrase does, however, receive a memorable melodic twist—the blues note of G♮ (in the key of E major) on the second iteration of the word "all," along with a jazzy, melismatic slide down to the F♯ right below it (example 21.5). The leap up to the C♯ on the second syllable of "dan-*cing*" just prior to the bluesy G♮ contributes to the striking melodic variation.

Example 21.5. "Dancing All the Time"

I was laugh - ing all the time.
I was dan - cing all the time.

Stroman says of the number's genesis: "It was all of us talking about our different lives, but the idea that it was the inspiration for a song to this day is very dear to me, and I'm very honored. I love that song. That lyric about laughing all the time and dancing all the time, having all the time in the world—I think as adults, we'd give anything to have that now."

This alluring song segues directly into "I Want to Know," Josh's song of wonderment regarding the mysteries of adult sexual relationships and grown-up women, particularly the compellingly attractive one who is mere inches away from him right at that moment.

"I Want to Know" has a special place in the artistic evolution of *Big.* For Weidman, this was the song that convinced him the movie could indeed be the source material for a successful musical. Prior to hearing it, he'd had reservations:

> I thought that the film was sort of perfect. The story that had been told in the film had been delivered exquisitely. I had never been that interested in adaptations, so the idea of taking this really well-told story and telling it again was something I was not initially enthusiastic about. But David and Richard went away and said, "We're gonna write a song"—it was like calisthenics, like warming up to see if we were gonna do the project—and they wrote "I Want to Know," which I think is just brilliant. I thought, "If music and lyrics can add this additional element, then yeah, let's do this."

The song creates a perfect soundscape for the inner monologue of a newly adolescent boy transfixed by a willing adult female. The tonality is static, sitting in A♭ major for a full thirteen bars. The melody is earthbound as well: the same four-bar phrase is heard three times, with only one note altered in the second iteration. This puts Josh in a near-hypnotic state within which his musings can flow freely:

> Girls smell like girls,
> Women wear perfume.
> That's one of their female glories.
> What do I do when I'm in her room?
> I just think I want to know.

In the second half of the second A section, we finally get some variation, on the lines "Talked all the talk, don't know what it means," as the bass begins a stepwise descent, first to G♭ and on through F, F♭, and E♭ before a cadence in the home key of A♭. The chords and melody above the meandering bass, however, stay the same.

The bridge provides the first significant harmonic and melodic motion, as Josh's yearnings become more pronounced. Shire does a reharmonization of the vocal melody note A♭, which is both the last note of the verse and the first note of the bridge. The new chord under the A♭ (first bar of example 21.6) is an F♭ major triad, setting up the ear-massaging chord progression F♭, G♭, A♭.

Example 21.6. "I Want to Know"

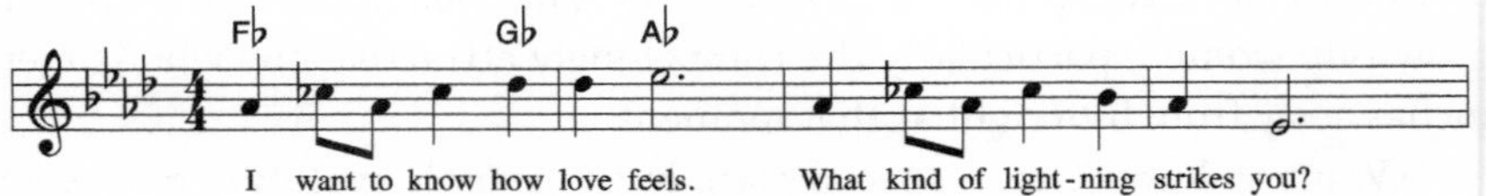

In the second four bars of the bridge (example 21.7), the vocal melody stays the same, except the C♭ becomes a C♮, and the D♭ becomes a D♮, allowing for a blossoming reharmonization (F minor–G–C minor) on the line "How does a woman kiss you . . .?"

Example 21.7. "I Want to Know"

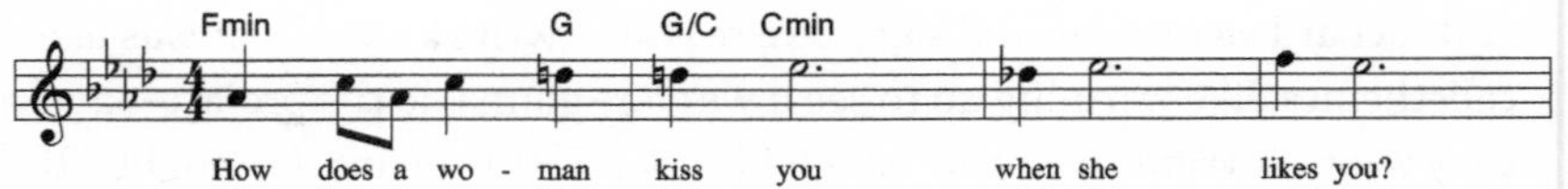

The concept for the song underwent a metamorphosis. Originally written for adult Josh to sing, the number was performed in several readings as a duet for adult Josh and Young Josh. Ultimately, it was deemed more powerful as a solo for Young Josh. This made it more convincing as an internal monologue, since Josh, even in his adult body, still has the mind of a thirteen-year-old. In addition, it's worth reinforcing that this is the kind of introspective moment that was largely absent from the movie and a big part of what convinced the writers that there was something to be gained via a musical version.

"Coffee, Black" has comic heft from the minute its brassy, jazzy instrumental introduction comes charging in right after the lights come down on "I Want to Know." It's the exuberant swagger of a young man who's just lost his virginity. The writers took this moment right from the movie, which has a big band playing on the soundtrack just as Tom Hanks comes sauntering through the revolving door of the office the morning after his night with Susan. That gave Shire the impetus to write "just a straight, old-fashioned jazz number, which I never get a chance to write enough of in musicals. That's really where I live." It's the number that Andrew Lloyd Webber singled out as his favorite when he saw the show.

"What we did, though," Maltby points out, "is put a lot of story in it. We put in Josh galvanizing the office about a new toy, Josh getting promoted by the boss, Susan suggesting a sexy trip to the Caribbean, all those internal things, so it actually has an enormous amount of plot to it."[9]

"We're Gonna Be Fine," also cut from Broadway but restored for the tour (and now part of the licensed version), was a casualty of Ockrent's axiom that you can't introduce a new song as an eleven o'clock number—it has to be a reprise. Accordingly, the Broadway production had reprises of "I Wanna Go Home" and "Stars, Stars, Stars" in this spot.

As heard on the UK cast recording, "We're Gonna Be Fine" sounds like an essential winding up of the story for Susan and Josh before he returns to his young teenage self. The song features this memorable exchange:

Susan and Josh: In ways I still can't name
I'll never be the same.
Susan: You reminded me that I could fly.
Josh: There's so much that you've already taught me.
Can you teach me how to say goodbye?

That last plea has a particularly poignant impact, since nobody really knows how to say goodbye satisfactorily. In Shire's words, the reprises that replaced this song were "just knee-jerk stuff."

The number Shire missed the most when it was cut, however, was "Little Susan Lawrence."

22
"LITTLE SUSAN LAWRENCE"

"Little Susan Lawrence," cut from the show before it reached Broadway, was a key restoration for the national tour and all subsequent productions of *Big*. It allows the audience to feel empathy for the character of Susan, who up to this point (the penultimate scene in Act I) has been presented only as an unlikable and manipulative corporate ice queen. The song manages to tug at the heartstrings in the very first two bars (example 22.1).

Example 22.1. "Little Susan Lawrence"

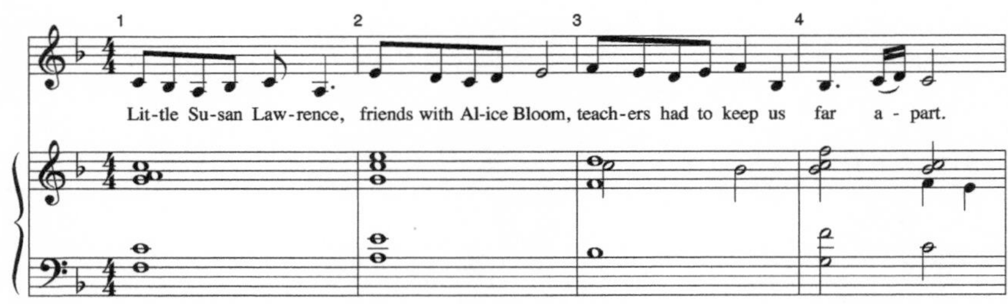

The chord progression from F major to A minor (with an added seventh) has a special poignancy; it's the same harmonic motion that gives a nostalgic aura to the very opening of, among others, "Puff, the Magic Dragon." Not only that, but little Susan and her best friend, Alice, were so devoted to each other and so chatty when they were together that the teacher wouldn't even let them sit next to each other. Doesn't everyone remember having a friend like that?

In short order, the teacher moves Susan across the room to another seat, and she finds herself next to her future boyfriend. Bars 5–8 are mostly a repeat of bars 1–4, except the melody takes a distinctive upward turn on the fourth beat of measure 7 (up to an A instead of down to a B♭) and into measure 8, elevating and emphasizing the boy "who'd steal my heart" (example 22.2).

Closer Than Ever. Joshua Rosenblum, Oxford University Press. © Oxford University Press 2024.
DOI: 10.1093/oso/9780197758236.003.0022

Example 22.2. "Little Susan Lawrence"

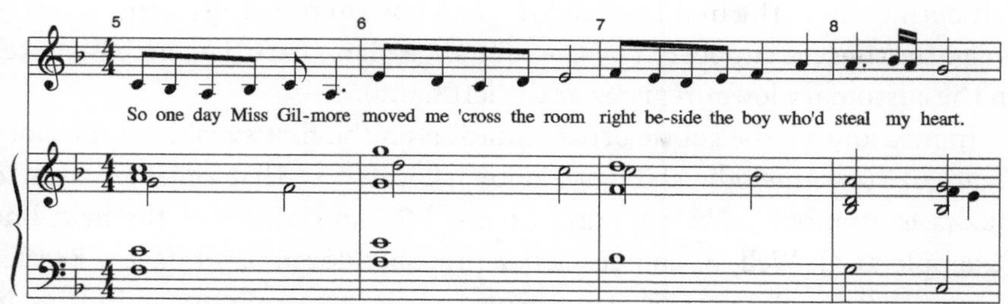

All of a sudden, in eight short bars, we have an entire backstory for Susan, replete with words and phrases that make her relatable instead of distant, set to an ingratiating melody and a reliably stirring harmonization. And what's the heartthrob's name? "He was Buzz Babcock, the very first love of my life." In measure 11, Shire reharmonizes the repeated B♭ in the vocal melody from a G minor chord on the first beat to a B♭ minor chord on the third beat;[1] this shift gives the word "love" an added wistful twinge (example 22.3).

Example 22.3. "Little Susan Lawrence"

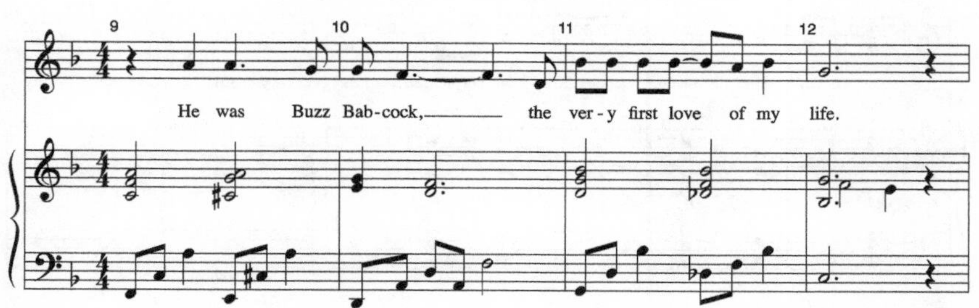

In bars 13 and 14, Shire's melody contains upward octave leaps from "close" to "my" and from "see" to "him" (example 22.4).

Example 22.4. "Little Susan Lawrence"

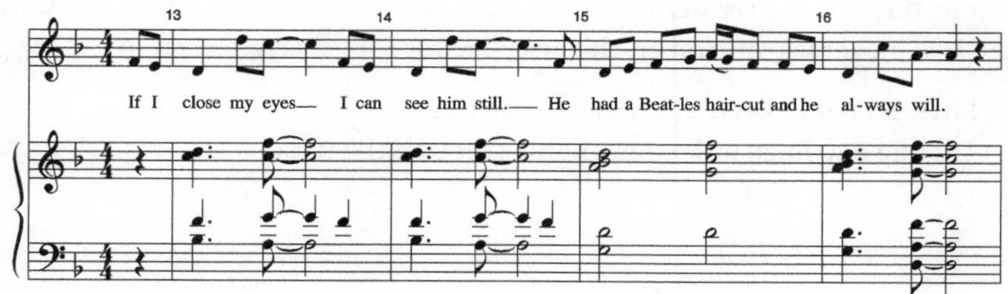

These registral shifts convey the buoyancy and lightheartedness Susan felt both then, in the first flush of love, and now, in recalling it. This sense of weightlessness is supported by the midrange piano part (i.e., no bass notes in the customary lower register of the left hand).

In measure 15, the subtle ornamentation on the first syllable of the word "*hair*-cut" (two melodic sixteenth notes allocated to that syllable) adds to Buzz's irresistibility. "In my mind I mean," Susan clarifies in the next line (example 22.5). Well, of course—Buzz probably doesn't *still* have a Beatles haircut, but we all know what it means to have someone frozen in time in our memories.

". . . where he's always seen / the very first love of my life," she continues, ending the verse. This time, as the phrase "very first love of my life" is repeated, it gets added emphasis with an octave leap in the melody, via an ascent from D through F up to the high D (measure 19 of example 22.5). This is in contrast to the earlier setting of "very first love of my life" with the repeated B♭s in measure 11 of example. 22.3.

Example 22.5. "Little Susan Lawrence"

In addition to the melodic leap, the harmonization of the word "first" is also noteworthy: it's an E♭ major seventh chord, with added sixth (C) and ninth (F) tones—a very jazzy and distinctive voicing. Plus, it's held for a full four beats, giving us time to fully absorb just how in love Susan is with Buzz.

But does Buzz love her back? He sure does—but we don't find out until the second verse (remember, the best theater songs have an action).

Little Susan Lawrence, lovesick little thing,
Till one day Buzz walked me home through the park.

That's the day he gave me a plastic compass ring
That whistled and decoded and glowed in the dark.

The bridge takes us into the subsequent winter, which little Susan spent as Buzz's girlfriend—and, accordingly, into a new key, D♭. The faster tempo (indicated by the "Più mosso" marking) adds to the sense of Susan being swept away by the memory of this emotionally formative time of her life (example 22.6).

Example 22.6. "Little Susan Lawrence"

Harmonically, Shire keeps D♭ in the bass for almost the entire bridge, but the chords built on top of the root D♭ (in the left hand of the piano part) change nearly every bar. For the first four bars, he alternates between D♭ major and an E♭ major chord with D♭ in the bass—a majestic II over I sonority (in bars 46 and 48) that classical, film, and theater composers alike turn to frequently to express something of import.

Starting in measure 49, the right-hand chords over the bass D♭ continue an upward progression by step, starting with E major, and moving to F major in measure 50 and G major in measure 51, as can be seen in the harmonic reduction in example 22.7.

Example 22.7. "Little Susan Lawrence"

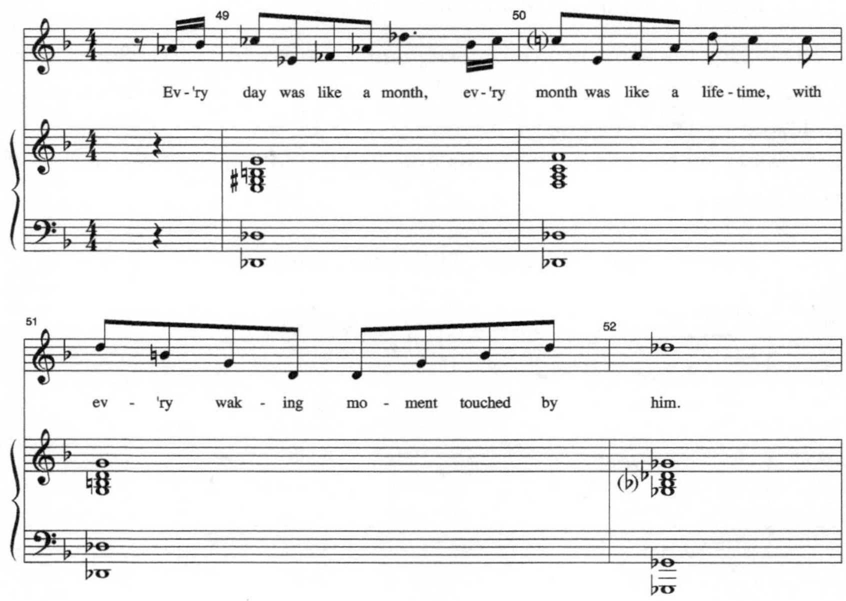

These chords become increasingly dissonant against the D♭ bass as they become increasingly distant from the temporary tonic of D♭, with the G major chord in measure 51, related to the root by the interval of a tritone, the most distant possible. This progression corresponds to the developing swirl of emotions Susan is describing. Finally, however, the dissonance resolves on a triumphant G♭ major chord on the last word of the phrase "Ev'ry waking moment touched by *him*" in measure 52.

The music takes four bars to calm down after this fortissimo emotional and musical climax, returning to the home key of F major via a scale of descending thirds (and prepared harmonically with a dominant C in the bass). Back in the comfort of an F major verse, Susan sings:

Little Susan Lawrence, thirty-three years old,
I could say I've changed a lot since then.
Though I've had involvements, though I'm hardly cold
My heart never beat that wildly again.

That first line is another classic Maltby time distortion, accomplished in the fewest possible number of syllables. It's also interesting that she throws in the line "though I'm hardly cold," which is primarily how we've thought of her until this song. Adjectives like that, however, have now been permanently banished as descriptions of Susan. And with "My heart never beat that wildly again," we get one more vivid description of the universal, disorienting experience of first love, even though we never find out how it ended.

And then, just in case you were wondering if Maltby will be able to rhyme anything with "Lawrence," he delivers in the coda:

Mem'ries come in *torrents*
Of little Susan *Lawrence*,
A girl with a compass ring
In love.

As discussed, "Little Susan Lawrence" was absent from the Detroit tryout and the Broadway run. Having no way, of course, of knowing anything about the missing number, Chris Jones nonetheless had this to say about Lawrence's character in his *Variety* review of the Detroit production:

> Crista Moore works better as love interest Susan, but you never understand why and at what point her initially self-serving interest in this childlike man turns into genuine romantic affection—such vital human transitions are given insufficient focus in Ockrent's heavy-handed staging.[2]

That line no doubt had Maltby and Shire smacking their foreheads in frustration. When the time came, however, to discuss restoring "Little Susan Lawrence" for the national tour, it wasn't an obvious call, according to Maltby.

"We really had sort of made the scene work without 'Little Susan Lawrence,' so it was a real question mark," he recounts. "We put the song in at the first performance in Wilmington. Josh falls asleep, she's sitting there, she starts the song, and . . . the audience went silent. They were listening. It's a long song—four and a half minutes—and they were riveted the whole time. They wanted to know what she was going to say, what she was going to do. I thought it was a life lesson in how audiences function. If we had heard coughs, we would have known they were bored."

John Weidman demurs slightly on this topic, saying it's *still* unclear what the best solution is. "In subsequent productions, both in Japan and in London in 2019, there always comes a point where they want to cut 'Little Susan Lawrence.' It's been a song that ever after has presented itself as problematic because we've just played a long scene. It keeps getting cut." Maybe it's too many songs for that scene, after all. "Her preoccupation with the ring and then the song—I think it's terrific. But Mike was not the only person who felt we were overstaying our welcome. It was odd to be in London and still be working on something that felt as elemental as whether 'Little Susan Lawrence' should be sung," he concludes.

One Broadway insider observed of "Little Susan Lawrence" on the *Big* national tour, "It stopped the show (not in a good way) for backstory instead of driving it toward the end of the act."

Susan Stroman, whose memory of the show and the experience is otherwise quite impressive and specific, says she does not remember the number.

BOB FOSSE'S WIFE, HIS MISTRESS, AND HIS DAUGHTER

FOSSE

Only three times in Broadway history has a revue (as opposed to a show with a plot and characters) won the Tony Award for Best Musical. The first was *Ain't Misbehavin'* (1978), as discussed in chapter 12. The second was *Jerome Robbins' Broadway* (1989), directed by Robbins himself. The third, and the only other revue so honored to date, was *Fosse* (1999), a compilation of musical numbers showcasing the work of the eponymous and legendary director/choreographer Bob Fosse. This last show, like *Ain't Misbehavin'*, was helmed by Richard Maltby, who in this case shared the directing credit with Ann Reinking. In contrast to *Ain't Misbehavin'*, however, which he co-conceived (with Murray Horwitz) and spearheaded himself, Maltby was a hired hand on *Fosse*.

The show that ultimately landed on Broadway as *Fosse* began as the brainchild of Chet Walker, a veteran dancer, choreographer, and teacher who had performed in several of Fosse's Broadway shows (*Pippin*, *The Pajama Game*, *Dancin'*) and was, in Maltby's words, "the keeper of the Fosse flame."

When Fosse was mounting a Broadway revival of *Sweet Charity* in 1986 as a star vehicle for Debbie Allen, Walker was on hand as dance captain and swing. He had been summoned out of semiretirement by Gwen Verdon, who, though by this time she had been long separated (but never actually divorced) from Fosse,[1] continued to have a fruitful working relationship with him and was helping him reconstruct the original *Sweet Charity* choreography.[2]

Once the company was back in New York rehearsing for the Broadway opening after an out-of-town run in Los Angeles, Walker thought it might be a good time to approach Fosse with an idea for a TV show centered around

Closer Than Ever. Joshua Rosenblum, Oxford University Press. © Oxford University Press 2024.
DOI: 10.1093/oso/9780197758236.003.0023

the iconic director/choreographer himself. In Walker's concept, Fosse would sit on a stage, and various stars who had become famous in Fosse-directed shows—Verdon, Liza Minnelli, Chita Rivera, Shirley MacLaine, Joel Grey—would come up and join him one at a time, each giving his or her own tribute to the great man and then introducing surprise guest performers to do their signature numbers.

To Walker's amazement, Fosse said yes to the idea. Walker was so prepared for a no that he didn't even hear Fosse say yes. "I repeated the whole thing over again, because I knew I was gonna have to fight for this. And he kept saying OK."[3] Walker says he gave his pitch four times until Fosse finally cut him off with "Chet! I said yes!"

Sadly, Fosse didn't have long to live at that point. On September 23, 1987, he collapsed (and shortly thereafter died) with a heart attack as he and Verdon were leaving their hotel to attend the opening night of the *Sweet Charity* national tour in Washington, D.C. After that devastating turn of events, Walker shelved the project. "I'm thinking, 'I don't want to go back and do it now,'" he remembers. "'Do I even have the rights?'"

Seven years went by. Walker had time to ruminate, and he began to feel he owed something to the legacy of his hero. Obviously, his original concept for the show would have to be altered now that it couldn't include the presence of Fosse himself, but he felt increasingly compelled to move forward.

Finally, in 1994, Walker contacted Verdon, who was in Germany visiting her daughter and grandchildren. He faxed her his proposal for the show. Verdon replied that she'd never heard about it—Fosse had never mentioned it—but that she supported the idea. So Walker set to work.

One of Fosse's stipulations to Walker about the possible TV show was that Walker would have to start a dance company, so that a group of performers could be trained methodically in the style and the material over a long period of time, unrestricted by the limits of a normal Broadway rehearsal period.

An ongoing class—eventually meeting three days a week—to train dancers in the Fosse style had never previously existed. But now that Fosse had been gone for seven years, Walker's classes served a unique function in the New York dance ecosystem. Naturally, there was a clamor to be admitted. "We had the cream of the crop to choose from," Walker says. Verdon, however, asserted veto power as far as who was allowed to continue week to week. The idea was that a new Broadway dance show—a posthumous tribute to Fosse—would evolve out of the routines that were being recreated by Walker and rehearsed by the select group of dancers in these classes.

After about two and a half years of this training, Verdon decided it was time to do a presentation for some friends and colleagues in the Fosse orbit.

"The glitterati of people who had worked with Bob were there," Walker recalls—performers, producers, writers, composers, designers, and other colleagues. Walker's company of dancers presented seven numbers from the Fosse canon. The reaction in the room was rapturous, and Walker had the thumbs up from Verdon to continue developing his show.

Soon afterward, Walker's agent, Bob Duva, put in a call to Garth Drabinsky, the flashy cofounder and owner of the theatrical production company Livent. By this time, the Toronto-based Livent had successfully brought *Kiss of the Spider Woman* to Broadway, as well as highly regarded revivals of *Show Boat* and *Candide*.[4] Once Drabinsky was on the line, Walker pitched the producer on the show he wanted to do and invited Drabinsky to come to a presentation. Drabinsky attended and was sold on the project. (After first saying he wouldn't be able to make it, he then arrived ostentatiously late with a full catering staff in tow.)

The next step was to bring Walker's troupe to Toronto for a full workshop of the emerging show—a rough version of what would ultimately become *Fosse*—at York University. It was a cast of about twenty-four people, drawn from Walker's ongoing New York dance class, and they rehearsed for three weeks. Again, the Fosse glitterati were invited, this time as Drabinsky's guests. "George Wolfe, Chita [Rivera], [John] Kander and [Fred] Ebb—Garth flew them all up to see this to get their opinion," Walker remembers, "and they all pretty much went apeshit." The support from this cohort gave Verdon and Walker further conviction that the project was worth further development.

As for what happened after that point, Walker won't say much. This was around the time that Maltby was brought on board. According to Maltby, Drabinsky's feeling after the workshop was that in spite of the great musical numbers and the terrific cast, the show wasn't holding together.

Marty Bell, a senior vice president for Livent and a close Drabinsky associate, had known Maltby for years. Their wives were friendly as well. Bell urged Drabinsky to bring Maltby in as director, with words to the effect of "If you want to put together a revue, there's only one person who really knows how."

Drabinsky flew Maltby to Toronto to meet the team. "When Garth wants to shmeichel[5] you, it's very nice," Maltby observes. "You stay at the Four Seasons Hotel, it's grand." And in those days, Drabinsky acted as if he had money to burn.

Maltby took the video of the workshop back to New York and watched it. The show had a strong beginning, with a number called "I Wanna Be a Dancin' Man," a terrific song by Harry Warren and Johnny Mercer. Originally a solo song-and-dance vehicle for Fred Astaire in the 1952 MGM movie *The Belle of New York*, "Dancin' Man," as it appeared in *Dancin'* and later in *Fosse*, was a full-company production number—an eight-minute, masterfully shaped sequence, every second of which is completely riveting, and a huge Fossean-style crowd-pleaser.

But as Maltby continued to watch the video, something seemed off:

> About five numbers in, I started thinking, Fosse keeps repeating himself. I thought he was better than this. And my interest started to kind of wane. And then I realized, well, of course! Fosse never expected these numbers to be put together, for "Steam Heat" to be right next to some other number he did. He stole from himself all the time. It never occurred to him that that wasn't perfectly fine. That was his vocabulary. But you put all the stuff together, and there's a sinking feeling that his vocabulary wasn't that large.

The solution, Maltby gradually realized, was to make the audience wait a while for the quintessential Fosse numbers—"to keep that cat in the bag as long as possible," in Maltby's words. Thus, he reconceived the show with "Dancin' Man" not as the opening number but as the Act I finale, building up to it gradually as a major cathartic arrival.

The show, as restructured by Maltby, starts with "Life Is Just a Bowl of Cherries," a hit Ray Henderson/Lew Brown Depression-era song and a favorite of Fosse's ("I guess because of the irony," Maltby speculates). Fosse had used the song in his 1986 musical *Big Deal*, the last Broadway show he directed before he died. However, it isn't even a dance number in *Fosse*—it's merely sung, and quietly at that (by Valarie Pettiford in the original Broadway cast). "Bowl of Cherries" segues to a sequence called "Fosse's World," a relatively amorphous montage that features two groups of dancers, entering from twin mini-prosceniums on opposite sides of the stage. The first group comes on, a few at a time, clad entirely in short-sleeved black or unitards (along with the requisite Fossean black hats), and lit so that our attention is drawn specifically to their bare arms and hands. The second group prioritizes movements that switch the focus to their legs and feet. Both the music and the dancing are deliberately fragmented. As Maltby describes it, "We brought in all the vocabulary of Fosse dance, but piece by piece." Thus, the show starts by showing the audience the basic building blocks of the choreography that will dazzle them later.

This intriguing and mesmerizing sequence leads directly to "Bye Bye Blackbird," another Ray Henderson number (with lyrics by Mort Dixon), which Fosse had used in *Liza with a Z*. "So, it's seven minutes in before we get a Fosse number," Maltby observes, "and it's the smallest number. Very subtle, tiny, little stuff. It's delicious, but it's nothing by comparison."

Up next are two consecutive imports from *Dancin'*—"From the Edge" and "Percussion 4"—both scored for percussion only. Both are virtuoso pieces, for the dancers and pit drummers alike, but the fact that they are not actual songs prevents them from seeming like full-fledged signature numbers.

"Big Spender" follows, with one of the most recognizable opening musical mottos in Broadway history. This, it would seem, must certainly qualify as "quintessential Fosse," but, as Maltby points out, it's more of a character number than a dance number. In fact, the jaded hostess girls in the lineup do not move *at all* throughout the first verse, and after that, it's mostly about posing.

Toward the end of Act I comes the first scene Fosse choreographed for Hollywood, a quickie sequence in the middle of the classic "From This Moment On" number from the 1953 film version of Cole Porter's musical *Kiss Me Kate*. This galvanizing bit of movie magic—referred to reverentially by Walker as "those forty-three seconds"—is canonical for Fosse devotees. As Elvis Mitchell wrote in the *New York Times* when the movie played at Film Forum in 2000, the scene "has the irresistible sparkle of history being made on screen."[6]

This sequence was also a turning point in *Fosse*, according to the *Times* review:[7]

> The ghost of the man being celebrated—blurred and fleeting but definitely there—first shows up when the girl bursts onstage with a scream. . . . At the sound of that scream, which echoes not with terror but with irrepressible energy, a slender, elfin-faced fellow with a goatee shoots into view, sliding on his side like a runaway roller skate. The orchestra is playing Cole Porter's "From This Moment On," as the couple perform an acrobatic, exuberant and exasperated mating dance, an ode to percolating hormones. You've just received, in darkest January, a quick infusion of springtime, and it's impossible not to grin.

With this dose of the great man's embryonic originality, we're clearly getting close to full-on Fosse. Now it's just a quick transitional number—"Walking the Cat" (featuring "dance elements from *Redhead*,"[8] according to the *Playbill*)—and we finally get "Dancin' Man," the Act I finale, where all the pieces go together. "In other words, Maltby summarizes, "hold off what the audience is desperate to get until they are desperate to get it, and then give it to them."

In the second act, as Maltby puts it, "We trot out all the biggies": "Shoeless Joe from Hannibal, Mo." from *Damn Yankees*, "Steam Heat" from *The Pajama Game* ("the quintessential Fosse number—this is where it all began," according to Walker), "Rich Man's Frug" from *Sweet Charity*, and "Big Noise from Winnetka" from *Dancin'*. The act concludes dazzlingly with the "Nowadays"/"Hot Honey Rag" sequence from *Chicago*. But *Fosse* is a three-acter. What's left for the final act?

The third act, it turns out, is all about leading dance deeper and deeper into the worlds of sex and violence. "It plows down the rabbit hole of depravity, as [Fosse] himself did in the latter part of his life," Maltby observes. "It asks, 'How much can you actually show?'"

The act begins with "Glory" from *Pippin*, a mock glorification of war. That song segues directly into what is known as the "Manson Trio," an appealing bit of Fossean vaudeville, during which the Leading Player, flanked by two women, performs an alluring song-and-dance routine to a bouncy, infectious Stephen Schwartz tune. During the course of the number, legs and body parts are flung all over the stage. This was the Vietnam era, when every night the network news anchors would tell viewers how many people were dying in the war. "[Fosse] was putting that onto an audience. Look what we do to war—we just kind of tap-dance through it," Walker observes. The routine's title implies that the three performers are stand-ins for Charles Manson and his creepy, murderous female acolytes, who were very much in the news in the early '70s.

Act III continues with a pulsating, decadent "Mein Herr" from *Cabaret*. This is followed by "Take Off with Us," from the movie *All That Jazz*, a slinky, sinuous number featuring a come-hither airline hostess and more than slightly suggestive lyrics. The next number is "Three Pas de Deux," also from *All That Jazz*, which features three couples (two men, two women, and a male/female couple) wearing only underwear and doing erotic ballet routines. In "Razzle Dazzle" from *Chicago*, the Billy Flynn character, flanked by two leotard-clad, impossibly long-legged female confederates, comments self-referentially on the show's salacious content. And so on.

But the third act isn't just about the allure of sex and violence. "It's about the emotion of dance," Maltby asserts. "It's about the barriers to expanding the horizons of sexuality and who the dancers really are, as opposed to faceless chorus people." Accordingly, in "Three Pas de Deux," the dancers state their names in turn as the number is beginning. Maltby traces this emphasis on individuality back to *Pippin*, where, he says, the revelation was that all the dancers were whoever they were in real life. Prior to that, ensemble dancers in musicals were mostly uniform and homogeneous. "But in *Pippin*, if you were gay, you were a gay man onstage," he says. Fosse wanted genuine personalities; he wanted a company made up of real, individual people.

But *Fosse* the show needed an ending. After following the titular director/choreographer through the general depravity of Act III, Maltby needed something to redeem him and to give the show an eleven o'clock number. It was Walker's idea to bring in "Mr. Bojangles" from *Dancin'*. Originally written and recorded by Jerry Jeff Walker in 1968, the song achieved popularity with its recording by the Nitty Gritty Dirt Band in 1970 and became a signature number for Sammy Davis, Jr. As conceived for *Dancin'*, it featured a vocalist and two dancers, an old man and a younger one. In that context, it was an aging dancer reminiscing about his younger self. In rehearsals for *Fosse*, however, the younger dancer was dressed in a black leotard instead of the same costume as his older counterpart. To Maltby, "He seemed to be like the spirit of dance, protecting the old dancer. Dancers' lives are short, and when they reach the point where they can't do it anymore, the spirit of dance is what comes and saves them." The character was reconceived as The Spirit.

And the old dancer, of course, is a stand-in for Fosse himself. Walker encapsulates it:

> [The "Mr. Bojangles" number] is all of Mr. Fosse, the kind of old man who remembers what he used to be able to do. When you get to a certain age, you can no longer do the things you once did, but it's not like it's not still inside of you. When you watch [the old dancer] walk offstage, he walks off straight as if he's that young man again. That's the whole essence of what the show was. It is the quintessential thread of the creator.

"Mr. Bojangles" serves effectively as an eleven o'clock number, albeit a low-key, quietly moving one. After that, a reprise of "Life Is Just a Bowl of Cherries" leads to the finale, the blazing big-band number "Sing, Sing, Sing," with music and lyrics by Louis Prima, made famous in its instrumental version by the Benny Goodman Orchestra. In Fosse's hands, it became an exuberant, maximally stylish, fifteen-minute dance extravaganza with the added excitement of six orchestra members playing from an onstage platform. For Maltby, it's the apotheosis of Fosse's choreography, and as the closing number of *Fosse*, "It's where we put all the elements together again."

Thus, a biographical thread runs through the whole show. "At the beginning, those percussion numbers from *Dancin'* are a kid on the street who just knows how to dance," as Maltby describes it. "[Fosse's] first jobs were at a burlesque house. He lost his virginity to one of those girls. So that's what 'Big Spender' is."

Accordingly, the show becomes more and more emotionally open toward the end of the first act, then continues to unfold as a reflection of Fosse's own personal evolution, as described above. "The audience picks up on [the biographical element]," Maltby says. "It's not spelled out, but they get it, just as they do in *Ain't Misbehavin'*. That's what I did."

Maltby and Walker worked together through two full workshops—one in New York and one in Toronto—before Verdon decided that the show was still missing something and that she needed to bring in Reinking to oversee the choreography.

There was certainly potential for tension in the Verdon-Reinking relationship, to say the least. Verdon, in addition to having been married to Fosse, had been his primary artistic inspiration until Reinking usurped her in the roles of both lover and muse. The two women had, however, developed a surprisingly close relationship over time.[9] Michael Paternostro, a dancer/singer/actor/pianist/musical director who was a member of the original *Fosse* cast, says Verdon and Reinking actually loved each other. "In a weird, wild way," he says, "they became family."[10] Reinking came onboard, starting with the final Toronto workshop.

At the same time, Maltby was finding himself unable to get his work done with Verdon breathing down his neck. "I went to Garth and said, 'You have to do something. I cannot work with somebody grimacing and groaning like that.' I couldn't get anything done because she was against anything I did that was a change."[11] Drabinsky spoke to Verdon and worked out an agreement that she would not attend rehearsals but would come in at the end and see the workshop performance. In the meantime, Nicole Fosse (Fosse and Verdon's daughter) would go to rehearsals as Verdon's proxy. "I was doing the show with Bob Fosse's wife, his mistress, and his daughter," Maltby laments wryly.

Once Reinking was installed as choreographer, it meant the end of Walker's involvement in the project. Regarding Walker's departure from the show, Nicole Fosse says, "All I can really distinctly remember is my mother saying, 'We have to get Ann Reinking in here. She'll fix it. She can get anybody to do anything she wants. But the only way she can do that is if she's in charge.' And so the ripple effect of that is that Chet couldn't be in charge. I know it did not start with 'Get Chet out.' It started with 'Get Ann in, and the only way that's gonna work is get Chet out.' And that [came from] my mother."[12]

Walker, unsurprisingly, would not discuss it.[13]

Reinking, after a certain amount of time working on the show, asked to be credited as co-director with Maltby, in addition to her choreographer billing. Maltby, feeling this was fair, agreed.[14]

The lengthy and circuitous path to Broadway that had begun as Walker's concept in 1985 took a big step forward as *Fosse* opened its pre-Broadway tryout tour in Toronto in July 1998. This thrilling evening for the company was followed by a shocking turn of events the next day: at six a.m. on the morning after the opening performance, Canadian Mounties sealed the offices of Livent, and producer Drabinsky was arrested for financial improprieties and eventually served a term in prison.[15] This, Maltby recalls, was "a life-changing event. For a good long while, we didn't know what we were gonna do." As it turned out, the tour proceeded, with lengthy stops in Boston and Los Angeles prior to New York. During that period, the show cycled through four different producers. The run of *Ragtime*, a Livent production then on Broadway, was cut short. *Fosse*, somehow, went forward.

Regarding the finished product—the final version of *Fosse* that ultimately opened on Broadway—Walker, understandably, has his reservations. Referring to a video recording of the first Toronto workshop, Walker observes, "If you looked at that, you would see what the show . . . I won't say should have been but *could* have been.

"Mr. Fosse," Walker continues, "does not need to be protected. His work stands on its own. When you start screwing around with it, it's no longer his." Walker concludes that Fosse would have hated the show. Or, more specifically, "He would've had a hissy fit."

Paternostro puts this remark in perspective. "'Bob would've hated it.' I can't tell you how many people who have worked with Bob have said that about every one of us dancers, every number in the show, the whole show. That comes with it!"

Nicole Fosse, for her part, thought the final version of the show was still too big and too much, despite Maltby's efforts to give the show a narrative arc and hold off on the big numbers until the right moment.

"There were too many dancers, too many numbers, too many *high-powered* numbers, so that it was overwhelming," she says. "And you lost sight of the different dancers. You couldn't follow a person through a track on the show and come to know them, as a performer, like, oh, that's the guy that did this thing. It was just more people that kept showing up and doing jumping splits and knee slides."

She offers some insightful speculation: "Let's say my father all of a sudden one day came in and appeared in rehearsal as the fixer, the doctor. He would've cut half of that out. 'Too much! How can you remember anything? How can you walk away as an audience member with an impression when everything is like *wham wham wham* and you don't remember the people?'"

In other words, Bob would've hated it.

On the other hand, she concedes, "How do you do all those numbers otherwise? You can't. Because somebody's gotta be changing clothes, getting ready for the next number. So it was a huge conundrum that I don't feel was ever solved in a way that really honored how Bob Fosse would present his work."

Nicole Fosse has nothing but praise for the performers ("All the moves were there, and every dancer in that show was absolutely phenomenal"), and she's careful not to assign blame for what she perceives as the show's failings. "I don't want to say it was anybody's fault, but somebody needed to come in with an axe and cut stuff out," she concludes.

Any tension between Verdon and Maltby, Nicole Fosse says, was nothing personal. She recalls her mother would say, "'What does he do? I don't know what he's doing.' She would say funny things. She wasn't in the meetings. She didn't know."

Walker, in spite of his painful departure from the show, makes apparent his great respect for Maltby. "Richard is kind and gracious," he avers. Regarding the various warring factions Maltby had to corral over the course of the show's development, Walker says, "Richard had to put up with a lot of shit. Once he was brought on, that's when things started going crazy with the Fosse family side of it. I talked to Garth a year and a half ago, and he said about Richard, 'You have no idea what he went through.'"

NEXT THING I KNEW, I WAS WRITING THE SHOW

TAKE FLIGHT

"We have so many songs for *Take Flight*, it's absolutely ridiculous," Maltby says. "We joke about the fact that maybe we should take all the songs that we've done, give them all to [Music Theatre International], and say, 'Make your own musical! Here—in this spot, you can use this song, or this song, or this song, and if you want this song, you can have this scene that follows it. Or not! You can do whatever you like!' "

"If we live long enough," Shire adds, "we might be able to rack up as many versions that don't quite work as *Candide* has. A score that everybody loves but you just can't get the whole thing to work!"

As with *Closer Than Ever*, *Take Flight* had its genesis with an idea from Maltby's assistant, Steven Scott Smith. Smith suggested a musical about Amelia Earhart. He and Maltby agreed it was an interesting story, but in the end, it seemed too thin for a musical on its own. Some years later, Maltby had the inspiration that if Earhart's tale were interwoven with those of fellow aviators Charles Lindbergh and Orville and Wilbur Wright, it could become a more universal story about the human impulse to fly.

"Flight is kind of the physical manifestation of human aspiration," Maltby explains. "It was the one thing that human beings could not do. They could do all these other things, but they could not fly, and then they did, and that seemed to be worth making a dividing line."

Shire liked the idea. In addition, they felt, the show should be done in an unconventional way. "Like a scrapbook," Maltby says. "Or a collage," Shire adds, that is, without a traditional book. This kind of piece is often referred to as a "concept musical."

Closer Than Ever. Joshua Rosenblum, Oxford University Press. © Oxford University Press 2024.
DOI: 10.1093/oso/9780197758236.003.0024

Concept musicals are shows that are based around a theme rather than focused on telling a narrative story. Kurt Weill and Alan Jay Lerner's *Love Life* (1948) is often cited as the first concept musical.[1] *Love Life* traces the evolution of a newly married couple through various eras in American history from 1791 to 1948 (the year the show opened), although the couple doesn't age much. The songs themselves are vaudeville-style, commenting on societal changes rather than advancing a storyline.[2]

The concept musical had its first big mainstream success with Stephen Sondheim's *Company* (1970),[3] which is more a series of vignettes and songs organized around the theme of marriage than a conventional book musical. In an essay about Sondheim in *The New Yorker*, Stephen Schiff called *Company* "the first modernist musical; certainly it was the first successful musical that did away with plot completely."[4] *A Chorus Line* (1975), another landmark concept musical, uses the audition process as a vehicle to explore the vivid inner lives of individual ensemble members. It's telling that Michael Bennett's credits for the show included a "Conceived by" acknowledgment along with one for direction and choreography.

Assassins (off-Broadway in 1990, Broadway in 2004), another notable (and controversial) Sondheim concept musical, investigates the psyches of various would-be and actual presidential assassins by placing them together in an imagined, extra-temporal gathering place and then jumping back and forth in time as their individual stories are told. Maltby and Shire cite *Assassins* and *Company* as models for what they had in mind with *Take Flight*. Shire also mentions the largely forgotten *Oh, What a Lovely War!* (1963), which used World War I as the springboard for a satire on war in general.

The flexibility of what has come to be known as the concept musical genre would seem to offer writers a fair amount of latitude to explore their chosen themes, yet it's difficult to get it right. Maltby and Shire have certainly found this to be true with *Take Flight*, which contains some magnificent material and depicts wonderfully vivid historical personages but, as the writers are quick to agree, has yet to find a satisfactory finished form.

The writers agree that the first reading they ever did of *Take Flight*—the "collage" version—may well have been its best realization. As Shire puts it, "What was magical about the first reading was that it was this kind of free-form thing where there were three main stories, but all these other ones hooking in as well."

Kevin Stites, the veteran Broadway conductor who was musical director for that original reading as well as numerous subsequent outings of *Take Flight*, concurs. "There are elements of the very first *Take Flight* that I still miss," he says. "The very first reading, where there was no second act, just the sketch of a first act and a finale. There were magical, beautiful things, like a ballerina slowly floating her foot way up into the air."

That first version of the show also included as a character "Lawnchair Larry," based on the real-life Larry Walters, who attracted worldwide media attention in 1982 when he took a solo flight in a homemade airship constructed from a patio chair and forty-five helium-filled weather balloons. "It was great, and he had a wonderful song," Stites recalls. "But they had to take it out because, unfortunately, somebody wrote a whole musical about him."[5]

After that initial outing, the team received feedback from well-meaning friends and colleagues in the audience, advising them to make the piece more logical and less fragmented. The revised version, as presented at a follow-up second reading, had lost some of the magic. Maltby observes:

> It's the living proof that you have to be really careful. My principle is that shows aren't ruined because somebody gives you a bad idea and you take it. Shows are ruined when somebody really smart gives you a really good idea that you must not take. Somebody had looked at that show and said quite wisely, "These are fragments. How do you know to go from here to there, how do you know how much time has gone by?" And since there was time between the first reading and the second reading, I went and made a bunch of little changes to just make it clear as to where we were in time and everything. But the show fell flat. It didn't play anywhere near as well as it did the first time, and a couple of years later, I read that draft over again, and it was terrible!

Based on his successful experiences with *Ain't Misbehavin'* and *Fosse*, Maltby feels that spelling everything out is not always necessary or even desirable:

> *Ain't Misbehavin'* is held together by what the audience perceives, what they bring to it. Same with *Fosse*. I assume that they are listening, that they get it, and they make the connections, and the emotions happen. I'm convinced that *Ain't Misbehavin'* was a big hit because nobody came into rehearsals and offered us advice or told us you couldn't do it or that it was a bad idea, and then it all just went together according to its own logic.

The team had hoped that Lynne Meadow would come to the first *Take Flight* reading, which took place in November 2000, and help them move the show forward, but she wasn't able to make it. She attended the second one, in February 2001, but, as Shire recalls, the revised version of the show "just kind of lay there" and did not elicit any enthusiasm from Meadow.

Considerable further development of the piece followed nonetheless. That summer, the writers took the show to the Eugene O'Neill Center, this time with Jerry Mitchell as director instead of Maltby. Playwright Marsha Norman was brought in to write the book that everyone had insisted the show needed. The team had their reservations about the results at the O'Neill ("kind of a disastrous thing," Maltby recalls), but George White, the founder of the O'Neill Center, had had a reciprocal arrangement with a theater conservatory in Russia for years, and he arranged to transport *Take Flight* to St. Petersburg. This involved bringing over the principal actors from the United States and using Russian musical theater students to form the ensemble. ("It was bizarre, it was crazy, and they were great, and we had a blast," summarizes Andrew Gerle, who served as music director for performances in both St. Petersburg and Moscow.)[6]

The next stop for *Take Flight* was a successful concert performance in July 2004 with a full twenty-piece orchestra at the annual Adelaide Cabaret Festival in Australia. In Adelaide, Maltby and Shire had an introduction to David Babani, the founder and head of London's well-regarded Menier Chocolate Factory. Babani was enthusiastic about the show, and three years later, *Take Flight* received its London premiere at the Chocolate Factory. The cast recording from this production, with an eight-piece orchestra,[7] is available on the PS Classics label.[8]

By the time *Take Flight* touched down in London, John Weidman was on board to write the book. Weidman, Maltby and Shire's librettist on *Big*, had also been Sondheim's librettist for *Assassins*.

Weidman felt the *Assassins* precedent was possibly relevant but only to a point. "Richard and I talked a lot about *Assassins* as a kind of model for a way in which different characters from different times could wind up in the same scene together," he says, "and as a result of winding up together, would do something that would lead to something else, and pretty soon, we're at the Texas School Book Depository. We talked about it, but I said it's not the same thing."

Weidman elaborates: "The structure of [*Assassins*] is based on the fact that you need to get all these people in an invented space together, to let them prod each other and irritate each other, and to learn that 'Oh, we've all got something in common. I didn't think we did, but we do.' But we never found a way to do that with *Take Flight*."

Another possible reason the team ran into trouble using *Assassins* as a structural model stems from the fact that *Assassins*, by virtue of its very subject matter, raises a compelling question that the show needs to answer: what could make someone crazy enough to shoot a president? This means there's inherent dramatic urgency to the show before it even starts. There's no such urgency with *Take Flight*—it's easy to understand why someone would want to fly.

Weidman had seen several prior workshop versions of *Take Flight* and, as a friend and former collaborator, had given the writers input on the show in its various iterations. "The quality of the material, what they were writing, I thought was amazing," Weidman says. He agreed that the three stories—those of Earhart, Lindbergh, and the Wright brothers—seemed to belong together.

What Weidman began to see, however, was a fundamental problem in the structure: "[The three stories are] proceeding along parallel paths, but the boundaries between them never seem to break down," he says. "I never had the feeling that to understand Amelia Earhart, I need these other two stories. So it feels unsatisfying, because I feel like we're jumping from one story to the other, without there being any particular reason all three stories are on the same stage at the same time."

The glimmer of a solution came in the form of an intriguing nugget from Lindbergh's autobiography, *The Spirit of St. Louis*. Halfway through his famous transatlantic flight, the sleep-deprived Lindbergh experienced hallucinations. "[T]he fuselage behind me becomes filled with ghostly presences—vaguely outlined forms, transparent, moving, riding weightless with me in the plane. . . . These phantoms speak with human voices—friendly, vapor-like shapes, without substance, able to vanish or appear at will."[9]

This gave Weidman his inspiration: "Why can't Lindbergh hallucinate, and it's Amelia Earhart? And she's coming out of her story into his story, and she's saying, 'Don't land. The only place where you're really happy, the only place where you feel peace, is up here. So you should stay up here, because that's what *I'm* gonna do.' And Lindbergh says, 'What are you talking about?' And it's a literal reaction, like, 'I'm running out of gas. I gotta land.' And she says, 'I'm just telling you, don't land,' And then she disappears, and he lands, and she doesn't.

"So it was one of those moments where I thought, 'Wow, that's a really smart idea,' and next thing I knew, I was writing the show," Weidman concludes.

"We were overjoyed when John finally agreed to do the book," Shire says. "We thought, 'It's finally going to get solved, telling these three stories in different time periods, different places.' And he worked so hard on it, for four or five years, with many drafts, workshops of those drafts, and two productions."

For Earhart, there's no question that landing was going to be an anticlimax. She had recently married George Putnam, founder of what is now the publishing firm G. P. Putnam's Sons. Putnam had successfully promoted Earhart and her flying escapades and even helped her write a book.

However, as Maltby puts it, "For a woman at that time, to be married was like death; it was the end of any aspiration you might have, so she resisted it. It's our fantasy that he makes her give up the idea of flying, and she says 'I'll give it up after I do just one more thing: a flight around the world. And when it's over,' she says, 'I promise you that'll be the end of it. I'll just be your wife.' And you have the feeling that she just couldn't do it. In that sort of psychological way, it seems almost too perfect that she got all the way to the end, and at the moment when there was no longer any impediment to a married life, she disappeared instead."

Lindbergh, of course, succeeded in his 1927 nonstop transatlantic flight, the first ever completed by a solo aviator. Arguably, that was the peak event of his life. Five years after that came the crisis of his son's kidnapping and murder; later he was accused of being a Nazi sympathizer.[10] In terms of the "Don't Land" song, Maltby says, "It's kind of wonderful, because it's literally true. Everyone thinks that her death was a tragedy and he was the triumph, but in fact, her disappearance was the triumph and his landing was the beginning of his tragedy."

The show was seen with Weidman's book both in London at the Chocolate Factory and three years later in Princeton, New Jersey, in a 2010 production at the McCarter Theatre. During the course of the show's development, the role of Earhart was played at various points by Kelli O'Hara, Christiane Noll, Sutton Foster, Carolee Carmello, Jenn Colella and (in London) Sally Ann Triplett—a veritable who's who of contemporary female musical theater luminaries.

But the overall problem of intertwining the three stories ultimately never found an entirely satisfactory solution, despite the inspired "Don't Land" sequence, which appeared too late in the show to fully achieve its intent. In Weidman's words, "I think the Wright brothers' story from the beginning, before I ever got involved, was really a bravura piece of writing by Richard and David. Their version of who those two guys were was terrific, and I thought we got the Amelia story to a good place, too. We kept trying to find a way to deliver Lindbergh in a way that would make him at least tonally a partner of these other two stories, but I feel like we never solved it."

Shire recalls, "Finally, a year or two ago, [Weidman] said, 'You know what? Your original idea of a collage was really the way it should be done, because I just could not make it work.'"

Maltby adds: "The trouble is there's no writer who's better than John, and he would write some really good scenes, but they didn't add information that you didn't already sort of have. Also, in order to make the story work, we kept chopping up the songs so that they didn't play as consistent pieces of music, so the score never really happened. So we thought maybe the thing to do was to go back and do a concert version of it and focus on the score."

As Weidman talks it through some more, he revises his take on the show's prospects. "I should go back and find that McCarter script and take another look at it," he muses, "because it did seem to me like we couldn't quite figure out how to open the show. If there were enthusiasm for just sorting out the first ten, fifteen minutes, I think we could do that, but we haven't talked about that in a long time."

Part of the problem for Weidman is the title number. "The song 'Take Flight' is written in the authors' vocabulary," he explains. "It's not a song written for any of the characters in the show. When we did it at the McCarter, Lindbergh and Amelia and the Wright brothers came out, and they sang it with the company, but why are they singing this? As a convention, it's fine for them not to be who they are yet. Finish the opening number, and then they can step into their actual roles. But it never felt right."

Stites, who was the musical director of *Take Flight* at the McCarter, respectfully disagrees. "I love John Weidman," he emphasizes, "but I remember this coming up at the time, and I thought, 'Well, yeah, but at least we get to meet them.'" Stites acknowledges that "they were sort of talking to themselves about themselves. But the music was appropriate, and it was very exciting, and they all end up singing this thrilling 'Take Flight' song. It was a nice thing because all three stories were together in one sequence, and then, at the end of Act I, they're [again] combined beautifully in 'Before the Dawn,' which is stunning."

The song "Take Flight" opens, appropriately enough, with the upward-reaching, aspirational interval of a major seventh on the words of the title (example 24.1).

Example 24.1. "Take Flight"

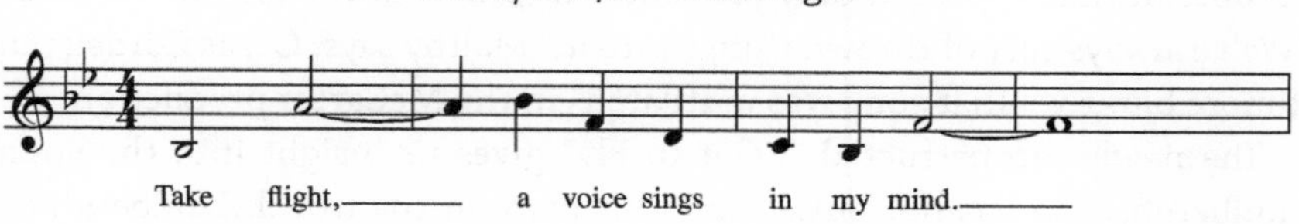

After those first two notes, the melody makes its way back down, then lifts back up with a perfect fifth at the end of the phrase "A voice sings in my mind." This is followed by a melodically unusual series of rising thirds on the phrase "Leave the earth behind." The urge to take leave of solid ground is palpable.

According to Stites, director Sam Buntrock declared the "Take Flight" number impossible to stage as it stood, so the entire opening sequence was cut.

Deniz Cordell, the longtime Maltby/Shire associate, says, "I always thought it was strange that when the show finally played at the McCarter, it did not have the title song in it. It opens with three little mini-prologues instead."

The arrangement of "Take Flight" that was intended for the McCarter production is divided into three sections. Each character—Earhart, Lindbergh, the Wright brothers—takes a section of the song, underscored by the accompanimental figure associated with them throughout the musical. The number was even orchestrated, an indication of how late in the process it was cut from the production.

After the opening was replaced, "Take Flight" appeared only briefly, at the end of each act,—each time in fragmentary form, as a series of rising major sevenths—providing, oddly, the hazy reminiscences of a song that has not previously been heard by the audience.

As Stites puts it, "David used that major seventh throughout the score. It's a compositional sort of thing that runs through it, like Bernstein has the sharp fourth in *West Side Story*. But it only resonated because there was an opening number where the title of the show was [he sings the major seventh interval] 'Take Flight.'" Once the opening number was cut, the ending seemed strange.

The song "Take Flight" is stirring, to be sure, but Weidman is right—it's not character-specific, as the best theater songs are, including most of Maltby and Shire's. In the rewrite intended for concert performance, the song is reinstated, but it's saved for near the end of the first act. The show instead starts (after a prologue that provides some amusingly austere exposition for the Wright brothers) with "I Get to Fly," a terrific number for Lindbergh that appeared only piecemeal in previous versions of the show. "We've always sort of thrown things into it," Maltby says. Or, as Cordell puts it more bluntly, "That song was mutilated" in the McCarter production.

The newly reconstructed "I Get to Fly" gives us insight into the young Lindbergh, who has not quite found his place in the world. Lindbergh has sought out Ray Page (of the Ray Page Flying Academy) and offers to be Page's flight mechanic for free, just so he can fly. The song starts with a verse that gives us some of Lindbergh's unpromising background ("My college told me I should take a vacation. They also told me I should never come back"). Then the song's chorus gives a remarkable musical depiction of the exhilaration that flight must have offered in the early days and a clear sense of its appeal to Lindbergh in particular. Expansive triplets in the vocal line give a sense of ever-expanding horizons, while running sixteenth notes in the accompaniment underpin the melody, conveying Lindbergh's visceral, heart-pounding excitement. It's the difference between an aspirational description of the meaningfulness of flight generally (as in the "Take Flight" song), versus what it feels like to actually be flying, which is what the writers capture so exquisitely in "I Get to Fly."

Earhart's appearance to Lindbergh as an apparition is anticipated in the show by an extraordinary number called "Back of the Line," which employs the hallucination device and is full of colorful characters. It also gives us another chance to see the Sondheim influence at work in *Take Flight*, not just in terms of the legacies of *Company* and (more pertinently) *Assassins* as concept musicals but more specifically with respect to the clear structural debt "Back of the Line" owes to Sondheim's "Please Hello" from *Pacific Overtures* (discussed in chapter 4).

In "Back of the Line," as Lindbergh prepares to set off on his history-making transatlantic flight, he imagines the successive presence of the other better-funded, more experienced aviators who are eager to be the first to make the nonstop trip from New York to Paris and claim the $25,000 Orteig Prize. Lindbergh begins the number, singing to an upbeat, '20s-style Dixieland accompaniment:

I do not have an iceberg's chance in hell.
Swell!
So please, somebody, step on up and tell
Me why I keep goin'.
Other teams, they got more money.
So far ahead o' me it ain't funny.
To even start I gotta be blind.
These are the thoughts in my mind
At the back of the line.

As French aviator and fighting ace René Fonck, the first Lindbergh rival, is introduced, the beat slows down to a suave, Maurice Chevalier–style two-step, and Fonck sings cheerfully, in a French accent, of his own attempt to make the crossing:

I took off for Paris,
But I returned.
At takeoff my plane . . .
Well, she crashed and she burned.

After Fonck concludes his verse, the next to appear is Commander Richard Byrd, or, as Lindbergh describes him, "The most famous explorer in the entire world." The block-chordal accompaniment and stepwise rising bass line have a classical grandeur that befits the intimidating stature of the renowned Arctic and Antarctic explorer.

The Byrd verse is followed by a moderate-tempo tarantella for the Italian American aircraft designer Giuseppe Bellanca, whose plane was grounded by a court injunction resulting from a contract dispute between squabbling copilots. Bellanca sings in a fractured Italian accent that recalls that of the fraudulent barber Pirelli from *Sweeney Todd*. Next, two women sing about the Americans Noel Davis and Stanton Wooster in a quick four-line verse that has a light folk/country feel, accentuated by Shire's banjo-dominated orchestration. This leads to the fifth contending team, Charles Nungesser and François Coli, who attempted to make the flight in the reverse direction, from Paris to New York. Maltby sums this up in a cancan, which includes this clever triple rhyme:

We'll fly Paree to Broadway.
We know that it's the flawed way.
If you'd like to applaud, wait
'Til we win this prize.[11]

The sequence ends with Lindbergh's slow realization that most of his rivals have eliminated themselves and that "Suddenly I'm all you find at the front of the line."

It takes nothing away from the brilliance of "Back of the Line," with its parade of characters singing in pastiches of recognizable national styles that instantly contextualize them, to say that it clearly owes a debt to Sondheim's "Please Hello," even down to the fact that both numbers present five separate genre-specific verses. For his part, Maltby acknowledges that "Please Hello" is a "breathtaking concept" but denies that it was specifically an inspiration for "Back of the Line." "That idea of having a lot of story and putting it into one number is something we've done in other places," he says.

Broadway producer and general manager Joey Parnes, a longtime Maltby/Shire friend, colleague, and fellow Yale alum, agrees that the proposed concert version of *Take Flight* may be the best version of the show.

"I think it's possible that what Richard has come up with is as close to that as he can hope for," Parnes affirms.[12] "By creating this concert but with narration and some dialogue, he's clarified the story more than it has ever been clarified before." Parnes recalls hearing the music from the show back in 2000. "They showed it to me—they must have sent me a recording. I just fell in love with it. It was one of the best scores I'd ever heard, and then we set about for a few years trying to get it to happen." Parnes has been involved with several workshops of the show, but, as he puts it, "We just couldn't get it off the ground, if you'll forgive the expression."

Stites, when informed of the proposed concert version with narration, says, "I'm stunned! I think literally without any dialogue, the songs wouldn't have that welcome lift that you need in a musical, when you hear dialogue and then it elevates into sound. I wouldn't want to hear 'Earthbound' without some of the scene before it that has the conflict." Stites's view on the best path forward? "I wish they could let go of almost everything and start again. Or go back and listen to the stuff that was cut."

WORKING WITH OTHER PEOPLE

One night in 2009, as Shire and his wife Didi Conn were lying in bed, Shire was reading a piece by the popular *New Yorker* staff writer Adam Gopnik that made him laugh out loud. Conn wanted to know what was so funny, and Shire told her, adding, "You know, I wish people like this were interested in writing musicals." "Well, how do you know he doesn't want to write musicals?" Conn asked. Shire was fairly certain that a public intellectual like Gopnik would have no interest in the art form, and he resisted Conn's suggestion that he just call Gopnik and ask him.

By coincidence, one week later, Conn was at the head table at a benefit for Theater for a New Audience, hosted by none other than Gopnik. Conn, actually seated next to Gopnik, asked him, with her characteristic outgoing charm, if he ever wanted to write a musical.

"Did I ever want to write a musical!" Gopnik responded. "I came to New York to write musicals, and I took the job at *The New Yorker* as a day job until I could have a hit show!" Conn, pleased to have been right all along, informed Gopnik that she was married to Shire, and a meeting was quickly arranged. "I said, 'I can't imagine anything in the world I'd rather do than write a musical with David Shire,'" Gopnik recalls.[1]

Shire and Gopnik met a week later at a restaurant in the Theater District and started kicking around ideas. Shire was interested in Gopnik's 2007 autobiographical essay collection *Through the Children's Gate*, about his family's return to New York from Paris shortly before 9/11, particularly one piece about a chefs' competition. Eventually, this idea became the basis of *Our Table*, with book and lyrics by Gopnik and music by Shire. The show had its premiere in May 2017 at the Long Wharf Theatre in New Haven under the name *The Most Beautiful Room in New York*. In January 2019, after undergoing the inevitable revisions, the show had a concert performance at Feinstein's/54 Below in New York (now simply 54 Below), with connective narration read

Closer Than Ever. Joshua Rosenblum, Oxford University Press. © Oxford University Press 2024.
DOI: 10.1093/oso/9780197758236.003.0025

by Gopnik in place of the book scenes.[2] The audio recording from that night serves effectively as the show's original cast recording and can be heard on YouTube.[3]

Our Table is the story of a small family-run restaurant in New York in danger of going under when the rent is raised fifteen-fold. In dire need of assistance, David, the husband and co-owner, turns to his old partner Sergio, who is now a celebrity chef in the mold of Anthony Bourdain. This not only raises the problematic issue of selling out commercially and becoming an exploitable part of Sergio's national brand, but it also gives Sergio an opportunity to renew his relationship with David's wife, Claire, with whom Sergio had a torrid fling long ago, before David and Claire were married.

Shire, who has boundless admiration for Gopnik as a writer, thought he was slightly green as a lyricist when they first started working together. "I want to say this in the kindest, the least patronizing way possible," Shire says. "What he had were wonderful instincts as a lyricist. [His lyrics] rhymed, they had onomatopoeia, alliteration, all that good stuff, but they were very hard to figure out, exactly. I would sometimes make changes, and he was very touchy about that, so we went through a period of trying to work that out. I kept telling him why I changed it and why the lyric wasn't right and that lyrics have to exist in real time, because if you have to stop to think about what a line means, you miss the next two or three lines."

Gopnik, in turn, is cheerfully up front about what he learned from Shire. "What *didn't* I learn from David?" he asks rhetorically. "David emphasizes action. A theater song isn't a description of someone's inner emotional state. It's an action that takes you with dramatic velocity from one moment to another, from one emotional state to another. He was always emphasizing that to me, and I would get fed up with it at times, but of course, he was right. That was the single most profound thing that David taught, and we had some fights along the way, because I thought there were some songs that were just beautiful! They're songs! People stand up and sing them, and they're beautiful!"

The attentive reader will note that not only are these the same lessons that Shire learned from Maltby, but this teaching dynamic of the Gopnik/Shire partnership very clearly mirrors the early stages of the Maltby/Shire working relationship.

Gopnik cites the song "Chopping Onions," one of the first songs he and Shire wrote for *Our Table*, as an example of transforming a previously undramatic song and giving it an action. "There was a line in the piece in *Children's Gate* about the chefs' competition, about how you think you're going to be an artist and you spend your life chopping onions, and we said, 'Well, that's a song.'"

Shire, however, felt the resulting song was inert and undramatic. Gopnik recalls what happened next:

> So I grumbled and went off, and then came back and said, "What about if she's folding napkins while he's chopping onions, and they have a fight?" And David said, "Now, that's interesting. Now we have a scene, now we're writing a scene in the song, we're not just writing a song." And I thought "Chopping Onions" was great as it was, and I was resentful as hell, but of course, he was teaching me. I learned more from him than I can easily describe.

The number, now called "Chopping Onions/Folding Napkins," is set to a lightly peppy cha-cha beat. In between verses, over underscoring, Claire confesses that years ago, she and Sergio went on "a date," and David presses her for details. For the rest of the song, they stew privately and spar outwardly with each other. In other words, the number is now about the vicissitudes of their twenty-year marriage—a far more interesting topic than the original chopping onions premise.

"It's Never Raining in Seattle," which Gopnik considers the best song in the show, also operates on multiple levels. David and Claire, contemplating the reality that they might have to move, console their young Manhattan-loving daughter by telling her how great the weather always is in Seattle.

"What could be a bigger lie?" Gopnik asks with amusement. "But sometimes you have to lie to your children in order to assure them that the world is going to be a welcoming place for them." In the middle of the song, after white-lie-laden verses from both parents, their skeptical and savvy daughter challenges them, singing, "I don't believe you. It's always raining. I've heard it's never sunny there." So the parents shift to describing other virtues of life in the Pacific Northwest—the sight of salmon leaping from Puget Sound, freedom from traffic jams and polluting haze—and end by emphasizing what really matters: "When storms are over, love remains / And if it rains, it rains." In other words, it's a song not about weather but about familial love.

At first, Shire and Gopnik were going to be co-lyricists for their musical, but Shire found Gopnik to be a quick learner. "His lyrics got better and better," Shire says, "and finally, one day, he asked me if he could have the sole credit, and I said yes. He was starting to come up with things that I wouldn't have thought of, and they were expressed in the right way. And now he's a first-class lyricist. What I was basically doing was giving him a course in Steve Sondheim or Richard Maltby lyric writing. He could have gotten it from one of Steve's books just as easily as he got it from me. But it came from showing him line by line, 'This isn't saying exactly what I think you want it to say,' and he'd make it better, and then he got into the swing of it."

One significant sticking point in the Gopnik/Shire collaboration arose around the subject of rhyme. Gopnik, a consummate man of letters, was (and is) of the slightly contrarian view that not all lyrics need to rhyme perfectly. In fact, he wrote a typically thoughtful, well-researched *New Yorker* essay on the subject, titled "The Rules of Rhyme," with the title followed by the (perfectly rhyming) teaser line, "True rhymes are marvels; a slant rhyme's a sin. Or is it vice versa? Let the battle begin."[4]

True rhymes, or perfect rhymes, occur between words that have different initial consonants but are otherwise identical, such as "name" and "game." For words of more than one syllable, everything from the last accented syllable to the end, except for the initial consonant, must be the same, as in "*sorrow*" and "to-*morrow*" or "em-*braceable*" and "irre-*placeable*." With slant rhymes (or near rhymes or false rhymes, as they are variously called), the rules are bent slightly, as in "home" and "alone" or "country" and "hungry," the latter famously featured in the song "My Shot" from *Hamilton*.

Identities, under the rules of strict rhyme, are also forbidden. An identity occurs when the final accented syllables have the same initial consonant or consonants, as with "a-*mend*" and "com-*mend*." Those two words do not actually rhyme; "a-*mend*" and "pre-*tend*," however, form a perfect rhyme because the initial consonants of the last accented syllables are different.

Gopnik quotes Sondheim's essay "Rhyme and Its Reasons," the definitive contemporary screed on the necessity of perfect rhyming: "Both identities and false rhymes are death on wit. A perfect rhyme can make a mediocre line bright and a good one brilliant. . . . A perfect rhyme snaps the word, and with it the thought, vigorously into place, rendering it easily intelligible; a near rhyme blurs it."[5]

Gopnik disagrees, stating his views on the subject in the context of a review of Daniel Levin Becker's book *What's Good: Notes on Rap and Language*, which extols the virtues of American rap as, in Gopnik's words, "a superior form of 'slanting' language." Gopnik refutes Sondheim's dictum as "a parochial notion, since the history of English verse shows a wonderfully witty tradition of near rhyme." He also quotes Levin Becker saying that rap "serves . . . as a delivery mechanism for the most exhilarating and crafty and inspiring use of language in contemporary American culture."[6] Gopnik concludes his essay by writing, "Near-rhyme, half rhyme, off rhyme, odd rhyme, assonance and identities, slant rhymers and straight rhymers: all of it is potentially compelling, and none of it is a sanctuary from sense. What's always at stake with literature and lyrics is their relation to the world."

Shire was not having any of it; he insisted that his music required perfect rhymes, just as Maltby had always provided. As Gopnik puts it, "David is a strict true rhyme guy." Gopnik, on the other hand, is a self-described child of Joni Mitchell, James Taylor, Paul Simon, and the Beatles. He explains in his essay, "Given the exactitude of Sondheim's music, exact rhyme is essential to snap his word into place, where Joni Mitchell can croon right past it."[7] This suggests that the requirement of perfect rhyming varies from genre to genre: generally expected in musical theater lyrics but not in pop, rock, or rap. As Gopnik says, "[No ear has] ever been stopped for a second by, say, the Beatles' rhyming 'changed' and 'remain' in 'In My Life.' "[8]

Regardless, Shire could not function with off rhymes or slant rhymes. "We had arguments about it," Gopnik admits. "I'd say, 'David, you're imprisoning yourself.' But he said eloquently once, 'I hear what you're saying about the legitimacy of slant rhyme, but it doesn't work for my music. My music is so fixed, syllable by syllable and note by note. A singer can't back-phrase it or jazz it up, and the lyrics similarly have to be right on the syllable and the note." In the end, Gopnik was convinced that when working with Shire, perfect rhyming was a reasonable requirement. The songs from *Our Table*, by turns lovely and eloquent, upbeat and fun, clever and character-specific, have certainly benefited from this aesthetic constraint.

Gopnik has additional insights about Maltby and Shire and their insistence on the craft of perfect rhyming. "Art doesn't have rules," he observes, "but every artist must have them." This, says Gopnik, is particularly important to a certain generation of songwriters intent on distinguishing musical theater from "the general great dreck of American pop music." He elaborates:

> You give yourself self-constrained rules, and you say, these are the rules I'm going to work with now. And if I don't work within these rules, then I'm just one more slob who's trying to write a hit song. And that sense was a very big deal for David and Steve Sondheim's generation, because you and I revere those guys, and we think of them correctly as major American artists, but when they were coming of age, that wasn't the way it was perceived. If you were like David and Yale-educated, there was something vulgar, something Brill Building, about writing musicals.[9] So they were constantly trying to demonstrate for the world that the Broadway musical could be every bit as legit an art form as opera or anything else. And the discipline of rhyme was one of the ways you did it.

Not long after Maltby worked with Alain Boublil to create English lyrics for *Miss Saigon*, he collaborated with composer Charles Strouse on the score to *Nick & Nora*, the ill-fated 1991 Broadway musical that had a then-record nine-week preview period[10] and closed after nine performances.

Maltby had been approached by James Pentecost and Charles Suisman, who had acquired the rights to *The Thin Man*, the Dashiell Hammett novel that inspired six films, a radio show, and a television series. Nick and Nora Charles, the charming central couple played in the movies by William Powell and Myrna Loy, banter wittily, drink copiously, and solve murder mysteries. In theory, these characters could have been the basis for a great musical. The creative team Pentecost and Suisman were assembling was also looking quite impressive. Pentecost, who had been the stage manager for the original 1983 Broadway production of *La Cage aux Folles*, brought Arthur Laurents, the director of *La Cage*, to the *Nick & Nora* project as director.[11] Also on board were playwright A. R. ("Pete") Gurney as librettist and Charles Strouse as composer.

When Maltby was asked to write lyrics for *Nick & Nora*, he was enthusiastic about the idea. "I thought Pete was a really good writer, and I wanted to work with him," Maltby recalls. Collaborating with Strouse seemed potentially rewarding as well. All three of them had houses in Roxbury, Connecticut, which Maltby also thought was a good sign.

"But you can see what's coming," Maltby says. Laurents, though nominally the director and not the writer, had a lot of very specific ideas for the libretto. After several meetings and a few proposed outlines, Gurney told Laurents outright that it was clear Laurents wanted to write the book himself, and therefore he, Gurney, would bow out of *Nick & Nora*. Suddenly, Maltby found himself attached to a project for which the main attraction was no longer there.

"Charles was fine," he explains, "but Pete was the one I really wanted to work with."[12] In addition, with one person now in charge of the whole project as both director and author, there was no escape from what turned out to be Laurents's tyrannical approach. Maltby summarizes working with Laurents as "a progression of catastrophes," and Strouse largely confirms this in his own memoirs.[13]

Maltby did, however, end up having a very pleasant collaborative relationship with Strouse. "Charles is delightful," Maltby says. "He's wonderful to work with, wonderful to be around. He's positive, he's cheerful, he's energetic, enthusiastic, and appreciative."

He is also, as Maltby vividly puts it, "a tune machine." More specifically:

> He [Strouse] cannot sit down at the piano without playing a fully shaped thirty-two-bar song. He's astonishing that way. And the only problem

was that because it was so fast, he never thought anything was permanent, so if he'd write a melody and I thought that it was really good, I'd go off and write what I thought was a good lyric for it. I'd bring it in, and he'd say, "Oh, yeah, but I changed the melody." And I'd say, "I just worked really hard to write a lyric for that melody, and the [new] one you wrote doesn't have the same rhythms in it." In many cases, I then went off and rewrote the lyric, as opposed to saying, "Stick with the old melody."

At the same time, in Maltby's view, Strouse's limitless facility means that there are very few "home-run" melodies. "He just can't stop turning them out," Maltby marvels. "As a result, it's a little hard to weed out the one that's gonna be spectacular. There are some really good ones, but it's not like he has twelve 'Tomorrows' sitting around."

Maltby's less-than-full-throated enthusiasm notwithstanding, the score for *Nick & Nora* has quite a bit to recommend it. "As Long as You're Happy," a first-act number for the central couple, sounds like a vintage, golden age, smile-inducing charm song—genuinely hummable, with a toe-tapping two-beat, a melodically buoyant bridge, and an energized dance break propelled by its brassy Jonathan Tunick orchestration. "Class," a song in which union president Victor Moisa (played on Broadway by Chris Sarandon) sings touchingly of his feelings for Nora, is a uniquely lovely number. It has some unexpected harmonic left turns that correspond with Victor's coursing emotions and a characteristically Maltbian lyric that juxtaposes insight and cleverness with yearning and poignancy.

"A Busy Night at Lorraine's" is a seven-and-a-half-minute, enjoyably syncopated, metrically surprising number with shifting time signatures and an extended large-scale form that allows it to cover a lot of dramatic ground. Specifically, it involves Nick and Nora replaying the events that took place the night Lorraine, the murder victim, was shot in her home, exploring different scenarios involving various suspects who may or may not have been the actual killer. It's a clever, thoroughly entertaining, and consistently surprising musical sequence and an outstanding example of Maltby's doctrine that the best theater songs have to incorporate action—like reasoning through and getting closer to the solution to a murder mystery.

Lorraine, the murdered (but, for dramatic purposes, frequently resuscitated) movie studio bookkeeper, sings "Men," a biting, tough-talking number that, as Frank Rich memorably put it in his *New York Times* pan of the show, "almost does to its satirical target what Miss Hannigan did to 'Little Girls' in Mr. Strouse's 'Annie.'"[14] As indelibly performed by Faith Prince, Lorraine's sarcasm punctures the balloons of any male egos within hearing range with the opening lines:

You're so big, you're so strong,
You're so mean, you're so tough,
You got guns, you got balls,
You're a man,
Ooh! I'm so scared.

The character of Lorraine, however, takes on additional depth as she goes on to reveal how easily she allowed herself to be duped and seduced by Connors, her charming but married boss, and the pain that ensued when he subsequently dumped her and took up with another woman. It's another number that traverses considerable dramatic territory, ending as Lorraine plots out her revenge fantasy: leaking Connors's latest affair to Louella Parsons.[15]

Despite these standouts from the score, other songs did not fully rise to the occasion, including the musically wan closing number, "Married Life," which sounds more like a Strouse trunk tune than a carefully constructed, character-specific finale. More important, as Rich and others pointed out, *Nick & Nora* had the misfortune of competing with another murder mystery spoof, the award-winning *City of Angels*, which had won six Tony Awards, including Best Musical, Best Score, and Best Book, and was in the second year of its successful run at the Virginia (now the August Wilson) Theatre.[16] As Steven Suskin observes, *Nick & Nora* was, like *City of Angels*, set in Hollywood, with a detective hero solving a movieland murder.[17]

In addition, both audiences and critics found the *Nick & Nora* murder mystery plot convoluted and confusing. Laurents wasn't particularly interested in writing a murder mystery and was late in delivering the second act. When it finally arrived, Maltby and Strouse learned for the first time who the actual murderer was: the Japanese houseboy of the movie star character Tracy Gardner, played by Christine Baranski.

Maltby was incredulous. "Are you saying that the butler did it?" he recalls asking Laurents. "That's going to be laughed off stage." He was right. At the first preview, and consistently thereafter, that was precisely the (unintended) audience reaction at the moment of revelation.

Laurents was convinced that the critics would understand and appreciate the show, even though the preview audiences seemed not to. (This did not prove to be the case.) Maltby says he was reminded of the Charles Addams cartoon that shows an audience at the movies crying and looking stricken, except for Uncle Fester sitting in the middle with a big smile on his face. "That was the show," Maltby recounts. "At every performance, the audience is going [he mimes incomprehension], and Arthur was laughing at all the jokes, enjoying himself, having a wonderful time."

It's hard to believe that Laurents, the legendary author and director of some of the most beloved shows ever written, could have been so unaware of what was taking place around him, both onstage and in the audience. "Isn't it interesting to know that you can be a genius and a fool at the same time?" Maltby observes dryly.

Collaborating on a musical is like a marriage, and going outside the boundaries of a long-term collaboration is a potentially fraught step. Gopnik says that when he first started writing with Shire, he sensed a certain tension with Maltby.

"Richard, I think, at first, to be honest, was a little peeved by the whole thing," Gopnik says. This, he notes, was in spite of the fact that Maltby himself had gone off and worked on *Ain't Misbehavin'*, *Fosse*, *Miss Saigon*, and *Nick & Nora* without Shire, to name a few.[18] "I think there was a little element at first of his thinking, 'I'm the wife and he's the mistress,' because David was excited to be working with a new writer, but [Richard and I] really warmed up, and we have a very deep friendship now, I think."

Maltby, for his part, says he had no issues with Shire and Gopnik working together. "Why not?" he asks rhetorically. "I didn't use up all of [Shire's] time." Regarding Gopnik, he says, "He was scared of me at first and didn't want to hear my opinions or anything, but I think he now knows that I just want him to be great." For Shire's part, his standard (and sincere-sounding) response about either himself or Maltby working with other people has always been "What's good for either one of us individually is good for the team."

PRODUCED BY A CONVICTED FELON

SOUSATZKA

Serving seventeen months in prison gives you plenty of time to think. And foremost on Garth Drabinsky's mind during that grim period was how he would make his comeback after he served his term.

Central to that comeback was his plan to produce a musical adaptation of the 1988 film *Madame Sousatzka*, which in turn had been based on a 1962 novel of the same name by Bernice Rubens. The movie, a star vehicle for Shirley MacLaine, tells the story of Manek, a Bengali immigrant and gifted young piano prodigy. Manek lives with his mother in London and studies with Madame Sousatzka, a highly talented pianist herself, whose stage fright prevented her from having a solo career and who now lives vicariously through her students. The film depicts Manek as torn between two strong-willed women: his mother, who wants to see him launched professionally so he can support them, and Sousatzka, who feels the need to protect Manek from the temptation of making his debut before she deems him sufficiently prepared. In Sousatzka's view, being forced to make her own debut too early was the cause of her professional failure. She also, it is implied, does not want Manek to take off on his own career because then he will no longer be under her influence and control.

Drabinsky, characteristically, had grand ambitions for his stage adaptation of the property. In his reconceived version, now titled simply *Sousatzka*, Manek the piano prodigy became Themba, a young South African refugee, and Black instead of Indian; Sousatzka, a Russian emigrée in the film, was now a Polish Jew who had fled to London to escape the Nazis.

Drabinsky's conception potentially gave the project more historical heft and social relevance. With backstories that included both apartheid and the Holocaust, the musical would grapple with weighty themes absent from

Closer Than Ever. Joshua Rosenblum, Oxford University Press. © Oxford University Press 2024.
DOI: 10.1093/oso/9780197758236.003.0026

both the book and the movie. And Drabinsky wanted Maltby and Shire to write the score.

"We had auditioned for Garth many, many years ago," Shire notes. He and Maltby were among the nine or so teams asked to write songs on spec for Drabinsky's musical adaptation of E. L. Doctorow's novel *Ragtime*. Maltby and Shire didn't end up getting that job; it went instead to composer Stephen Flaherty and lyricist Lynn Ahrens. Nonetheless, they made a strong impression on Drabinsky, which was only reinforced by the producer's positive experience later working with Maltby on *Fosse*.

When the team flew to Toronto to meet with Drabinsky, the impresario, still on supervised parole, was wearing an ankle bracelet. "It was our first time meeting with a producer who was a convicted felon," Shire observes. Maltby, when asked what it's like to be produced by a convicted felon, quips, "It's probably better than being produced by an unconvicted felon."

DS: We read the book, and we saw the movie, and heard his ideas, and had a trip or two to Toronto to discuss it with him, and we kept turning it down. Why did we keep turning it down?

RM: Because it's a ridiculous idea! The movie has almost no plot. If you're just looking at the movie and the book, it's really hard to know why anybody would like this. Garth is a showman in terms of talking you into something, but even he couldn't make it sound like a viable project.

Maltby and Shire finally agreed to do the show mainly on the strength of the team Drabinsky had hired: Adrian Noble, a world-class director and, from 1990 to 2003, the artistic head of the Royal Shakespeare Company; and playwright Craig Lucas, author of the play (and later movie) *Prelude to a Kiss* and the libretto for composer and lyricist Adam Guettel's highly regarded 2005 Broadway musical *The Light in the Piazza*. They also signed on because, in contrast to his approach with *Ragtime*, Drabinsky didn't ask the team to write any songs on spec; instead, he offered them a considerable advance for their work.

Once they agreed to write the score, the writers spent a substantial amount of time in Toronto and threw themselves into the project completely. Drabinsky would eventually put on two workshops and a full production there.

"The more we wrote, the more we saw the possibilities in it," Shire says. In contrast to the movie and the book, Drabinsky's concept provides a conflict between Themba, the young piano prodigy, and his mother. Maltby explains:

South Africa had no tradition of classical music until recently. At the time, it was a wildly musical country, but it was all jazz. So it would not be much of a stretch for the mother to dislike classical music because it's the music of the oppressors. All classical music is *their* music. And so wouldn't God just send her a prodigy in classical music, a complete anomaly. She wants to give him what he needs, but what he needs is training in this thing she hates. But she does it anyway because it's important to him, and she knows that he has a gift. And then, by accident, he finds himself attached to a central European woman, an exile from the Holocaust, who as a pattern always tries to lure the child away from his roots. Madame Sousatzka has subjugated her maternal instincts because she had to give away a child [resulting from her rape by a Nazi officer]. This gets turned into attracting her newest young talent and wooing that child away from the parents. I thought that was a great battle and a wonderful premise for a show.

For Shire's part, *Sousatzka* enabled him to compose in two of his favorite genres. Since Themba is a piano prodigy, the score required a lot of faux classical music, "which I love to write," Shire emphasizes. Additionally, Themba grew up hearing jazz in South Africa, and his father is a jazz pianist; this provided Shire with some great opportunities to juxtapose classical with jazz, another beloved idiom.

In the *Sousatzka* score, Shire incorporates some actual Bach, in addition to writing some imitation "Shirean" Bach. One early sequence has Themba playing the C minor Prelude from Book One of *The Well-Tempered Klavier*, reproducing it perfectly by ear, having heard it only once on the radio. His family is astounded, and his father proceeds to play a jazz variation on the Bach piece. Composed by Shire, it's just a twelve-second riff, but it's thoroughly tantalizing and gives us a taste of more substantial juxtapositions yet to come. (Themba, to his father's great amusement, reacts to his father's improvisation by saying, "No! I like the way Mr. Bach wrote it!")

In the show's culminating number, Themba plays a concert as piano soloist with a symphony orchestra. Shire uses the Bach Piano (originally Harpsichord) Concerto No. 5 in F minor as a springboard for this two-and-a-half-minute sequence, which involves characters in the audience singing vocal lines as they comment on the performance. These interweave contrapuntally with the melodic lines of the concerto.

The real tour de force, however, is the following piece, titled "The Encore," a fully original Shire instrumental composition that manages to layer in all the influences in Themba's life. It starts with a driving, energetic, Bach-like chromatic figure in running sixteenths. After eight bars, percussion kicks in—a shaker beat along with conga drums—and suddenly, we're in the world of African jazz. Countermelodies pile on, leading to three-part counterpoint. When the chorus enters with joyful chanting, the jazz beat takes over, including hand claps on the backbeats. Toward the end, Madame Sousatzka joins Themba at the keyboard to provide additional classical-style pianistic fireworks. After a choral build, a descending volley of major chords brings the piece to a virtuosic conclusion, by which point the listeners have been treated to a pan-stylistic celebration of life, music, and cross-cultural unity.

A song called "Manders' Salon," accompanied by strings only, also invokes the classical style, conjuring a snobbish musical soirée in Paris. Maltby is in top form here with some of his nimblest triple and quadruple rhymes:

Perhaps you can help us
We're talking pianists
And having a squabble
About who is best.

Clearly the victor
Is Sviatoslav Richter
Oh no, Mischa Dichter
Has licked
All the rest.

Let us not squabble
It's clear Artur Schnabel
Will gobble
The playing field
Quick as a wink.

Bollocks, my friend
To hear Brendel
Play Mendel-
ssohn
That puts an end
To it.
What do you think?

For the jazz numbers, Drabinsky referred Shire to South African musicians whose work he felt Shire ought to know, particularly the pianist and composer Dollar Brand, also known as Abdullah Ibrahim. ("He's like the Oscar Peterson of South Africa," Shire says.) Drabinsky also hired Lebo M, the South African composer and producer, to come in and work with the writers, cast, and musicians for a few weeks during rehearsals. Lebo M (born Lebohang Morake) also served as the African music adviser on both the film and Broadway versions of *The Lion King*.

Of Lebo M's contribution, Maltby says, "He came in, we would play the number, and he would say, 'Why don't you play that, why don't you sing this here?' He made the pieces absolutely thrilling." For the most part, it went quite smoothly. "There was only one place where we had a contention," Maltby remembers, "where he was putting in something in such a way that you couldn't understand a lyric I thought was important to hear, and he completely ignored me."

This primarily collegial approach contrasted with Drabinsky, who made it all but impossible for his creative team to do their work. Maltby recalls:

> In rehearsals, I had to go up to Garth and say, "I want to change this line in the lyric to this line. Can I?" And he would let me do it, or he'd say, "No, you don't want to do that." I had to get permission for every comma. "I think that should be a semicolon." "Wait just a minute, let me think about it." It was that kind of thing. And as a result, he did not look at the whole picture and say, "You know, the story doesn't make sense over here, or this isn't very emotional." Which he's really good at.

Librettist Lucas, who expresses his frustration with the process in remarkably similar terms, had been hesitant to meet with Drabinsky about writing *Sousatzka* in the first place.

"I didn't like *Ragtime*," he says, "and I didn't like [*Kiss of the*] *Spider Woman*. I love Kander and Ebb, but I thought that show was misbegotten. And I didn't like *Show Boat*." Lucas rattles off nearly all the Broadway successes Drabinsky is known for. "So I think I should have not said yes. I had serious misgivings about the producerial aesthetic."[1]

Lucas did, however, like Drabinsky's concept of people who, caught up in history and political machinery, had their lives torn apart, one by Nazism and one by apartheid, coming together as exiles to try to make art. "That seemed to me to be a worthy pursuit," he says. "It was Garth's concept, and that really interested me. But I do think it was hubris that I could somehow contend with the indefatigable, insistent, and all-controlling energies of a producer and still function as an artist. I simply wasn't capable of doing it."

Although Drabinsky's large-scale historical vision appealed to him, Lucas still thought it was an intimate story. "I felt this was two people in a room, a teacher and a student," Lucas affirms. "And each had something the other wanted. I was so interested in writing that room, not all the anthems that the producer wanted and all the swelling choruses and generalities about suffering and freedom. It isn't that the choir doesn't need to be preached to, but it has to be done artfully."

Maltby describes the story he and Shire wanted to tell in similar terms, although for them, it was the young piano prodigy torn between *two* uncompromising adult women in his life: his mother and his piano teacher. Even so, Maltby and Shire often felt as if they were at cross purposes with Lucas. According to Shire:

> We would have meetings with [Lucas] where we would talk about a musical conception for a scene and how we thought the music could handle that scene, and he'd say, "That's great, that's great," but then he'd go off and have a meeting with Garth, and [the scene] would come back, and it would go off on all kinds of tangents from what we had talked about, making the number not work. Garth just drove him crazy. Eventually, [Lucas] just left the project, and we never got another book writer.[2]

Drabinsky drove director Noble to distraction as well. Noble's attempts to experiment with the material in rehearsal—a crucial component of any creative process—were repeatedly thwarted by the producer, who would routinely cut him off.

"Garth would say, 'No, no, no, we can't do that,' before he even knew what Adrian was doing," Shire recalls. "So he completely alienated Adrian, who doesn't have a lot of patience."

In one infamous blow-up, Drabinsky even managed to drive away Jonathan Tunick, the show's orchestrator. As reported by Michael Riedel in the *New York Post*:

> Frustrated by Tunick's contractual demands, Drabinsky wheeled on him during a rehearsal and screamed, "Why am I paying you all this money?" The outburst silenced the room until Tunick stood up and said, "Because I'm one of the greatest orchestrators in the history of Broadway." And then he walked out.[3]
>
> Tunick, sources say, was prepared to leave "Sousatzka," and Drabinsky was looking to replace him. But Richard Maltby Jr. and David Shire, who wrote the score, weren't having it. They exercised a clause in their contract giving them approval over the orchestrator. They wanted Tunick and no one else. Drabinsky, sources say, was forced to apologize and meet Tunick's demands.
>
> "Nobody insults Jonathan like that," a source says.[4]

In exchange for Tunick returning to the show, Drabinsky agreed to make a lump-sum cash payment to him, payable in advance. "It actually came to more than if he had paid me double scale, and it was ironclad," Tunick recounts. "And guess who was the only one who didn't get screwed?"

Tunick finished the orchestrations in New York and booked a flight to go back to Toronto for orchestra rehearsals. The night before his flight, he opened his desk drawer to get his passport, and it wasn't there. "I must've left it in the taxi on the way home," he speculates. As a result, he wasn't able to get back to Toronto to hear his orchestrations. "I'm sure everybody thought I was lying, that I was pissed off at Drabinsky and didn't want to come, but it's not true," Tunick insists. "I really lost my passport."

In contrast to the *Big* rehearsal process, wherein songs were excised or replaced once they were rendered irrelevant by the rewritten scenes around them, with *Sousatzka*, the songs were never cut. Nobody, however, thought to question if they were still connected to the show or not.

"The director, the book writer, the producer, the choreographer—none of them gave one minute's thought to what a song was doing in the show," Maltby says. "They would stage a whole number without ever coming and saying, 'Richard, what's the content of this number?' And so, as a result, the staging . . . sometimes it was spectacular, but it would have nothing to do with what was going on."

Once *Sousatzka* was in previews, Drabinsky was oddly complacent. Maltby knew the show was in big trouble, but there was seemingly little he could—or would—do about it.

RM: We had six weeks of previews at the Elgin Theatre [in Toronto]. During that time, we did not have a single production meeting after a performance. The Hal Prince/Stephen Sondheim/Jerry Robbins pattern was, you go to the preview performance, then everyone goes to the bar, and you talk about what worked and didn't work, and you prepare what you're gonna do about it.

JR: Isn't that the whole point of previews?

RM: That would be the point of previews! But Garth sat there. He was mostly happy with the way the show was going because it was his vision of the show. So there was no sense of let's all get together. And I must say, our weakness—*my* weakness—is that I do not in circumstances like that go in and rock the boat. That would have been the time for somebody who was a better human being than I am to go in and say to Adrian and to Craig and to David [Caddick, the music supervisor], "Do you think the show's working? Why isn't it working? Do you think the audience is happy in the end? They don't seem to be. What's going on?"

JR: Isn't that why you became a director?

RM: Yes. It's totally why.

JR: But at this point, you have huge credits, a Best Direction Tony Award, nine Broadway shows under your belt.

RM: And no one is asking me what to do.

JR: How can you restrain yourself?

RM: I can because I am a spineless weakling.

JR: We know that's not true. But it's a droll thing for you to say.

RM: It's not droll. It's actually true. There's a certain point in my mentality at which I become spineless. One of them is any circumstance if I have to put myself up against the de facto director. I have a really hard time taking that on.

JR: I'm surprised the directorial impulse doesn't just kick in.

RM: I am, too.

DS: I'm a little bit the same way. We're too nice. If Andrew Lloyd Webber had been doing *Sousatzka*, at one point, he would've stood up and said, "Hey, guys!" And he would've told them what he wanted, and if they didn't do it, he would've fired them.

The critics largely agreed that *Sousatzka* didn't know what it was supposed to be about or that it was trying to be about too many things. In her *Variety* review, typical of the overall critical response, Toronto stringer Carly Maga wrote that the show "assembles an impressive amount of talent but ends up overwhelmed by plot lines, disparate music styles and dated racial representations." Later she elaborated:

> "Sousatzka" is at best an over-produced, overly-complicated combination of plot, genres, technical elements and emotional tone. At worst, it's an offensive and tone-deaf portrayal of South African politics and people, and so emotionally manipulative that [it] feels as if it's decades behind the times.[5]

The generally negative reviews stunned Drabinsky. "He couldn't figure out why every review didn't jump up and down and say what a masterpiece it was," Shire recalls. "That's how different the show he saw onstage was from the show Richard saw onstage." "He didn't know what they were talking about," Maltby adds. "It took him the longest time to vaguely crack through and realize that it wasn't something else at fault, that it was the actual show."

A postproduction workshop of *Sousatzka* did not improve the piece. Drabinsky cut several songs, turning the show into more of a play with music. "The dialogue was endless," Deniz Cordell says of the workshop. "Twenty minutes would go by before you'd hear a song."

Maltby feels the show is salvageable but that it doesn't currently have a script that is producible.

Victoria Clark, the Tony-winning actress who played Madame Sousatzka in both workshops and the production, has a different take on how to fix the show. She agrees that the scale of the show needs to be smaller ("I'd reduce the cast size by half," she says), but just as important, she believes the young boy playing Themba has to be an actual world-class piano prodigy, someone who can really play the fiendishly difficult virtuoso piano parts Shire wrote into the score for Themba's character.

In the production, these parts were played by Jihwan Kim, the pianist in the orchestra pit ("He was just amazing," Shire recalls) and mimed by Jordan Barrow, the young actor playing Themba, at an onstage baby grand piano. "This is nothing against Jordan," Clark hastens to add. "He was absolutely incredible, a heartbreaking and beautiful actor, and I loved working with him." But Clark says the piano playing has to come first. "That's what's kept him alive," she elaborates, referring to the character of Themba, "and that's his ticket to freedom. Unless [the actor] is an exceptional musician, you don't buy the story. You don't *have* a story."[6]

This, of course, would create enormous casting challenges, but Clark insists it's possible. "You have to do a worldwide search," she says, "but those people are out there. No one thought they'd be able to find Billy Elliot. Well, they found three. That piano concerto at the end—can you imagine a little boy actually sitting down and playing that? It would be the most astonishing thing."

On April 3, 2022, Drabinsky opened his other long-gestating musical, *Paradise Square*, on Broadway. (Maltby, who had been an informal consultant on the show and had seen out-of-town tryouts in both Berkeley, California, and Chicago, said during the run-up, "He does not know what a plot is, and sadly, he's going to open *Paradise Square* and discover the same thing.") The feeling in the Maltby/Shire camp was that if *Paradise Square* proved to be a success, it could rejuvenate the prospects for *Sousatzka*. If *Paradise Square* flopped, it would be Drabinsky's last hurrah, and *Sousatzka* would go permanently into the bottom drawer, possibly to serve as a source of material for what Maltby and Shire until recently referred to as *Revue #3*, the projected sequel to *Starting Here, Starting Now* and *Closer Than Ever*.

Paradise Square opened to mixed reviews, and its sales never achieved critical mass. It was nominated for ten Tony Awards but won only one: Best Actress in a Musical for Joaquina Kalukango, whose roof-raising performance of the show's eleven o'clock number "Let It Burn" on the Tony broadcast was widely praised. However, neither that nor a considerable amount of positive word of mouth was enough to keep the show running. On July 11, Drabinsky announced that the production would shut down at the end of that week after a three-and-a-half-month run. "We wanted to give 'Paradise Square' every chance to succeed, but various challenges proved insurmountable," he said.[7]

The following day, it was reported that two different unions, United Scenic Artists and Actors' Equity, were taking legal action against the show's production company for unpaid union dues, wages, and benefit fund contributions.[8] In addition, Drabinsky was placed on Equity's "Do Not Work" list after cast and crew members of *Paradise Square* sent a letter to their union complaining about "outstanding payments and benefits, and a continued pattern of abuse and neglect that created an unsafe and toxic work environment."[9]

At present, there are no plans for a production of *Sousatzka* on Broadway or anywhere else. However, Maltby and Cordell have edited a live audio recording of the Toronto production. Once it's mastered, the plan is to release it as a cast album, provided the proper clearances from the actors and musicians can be obtained.

27

AMERICA WILL BREAK YOUR HEART

• • •

WATERFALL

During roughly the same time that *Sousatzka* was in development, Maltby and Shire were working on *Waterfall*, another show with cross-cultural implications and another opportunity for Shire to demonstrate his skill at incorporating non-Western genres into an American musical. *Waterfall*, which used a Thai novel as its source material and includes scenes in Tokyo as well as Bangkok, had productions at the Pasadena Playhouse in June 2015 and Seattle's 5th Avenue Theatre in October of the same year. These were billed as "pre-Broadway tryouts," but mixed reviews stalled the progress toward New York.

Waterfall was the brainchild of Thai director Tak Viravan, who earned degrees in theater from Boston College and broadcasting from Boston University before returning to his native Bangkok. There he started producing and directing original musicals based on Thai subjects, historical themes, and novels. After a dozen or so of these, he took the next step, expanding outside his native country and adapting one of his Thai-developed shows as a full-scale American musical with Broadway as its target. Along the way, he got his feet wet by investing in Broadway shows, such as the 2011 revival of *How to Succeed in Business without Really Trying* with Daniel Radcliffe and John Larroquette and the 2012 Gershwin adaptation *Nice Work if You Can Get It*. When it came time to produce one on his own, he contacted American producer Jack Dalgleish, who connected him with Maltby. "Basically, he showed me ten different shows that could be adapted, and I picked *Waterfall*," Maltby says. *Waterfall* was a full-fledged romance and, unlike some of the others, didn't particularly depend on any knowledge of Thai history.

Closer Than Ever. Joshua Rosenblum, Oxford University Press. © Oxford University Press 2024.
DOI: 10.1093/oso/9780197758236.003.0027

Waterfall is based on the 1937 novel *Behind the Painting* (or *Khang Lang Phap* in Thai) by Siburapha, the pen name for Kulap Saipradit, one of the preeminent Thai writers of his time ("The Nicholas Sparks of Bangkok," as Shire puts it). The book was adapted for film twice, in 1985 and 2001. The original Thai musical adaptation, with music by Nann Sarawut and lyrics by Wichien Tantipimolpan, was also titled *Behind the Painting* and debuted in 2008 in Bangkok. The book and the musical tell the story of Noppon, a young Thai man studying abroad in Japan, where he meets an aristocratic Thai woman, newly married to a family acquaintance. They develop strong feelings for each other, but the idea of having an affair is so culturally forbidden that she can only admit she loved him decades later when she's on her deathbed.

To adapt the Thai musical *Behind the Painting* as the show that would become *Waterfall*, Maltby decided the wife should be American in order to give the show a connection to American audiences. Thus, the wife of Chao Khun, Thailand's ambassador to Japan, is an American painter, and Noppon, who is Chao Khun's attaché in the new musical adaptation, is assigned to escort the ambassador's wife while her husband is stationed in Tokyo.

Making the wife an American created additional expanded possibilities, as Maltby described in an interview with the *Seattle Times*. "We thought if we made the woman the American wife of a Thai diplomat, it opened the story to the huge political and cultural changes going on between the two world wars. It was a time when American culture, our movies and songs and dances, were sweeping Japan, before the hard-liners who came into power banned American influences."[1]

Maltby felt that the score to the original Thai version of the show would have to be recomposed, not just translated. Making the ambassador's wife an American woman necessitated a considerable rewrite. "So I brought in David—you know, what the heck," Maltby quips.

In the same *Seattle Times* interview, Viravan gave a good overview of the guiding philosophy behind the adaptation. "We are taking a risk," he explained. "We're trying to combine the best of America, Thailand and Japan in one piece that's respectful to all cultures, and have it make sense to both American and Asian audiences."[2]

Now that the show had Thai, Japanese, and American elements, it required considerable cross-cultural musical finessing. "At first, we were going to keep some of the original score and just add some other things, but as it worked out, we only kept one song," Maltby recalls. "And that one we kind of half rewrote," Shire adds.[3]

Shire, in describing his approach to creating a new score for *Waterfall*, says, "I just do a lot of research, which, thank God, is so easy now, with YouTube and Wikipedia. I used to have to go to dusty music libraries and take out these books that no one had taken out for years just to learn what different scales were. Now it's all at my fingertips."

There's a tendency among Westerners to homogenize all Asian music into one category. Shire wanted to avoid this. He explains:

> Part of [the show] is set in Bangkok, part of it's in Japan. So there were two types of Asian music, and I had no idea what the distinction was. It turns out the Thai scale is the basic pentatonic scale that we all know, that goes C-D-E-G-A [in the key of C]. I was able to find enough ways to make that interesting, although it took some doing. But luckily, when I started working on the Japanese music and looked at the Japanese scales, they are very interesting, because there are many of them, and they're chromatic. They have weird intervals, like the Jewish scale has the lowered second.

Shire makes use of the basic pentatonic scale in the opening song, "This Is My Life," as Noppon, the young Thai student, sings of his ambitions. Both the piano and the vocal line use only the notes D-E-F♯-A-B, which is the pentatonic scale based in the key of D. Interestingly, Noppon is singing about wanting to break out of the confines of his Thai life and be more like the men in America he has read about, who can make history with the work they do. However, since he has never met any Americans or been to America, he can still only sing in the pentatonic Thai mode.

By contrast, when Katherine, the American painter and soon-to-be wife of the Thai ambassador, enters to sing her verse, her melody is derived from the Western diatonic or major scale—the standard vernacular for American musicals.

Soon thereafter, in the duet number "One Day," as Noppon escorts Katherine home from a formal event where her ambassador husband has been detained for a meeting, Noppon responds to Katherine's opening verse by singing in the major mode, just as she has. Leaving the Thai pentatonic scale behind indicates his excitement upon meeting an American for the first time, particularly one who is expressing the same kind of yearnings he has experienced and for whom he is developing romantic feelings.

As Shire indicated in the quotation above, Japanese pentatonic scales come in wider and more colorful varieties than the Thai pentatonic scale. He collected several examples as part of his research, all variants of the Hirajōshi scale, as seen in example 27.1.

Example 27.1. Japanese pentatonic scale variants

In the Japanese foreign minister's song "I Like Americans," which progresses from friendly and solicitous to openly threatening, both melody and accompaniment are clearly derived from the first of the Japanese pentatonic scales shown in example 27.1, with its prominent raised fourth. Other numbers similarly use the other two scales shown in the example as their melodic basis.

In an Act II sequence titled "Gone Pt. 2," which switches between Thai and Japanese locales in the run-up to (spoiler alert) Chao Khun's surprise assassination in Bangkok, Shire alternates between the respective modes of the two different countries, effectively signaling where the action is taking place at any given moment. This isn't merely an academic exercise; the different styles of music—Thai, Japanese, and American—serve throughout the show to differentiate the characters and dramatize the cultural clashes.

Shire was also interested in authenticity when it came to the actual instruments used. Research involved a trip to Thailand. "Tak took us to a Bangkok music school that had all those instruments there," says Shire. "The main one is the ranat ek, which is that semicircular xylophone-like instrument. Their scales involve quarter-tones, so it's impossible to write music for the Western ear and still make it completely authentic, but we got an equivalent on a synthesizer." Orchestrator Jonathan Tunick ended up supplementing the digital sounds from the keyboard with a good old-fashioned Western xylophone. "There is great virtuosity on [the ranat ek], and we listened to quite a bit of that," Tunick says. "It doesn't translate into anything that esoteric in real life, but it's interesting. We just used a xylophone, and it comes out just fine."

Digital samples of Thai instruments that could be played on synthesizer came with the help of Sarawut, the composer of the original Thai score for the first musical adaptation, who was on hand as a consultant for the Thai and Japanese musical styles. It would not have been unreasonable for Sarawut to be resentful over having almost his entire score thrown out, but that was apparently not the case. "He was completely on it," Maltby says about Sarawut's participation. "I guess he accepted that his score wasn't useful for Broadway. If he had dark thoughts, we never saw them. An American composer would've hit the ceiling," he observes. "He just didn't have that kind of ego," Shire adds. "He was a great resource, and we became good friends."

Shire says that in the end, although authenticity and respect for other cultures is important, a composer's own instinct is the ultimate guide. As he puts it:

> I tried to be authentic, but it's still an Americanization—it's written for American ears, as opposed to totally authentic. Like when I did movies and had to study an ethnic style, I did a lot of research, and then I put it aside and just used my own instincts and my knowledge of the basic patterns and instruments, the basic parameters of the culture, harmonically and melodically.

To play the young Thai student, Viravan enlisted Bie Sukrit, who was literally a rock star in Thailand after winning the reality show *The Star*, that country's equivalent of *American Idol*. (Viravan, in fact, was the creator and producer of *The Star*.) The original Thai musical adaptation had been written for Sukrit. As Shire put it in an interview, "You walk down the street with him and the girls go crazy."[4] Pasadena, where the American adaptation had its premiere, has a large Thai population, and part of the Pasadena Playhouse's decision to produce the show was motivated by a desire to bring more of those locals into the theater. It worked—the Thai community showed up in droves.

Sukrit, unfortunately, spoke no English and had to learn the part entirely by rote, which he did—quite convincingly. It meant, however, that he couldn't interact genuinely with Emily Padgett, the actress playing the diplomat's wife. Another challenge for the American actors was Viravan's approach to directing. "In Thailand, the actors are used to just doing what they're told," Maltby explains. "'Say your line, turn, go over there to the door, turn back, say your line, and leave.' And they fill it. That's not how American actors work. You tell them what to do, and the actor says, 'Why?'"[5]

Padgett, a theater pro with six Broadway credits to her name, made the most of a challenging situation, even though she couldn't truly communicate with either her director or her costar. On a video of the Pasadena production, she gives a nuanced, beautifully sung performance and at least appears to interact convincingly with Sukrit. According to Maltby, however, "Emily couldn't wait to get on the plane and get back to New York." She did not return for the Seattle production of the show later that year.

Several reviews for *Waterfall*'s Pasadena premiere were enthusiastic and positive. *Variety*, however, in a review that recalls certain criticisms of *Sousatzka*, felt the show was trying to take on too large an agenda:

> "Waterfall," the new cross-cultural, lushly romantic tuner at the Pasadena Playhouse, has admirable ambition, visual splendor and patchy dramaturgy. Working from a Thai source novel, stage veterans Richard Maltby Jr. (words) and David Shire (music) seek to explore cultural identity in personal and political contexts, set against a complex historical backdrop. Which is all too tall an order at this stage of the show's development. Characterizations and plotlines will need to be firmed up if the next stop, Seattle's 5th Avenue Theatre in October, is to be followed by a hoped-for Broadway success.[6]

The creative team agreed that the show needed rewrites, and considerable work was done for the show's next outing, in Seattle. But the revision process, as always, was tricky. Maltby outlines it:

> Some of the revisions we made along the way I didn't think were very good. You have to be really careful about what you change. One thing I've learned is that you must never take something out just because you don't like it—the idea that I hate that moment, so let's cut it. But maybe that moment, even though it's not good, is connecting something from earlier into something later. If you're gonna take something out, you have to reconceive everything around it to make sure that you haven't lost something. I thought we were less clear in Seattle than in Pasadena.

Reviews of the Seattle production at 5th Avenue Theatre were indeed more consistently negative. Critic Misha Berson of the *Seattle Times*, who had seen the show previously in Pasadena, was able to make the following comparison:

> The "Waterfall" creators have added more political context to the show since its world premiere last summer at Pasadena Playhouse. This highly eventful era in Asian geopolitics, as World War II looms on the horizon, holds more dramatic promise than the vapid, unconvincing romance.
>
> But the periodic news bulletins don't add much historical depth. And the more topical songs are mainly blunt declarations and mockeries of national identity.

For material this familiar, more developed characters, less clunky dialogue ("I am an artist in my soul!") and a much fresher exploration of cultural identity and relations are simply must-haves.[7]

Further development of *Waterfall* was put on hold for work on *Sousatzka* in Toronto. Maltby, Shire, and Viravan returned to work on the show in the run-up to a New York reading of a revised version, at that point retitled *Dancers at a Waterfall*, in May 2019.

In Seattle, Act I of the show had ended with a sumptuous romantic duet for Noppon and Katherine, titled "No One Will Know." Several reviews mentioned it as a standout number. Tunick agreed:

I remember David coming up with a new song, a new finale to Act I. He emailed it to me and said, "Here's the new song," and I read it through, and I thought, "Wow." I called him. I said, "You guys have really hit it out of the ballpark." I don't talk like that all the time, but it was really true. It hit every point, and the lyrics had a flow, and it touched on inner feelings and was technically perfect. Every line was delicious, and the music, liquid and beautiful and colorful and organic. Just satisfying on every level.

"No One Will Know" was cut from the show after Seattle.

When Maltby and Shire were reminded in an interview that this is Tunick's favorite number from the show, the following dialogue ensued:

DS: You know about songs when the plot changes. They become orphaned.
RM: It's funny with a song you just really love, and you think it's great, and then the scene changes out from under it, and it no longer is needed, and it becomes this thing you can't wait to get rid of.
JR: Do you feel that way about that song?
RM: I actually liked it, but it was for a different scene.
JR: So Act I doesn't end in the waterfall grotto anymore?
RM: It does, but the dynamic between the two of them is entirely different.
JR: So which is more important, the scene or the song?
RM: The scene, always, is more important.
JR: Aren't scenes sometimes rewritten to preserve a great song?
RM: I wonder whether I can think of an example of a scene that was rewritten to preserve a great song.
JR: There must be.
RM: There are many examples of songs that were cut.
DS: "The Man I Love" was cut from two shows before it finally found a home.

"No One Will Know" was replaced for the reading by another song from elsewhere in the show, "America Will Break Your Heart." As rewritten for Katherine, it carries the unspoken but unmistakable double meaning that not only will America break your heart, but I, Katherine, will break your heart if you insist on loving me, because I am engaged to another man. In performance, the song packed a powerful punch as the Act I curtain number, even if it didn't soar to quite the same musical heights as its predecessor in that slot.[8]

In May 2022, Maltby, Shire, Viravan, and musical director Brad Haak[9] presented another workshop of the show, this time with Sierra Boggess as Katherine[10] and Josh Dela Cruz, the host of Nickelodeon's *Blue's Clues* reboot, as Noppon. Even in this bare-bones mounting, with actors at music stands and piano accompaniment, it was apparent how deeply moving and dramatically powerful the show is. At the end, after Katherine has enforced a separation between herself and Noppon, both have married other people, and Noppon has gone on to become a successful, high-ranking Thai official, Katherine and Noppon are reunited for one night together after having spent many years apart. Here they at last openly admit their love for each other. When Katherine dies shortly after this, Noppon has the following lines:

> I have become an important person. I am doing important things. But that is not why my life will matter. My life matters because once, ridiculously, uselessly, I loved Katherine Bingham. And she loved me. Loving her made me the equal of any creature in the universe.

This universal sentiment—that we become the best version of ourselves when we truly and deeply love another person—is the heart of the show and has a powerful impact.

The newly reworked *Dancers at a Waterfall* had been slated (after a Covid postponement) for a production at the Philadelphia Theatre Company as part of the 2023–2024 season. However, because of a change in artistic leadership at the theater, the show was removed from the roster.

In lieu of the canceled Philadelphia production, Viravan scheduled a large-scale, Broadway-sized tryout of the show's new incarnation for three weeks of performances in Bangkok in September 2023, with American principal cast members (including Dela Cruz) joined by English star Danielle Hope as Katherine plus authentic Thai dancers and musicians. Prior to this crucial outing, Maltby and Viravan reworked the script yet again, and playwright Karen Hartman, who was brought in by Maltby as a co-librettist after the Seattle production, worked closely with him throughout the Bangkok rehearsal process as well. The new concept dictated that the show would use dancers all the way through. In Maltby's description, "It'll be as if they're telling the whole story like a formal dance of the Royal Bangkok Ballet." The plan was to fly theatrical angels and investor types over to Bangkok for the occasion, with an eye toward funding a Broadway production.

The opulent Bangkok version of the show, once again titled *Waterfall*, exceeded the artistic expectations of the show's creators and production team. "It was really kind of great," says Deniz Cordell, who served on the music staff along with music supervisor Dale Rieling, conductor Phatcharapong ("Bom") Chantapoon, and new orchestrator Apisit ("Jack") Wongchoti. Cordell recalls sitting next to a woman in the audience at one of the last preview performances. "For the last twenty-five minutes, she was sobbing uncontrollably," he relates. "She was shoving her scarf in her mouth to prevent herself from bawling. Those were the responses I saw every night—people leaving with tears in their eyes."

Rieling concurs: "The show was in the best shape it's ever been in. It absolutely works, and the audience is with it the whole time. It's especially amazing to experience that in a place where English is the second language."[11] The production was done with Thai supertitles, but Rieling says the timing of the responses indicated that the audience was listening to the English text rather than reading the translations.

"It was very exciting, and now the process of moving on is whatever it always is," Maltby observes. "People have to say yes, they have to go back and find out what money they have and what the theater availability is. Tak in particular wants it, and he's got the resources to make it happen," he concludes.

Interested parties from London, Toronto, Seoul, and Tokyo attended the show in Bangkok, and as of this writing, a number of producing organizations have shown enthusiasm, including several from the United Kingdom. The possibility of an Asian touring company is also under discussion. No New York producers made the trip to Thailand, but Viravan recorded a high-quality, seven-camera video of the show, which had two New York screenings in November 2023, two months after the Bangkok production. A stunning capture of one of the lavish performances, the video reinforces *Waterfall*'s status as Maltby and Shire's most emotionally wide-ranging, viscerally powerful work.[12]

POSTPARTUM

• • •

BABY REVIVAL

As *Baby* was headed toward its Broadway opening in 1983, Maltby and Shire were concerned that gay men, traditionally a reliable component of the Broadway audience demographic, would not be interested in the show. This, of course, was long before gay marriage was legalized and when gay adoption was comparatively rare. In *Not since Carrie: Forty Years of Broadway Flops*,[1] Ken Mandelbaum describes *Baby* as "utterly heterosexual."[2] It was also, at least in its initial outing, utterly white.

Maltby and Shire were eager to address the lack of racial diversity in future productions of the show. In 2003, the Roundabout Theatre Company put on a workshop as a tryout for a planned revival of *Baby* that never materialized. Todd Haimes, artistic director of the Roundabout, told Maltby that they didn't allow authors to also direct their productions, so Maltby tapped Charles Randolph-Wright to direct. Randolph-Wright had been a member of the original Broadway cast of *Dreamgirls* and has since gained acclaim as the director of the 2013 Broadway hit *Motown: The Musical*. He was a big fan of the show and was eager, as Victoria Clark put it, to "take *Baby* and get less white white white." The result was a half-Black, half-white cast that included Anika Noni Rose and Chad Kimball as Lizzie and Danny; LaChanze and Norm Lewis as Pam and Nick; and Clark and John Dossett as Arlene and Alan. "I thought it was fantastic," Clark enthuses. "They made some really smart updates. It became much more accessible and open. And all of those people brought their A game. It was an exciting workshop to be a part of."

When the Roundabout was unable to mount a full production of *Baby* as part of its regular season, the new version ended up at the Paper Mill Playhouse in Milburn, New Jersey. Mark Hoebee, the producing artistic

Closer Than Ever. Joshua Rosenblum, Oxford University Press. © Oxford University Press 2024.
DOI: 10.1093/oso/9780197758236.003.0028

director of Paper Mill, had choreographed the first post-Broadway production of *Baby* at the Marriott Theatre in Lincolnshire, Illinois (with musical direction by Kevin Stites, who began his long Maltby/Shire affiliation on that production) and was eager to direct the show at Paper Mill, whose artistic staff he had joined in 2000. A few casting changes were necessary due to the unavailability of Rose, Clark, and Dossett, but the racial mix stayed the same: Moeisha McGill played Lizzie; Broadway veterans Michael Rupert and Carolee Carmello played Alan and Arlene, the older couple. Local reviews were overwhelmingly positive, and, incidentally, none mentioned the mixed-race casting, which, happily, seemed perfectly natural by 2004. Interestingly, one very positive review of the production presciently anticipated the still-to-be-addressed issue of the show's heterosexual-only couplings by writing: "Whatever plot changes have been implemented, 'Baby' might have benefited by being more topical with the substitution of a same-sex partnership."[3]

The current published version of the *Baby* script that is rentable for production purposes incorporates changes that were made for the Paper Mill production, which, according to the Author's Note, allows for "the possibility of non-traditional or racially mixed casting."[4] It goes on to say that a then-recent all-African-American production had "added a universality to the show that the authors wish to encourage." The note continues:

> In other productions, Lizzie has been Hispanic or Japanese-American, to equally satisfying effect. Such casting can simply be a given of the production—no overt references to an ethnic heritage need to be added. (Directors should, however, feel free to adjust topical references if they wish. A few alternatives are offered.)[5]

The next step in *Baby*'s evolution was to make it, as Clark might have put it, less straight straight straight. This is where Out of the Box Theatrics, an off-Broadway not-for-profit company, entered the picture. Out of the Box, as its website puts it, is committed to "lifting the voices of marginalized communities through the stories it tells" and allowing audiences "to experience work from a fresh perspective in site-specific locations." In December 2019, it mounted a version of *Baby* in which Pam and Nick (now Nicki) are a same-sex female couple.

"This was not our concept," Shire explains. "This group called us and said they had done a version of *Baby* with a lesbian couple in the middle. They invited us to see it. It was the strangest thing—all they did was change the pronouns. We said, 'There are writing issues involved. You can't just change all the hims to hers and think the story's going to work!'"

Maltby elaborates: "The fertility issues just didn't follow. [In the original], Nick has to keep trying to inseminate her. And she feels that she's not feminine enough, and then it turns out that it's his problem with weak sperm, and she's perfectly healthy. That all seems very gender-specific. It doesn't work with two women. It just doesn't make sense."

Out of the Box was hoping to revive its production of *Baby* in 2020, but those plans, like so many, were derailed by the Covid-19 pandemic. In November 2021, however, as live performances were once again taking place, the production had a return engagement, this time with a considerably reworked script by Maltby.

In revisiting *Baby*, Maltby realized that bringing the show into the twenty-first century would involve substantial overhauling. As he put it in an interview for Broadwayworld.com, "It's hard to imagine, but we wrote the show in 1983, and since then just about every social issue connected with the show has changed utterly. Gender, sexuality, language, fertility, marriage norms, same-sex marriage and adoption, women having babies after forty—everything has changed."[6]

Maltby's new book for *Baby* made accommodations not only for the gay female couple but also for the fact that the actress playing Lizzie—Elizabeth Flemming, who is the founder and producing artistic director of Out of the Box—is legally blind, and the actor playing Danny—Johnny Link—is hearing-impaired. This is laid out explicitly in the second scene:

Danny: So, I'm looking across the room and I'm seeing this amazing girl – woman! She walks around, she looks at you, she's a writer! She's a powerhouse. And it turns out, she's LEGALLY BLIND! And you would never know it!

Lizzie: I never want anyone to feel sorry for me.

Maltby even mines Danny's condition for humor:

Danny: And I'm thinking, who is this person? Because I have just decided to switch—to a *music* major!—and I am . . . deaf![7]

Then, toward the end, they have a particularly moving exchange, relating to the specific challenges that will face them as parents:

Lizzie: Is that what we are now, just two more boring old parents, like every boring old parent on the face of the earth?

Danny: No, we're blind and deaf parents who are going to spend every waking hour making life safe for our kids. We're special.

Both Flemming and Link performed so seamlessly in Out of the Box's *Baby* that the audience might not have been aware of their respective challenges. Shire, in fact, says the two actors played it so well that some audience members thought that even though the characters were explicitly deaf and blind in the script, the actors themselves might not have been. Link, for his part, sang the role gorgeously and amazingly well in tune. As for Flemming, the only hint of her visual challenges came when other cast members held her hand to escort her offstage during blackouts. Both subtly used sign language to communicate with each other in their dialogue scenes, in addition to speaking with perfect clarity.

The scenes for the middle couple—now both female—needed to be rewritten almost in their entirety. Shire felt this resulted in the loss of some of the humor surrounding the heterosexual problem of the man not being able get the job done, including the doctor's line, "You're shooting blanks,"[8] which always received big laughs in the original version. Maltby, however, was able to find humor elsewhere, particularly in his rewrite of Pam and Nicki's verse in the opening number, "We Start Today," in which they address the ongoing artificial insemination process:

Nicki: Babies don't just trot along.
Doctors warned us: must be strong.
Pam: If in five months nothing clicks?
Nicki: (*turns, holding up a Dixie cup and a tube*) We just start month number six.
Both: What a journey, what a ride!
Pam: How much fun can one girl handle?
Nicki: (*approaches Pam, brandishing the tube*) Look—a turkey baster's coming your way.
Pam: *(spoken)* Yes! Yes! Bring it on!
Both: *(sung)* We start today!

There are also opportunities for different kinds of dramatic tension, including the following heated exchange in the new second act:

Pam: You have NO IDEA what I am going through.
Nicki: No, I don't!! And if I had gone first, none of us would know it! Because we'd have a baby by now. (*She is shocked by what just came out of her mouth*) I should not have said that.

The song "Romance," which originally tracked Pam and Nick's attempts to follow very specific ovulation-timed insemination rituals, as rigorously prescribed by a fertility guidebook ("On the ninth, eleventh, thirteenth, fifteenth and seventeenth . . ."), also had to be substantially rewritten. Despite Maltby's admirable relyricizing efforts, the new "Romance" is not one of the show's more successful adaptations. Far better is "At Night She Comes Home to Me," which emerges as a much more suitable number for the current cultural climate once it is stripped of its original patriarchal implications and becomes a number for one woman singing about another woman.

In the Out of the Box production, Pam was played by Danielle Summons, who is Black, and Nicki by Jamila Sabares-Klemm, who is Filipino American. There is only an occasional reference in the script to their racial identities. In a discussion with their doctor about the sperm donor, Pam says, "We picked the trumpet-playing hockey star with a PhD, who says he looks a little like Idris Elba." Elsewhere, Pam, in a moment of frustration, refers to "all those smarmy, smiling, Purell-smelling white-ass nurses."

The older couple is different in the rewrite as well but in a subtler way. Arlene, played by Broadway veteran Julia Murney, and Alan (Robert H. Fowler) are a mixed-race couple, but this seems almost incidental. More interesting is the fact that Arlene is forty-nine in this version, whereas in the original Broadway production, she was in her early forties.[9] Fertility issues are quite different for a woman pushing fifty from what they are for one just over forty, and the stakes for Arlene indeed seem higher in the new version.

Updating *Baby* also seemed to merit a nod to freedom of gender expression, which is efficiently accomplished in the following exchange, as Nicki and Pam speculate about the baby they're trying to conceive:

Nicki: To begin with, she might be a "he."
Pam: Or a them. They can make up their own pronouns. I DO NOT CARE! I WILL TAKE WHATEVER WE GET!

Other scattered contemporary references slipped into the script comfortably. At one point, we hear Lizzie say, "Siri, call Danny." And in "I Want It All," when Lizzie sings "The thing that I did was to make myself a list," she's holding her iPad. Elsewhere in that same number, Maltby took the opportunity to update some of the iconic women whom Lizzie, Pam, and Arlene cite as worthy of emulating: "I want to be Gloria Steinem, Janis Joplin, Annie Hall" is updated as "I want to be Michelle Obama, Nora Ephron, Annie Hall." (Annie Hall, still resonant, remains in place so she can rhyme with "I want it *all*" in the last line of the chorus, as do Lucille Ball and Lauren Bacall in other stanzas.) Additionally, Ruth Bader Ginsburg replaces Mother Teresa, and

"I want to be Katharine Hepburn, Connie Chung, Madame de Staël" is rewritten as "I want to be Serena Williams,[10] Meryl Streep, Madame de Staël."[11] The three Donnas remain intact ("I want to be Donna McKechnie, Donna Summer, Donna Reed"), but of the three original Margarets ("Margaret Sanger, Marg'ret Thatcher, Marg'ret Mead"), Thatcher gets replaced by Atwood.

It's also noteworthy that the line "I want a quiet simple life and some glory / And Steven Spielberg filming my first story" still has cultural resonance nearly forty years later and did not need updating.

None of the new aspects of the show—a lesbian couple, a blind Lizzie, a deaf Danny, two mixed-race couples, and an older Arlene—made it seem as if *Baby* was trying too hard to be hip or accommodating. Rather, it seemed as if the show successfully reflected its twenty-first-century world. One millennial leaving the theater was overheard saying that it seemed like a fully contemporary musical.

Broadway producer and general manager Joey Parnes agrees. "I think the update works," he says. "I think it doesn't feel like an old show at all." This is a tribute to the durability of the songs, which, aside from "Romance," "At Night She Comes Home to Me," and a few of the names in "I Want It All," have remained largely intact.

The site-specific production took place at Theatrelab on West 36th Street, which is a loft, as opposed to an actual theater. It had minimal set pieces and a capacity of not more than sixty, with seats on opposite sides of the room and the action in the middle. The orchestra, of necessity, was stripped down to a mere four pieces—piano, bass, drums, and cello—but the instrumentation did the score full justice. In fact, having only the rhythm-section-based quartet lent the songs a timeless element, whereas Jonathan Tunick's spectacular original orchestrations for twenty pieces are inevitably a reflection of their era and would have pulled the show right back into the '80s.

For Maltby, this newly updated *Baby* is still a work in progress. His daughter Emily, a director and choreographer, has assured him that in today's world, two college sophomores would never decide to have a baby together. (Maltby quips that he feels much closer to understanding the same-sex female couple than he does to understanding today's college students.) However, as of this writing, the Supreme Court's shocking reversal of *Roe v. Wade* forces a rethinking of the choice issue for both Lizzie and Arlene. Although the song "Patterns" doesn't explicitly mention abortion (Sybille Pearson's original objections to the number notwithstanding), in the new script, the following exchange takes place, while Lizzie is visiting Arlene in the hospital after Arlene's miscarriage:

Lizzie: Given the risk, did you ever consider . . .?
Arlene: It was something that I chose not to do. And then I tricked myself into thinking that meant nothing could go wrong.

The implication that Arlene thought about ending her pregnancy is clear, but in a world without *Roe*, the subject is considerably more fraught.

To the surprise and delight of everyone involved, Out of the Box's *Baby* received a 2022 Drama Desk nomination for Outstanding Revival of a Musical, knocking out such Broadway behemoths as *The Music Man* and *Funny Girl*, which were eligible in the same category but weren't nominated.[12] The company also went into the studio on May 5, 2022, to make *Baby: The New Off-Broadway Cast Recording*, which was released by Yellow Sound Label on streaming and digital platforms on February 14, 2023. "I can't believe how good it is," Maltby enthuses, lauding the achievement of the cast, musicians, music supervisor Geoffrey Ko, and particularly album producer Michael Croiter. As hoped, the release of the new *Baby* studio recording is spurring additional productions of the show's new version.

OH, THAT'S WHAT THOSE SONGS WERE ABOUT!

• • •

Jim Morgan, the longtime producing artistic director of the York Theatre Company, first met Maltby in 1984, at the opening night of the York's revival of Stephen Sondheim and John Weidman's *Pacific Overtures* when it transferred to the Promenade Theatre. Morgan, at the time, was York's in-house set designer and right-hand man to York's founder and then producing director Janet Hayes Walker. Maltby came up to Morgan at the opening-night party, told Morgan he loved his work, and asked if he would design a new show Maltby was directing at the Manhattan Theatre Club. The show was *Hang on to the Good Times*, a revue of songs by Gretchen Cryer and Nancy Ford, original cast members of *Grand Tour* back at Yale and the authors of the off-Broadway hit *I'm Getting My Act Together and Taking It on the Road*, which opened at the Public Theater in 1978 and ran for nearly three years. A little in awe of Maltby, who at that point was already well known for *Starting Here, Starting Now*, *Baby*, and *Ain't Misbehavin'*, Morgan eagerly accepted the offer.

Morgan and Maltby remained friends, and after Morgan took over the artistic leadership of the York in 1997 upon Walker's passing, there were several discussions over the years about possible Maltby/Shire projects at the theater. Eventually, a remarkably fruitful artistic partnership emerged, leading to an ongoing track record of successful productions. The first of these was the well-received revival of *Closer Than Ever* in 2012.

Closer Than Ever's path to the York began with producer Neil Berg, who, in conjunction with his producing partner Adam Friedson, spearheaded a two-week run of the show, billed as a twentieth-anniversary production, at the Queens Theatre (then called Queens Theatre in the Park) at Flushing Meadows Corona Park in April 2010. The cast included Lynne Wintersteller and Sally Mayes from the original 1989 company, plus newcomers to the show George Dvorsky and Sal Viviano, taking over the parts that had been

Closer Than Ever. Joshua Rosenblum, Oxford University Press. © Oxford University Press 2024.
DOI: 10.1093/oso/9780197758236.003.0029

originated by Richard Muenz and Brent Barrett, who were both unavailable.[1] The production also included original musical director Patrick Brady on piano, plus original bassist Bob Renino, who by then had been married to Mayes for years. A month later, the production made a three-week stop at the Bristol Riverside Theatre in Bristol, Pennsylvania. In the meantime, Maltby had been discussing the show with Morgan. "The idea was always that we would come in and do it at the York if we could raise enough money," Maltby says. That happened two years later.

Mayes and Wintersteller passed on doing the show at the York. Wintersteller in particular felt that it was time to get someone younger to sing her *Closer Than Ever* songs, although, according to Morgan, Maltby disagreed and pressed her to stay with the show. "Richard really didn't think anyone could sing the women's parts except Lynn and Sally," Morgan says.

Andrew Gerle, who took over as pianist and musical director for the York Theatre run of *Closer Than Ever* when Brady became unavailable, recalls, "Richard was obviously very attached to Sally and Lynn because they were the originals, and it was all he had ever heard, and he was very worried that they could never be replicated, vocally and acting-wise, and their humor and humanity—all these things. For him, it was a little scary."

Once it sank in for Maltby that Mayes and Wintersteller were not going to appear in the York's *Closer Than Ever* ("It took a long time to realize they actually didn't want to come back," he says), he brought in Christiane Noll and Jenn Colella. Both were *Take Flight* alumnae—Colella having played the role of Amelia Earhart in the McCarter Theatre production and Noll having originated the same part in the show's first workshop at the O'Neill Center in 2001. About the casting, Gerle enthuses:

> Christiane and Jenn are absolutely spectacular, top of the list. They can both sing anything, and they're great musicians and both ready to play. And both of them put so much work in. I remember they came to their first rehearsal, and I was ready to teach the notes. Not only did they know all their notes, they had already made amazing choices, fully formed choices, with these complicated songs. And I was, like, this is going to be fun! I don't have to do anything. We can just continue to play and refine.

Maltby was thrilled. "Christiane and Jenn were perfect casting," he admits, "and they both are really subtle actors, so they really got it, and they brought out the best of George and Sal."

"Richard discovered what we all discover—that when you get great performers, they're gonna find even more levels, more layers," Gerle says. "That's exactly what Jenn and Christiane did. They brought so much smarts and humanity and kept asking questions and kept digging deeper. And Richard and David discovered new things about these songs that they'd known for twenty years."

Originally scheduled for a six-week run, the production ran for five months—a record length for a continuous York Theatre run. The *New York Times*, which had been decidedly unenthusiastic about the original *Closer Than Ever* (Stephen Holden's raves about the embryonic *Next Time, Now!* and the subsequent original cast recording notwithstanding), now found a lot to like in the show:

> Musical theater has courted young audiences relentlessly in the 23 years since "Closer Than Ever" opened off-Broadway. But among the abundant charms of this pocket-size 1989 revue, now getting a polished revival by the York Theater Company, is its assertion that folks with a few miles on the odometer also have stuff to sing about. More stuff, in fact.[2]

Other reviews were even more gushing. In the *New York Post*, Michael Riedel wrote:

> I'm happy to report that "Closer Than Ever" doesn't show its age at all. I saw the original production when I was fresh out of college and writing about theater for a small magazine. I loved Shire's bright (and deceptively simple) melodies and Maltby's sophisticated lyrics.
>
> What I missed was the sadness beneath the polish.
>
> But what 21-year-old is going to be unsettled by a batch of songs about hitting middle age and realizing you're not going to live forever?
>
> Now that I'm—well, you can do the math—"Closer Than Ever" is, for me, deeper than ever.[3]

Riedel's reaction turned out to be a common one. Nine years after the fact, Maltby reflected on the 2012 *Closer Than Ever* revival:

> When we did it at the York, a whole lot of people would come up and say, "Oh, when that album came out, we were in college, we went crazy, I wore out three CDs, I played it all the time." We didn't know that, because at the time, we were struggling to keep the show open, but *all* of them said, coming back to see the show at the York twenty years later, "Oh, *that's* what those songs were about!" That's what they said over and over again, like, "I had no idea, but now, now that I have a child, now that I've been divorced and remarried, I understand what it is." Because the songs in *Closer Than Ever* are all about dealing with irreconcilable, contradictory obligations and feelings. And in fact, I have

come to think that that is almost the definition of adulthood: you become an adult when you start dealing with these things that cannot possibly be reconciled, but then that's what you do.

The *Closer Than Ever* revival featured a handful of new, or not so new, songs. "I'll Get Up Tomorrow Morning" went into the original 1989 run of *Closer Than Ever* shortly after it opened, as a replacement for "Like a Baby," an outtake from the second act of *Baby* that is not nearly as strong a number. (In her negative *Times* review of the original production of *Closer Than Ever*, Laurie Winer had made a particular point of slamming that song.) "I'll Get Up Tomorrow Morning" did not, however, make it onto the first cast album—"Like a Baby" appears instead ("for some unknown reason," Maltby says)—so the former song was new in 2012 for fans who knew *Closer Than Ever* only from the original recording.[4]

"I'll Get Up Tomorrow Morning" seems to emblematize one aspect of the midlife predicament, which is that you find a way to persevere, even in the face of all the curveballs life keeps throwing at you. It starts out with a rip-roaring ostinato figure in the piano, a good musical representation of the tumult of contemporary life—particularly the rush to get to work on time in the morning—then proceeds to cycle through a list of travails:

I'm late for work, of course the car won't start.
The brand new DVR just fell apart.
I meet my boss with coffee on my pants.
My wife announces she wants more "romance."

But regardless of it all, the singer (Dvorsky) declares, "I'll get up tomorrow morning, take a deep breath, and go on." In the second verse, the stressors keep ratcheting up:

My ten-year-old's best friend is smoking pot.
The roof will cost ten grand I haven't got.
My daughter says the acting bug just bit her.
My teenage son is sleeping with the sitter.

Determination wages a battle with desperation, and the coping mechanisms move to a new level, as indicated by the end of the third chorus:

I'll get up tomorrow morning,
Say, "The past is prelude,"
Stay loose,
Drop a Quaalude,
And go on.

To top that, in the final chorus, our poor protagonist announces that as part of his morning regimen, he will now "take a hot bath, do my push-ups, feed the puppies, eat my oat bran, throw up, and go on." The long-held last note (on the word "on") ends with a primal scream.

"The Sound of Muzak," another number from the original *Closer Than Ever*, was also cut, despite its sumptuous Ravelian swirls. Originally written for Ronny Graham's revue *Graham Crackers* in 1963, it was, by 2010, both dated yet oddly prescient: it culminated in the sci-fi fantasy that you'd eventually be able to plug music straight into your brain via implants and bypass even headphones, a concept that seems not very far away from reality right now. Regardless, the song was the show's only straight-ahead cabaret number—which is to say that it wasn't character-based like the other songs—and seemed to stick out.

Thus, "The Sound of Muzak" was replaced by "Dating Again," a sardonic (but nevertheless exuberant) look at the mating dance from a midlife perspective.[5] It has a bouncy swing feel, jazzy substitute harmonies, and sarcastic takes like:

Boy, oh boy to sit there churning out the small talk
With someone who is all talk
And boring

And:

I'm divorced and so I'm sitting smiling vainly
At someone who is plainly
Mr. Wrong.

The men are just as over the whole thing as the women are:

I feel a tingle
But I'm wondering while we mingle
Why is she forty and still single?

And of course, all four warily anticipate that imminent moment:

When that old siren goes off
And you must take your clothes off
Oh my God!

Though it wasn't included in the original, "Dating Again," like "I'll Get Up Tomorrow Morning," now seems like an essential part of the show.

The third new song for the York revival was "There Is Something in a Wedding," which is based on the wedding processional Shire wrote for

Maltby's second marriage to Janet Brenner. Maltby later lyricized it so it could go into the revival as a companion piece to "Another Wedding Song," the clever and moving number Shire wrote for his wedding to Didi Conn. Though it does not seem as foundational to the show as the other two new songs, it is, like many Maltby/Shire numbers, an effective fusion of clear-eyed realism with heartfelt emotion, as in the following quatrain:

> There was never such a bride
> There was never such a groom
> Something like an act of faith that gets inside
> Every cynic in the room.

A new cast recording was made of the York revival. In contrast to the original recording from 1990, the orchestration is not expanded; instead, listeners hear only piano and bass, just as they would in a live performance. This was considered a plus in some quarters, as one reviewer elaborated:

> Jay Records' producer John Yap, as is his highly praised practice, likes to do note-complete recordings of scores using their in-theater arrangements/orchestrations. Therefore, his *Closer Than Ever* offers the sound you would have heard at the York—four vocalists and two instrumentalists. It is a bit more like a cabaret sound than a show tune one. The result is that music director/pianist Andrew Gerle has the intended central spot in the support for the vocalists and he fills it with superb panache. Indeed, for my money, Gerle's work is the deciding factor making the new recording the best choice for those wanting just one *Closer Than Ever* on their theater shelf.[6]

Not long after *Closer Than Ever* closed, the York assembled the original cast of *Starting Here, Starting Now*—Loni Ackerman, Margery Cohen, and George Lee Andrews—for a special performance of the show on December 2, 2012, more than thirty-five years after it first opened at the Barbarann Theater Restaurant. Originally intended as a one-night-only event, it was brought back for two additional performances on December 9 and 16 due to popular demand.

The performance was originally going to be just a concert reading, with the actors sitting at music stands. Once in rehearsal, however, they discovered that they couldn't do the show without the original staging. "They had to move," Maltby remembers. "It was still in their bodies after all those years."

Kevin Stites, who served as musical director and pianist for the performances, found it to be a deeply moving experience. "Those three people, and the history they brought to singing what they originated, were so committed and so real—not that today's actors aren't, but there was a depth to it. Also adding to it the fact that they are now in their twilight years. So even for them to sing the title song, you're weeping. 'Starting here, starting now'? Really? You're seventy years old."

Stites has one memory of Cohen in particular. "She was a cancer survivor at that point, so when she sat on that stool and sang 'Autumn,' it was like nothing you've ever heard."

"It was a charming, wonderful evening," Morgan agrees.

There was talk of building on the buzz from the three successful performances and transferring the show with the original cast for an extended run, but it never materialized. "I'm not sure anybody thought they were up to eight [performances] a week, Stites says. "It's really hard work. They could have done six a week, but the idea sort of fizzled. But oh, my God, it was good."

Although there were no further performances of *Starting Here, Starting Now* with the original cast, the mini-revival led to the idea of bringing the show back to the York with a new cast of young performers. This took place in March 2016 for a two-week run as part of the York's Musicals in Mufti series. The cast consisted of Bobby Conte Thornton, Krystal Joy Brown, and Charlotte Maltby, Richard's daughter. Stites once again served as musical director and pianist, and bassist Danny Weller, who played for the *Closer Than Ever* revival, returned for *Starting Here, Starting Now*.

Thornton and Charlotte Maltby were right out of college, having attended the University of Michigan together. Both had also appeared in a starry production of *Les Misérables* at the St. Louis Muny—Thornton as Enjolras, Maltby as Fantine—while they were still students. (Stites was also the conductor of that production.) Brown, already a seasoned professional, had appeared in three Broadway shows by that time, including a year in the Diana Ross role in *Motown: The Musical*, and would go on to be an Eliza replacement in *Hamilton*.

Regarding Charlotte Maltby, Stites recalls, "She's extremely talented. She's charismatic. That look she's got is sort of otherworldly, in a good way. And sweet as can be. She can also be goofy as hell. Sometimes you have to say, hey, whoa, come back! She especially was super professional and like a sponge when she did Fantine at the Muny."

Stites found the father-daughter dynamic particularly fascinating on *Starting Here, Starting Now*. "He was her director, but you could tell sometimes he'd pull her over and give her notes in a more fatherly way. It was very sweet." On the song "Autumn," Stites says, "she was coached within an inch of her life by her dad."

Maltby and Shire perform "Autumn" themselves occasionally; they did a rendition at a master class for musical theater students at Yale in December 2013.[7] Afterward, Maltby, admitting that he was nobody's idea of a great singer, added, "But I think I had you." He was right. In performing the song, Maltby puts across the subtext, all the other meanings that don't fit into the song as lyrics but are part of the idea. "You have to remind singers how many other thoughts are available in those lines," he says.

When Charlotte Maltby sang "Autumn" in the York's *Starting Here, Starting Now* revival, she had us, too.

Performances in the York's Musicals in Mufti series are not normally reviewed by the mainstream press, since they are presented by the actors in street clothes, with scripts in hand and limited staging, as opposed to full productions. However, several online reviewers from smaller outlets were full of praise.

"Maltby and Shire's work remains a timeless and relevant musical self-help session that explains how and why we fall in and out of love," Ryan Leeds of *Manhattan Digest* declared.[8] Praising the "talented trio" of performers, he concluded that the show "doesn't propose to be anything other than joyous. Sometimes, like love, that is all we need." Joseph Verlezza, writing in Onstageblog.com, also praised the cast, saying, "These three are generous performers and understand collaboration as they fuse their individual skills to become a theatrical force."[9]

In between the revivals of *Closer Than Ever* in 2012 and *Starting Here, Starting Now* in 2016, the York presented *Big* in October 2014 (as mentioned in chapter 20), starring John Tartaglia as grown-up Josh and Kerry Butler as Susan Lawrence. Unexpectedly, Maltby himself ended up playing George MacMillan, the head of MacMillan Toys, stepping in at the last minute for Walter Charles, who had been cast in the role. As Morgan reports it, Charles had said he wasn't feeling well at the Friday-night dress rehearsal and then didn't show up for the first performance the following Saturday afternoon. "Walter was having major issues," Morgan recalls. They never did find out exactly what happened.

Maltby went on and played the role for the rest of the run. "Richard was so spectacular," Morgan enthuses. "I was fabulous," Maltby concurs modestly. "We had to drag him off the stage," Shire adds.

Maltby, who can be seen performing as MacMillan in an archival video made of one performance, is indeed ingenuously charming in the role, free of acting artifice, and he sings with excellent intelligibility and remarkably good pitch. He's also hilarious pounding out the melody to "Chopsticks" with

Tartaglia on the Walking Piano (a lighting projection onto the floor in this bare-bones production).

Presenting *Closer Than Ever*, *Big*, and *Starting Here, Starting Now* in succession over the course of four seasons has provided the York with a clear identity as a champion of the Maltby/Shire canon and, unsurprisingly, earned tremendous gratitude from the writers themselves.

"'You've given our shows back to us' is something that David has said many times," Morgan says, and he hopes there will be more to follow. He's particularly interested in the forthcoming *Revue #3*.[10] "I would give anything to do that," Morgan adds, even speculating on the idea of doing all three together, in a rotating rep format. "But anything we could do of theirs I would do sight unseen."

On November 1, 2021, the York honored Maltby and Shire at the Edison Ballroom with the Oscar Hammerstein Award for Lifetime Achievement in Musical Theater. The award was created by Walker in 1988, and past recipients have included such luminaries as Stephen Sondheim, Betty Comden and Adolph Green, Harold Prince, Cy Coleman, Charles Strouse, Stephen Schwartz, Arthur Laurents, Tom Jones and Harvey Schmidt, Susan Stroman, and André De Shields. The presentation cited Maltby and Shire as "the longest-running collaboration in musical theater history" and included a concert featuring, among others, Norm Lewis singing "Starting Here, Starting Now"; Charlotte Maltby singing "Autumn"; Liz Callaway singing "The Story Goes On"; Kerry Butler singing "Little Susan Lawrence"; Montego Glover singing "Song of the Child" from *Sousatzka*; Sierra Boggess and Josh Dela Cruz singing "One Day" from *Waterfall*; Daniel Jenkins and Santino Fontana singing "The Funniest Thing" from *Take Flight*; Ackerman, Andrews, and Cohen from the original cast of *Starting Here, Starting Now* singing "Travel"; and, as a finale, Maltby and Shire themselves singing "One Step," in suits and top hats. Sondheim made an appearance in a brief video, in which his final words to the honorees were "Keep writing—please."

As part of his acceptance speech, Shire gave a moving testimony to his writing partner of sixty-five years, reminiscing about their early days working together at Yale and saying, "Richard managed in those three years to patiently teach a rube theater greenhorn how to write competent theater songs." He concluded by describing Maltby as "Not only the perfect writing partner but a treasured, lifelong soul mate, a man whose supreme talent, theatrical intelligence, wisdom, savvy, and composer's sense of musical, harmonic, and melodic structure, and limitless patience turned a cocky young tunesmith from Buffalo into a respectable theater composer."

THE SONGWRITERS' SONGWRITERS

Over the course of the last two years, I have encountered two kinds of reactions when I've mentioned to friends and colleagues that I was writing a book about Maltby and Shire. One frequent response was along the lines of "Wow, that's terrific! They're so fantastic. It's about time someone wrote a book about them." The other periodic reaction was "Who are Maltby and Shire?" To those people, I said, "That's exactly why I'm writing this book."

Still, the discrepancy between these two types of responses was striking, and it begs the question of why two artists who are so accomplished and so revered by those who know their work have not had more mainstream recognition in their chosen genre. In fact, Maltby and Shire have arguably had more success working separately than together.

The gushing accolades for them as musical theater writers are easy to find, coming from many quarters. Adam Gopnik, typically, sums it up well. "They are the songwriters' songwriters," he declares. "Everybody within the world has limitless regard for them, including Steve Sondheim."

Particularly telling is the admiration that comes from the musicians who have long-term working relationships with the team. "He's such a fantastic pianist, and he orchestrates for the piano," composer and musical director Andrew Gerle says of Shire. "It's the richness of his harmonic vocabulary, combined with the most gorgeous melodies—it's a rare combination. And his musical palette is just enormous. He can do pretty much anything. All the colors, all the textures—it's such a blast to play."

Jonathan Tunick offers a unique perspective on Shire. "I always thought of David as our Gershwin," he recalls, referring to a group of his contemporaries in New York in the early '60s—a circle of up-and-coming composer/musicians that included Billy Goldenberg, Arthur B. Rubinstein, Lee Holdridge, Fred Silver, Ed Kleban, and Claibe Richardson. "David was the piano virtuoso. He had all the technical chops and the jazz influence and all

Closer Than Ever. Joshua Rosenblum, Oxford University Press. © Oxford University Press 2024.
DOI: 10.1093/oso/9780197758236.003.0030

that sparkle, and just general mastery, combined with a great sense of tonal color and human inspiration."

Musical director Joel Fram elaborates on what makes so many Maltby/Shire songs particularly special:

> They write so beautifully for these very distinct, immediately recognizable characters, fully fleshed in a single song. I think that's why the songs appeal to performers, because they feel like they can become Miss Byrd for that moment, and you [the audience] literally get a sense that you have known this character forever. So they don't just write generally comic songs or generally sad songs. They have an amazing specificity, both in terms of musical theater writing but also in how these songs lift out and work in cabaret performances, because the stories that surround the characters are told so eloquently in the songs themselves.

"They are some of the finest [musical theater] writers of the last fifty years," Kevin Stites says. "I thought *Baby* was one of the most terrific things I'd ever seen. I cried at the end of Act I, and at the end of Act II, I was inconsolable. Of course," he admits, "my wife was expecting our second child at the time."

Liz Callaway, who frequently gives concerts and master classes at colleges, routinely advocates for Maltby and Shire. "I try to make it my mission for more people to know their work," she says. "I'll go to a college, and I hear songs that people are singing. And I think they're good, but they're not crafted in the same way. I say, 'Listen to Maltby and Shire.'"

Callaway is optimistic that the team may still find their place in terms of greater public awareness. "They're still writing," she points out. "All it takes is one hit show. And then people will say, 'Oh, and they also wrote this, and they wrote that.'"

One hit show. And how does one manage that? Nobody knows, of course. Joey Parnes, who has been associated with many of them, says, "It's a miracle that any Broadway show ever happens at all! Let alone be successful. That it opens in a theater on Broadway *at all* is a miracle!"

As Lynne Meadow puts it, "Broadway's tough. It obviously is part of a much larger picture of what the traffic will allow and how that has shifted over the years."

Plain old luck can certainly play a role in the success of a show and indeed a whole career. Jack O'Brien, the famed director and longtime artistic head of San Diego's Old Globe Theatre (1981–2007), seemed for a while to have a direct pipeline from the Old Globe straight to Broadway, with hits such as *The Full Monty, Dirty Rotten Scoundrels*, and *Dr. Seuss' How the Grinch Stole Christmas*. He was interested in *Take Flight* and scheduled a meeting with Maltby and Shire about it. The team, eager to present O'Brien with the original (and, in their view, the best) version of the show, flew to San Diego for the meeting, but someone had gotten the date and time wrong, and they never got to see O'Brien.

"We thought that was a bifurcation point," Shire says. "If we'd gotten to audition the show for him, he probably would have directed it [at the Old Globe]." A Broadway transfer would then have been easy to envision, given O'Brien's track record. "Bad luck—he never saw it," Shire concludes ruefully.

Even on projects in which the experience wasn't entirely positive, artistic collaborators inevitably come away with nothing but admiring things to say about Maltby and Shire. The frictions on *Sousatzka*, Craig Lucas says, "had nothing to do with Richard and David because they were tireless, and they're so skilled. I grew up on the score to *The Conversation*, which is a masterpiece, and right out of school, *Starting Here, Starting Now* and *Closer Than Ever* were the coin of the realm. I'm also old enough to remember the first releases of the Barbra Streisand recordings of David and Richard's songs, and they're inarguably effective and theatrical."

The raves extend beyond their work as songwriters to the two men personally.

"They're two of the nicest and most wildly talented gentlemen of the theater that you could hope to work with," Jim Morgan says.

Parnes, in discussing his relationship with Maltby and Shire, is quick to mention "their inherent decency. And their lack of bile. There's no typical theatrical, catty, nasty backbiting. They're never really critical or sarcastic about anyone else. About themselves? Absolutely, but not about anyone else that I've heard. They're just very decent and kind and humane, and they really care about what they're doing."

Parnes says part of the fun is watching Maltby and Shire interact. "It's like *The Sunshine Boys*," he observes. "David is so unbelievably dry in his humor, but he's always so dead-on right when he says things. Richard goes on and on, and you think, 'Oh, my God, he's so domineering. Poor David, he's just being shoved to the side.' But then that isn't it at all. It's just his style. So Richard says whatever he says, and then, boom, David says something completely perfect and smart, and you just don't see it coming."

When asked how Richard and David have managed to remain collaborators and friends for so long, Didi Conn puts it this way:

> I think it's a mutual admiration society. They really love each other, and the only time they disagree is when David's been working on something all day, and then he plays it for Richard, and Richard says, "Oh,

that's good, but I wanted this," and then that upsets him. But you know, Richard's like his other wife. I mean, I wish he did more cooking.

As of this writing (January 2024), Maltby and Shire are both eighty-six. They currently have numerous projects in the works and show no signs of slowing down. ("David in his eighties is writing some of the most beautiful music he's ever written," Gopnik asserts.) However, both are inevitably aware of "The March of Time," as it were. This is, as Shire puts it, "a global concern about this period in our lives. With so much in the pipeline, we hear time's chariot hurrying near. We don't have a lot of time. And Richard is picking up signs of ageism—there are little teeny glimmers of not being taken seriously because we're old."

This unfortunate prejudice notwithstanding, Shire has shown a remarkable late-in-life creative flowering with the writing of his *Peace Cantata*, a major composition unlike anything he's written before. The piece is Shire's contribution to *Symphony of Three*, a large-scale work that was commissioned to celebrate the completion of the Abrahamic Family House, a new interfaith complex in Abu Dhabi that has sanctuaries for Jewish, Christian, and Muslim faiths. Three composers—one from each faith—were commissioned in 2021 to contribute a twenty-five-minute piece. Shire, as the title of his work indicates, was assigned the topic of "Peace," the American film composer John Debney was given "Love," and the Emirati composer Ihab Darwish's subject was "Tolerance." Shire's resulting nine-movement work reveals astonishing stylistic breadth and stirring humanity. It is additionally remarkable in that, in contrast to nearly everything else he's ever written, with the lone exceptions of *Sonata for Cocktail Piano* and the unpublished orchestral jazz piece *Shades of Blue*, the *Peace Cantata* is a standalone concert work, not connected to a musical or a film. An impressive video of the full *Symphony of Three: Peace, Love, Tolerance* can be seen on YouTube.[1] It features more than three hundred performers—including vocal and instrumental soloists, multiple choruses, and full orchestra—from seventeen different countries, with all the performing groups prerecorded separately and digitally assembled into a virtual concert. An astonishing musical and technical achievement, the video has garnered 1.6 million views to date.

Of the several theatrical projects currently on the table, the one that generates the most excitement is what for a long period was referred to as *Revue #3*, the working title for a compilation of songs that forms a trilogy with *Starting Here, Starting Now* and *Closer Than Ever*—or, as Shire puts it, with characteristic morbid wit, "Our last revue before that Great Review in the Sky." Just as *Starting Here, Starting Now* was largely about the excitement of young love and *Closer Than Ever* offered more lived-in midlife perspectives, the third revue focuses on lives seen in full. The opening number of an early version of the show was, in fact, called "A Life in Full."

As Maltby describes it, "We spend most of our time planning what's going to happen tomorrow. Then, when you get to a certain point, like at our age, you suddenly glance back and see the whole arc of it, and suddenly, life gets defined differently. Things that mattered incredibly don't matter at all, and other moments that actually changed your life, the things that determined where you're going, took you by surprise."

Like the two earlier Maltby/Shire revues, the latest is a compilation of trunk songs and new ones written specifically for the purpose. Among the former are outtakes from *Sousatzka*, *Waterfall*, and the as-yet-unproduced *The Country Wife* (discussed later in this chapter). It also includes "Little Susan Lawrence," which, although part of the currently licensed version of *Big*, does not appear on the original Broadway cast recording and is thus unknown to most people, even Maltby/Shire fans. Also on the song list are "Both Ends Now," a Joni Mitchell parody about what happens to hippies when they get to be in their fifties, written specifically for the revue; "All I Wanna Do Is Go Dancing," originally from *Sousatzka* but repurposed and relyricized; and a song called "Smart People," based on an Aaron Sorkin essay about being a Jewish TV writer and having everyone assume that any smart, witty characters you write must be Jewish, too (although you can't come right out and say it):[2]

It's not a new idea, though to me it's kind of new-ish,
That when your cast
Talks really fast,
It simply means they're . . .
Smart people.

And:

Smart people,
What can I do?
You write a Christian president,
He comes off as a . . .
Know-it-all.

Also on the list is Maltby's remarkably deft lyricization of "Manhattan Skyline," the rousing Shire instrumental from the *Saturday Night Fever* soundtrack that was never intended to have words but in Maltby's hands turned into a terrific number for four singers about moving to New York.[3]

A preliminary tryout of *Revue #3*—fourteen songs, about an hour's worth of material—took place on November 21, 2022, at New York's 54 Below before a packed, unashamedly partisan room full of Maltby/Shire friends, colleagues, and devotees.[4] Many in the crowd began tearing up as Broadway luminary Chip Zien (*Falsettos, Into the Woods*) sang "A Life in Full." The opening song segued directly into "Way Up There," the number for Lawnchair Larry that was cut from *Take Flight* (see chapter 24). This song received a thoroughly rousing rendition from Dan Jenkins, who created the leading role of Josh Baskin in the Broadway production of *Big*. Other Broadway veterans in the cast included Kerry Butler, Penny Fuller, and Karen Ziemba. Sydney James Harcourt and Nikki James had also been scheduled to perform, but both had to drop out at the last minute. As a result, Maltby himself—in a scenario reminiscent of his stepping in as George MacMillan for the York Theatre revival of *Big*—ended up singing "Only When I Laugh," the toe-tapping title song from the Neil Simon movie of the same name. He also (as originally scheduled) performed "Kensington Kenny," a song from *The Country Wife*, in which a nineteenth-century New Orleans theater owner reminisces about a cross-dressing stage act he used to perform when he was in the British Music Hall.

The performance also included a number called "Bach," originally written for the postproduction workshop of *Sousatzka*, sung impressively from the piano by musical director Deniz Cordell. Two songs from *Waterfall*—"Once You Fall in Love," which has the feel of a sentimental classic, and "One Day," the best of the evening's nostalgic "looking back" numbers—rounded out the set.

The team concluded after the 54 Below performance that the theme of "A Life in Full," despite the appealing opening number with that title, sent the wrong message about the show as a whole. "It made it sound like it was going to be an evening full of geriatric songs," as Shire put it.

A better and far preferable title, it turns out, is *About Time*, which is what the show is now called as development continues. Maltby and Shire discussed this shift in the theme of the show during a Zoom interview in March 2023:

JR: *About Time*. That's a thought-provoking title.

DS: Richard came up with it.

RM: Looking-back songs are not very exciting. There'll be a lot of nostalgia in it because there has to be, but there was a line in one of the songs that Adam Gopnik picked up on, and it connected to something I was thinking about, which is that young folk expect that at a certain point, you get to slow down, you can rest, you can take it a little easy, and yes, that's true. But there's another truth that is not anything you expected, and that is that simultaneously, time starts to go into double time. It's January 1, and then it's March 1, and then it's summer, and you can't figure out how it's gone by so quickly. It seems that time is suddenly sailing by.

DS: There's a great new number called "Faster and Faster" which Richard wrote a wonderful lyric for.

RM: It's to the "Mind over Matter" melody from *The Sap of Life*, which I was looking to find something for, and "Faster and Faster" just fell into place. "Time hurries by like an untied balloon. Wake up on Monday, it's Friday by noon." It's that kind of thing. My daughter Emily went off to Northwestern, and I swear I was being invited to her graduation a month later. Whereas I remember being in college *forever*.

DS: So it really is "about time."

JR: That's certainly compelling. Are there other new songs since last October?

RM: We have six or seven in various stages of forward motion. Some trunk songs— "To Be Alive" has always been a melody that is very positive.

DS: That's from *Love Match*.[5]

RM: And a couple of others that we haven't worked on that don't even have melodies yet. I'm just gathering rhymes and jokes and stuff. These are all new ideas.

DS: Another idea I'm starting on is called "Lost and Found," which is about "Where are my keys?"

JR: Everyone can relate to that.

DS: We've got about half a dozen things in the works. That should define what the tenor of the show is.

JR: But those fourteen songs we heard at 54 Below, that's still the core?

RM: Yeah, some of those may not make the cut, but most of them will.

JR: It had a hugely enthusiastic reception.

RM: Yes, song for song, they were impressive. But as a unit, is it a show? That's another element.

DS: It was a nightclub act rather than a show.

RM: Well, so was *Closer Than Ever*, and so was *Starting Here, Starting Now*. They were both nightclub acts originally.

JR: You're the one who knows how to turn a bunch of songs into a show.

RM: So I keep telling myself!

Maltby and Shire are planning to present the latest version of *About Time* as a special concert event during their 65th Yale class reunion in May 2024. The performance will take place at the University Theatre, home to the Yale Dramat, the same place their collaboration began back in 1958 with *Cyrano*.

The other Maltby/Shire show still awaiting a full production is *The Country Wife*, loosely based on the 1675 play of the same title by William Wycherley. Maltby first had the idea to adapt a Restoration comedy several decades ago, after *Ain't Misbehavin'* opened.

"I was trying to figure out why the comedy in [*Ain't Misbehavin'*] seemed familiar to me," he explains. "It all came from the idea that the title song is a lie—he's been misbehavin' like crazy. And that travels all the way through the show. I thought that seemed familiar."

It finally hit Maltby what he was thinking of: way back in the '60s, he and Shire had stopped off during a cross-country drive back from LA to see William Congreve's play *The Way of the World* at the Guthrie Theater, in a production starring Zoe Caldwell. Somehow there was a connection between that style of hiding indiscreet feelings under a layer of gentility and Fats Waller's brand of deceptive musical chicanery. As Maltby puts it, "Restoration comedy is the same thing: you don't tell the truth."

Although his original thought was to create a new version of *The Country Wife* with a mixed-race cast, updating its setting to New Orleans just before the Civil War (he did an early reading that included *Ain't Misbehavin'* original cast members André De Shields and Charlayne Woodard), Maltby eventually decided—no surprise here—that it should be a musical. The songs, however, would be genre set pieces, as opposed to the fully integrated, book-musical-type songs that advance the plot through dramatic action—the type of number that Maltby and Shire normally specialize in. On the contrary, in this case, the audience would be presented with the ragtime number, the tango, the French cabaret number, the grand waltz tune, and so on, and then the plot would continue.

In what seems to have been an extraordinary burst of improvisatory creativity, Shire generated what turned out to be a significant part of the score to *The Country Wife* in one afternoon. "It was while I still lived on Perry Street, so it was probably '87, '88," Maltby says. "David came over one day, and we were talking about it, and I said, 'Why don't I just run a tape, and you just play through some melodies, some ideas, whatever comes to mind.'"

Shire says about the session:

> I knew the period—the 1840s and proto-jazz and the proto-rag. I think I was just loose and having fun, and jazz is one of the styles I grew up with. The vocabulary was in my fingers. I was thinking about the era: New

Orleans, Dixie jazz, ragtime, that whole thing of Americana. I took liberties—there are songs in there that aren't 1840s songs, but you have freedom in writing a musical. No musicologists are going to say, "That kind of rag was really not written till Scott Joplin [five decades later]."

These recordings still survive—two tapes with a combined running time of about two and a half hours—and they constitute an astonishing document of a sustained, spontaneous outburst of creative inspiration. Listening to Shire improvise, one hears a series of almost perfectly formed songs, with hardly a wrong note or a single instant of hesitation. "The kinds of melodies that you work over—they were all just there," Maltby marvels. Many of them from that original session are still in the show.

"I wasn't smoking anything, either," Shire deadpans.

Several of the numbers are Joplinesque, as mentioned. Others reveal the influence of Louis Moreau Gottschalk, a nineteenth-century composer sometimes referred to as the "American Liszt," who was the first American composer to combine Louisiana Creole and Cuban influences with the European classical music tradition. All, however, have the customary Shirean polish, elegance, melodic shapeliness, and knack for surprising yet inevitable harmonizations. Even in this context of spontaneous generation, they just pour out of Shire's fingers on Maltby's slightly out-of-tune piano.

The writers eventually realized they couldn't play *The Country Wife* completely straight, as originally written. A bawdy seventeenth-century British comedy about a rake's ploy to seduce as many women as possible was simply too misogynistic and no longer suitable for contemporary audiences. In the new concept, an exiled theatrical producer from England is mounting a new production of *The Country Wife* in his adopted town of New Orleans, but one of the leading female players is offended by the show and, in the second act, rewrites the script to suit her own purposes. As the theater manager puts it near the end of the play:

When producing a classic today, it's advisable
To rewrite it until it's unrecognizable.

All the dialogue in the play, it should be noted, is written in rhyming couplets like these. At one point, Maltby's concept was for only the play-within-the-play to rhyme in that fashion, but he says it just seemed natural to continue to have the characters speak in rhyme even when they stepped outside. This allows Maltby to make a joke out of it. As one character says:

Well, it's messing my brain up, it's ruining my timing:
Look, the play's halted and I am still rhyming!

In May 2021, Melia Bensussen, the artistic director of Hartford Stage, directed a remote reading of *The Country Wife* via Zoom, with musical direction by Cordell. In December 2023, Symphony Space presented a concert version of the show as a benefit for Red Bull Theater, an off-Broadway company that specializes in reviving classic plays. The performance received a rousingly enthusiastic response from the capacity audience.[6]

"Red Bull wants to put it on [as a full production]," Maltby says, "but it's a way bigger show than they're normally used to doing." Considerable outside financing would be needed, but the possibility remains open.

A sixty-plus-year songwriting partnership is both extraordinary and unprecedented. However, one might say that this is a misleading description. Although Maltby and Shire have been writing songs together since 1957, large parts of their creative lives, as has been noted, have been spent working on projects that did not involve each other. Shire had his entire career as an Oscar- and Grammy-winning[7] and five-time Emmy-nominated film and TV composer; Maltby is a Tony-winning director for *Ain't Misbehavin'* and a nominee for *Fosse*, *Song and Dance*, and *Baby*. And both have worked with other collaborators on musicals (Shire with Gopnik, Maltby with Charles Strouse and Alain Boublil/Claude-Michel Schönberg).

What's notable is that they keep coming back to each other.

In the intervening years, of course, there have been seismic changes in popular culture. Back in 1956, when *My Fair Lady* had its first out-of-town tryout at the Shubert Theater in New Haven, Broadway musicals had a firmly prominent position in American cultural life. In Gopnik's words, musical theater was "the bright center and crucible of pop music and, indeed, of pop culture." Broadway show tunes were the songs that Shire's father taught to David and to his piano students. The *My Fair Lady* cast album went on to be a massive bestseller; it was the first LP to sell a million copies. New Broadway shows were such a common occurrence that Shire, it will be recalled, didn't even bother to see *My Fair Lady* at the Shubert in New Haven, assuming there would always be another new musical coming in. ("Just as one might ignore a talked-of Netflix series now," Gopnik says.)

This was the artistic infrastructure to which Maltby and Shire came of age, but it was on the verge of collapse. As Rob Kapilow puts it in his book *Listening for America*:

> The arrival of rock and roll at the end of the 1950s created an enormous schism between Broadway and commercially popular music. Broadway would ultimately move in new directions and find new audiences, but its music would never again be America's music. . . . Rock and roll had

created a wedge between the generations, and the arrival of the Beatles and Beatlemania in 1964 made the split permanent. Broadway was no longer everyone's music; it had become your parents' music.[8]

As they became aware that opportunities were different, the collaborators tried different things—Shire went to Hollywood, Maltby became a director—and both found great success in those domains. But in the end, what they really wanted—and still want—was to write musicals together. About his many film scores, Shire says, "I'd trade any twenty of them for another show that made it to Broadway." Gopnik observes, "They're still persuaded the [original American] Broadway musical is what matters most. I find that a telling and human story."

The Maltby/Shire legacy, then, is an important one but atypical among musical theater songwriters. They don't have the string of hit Broadway shows that other, more celebrated writing teams (or individual composer/lyricists) can point to. As Ken Mandelbaum puts it, they "[have] few peers in contemporary musical theatre" and are "among the most talented music-theatre writers of the last thirty years,"[9] but their most enduring work, with a few exceptions, is contained not in their two Broadway musicals but in their revues.

The extraordinary story songs in *Starting Here, Starting Now* and *Closer Than Ever* are the kinds of numbers that no other musical theater writers have managed to create with the regularity and consistency of Maltby and Shire. And it is perhaps the wholly self-contained nature of these songs that makes them work better in the context of revues like *Starting Here, Starting Now* and *Closer Than Ever* rather than within a book musical (which is where many of them originated). The best of these, such as "The Bear, the Tiger, the Hamster and the Mole," "I Don't Remember Christmas," "What About Today?" "Crossword Puzzle," "Miss Byrd," "I Wouldn't Go Back," "If I Sing," "The March of Time," and others that have been examined in this book, can hold their own in terms of craft, originality, melodic/harmonic invention, and sheer entertainment value against nearly anything else in the canon. Thus, one might say Maltby and Shire are indisputably great musical theater songwriters whose primary legacy ultimately lies outside the Broadway musical, because so many of their best songs contain complete musical narratives in themselves. But it may be too soon to draw any sweeping conclusions. Clearly, for the time being, at least, their story goes on.

ACKNOWLEDGMENTS

First thanks, of course, go to Richard Maltby and David Shire for agreeing to let me write this book and then for being such good sports and great interview subjects over the course of our many hours of time spent together, mostly on Zoom during the pandemic. I started out thinking they were two of the smartest, most interesting, and most gifted people I knew, and by the end of the process, I realized I had only known the tip of the iceberg.

Warm gratitude goes to the other fine and accomplished people who were willing to be interviewed for this book. It was a privilege to be able to speak to and/or correspond with George Lee Andrews, Alain Boublil, Jason Robert Brown, Liz Callaway, Vicki Clark, Didi Conn, Deniz Cordell, Nicole Fosse, Joel Fram, Jim Freydberg, Andrew Gerle, Adam Gopnik, Craig Lucas, Sally Mayes, Lynne Meadow, Jim Morgan, Joey Parnes, Michael Paternostro, Dale Rieling, Tom Shepard, Kevin Stites, Susan Stroman, Chet Walker, John Weidman, and Ben Whiteley. Each of these distinguished folks contributed uniquely and immeasurably, making the process a rare pleasure.

My wonderful family rallied round for the purposes of this project. Joanne Lessner, the spectacular human being I'm lucky enough to be married to, read the full draft at least twice, not to mention most individual chapters along the way, and made it considerably better with her suggestions. Among her many virtues is her astounding acuity as an editor, on both the micro and macro levels, plus everything in between. Special thanks also go to my daughter, Phoebe, and my son, Julian, both terrific songwriters themselves, for mercilessly incisive feedback along the way. Phoebe gets an extra-big hug for her meticulous interview transcriptions.

I have learned that the trick to getting a book published is to get it into the hands of the right person. In this case, the right person was the brilliant author and scholar Geoffrey Block, editor of Oxford University Press's estimable Broadway Legacies series. Geoffrey was kind, encouraging, and wise, from our first email exchange all the way to the end of the review and approval process. Amazingly well versed in the fields of both classical music and musical theater, he seems to have read *everything* pertinent to his areas of expertise, given the numerous references, some quite obscure, that he routinely tossed out while making his invariably useful suggestions.

A major shout-out thus goes to my good friend and esteemed Yale colleague Dan Egan, who suggested querying Geoffrey about my book in the first place.

I also extend my humble gratitude to Oxford University Press senior acquisitions editor Norm Hirschy, whose guidance, judgment, responsiveness, and gracious support were essential in helping me navigate the daunting path to publication. My project editor, Laura Santo, answered my barrage of questions with much-appreciated thoroughness and patience.

During the production process, my project manager Hinduja Dhanasegaran was unfailingly helpful, knowledgeable, and alacritous, and my astonishingly keen-eyed copy editor Wendy Keebler whipped the manuscript into its final form with impressive discernment and command of style.

I have Carol Rosegg to thank for the terrific photo of Maltby and Shire, which Linda Roppolo incorporated as the basis for her beautiful cover design, and the multitalented Diane Phelan for the author photo.

I am grateful to Matt Boethin of Music Theatre International for information regarding worldwide rentals of Maltby/Shire properties; to BJ Karpen for directing me toward some invaluable guidance on writing a book proposal; to Rosie DiVincenzo, Lynne Meadow's efficient assistant; and to Jonathan Levi for hiring me four decades ago for my first summer stock piano-playing job, which happened to include *Starting Here, Starting Now* in the season. That was my first encounter with (and the beginning of my admiration for) the songs of Maltby and Shire.

The contributions of Deniz Cordell, who probably knows more about Maltby and Shire than anyone else alive, are in a category by themselves. Deniz cheerfully shared his insightful perspectives on many occasions and patiently helped me sift through Shire's archives. He also gave my manuscript a thorough fact-check that couldn't have come from anyone else—not even the book's two subjects—and provided reams of illuminating background detail.

Others who read all or parts of the book pre-submission and gave welcome feedback include my faithful friend, best man, and one-time songwriting partner, Tim Peierls; the inimitable George Lee Andrews and his charming wife (and pianist), Marty Morris Lee; and the ever-delightful Sabrina Karlin, who made sure I didn't get any of the dance descriptions wrong.

Juan Chattah's illuminating book *David Shire's "The Conversation"* provided inspiration throughout my writing process. It was serendipitous to discover that Juan teaches at the University of Miami's Frost School of Music, where my daughter happened to be a student while I was working on the book.

This afforded me the welcome opportunity to meet him in person and have a great time comparing notes during a visit to see Phoebe.

I'd be remiss not to mention my always supportive friend, the perspicacious and encyclopedically knowledgeable Peter Filichia, who continues to set the standard for writing informatively and entertainingly about musical theater.

Several fellow-musician friends who have become authors gave me valuable publishing advice, including Joe Church, Andrew Gerle, and Rob Kapilow, my former Yale professor and mentor. Rob did me an especially good turn by urging me to get on the case and secure reprint rights on the double.

On that topic, I owe thanks to George Maloian of Warner Chappell Music for his enthusiasm regarding this project and his guidance in obtaining permissions for the musical examples. Appreciation also goes to Maria Palma in the Warner Chappell LA office, Gail Hopkins Kolehma at Alfred Music, and, most of all, the memorably helpful Michael Worden, the light at the end of the tunnel.

Thanks also to Ian Marsh for additional reprint rights, to Paul McKibbins for pointing me toward Ian, and to my lawyer, David Friedlander—a cherished friend since grade school, a smart, eagle-eyed attorney, and a great person to have on your side.

And finally, I am grateful to the many friends and colleagues who told me writing this book was a great idea, thus encouraging my perseverance in the often lonely role of first-time author. I am, however, similarly obliged to the people who said they were unfamiliar with the subjects of my book—this only reinforced for me the necessity of writing it.

All the musical examples in this book from *Starting Here, Starting Now*, *Baby*, *Closer Than Ever*, and *Big* have been reprinted with the kind permission of Alfred Music.

Musical examples from the songs "Autumn" and "What About Today?" have been reprinted with the kind permission of BJS Music.

All other reprints, figures, or photographs are the personal property of Richard Maltby, Jr. or David Shire and have been reproduced with their permission.

APPENDIX A

STARTING HERE, STARTING NOW MUSICAL NUMBERS AND SOURCES

Song Title	*Original Source*
ACT I	
The Word Is Love	*The Sap of Life* (adapted from Act II finale)
Starting Here, Starting Now	*Stand-alone
A Little Bit Off	John Reed show (also called *Tomorrow*)
I Think I May Want to Remember Today	*Love Match*
Beautiful	*Love Match* (left off the album for length)
We Can Talk to Each Other	*You're What's Happening, Baby*
Just Across the River	*How Do You Do, I Love You*
Crossword Puzzle	*Graham Crackers*
Autumn	*Cyrano*
I Don't Remember Christmas	Written for *Starting Here, Starting Now*
I Don't Believe It	*Love Match* (lyrics largely rewritten)
I Hear Bells	*Love Match*
I'm Going to Make You Beautiful	*You're What's Happening, Baby*
Pleased with Myself	*How Do You Do, I Love You*
ACT II	
Hey There, Fans	Written for *Starting Here, Starting Now*
The Girl of the Minute	** *You're What's Happening, Baby*
A Girl You Should Know	*You're What's Happening, Baby*
Travel	*The River*
Watching the Big Parade Go By	*The Sap of Life*
Flair	Written for *Starting Here, Starting Now*
What About Today?	*Stand-alone
One Step	*How Do You Do, I Love You*
Barbara	Stand-alone (written for first anniversary of Maltby's marriage to his first wife, Barbara)
Song of Me	*The River*
Today Is the First Day of the Rest of My Life	*Love Match*
A New Life Coming	*The Sap of Life* (originally "A Charmed Life")

*Recorded by Barbra Streisand.

**Also included in the Broadway show *New Faces of 1968*.

APPENDIX B

CLOSER THAN EVER MUSICAL NUMBERS AND SOURCES

Song Title	*Original Source*
ACT I	
Doors	Written for *Closer Than Ever* (melody from the Urban File)
She Loves Me Not	*The Sap of Life*
You Want to Be My Friend?	From the Urban File
What Am I Doin'?	*Village Bells*
The Bear, the Tiger, the Hamster and the Mole	Cut from *Baby*
Like a Baby	Cut from *Baby*
Miss Byrd	*Urban Blight*
The Sound of Muzak	*Graham Crackers*
One of the Good Guys	*Urban Blight*
There's Nothing Like It	*Urban Blight* (originally "Aerobic Cantata")
Life Story	*Urban Blight*
Next Time/I Wouldn't Go Back	*Love Match*/cut from *Baby*
ACT II	
Three Friends	Written for *Urban Blight* but not used
Fandango	Written for *Closer Than Ever*
There	*Urban Blight* (originally "There, There")
Patterns	Cut from (and later restored to) *Baby*
Another Wedding Song	Written for Shire's wedding to Didi Conn
If I Sing	Written for *Closer Than Ever*
Back on Base	Written for *Closer Than Ever*
The March of Time	Written for *Closer Than Ever*
Fathers of Fathers	Cut from *Baby*; lyrics rewritten
It's Never That Easy/I've Been Here Before	*The River*/*Village Bells*
Closer Than Ever	Written for *Closer Than Ever*

Song Title	*Original Source*
ADDED FOR 2012 YORK THEATRE REVIVAL	
*I'll Get Up Tomorrow Morning	Written for *Closer Than Ever*
**Dating Again	*A Time for Love* (Lois Robbins showcase)
There Is Something in a Wedding	Music written as the processional for Maltby's wedding to Janet Brenner; lyrics added for *Closer Than Ever*

*Replaced "Like a Baby" in original production a week after opening but not included on original cast recording.

**Replaced "The Sound of Muzak."

NOTES

CHAPTER 1: ORIGINS

1. All the quotes in this book from Maltby and/or Shire come from a series of more than two dozen interviews conducted both separately and jointly with the songwriters, via either Zoom or telephone, during the period from December 28, 2020, through January 12, 2024, unless otherwise specified.
2. Schulberg himself later adapted his own novel as a musical, with music and lyrics by Ervin Drake—the composer of "Good Morning, Heartache"—and book by Schulberg and his brother Stuart; it ran on Broadway for 540 performances from 1964 to 1965.
3. At the time, RCA Victor had a custom record division that would press LPs from customers' cassette tapes for a fee.
4. One famous example of this technique is the transition into "Ya Got Trouble" from Meredith Willson's *The Music Man*, which, as a point of reference, began its Broadway run in 1957, right around this time.
5. Among Brower's credits are the 1960 Broadway revue *From A to Z*, which featured a book by, among others, the twenty-five-year-old Woody Allen, and songs by Jerry Herman, Fred Ebb, and Mary Rodgers. Brower's co-orchestrator on the show was a young Juilliard student named Jonathan Tunick.
6. Richard Maltby, liner notes for *Cyrano* original cast recording (Original Cast Records OC9987, 1999), CD.
7. *Summertime* had been adapted from Arthur Laurents's Broadway play *The Time of the Cuckoo*, which later provided the source material for the 1965 Broadway musical *Do I Hear a Waltz?* with a book by Laurents, music by Richard Rodgers, and lyrics by Stephen Sondheim.
8. Strictly speaking, in classical music, the term "quodlibet" refers to a piece in which previously written, well-known melodies are presented simultaneously. (Variation 30 of J. S. Bach's *Goldberg Variations*, in which the composer combines two famous German folk songs, is a good example.) In the type of theater song under discussion, by contrast, the melodies are specifically composed to be sung together, after first being presented successively. "Quodlibet" nonetheless remains the best descriptive term for this type of number and has been adapted by many writers on musical theater.
9. The *Raid on Entebbe* title track can be heard on YouTube: https://www.youtube.com/watch?v=R2Q90AvWqVA.

10. Subber's major Broadway credit at the time was *Kiss Me, Kate*, and he later had a string of successes as Neil Simon's producer.

CHAPTER 2: THE FAIR-HAIRED BOYS: *THE SAP OF LIFE*

1. See example 19.4 in chapter 19 for a usage of this specific chord in "The Bear, the Tiger, the Hamster and the Mole."
2. The example Maltby has cited as particularly seminal for himself is his father's recording of "St. Louis Blues Mambo." This track can be heard on YouTube: https://www.youtube.com/watch?v=XFpTwbmHmYc.
3. The school is now known as David Geffen School of Drama at Yale in honor of a $150 million gift made by the David Geffen Foundation in 2021.
4. Today Yale College's popular Theater and Performance Studies program is large and thriving.
5. Howard Taubman, "Theatre: 'Sap of Life' Off Broadway," *New York Times*, October 4, 1961. https://www.nytimes.com/1961/10/03/archives/theatre-sap-of-life-off-broadway-musical-in-premiere-at-one.html.
6. Shire did the arrangements along with Julian Stein, the show's musical director. Stein, notably, had also been the original pianist and musical director for *The Fantasticks* and hired Shire to be his first replacement. (Shire played *The Fantasticks* for a full year.)
7. Hemiola refers to the replacement of a two-beats-to-the-bar feel with three beats to the bar, spread over an equivalent amount of musical time. The most famous example of this device is in the song "America" from *West Side Story*.
8. "It was probably a mistake," Shire quips when this harmonic alteration is pointed out to him.
9. As a reference point, *West Side Story*, co-produced by Prince, with music by Bernstein, lyrics by Sondheim, and direction and choreography by Robbins, opened on Broadway in 1957. The hit movie adaptation was released on October 18, 1961, two weeks after *The Sap of Life*'s opening. *Gypsy*, also with direction and choreography by Robbins and lyrics by Sondheim, plus music by Jule Styne, had closed earlier that year (1961) in March, after a nearly two-year run.
10. Reprinted in Frank Rich, "Conversations with Sondheim," *New York Times Magazine*, March 12, 2000, 38.

CHAPTER 3: BARBRA

1. Though *People* was Streisand's fourth studio recording, Maltby says she recorded "Autumn" at her first session.
2. Sometime later, when Shire encountered *Funny Girl* composer Jule Styne and related the "Starting Here, Starting Now" story, Styne responded, "Don't you know that about Barbra? We all know she always wants to do men's songs, 'cause those are the ones with guts." (According to Shire, "People" was also originally written to be sung by a man.)

3. Again, Shire credits Maltby with supplying one line when he needed it: "I've heard a lot of toasts to tomorrow / but none of them ever say . . ."
4. The chord in the fifth bar of example 3.5 is a particularly striking dissonance: an altered ♯9 chord, with the A♭ and A♮ (notated here as a B𝄫) rubbing discordantly against each other and emphasizing the tension effectively.
5. Shirley Bassey apparently never got the memo about staying away from songs that Streisand has recorded. She put "What About Today?" on her 1970 album *Something*, in a galvanizing arrangement by Johnny Harris. The album was reissued on CD in 2002. In Bassey's hands, it sounds like a James Bond title track. (Of course, there's a case to be made that *everything* Bassey sings sounds like a Bond title track.)
6. The single can be heard on YouTube: https://www.youtube.com/watch?v=4iU4RmGhPyg.
7. The piece was published by Belwin-Mills. Shire's own virtuoso performance of the piece can be heard on YouTube as part of the album *David Shire at the Movies*, https://www.youtube.com/watch?v=IHjEkUHj9JI.
8. Shire also wrote the concert jazz suite *Shades of Blue* for saxophonist Bobby Militello in 2007. It was performed by Militello and the Buffalo Philharmonic Pops with Shire conducting but never published or professionally recorded.

CHAPTER 4: DEALING WITH STEVE

1. The article's actual title was "The Cult of Saint Stephen Sondheim," but the listing appeared on the contents page as "Is Stephen Sondheim God?," and that is how it lingers in the collective consciousness.
2. James Kaplan, "The Cult of Saint Stephen Sondheim," *New York*, April 4, 1994, 48.
3. Stephen Sondheim, *Look I Made a Hat: Collected Lyrics (1981–2011)* (New York: Alfred A. Knopf, 2011), 333.
4. The nominees for Best Score at the 1963 Tonys were *Stop the World—I Want to Get Off* (music by Anthony Newley, lyrics by Leslie Bricusse), *Little Me* (music by Cy Coleman, lyrics by Carolyn Leigh), *Bravo Giovanni* (music by Milton Schafer, lyrics by Ronny Graham, producer of *Graham Crackers*), and the winner, *Oliver!* (music and lyrics by Lionel Bart).
5. Quoted in Meryle Secrest, *Stephen Sondheim: A Life* (New York: Alfred A. Knopf, 1998), 157.
6. Maltby says the claim that Shire's influence can be detected in Sondheim's work originated with orchestrator Jonathan Tunick. Tunick, for his part, does not remember making this assertion and says he does not know of any musical examples that support it.
7. Conversation between the author and Scott Frankel, March 1997.
8. This thrilling instrumental sequence is called "Tick-Tock" on the original cast recording.
9. Shire says the actual phone call came from director Hal Prince.
10. Rick Pender, *The Stephen Sondheim Encyclopedia* (Washington, DC: Rowman & Littlefield, 2021), 79.

11. The entertaining song clip from the movie can be seen on YouTube: https://www.youtube.com/watch?v=PNW4yaa1BWI.
12. According to Pender's *The Stephen Sondheim Encyclopedia*, Sondheim said, regarding Bernstein, "I drove him crazy because, to his dying day, he never beat me [at solving the cryptics]" (423).
13. Maltby, unsurprisingly, is a natural at puzzles from way back. Shire recounts that back at Yale, Maltby had a party trick: he would take a daily *New York Times* crossword, look at it, but not write anything in. After studying it for about half an hour, he would cut the diagram out so he could no longer see the clues and then fill in the whole puzzle from memory.
14. *Road Show* opened in 2008, but it was an off-Broadway production at the Public Theater.
15. Quoted in Norman Lebrecht, "Manhattan's Greatest Mourning since John Lennon Died," *Slipped Disc* (blog), November 29, 2021, https://slippedisc.com/2021/11/manhattans-greatest-mourning-since-john-lennon-died/.

CHAPTER 5: I HAVE A RICH WIFE: *LOVE MATCH*

1. Anthony Shaffer has said that *Sleuth*'s main character, the mystery writer Andrew Wyke, was partially inspired by Sondheim. The working title of the play was reportedly *Who's Afraid of Stephen Sondheim?*
2. Stone, an accomplished screenwriter and Broadway librettist, would go on to write the adapted screenplay for *The Taking of Pelham One Two Three*, an early triumph for Shire as a film composer. (More about Shire's film career appears in chapter 7.)
3. Arthur B. Rubinstein, who was the musical director for *Grand Tour* at Yale, had a long career as a composer for film and television, including several scores for John Badham.
4. Balding, after accumulating a few more Broadway producing credits, would go on to become a circus producer and ringmaster; his *New York Times* obituary in 2014 featured a picture of him embracing the trunk of his adopted African elephant, Flora.
5. Guittard would go on to create the role of Count Carl-Magnus Malcolm in Sondheim's *A Little Night Music*.
6. Strouse's show, titled *I and Albert*, ended up opening not on Broadway but on London's West End in 1972. It ran for only 120 performances and was considered a flop. Richard Rodgers reportedly referred to the show derisively as "The King and Me."
7. Hamilton was originally supposed to be the lyricist for the show, in collaboration with composer Milton Kaye. This was, no doubt, one reason he didn't treat Maltby and Shire particularly well throughout—his lyrics were being tossed out one by one.

CHAPTER 6: HOW BAD COULD I BE?

1. At one point, the show had the working title *Tomorrow*. Maltby's early draft of the libretto shows this title.
2. Knee also wrote the 1991 off-Broadway play *Shmulnik's Waltz*, for which Shire wrote incidental music.

3. Shire recalls Prince telling him that he (Shire) should consider getting a worthier collaborator.
4. Richard Maltby, interview with Paul Lazarus, *Anything Goes* (podcast audio), December 6, 2021, https://www.anythinggoespl.com/episodes/episode-14-richard-maltby-jr.
5. Richard Maltby, interview with Steve Cuden, *Storybeat* (podcast audio), April 6, 2021, https://www.storybeat.net/richard-maltby-jr-tony-winning-writer-lyricist-director-episode-155/.
6. All quotes from Jim Freydberg in this book are from a Zoom interview with the author on March 25, 2021, unless otherwise indicated.
7. Hytner directed *Miss Saigon*, for which Maltby co-wrote the English lyrics with Alain Boublil. (An examination of this collaboration appears in chapter 16.)

CHAPTER 7: THE FIRST THING THEY GIVE YOU IS WRITING THE OBITS

1. Wilson's position was a remnant of Hollywood's soon-to-be-defunct studio system, in which the major movie studios had fully staffed internal music departments and rosters of composers.
2. Other jazz composers hired by Wilson at one time or another included Oliver Nelson, Sonny Burke, Pete Carpenter, Benny Carter, and even Count Basie.
3. Both songs were sung by Tim Morgon on the soundtrack.
4. For a thorough analysis of Shire's music for this film, see Juan Chattah, *David Shire's "The Conversation"* (London: Rowman & Littlefield, 2015), part of the Film Score Guides series. The book is an impressively thorough excavation of not only *The Conversation* (both the movie and the music) but several of Shire's other film scores as well. It also contains extensive discussions of the film noir genre and film-music analysis techniques in general. Chattah's comprehensive approach includes an "interdisciplinary paradigm" that references such subjects as embodied cognition, semiotics, metaphor theory, and related fields. It's not for the timid, to be sure, but highly enlightening for the intrepid reader.
5. According to Shire, Coppola took the job of directing *The Godfather* thinking it would be just another B-movie gangster picture but that it would at least earn him enough money to make *The Conversation*, which it did.
6. Shire has played them in concert on occasion, in arrangements that include added string orchestra parts. This has mostly been in Europe, where he has been honored at film music festivals in Spain, Ireland, and Belgium.
7. Donald A. Guarisco, "Taking of Pelham 123 Review," *AllMusic* (blog), 2013, https://www.allmusic.com/album/taking-of-pelham-123-mw0000026048.
8. Editor's notes, *The Taking of Pelham 1 2 3 (Original Motion Picture Soundtrack)*, Apple Music, https://music.apple.com/us/album/the-taking-of-pelham-123-original-motion/318440740.
9. "The Taking of Pelham One Two Three," *Film Score Monthly* (online magazine), February 5, 2001, https://www.filmscoremonthly.com/cds/detail.cfm/CDID/33/Taking-of-Pelham-One-Two-Three-The/.

10. El Hippo, comment on Soundtrack Fred, "The Taking of Pelham One-Two-Three Soundtrack Suite (David Shire)," YouTube Video, February 7, 2016, https://www.youtube.com/watch?v=f84e64g1ZMw, 11:05. Also in the same thread: "Good Lord! That riff is filthy . . . I want to leave my wife and children and run away with it to Mexico!"
11. Strictly speaking, serialism refers to an expanded compositional method wherein numerous aspects of music besides pitch—such as rhythm, timbre, and dynamics—are also manipulated by way of a row, or series. In practice, however, the term "serialism" is often used interchangeably with twelve-tone composition and refers to the systematization of only pitches via tone rows.
12. In fact, numerous classical composers have appropriated aspects of the twelve-tone method for their own purposes, often in the context of predominantly tonal pieces. Igor Stravinsky, Aaron Copland, Frank Martin, Walter Piston, Witold Lutosławski, Dominick Argento, and Leonard Bernstein are just a few who fall into this category.
13. Phil Ford, "Jazz Exotica and the Naked City," *Journal of Musicological Research* 27 (2008): 113–133.
14. *The Hindenburg* included the comedy number "There's a Lot to Be Said for the Fuehrer," with music by Shire and lyrics by Ed Kleban.
15. Shire wryly refers to the song as "the medley of my hit."
16. Maltby's only solo foray into the world of movies was the screenplay of *Miss Potter* (2006), the story of Beatrix Potter, who created Peter Rabbit, directed by Chris Noonan, with Renée Zellweger in the title role.

CHAPTER 8: LYNNE

1. All quotes from Lynne Meadow in this book are from a Zoom interview with the author on March 18, 2021.
2. The musical was an adaptation of a play called *The Happy Time* by Samuel Taylor, who was also the librettist for the Richard Rodgers musical *No Strings* but whose chief claim to fame is as coauthor of the brilliant screenplay of the 1958 Alfred Hitchcock classic *Vertigo*.
3. As discussed in chapter 2, Francisco went on to direct the off-Broadway production of *The Sap of Life* in New York. He joined the faculty of Wesleyan University in 1975 and taught there until his retirement in 2002. The list of his many gifted alumni most famously includes Lin-Manuel Miranda.
4. Maltby and Shire, as mentioned in chapter 2, did a tryout of *The Sap of Life* at Williamstown in 1961. Psacharopoulos had also been the director of *Cyrano* at Yale.

CHAPTER 9: *STARTING HERE, STARTING NOW*

1. Richard Maltby, "Maltby and Shire on Maltby and Shire," Legends of Broadway Video Series, Masterworks Broadway, https://www.masterworksbroadway.com/video/maltby-and-shire-on-maltby-and-shire-legends-of-broadway-video-series/.
2. Apparently, the show *You're What's Happening Baby* was at one point called *Girl of the Minute* and is referred to as such in William H. Evans's liner notes to the original cast recording of *Starting Here, Starting Now*. Maltby, however, has no recollection of the show ever bearing this title.

3. Her ex has the unusual name of Hecky, which Maltby used because it was Broadway composer and lyricist Harold Rome's nickname.
4. The song "Barbara" was also incorporated into the score of *You're What's Happening, Baby* at one point.
5. William H. Evans, liner notes for *Starting Here, Starting Now* original cast recording (RCA Victor, RCA Red Seal ABL1-2360, 1977), LP.
6. Andrews would later achieve immortality as the world-record holder for the longest run in the same show—he played 9,382 performances of *Phantom of the Opera* from 1988 to 2011.
7. The review's first sentence actually said, "What could be nicer than a lot of fine show songs you've never heard before?" Martin Gottfried, "'Now,' a Winner out of Losers," *New York Post*, March 8, 1977, personal collection of Richard Maltby.
8. Gottfried went on to say, "It is ironic and striking that David Shire and Richard Maltby, Jr. should be making their NY debuts with a show that is a retrospective of their work. This is a team of formidable talent and theatrical flair, superior to most and then some. . . . This music is what Broadway can't get enough of: melodic, surprising, playable musician music. . . . Be sore that M & S have had such tough luck, and grateful that their work can be heard in this lovely production."
9. The original opening-night *Times* review was written by Clive Barnes.
10. All quotes from Thomas Z. Shepard in this book are from a Zoom interview with the author on April 28, 2021.
11. David Wolf, "Starting Here, Starting Now," in *The Theatermania Guide to Musical Theater Recordings*, edited by Michael Portaniere (New York: Back Stage Books, 2004), 344.

CHAPTER 10: "I DON'T REMEMBER CHRISTMAS"

1. https://www.youtube.com/watch?v=-BoA5OAoZEc.
2. Email from George Lee Andrews, June 25, 2021.

CHAPTER 11: HE'S THE ARBITER, REALLY

1. All quotes from Deniz Cordell in this book come from interviews or email exchanges during the period from January 22, 2021, through January 11, 2024.

CHAPTER 12: REMEMBER THAT FATS WALLER IDEA?: *AIN'T MISBEHAVIN'*

1. Richard Eder, "'Chez Nous' Is Not the Best Peter Nichols," *New York Times*, November 7, 1977, 43.
2. Maltby, *Anything Goes* (podcast audio).
3. Maltby, *Storybeat* (podcast audio).
4. Quoted in Andrew Gilbert, "David Shire Is Still Writing Scores That Make Movies Sing," *San Francisco Classical Voice*, March 8, 2019, https://www.sfcv.org/articles/artist-spotlight/david-shire-still-writing-scores-make-movies-sing.
5. Shire and the Bergmans had also teamed up to write "There's a New Girl in Town," the theme song to the popular TV series *Alice*, starring Linda Lavin.

6. The fifth nominated song that year was "It's Easy to Say" from *10*, with music by Henry Mancini and lyrics by Robert Wells.
7. *David Shire's Apocalypse Now—The Unused Score* (La-La Land Records LLLCD1439, 2017), compact disc.

CHAPTER 13: AT THE END OF THE SONG, EVERYONE'S PREGNANT!

1. Richard Maltby, interview with Liz Callaway, *Stars in the House* (podcast audio), January 27, 2021, https://www.starsinthehouse.com/january-archive?pgid=kjenl646-26cdc39c-9d27-4467-8367-0d8e8ac7b79b.
2. It seems surprising that this concern wasn't at least partially alleviated by the fact that Maltby at this point had already won a Best Direction of a Musical Tony for *Ain't Misbehavin'* in 1978.
3. All quotes from Jim Freydberg in this book are from a Zoom interview with the author on March 25, 2021, unless otherwise indicated.
4. According to Maltby, "Ted Tally produced one joke, which is 'You're shooting blanks'—the biggest laugh in the show. That was worth the percentage we gave him."
5. This vitalizing number is now the Act I finale of *Closer Than Ever* (more about this in chapter 17).
6. This key bit of dialogue does not, in fact, appear on the cast recording. It was decided that it would interrupt the momentum of the song on the album, which is primarily a musical document, not a dramatic one.
7. In performance, this moment always gets a big laugh.
8. This is the biology teacher's speech from the currently licensed *Baby* script. The Broadway cast recording includes a different, longer version, underscored by mysterious, swirling choral vocals.
9. This is consistent with Alfred Hitchcock's definition of suspense, which states that suspense occurs when the spectator knows more than the characters in the movie.
10. "Patterns" was later incorporated into the revue *Closer Than Ever* and has since been restored in the currently licensed version of *Baby*.
11. It was a reprise of "Baby, Baby, Baby."
12. Frank Rich, "'Baby,' a Musical Exploring Parenthood," *New York Times*, December 5, 1983, C13.
13. Ken Mandelbaum, *Not Since Carrie: Forty Years of Broadway Musical Flops* (New York: St. Martin's Press, 1991), 253.
14. Herman's acceptance speech included the line, "There's been a rumor around for a couple of years that the simple, hummable show tune was no longer welcome on Broadway. Well, it's alive and well at the Palace [where *La Cage* was playing]." Some interpreted this as a direct swipe at Sondheim, but Herman later denied this.
15. All quotes from Liz Callaway in this book are from a Zoom interview with the author on July 12, 2022, unless otherwise noted.
16. Maltby, *Stars in the House* (podcast audio).
17. Live spoken commentary during Callaway's show *The Story Goes On: Liz Callaway Sings Maltby & Shire*, Lincoln Center's American Songbook series, New York, March 30, 2016.
18. Callaway, *Stars in the House* (podcast audio).

CHAPTER 14: *BABY*

1. Actual lyrics: "My first kid simply popped out like a cork, my dear / The next they couldn't pry out with a fork, my dear."

CHAPTER 15: "THE STORY GOES ON"

1. This is an example of tritone substitution, a common jazz technique.

CHAPTER 16: FRENCH IS A LANGUAGE THAT DOESN'T SCAN: *MISS SAIGON*

1. Maltby says: "Andrew sat down and played me what he said would become the score to *Aspects of Love*. What he played me was the score to *Phantom of the Opera*. All the melodies he played me he ended up putting in *Phantom* instead."
2. The credits for the English version read: "Book by Claude-Michel Schönberg and Alain Boublil; Music by Claude-Michel Schönberg; Lyrics by Herbert Kretzmer; Original French text by Alain Boublil and Jean-Marc Natel."
3. It probably did not help the overall theatrical impact that the house lights came up at the end of every scene, and stagehands would move the scenery on and off in full view of the audience.
4. All quotes from Alain Boublil in this book are from a Zoom interview with the author on June 16, 2022.
5. *Les Miz* also includes the credit "Additional text by James Fenton," an English poet, journalist, and critic. Fenton was originally hired to write the English lyrics, but a dissatisfied Mackintosh replaced him with Kretzmer. Some of Fenton's structure but few of his actual lyrics remain in the show.
6. Schönberg is a distant relative of the great Viennese composer Arnold Schoenberg, but, as the Frenchman once expressed it to this author, "We are not very close, either in family or in music."
7. Pryce was eventually allowed to appear in the role on Broadway after Mackintosh threatened to cancel the production and the actors union realized the decision would result in the loss of many jobs for its Asian American members.
8. The author played keyboards in the *Pirate Queen* pit orchestra on Broadway and also served as associate conductor for the production.

CHAPTER 17: ONE OF THE FINEST SCORES OF THE YEAR

1. Quoted in Patricia Leigh Brown, "Twenty Playwrights Survey Urban Life," *New York Times*, June 19, 1988, section 2, 5.
2. Frank Rich, "Taking New York Apart in a Musical Revue," *New York Times*, June 20, 1988, C13.
3. The title *Next Time, Now!* came from the end of the song "Next Time," which was resurrected from *Love Match,* the Queen Victoria/Prince Albert musical.
4. Stephen Holden, "Review/Cabaret; Of Young Adulthood," *New York Times*, January 20, 1989, C13.

5. Bill Rosenfeld, liner notes for *Closer Than Ever* original cast recording (RCA Victor 60399, 1990), CD.
6. Cited by Rosenfeld, liner notes, *Closer Than Ever* original cast recording.
7. Ibid.
8. Howard Kissel, "Better Than Broadway," *New York Daily News*, November 7, 1989, 15.
9. Laurie Winer, "'Closer Than Ever,' Revue from Maltby and Shire," *New York Times*, November 7, 1989, C19.
10. Theater columnist Michael Riedel says Winer wrote for the *Times* for six months. Michael Riedel, "Closer Than Ever to a Hit," *New York Post*, July 6, 2012, https://nypost.com/2012/07/06/closer-than-ever-to-a-hit/.
11. Stephen Holden, "'Closer Than Ever' Is One from the Heart," *New York Times*, February 25, 1990, section 2, 27.
12. Interestingly, Holden began his review by devoting the first two paragraphs to "The March of Time," which, as noted above, was written specifically in response to his original review of *Next Time, Now!*
13. All quotes from Joel Fram in this book are from an in-person interview with the author on October 27, 2021.
14. Jason Robert Brown, "*Songs for a New World* Meets *Closer Than Ever*," *Jason Robert Brown* (blog), August 4, 2012, https://jasonrobertbrown.com/2012/08/04/songs-for-a-new-world-meets-closer-than-ever/.
15. In Maltby's recollection, it was a laundromat.
16. See chapter 29 for a discussion of the York Theatre's revivals of both *Closer Than Ever* and *Starting Here, Starting Now*.

CHAPTER 18: *CLOSER THAN EVER*

1. In addition, the accented patterns of the lyrics in the first three lines of these two excerpts are nearly identical.
2. In-person conversation with Didi Conn, August 22, 2022.
3. Note also the subtle, impressive inner rhymes of "groping"/"blind" and "hoping"/"find."
4. The hemiola feel, in fact, is similar to that of "A Charmed Life," discussed in chapter 2.
5. The song that follows "Another Wedding Song" in the show is "If I Sing."
6. According to Deniz Cordell, Sheldon Harnick was also a huge admirer of "One of the Good Guys."

CHAPTER 19: "THE BEAR, THE TIGER, THE HAMSTER AND THE MOLE"

1. The third chord in that remarkable series of passing sonorities, indicated by an asterisk, is a B♭7 ♭9 ♭5, which Shire specifically cites in chapter 2 as a jazz chord he learned from his father.
2. A pre-chorus is exactly what it sounds like: a transitional section between the verse and the chorus of a song.
3. *They Love and Kill: Sex, Sympathy and Aggression in Courtship and Mating* by Vitus B. Droscher (New York: E. P. Dutton, 1976).

CHAPTER 20: IT SHOULD HAVE BEEN CALLED *SMALL*

1. Didi Conn and David Shire, joint Zoom interview, June 24, 2021.
2. Barbara Isenberg, *Making It Big: The Diary of a Broadway Musical* (New York: Limelight Editions, 1996).
3. All quotes from Susan Stroman in this book are from a Zoom interview with the author on February 17, 2022.
4. All quotes from John Weidman in this book are from a Zoom interview with the author on August 7, 2021.
5. This song was cut before the show reached Broadway.
6. The number went by this name instead of merely "Stars," since one of the songs from the megahit musical *Les Misérables* had already claimed that title.
7. Quoted in Isenberg, *Making It Big*, 10.
8. Quoted in William Grimes, "Placing Big Bets on 'Big,' the Musical," *New York Times*, April 21, 1996, section 2, 8.
9. Quoted in J. Wynn Rousuck, "'Big' Shrinks, Grows Musical," *Baltimore Sun*, October 5, 1997, https://www.baltimoresun.com/news/bs-xpm-1997-10-05-1997278012-story.html.
10. Isenberg, *Making It Big*, 33.
11. Chris Jones, "Big," *Variety*, February 25, 1996, https://variety.com/1996/legit/reviews/big-2-1200444881/.
12. Quoted in Isenberg, *Making It Big*, 109.
13. Quoted in Grimes, "Placing Big Bets on 'Big.'"
14. Vincent Canby, "A Child Who Exuberantly Finds His Inner Man," *New York Times*, April 29, 1996, A21.
15. The general positivity of Canby's *Times* review was no consolation for Shire, who was crushed by Canby's observation that "[t]he Shire and Maltby score is attractive, serving the purposes of the show without being especially memorable," but that "[y]ou probably won't leave the theater humming anything but 'Chopsticks,'" which, as in the movie, is the springboard for the Walking Piano scene in FAO Schwarz. "In my memory, that was enough to kill the evening for me," Shire admits.
16. Rousuck, "'Big' Shrinks, Grows Musical."
17. Peter Marks, "'Big,' Closing on Oct. 13, Is Living Up to Its Name as a Broadway Disaster," *New York Times*, September 26, 1996, C17.
18. Conn and Shire, Zoom interview.
19. Rousuck, "'Big' Shrinks, Grows Musical."
20. Alvin Klein, "The Good News: 'Big' Is Back, *New York Times*, August 20, 2000, Long Island section, 14.

CHAPTER 21: *BIG*

1. He had, in fact, played a role in creating this genre several years before, albeit under the radar, in *How Do You Do, I Love You*.
2. "Say Good Morning to Mom" ultimately made the cut and is included in the version of the show currently licensed by Music Theatre International.

3. Quoted in Isenberg, *Making It Big*, 75.
4. Quoted in Isenberg, *Making It Big*, 28.
5. Maltby is not actually Jewish. As he explains, "I'm not Jewish, but I married Janet [his second wife], and she's Jewish, so my children are Jewish, so therefore I am the head of a Jewish household. I will say we did better Seders than most of my friends."
6. Jeremy Gerard, "Big—The Musical," *Variety*, April 29, 1996. https://variety.com/1996/film/reviews/big-the-musical-1200445543/.
7. Jones, "Big," *Variety*.
8. Quoted in Isenberg, *Making It Big*, 16.
9. The romantic interlude for Susan in $\frac{3}{4}$ time, which serves as an oasis in the middle of the otherwise hard-charging, caffeinated number, was omitted from both the Broadway and the UK cast recordings.

CHAPTER 22: "LITTLE SUSAN LAWRENCE"

1. It's actually a first inversion B♭ minor chord, which means the third of the chord (D♭) is in the bass instead of the root (B♭). This gives the sonority a certain weightlessness that emphasizes the emotion.
2. Jones, "Big," *Variety*.

CHAPTER 23: BOB FOSSE'S WIFE, HIS MISTRESS, AND HIS DAUGHTER: *FOSSE*

1. Fosse and Verdon were married in 1960 and separated in 1971.
2. The show had originally played on Broadway in 1966 with Verdon in the title role and was later made into a movie in 1969 with Shirley MacLaine as Charity.
3. All quotes from Chet Walker in this chapter are from a Zoom interview with the author on August 30, 2021.
4. *Ragtime*, another critical and popular success, would follow in 1998.
5. A Yiddish word meaning to butter up or smooth-talk someone.
6. Elvis Mitchell, "Young Fosse, Vintage 'Kate,'" *New York Times*, July 7, 2000, https://archive.nytimes.com/www.nytimes.com/library/film/070700kate-film-review.html.
7. Ben Brantley, "An Album of Fosse," *New York Times*, January 15, 1999, E1.
8. *Redhead*, a 1959 Broadway musical, was the Fosse/Verdon follow-up to *Damn Yankees* and netted Tony Awards for both of them.
9. For a thorough examination of Verdon and Reinking's ultimately close relationship, see Julie Miller, "*Fosse/Verdon*: Inside Ann Reinking and Gwen Verdon's Unlikely Friendship," *Vanity Fair*, May 7, 2019, https://www.vanityfair.com/hollywood/2019/05/bob-fosse-girlfriend-ann-reinking-gwen-verdon.
10. All quotes from Michael Paternostro in this chapter are from a Zoom interview with the author on September 27, 2021.
11. Maltby emphasizes that he never attempted to make any changes to the actual choreography, which Verdon would have had a right to object to.

12. All quotes from Nicole Fosse are from a Zoom interview with the author on January 21, 2022.
13. Walker passed away on October 21, 2022.
14. Walker retained a credit and a royalty: the program included the listing "Conceived by Richard Maltby, Jr., Chet Walker and Ann Reinking," as well as the credit "Choreography Recreated by Chet Walker."
15. Drabinsky, originally sentenced to seven years in prison for fraud and forgery, only served seventeen months before he was granted day parole.

CHAPTER 24: NEXT THING I KNEW, I WAS WRITING THE SHOW: *TAKE FLIGHT*

1. Richard Rodgers and Oscar Hammerstein's *Allegro* (1947) is also sometimes mentioned as a contender for the status of first concept musical, although its largely conventional linear plot would seem to stand in the way of earning this designation, despite the show's other (for its time) unconventional aspects.
2. In this regard, *Love Life* can be seen as a precursor to the John Kander and Fred Ebb/Bob Fosse musical *Chicago*, which similarly integrated show-biz numbers into its plot—in this case, as a critique of the way the media glamorizes criminals.
3. Others have made the same claim for *Cabaret*, which preceded *Company* by four years. The case for *Fiddler on the Roof*, also sometimes mentioned in this context, is less persuasive.
4. Stephen Schiff, "Deconstructing Sondheim," *The New Yorker*, February 28, 1993, https://www.newyorker.com/magazine/1993/03/08/deconstructing-sondheim.
5. That musical was *Flight of the Lawnchair Man*, with book by Peter Ullian and music and lyrics by Robert Lindsey-Nassif. The song from *Take Flight* for Lawnchair Larry, however, would be resurrected later for the still-in-development revue *About Time* (see chapter 30).
6. All quotes from Andrew Gerle in this book are from a Zoom interview with the author on July 6, 2021.
7. Shire orchestrated both the twenty-piece and the eight-piece versions of the show himself.
8. Richard Maltby, Jr. and David Shire, *Take Flight* original cast recording (PS Classics PS-859, 2008), CD.
9. Charles A. Lindbergh, *The Spirit of St. Louis* (New York: Scribner, 2003), 389.
10. Lindbergh publicly praised the German army after Hitler's invasion of Poland and became the spokesman for the America First Committee, the leading US isolationist group advocating against American entry into World War II. His statements that American Jews were pushing the country into war with Germany were widely considered anti-Semitic and were publicly rebuked by President Franklin Roosevelt. The first version of *Take Flight* included a musical scene that addressed Lindbergh's Nazi sympathizing.
11. The "t" at the end of "wait" elides with the "t" that begins the following word "'til." Thus, the ear hears "wait" without its final "t," making "applaud, wai-" a legitimate rhyme with "Broadway" and "flawed way."

12. All quotes from Joey Parnes in this book are from a Zoom interview with the author on December 12, 2021.

CHAPTER 25: WORKING WITH OTHER PEOPLE

1. All quotes from Adam Gopnik in this book are from an in-person interview with the author on June 13, 2022.
2. According to Deniz Cordell, who was pianist and musical director for the 54 Below performance of *Our Table*, many of those revisions were instigated by Maltby, who directed the evening.
3. https://tinyurl.com/36ytcbty.
4. Adam Gopnik, "The Rules of Rhyme," *The New Yorker*, May 23, 2022, https://www.newyorker.com/magazine/2022/05/30/the-rules-of-rhyme-daniel-levin-becker-whats-good-notes-on-rap-and-language.
5. Stephen Sondheim, "Rhyme and Its Reasons," in *Finishing the Hat* (New York, Alfred A. Knopf, 2010), xxv.
6. Quoted in Gopnik, "The Rules of Rhyme."
7. Gopnik, "The Rules of Rhyme."
8. This is arguable.
9. The Brill Building, just north of Times Square in New York, houses music industry studios and offices and served as home base for many of the most popular songwriters of the early 1960s. In Gopnik's usage, it has the connotation of a production house that churns out reams of would-be hit songs indiscriminately.
10. This record held until *Spider-Man: Turn Off the Dark* shattered it in 2011 with 182 previews, or almost twenty-three weeks.
11. Laurents was also the renowned librettist of *West Side Story*, *Gypsy*, and *Anyone Can Whistle* (which he also directed), as well as the screenwriter of the films *The Way We Were*, *The Turning Point*, and Alfred Hitchcock's *Rope*.
12. Gurney, who died in 2017, was the author of, among others, *Love Letters*, *The Cocktail Hour*, *Sylvia*, and *The Dining Room*.
13. Charles Strouse, *Put on a Happy Face: A Broadway Memoir* (New York: Sterling, 2008), 272–280.
14. Frank Rich, "Bostwick and Gleason in 'Nick and Nora,'" *New York Times*, December 9, 1991, https://archive.nytimes.com/www.nytimes.com/books/00/04/16/specials/laurents-nick.html.
15. Hearing Prince belt out the bittersweet, alternately raging, alternately sorrowful chorus to "Men," it's no surprise to remember that four months after opening in *Nick & Nora*, she would become a Broadway star with her Tony-winning turn as Miss Adelaide in the 1992 revival of *Guys and Dolls*.
16. According to Deniz Cordell, Maltby was the first lyricist approached for *City of Angels*, but he turned it down because, as Cordell puts it, "He got a funny feeling from Cy Coleman."
17. Steven Suskin, *Show Tunes: The Songs, Shows, and Careers of Broadway's Major Composers* (New York: Oxford University Press, 2010), 287.

18. Shire recalls that during the *Ain't Misbehavin'* period, he asked Maltby what it was like working with a dead composer instead of with him (Shire), and Maltby replied, "Well, for one thing, he can't criticize my lyrics."

CHAPTER 26: WORKING WITH OTHER PEOPLE

1. All quotes from Craig Lucas in this book are from a Zoom interview with the author on February 13, 2022, unless otherwise indicated.
2. At one point, there were conversations with Drabinsky about Maltby and Adam Gopnik co-writing a new book for Sousatzka, but nothing came of it.
3. Tunick set the record straight on this in an interview with the author: "I'm not that modest. I actually said, 'Because I'm the best f***ing orchestrator in the world.' That's what I said. Michael Riedel I think toned it down a little."
4. Michael Riedel, "Broadway Producer, a Convicted Felon, Is Yellin' at Rehearsal," *New York Post*, January 31, 2017, https://nypost.com/2017/01/31/broadway-producer-a-convicted-felon-is-yellin-at-rehearsal/.
5. Carly Maga, "'Sousatzka,' the New Musical Produced by Garth Drabinsky," *Variety*, March 24, 2017, https://variety.com/2017/legit/reviews/sousatzka-review-musical-1202015565/.
6. All quotes from Victoria Clark in this book are from a Zoom interview with the author on January 28, 2022.
7. Quoted in Michael Paulson, "'Paradise Square' Will Close on Broadway after Winning One Tony," *New York Times*, July 11, 2022, https://www.nytimes.com/2022/07/11/theater/paradise-square-broadway-closing.html.
8. Caitlin Huston, "Unions Take Broadway Show 'Paradise Square' to Court for $350,000 in Unpaid Benefits, Wages," *Hollywood Reporter*, July 12, 2022, https://www.hollywoodreporter.com/business/business-news/paradise-square-lawsuit-broadway-1235178774/.
9. Alejandra Gularte, "*Paradise Square* Producer Added to Actors' Equity 'Do Not Work' List," *Vulture.com*, July 14, 2022, https://www.vulture.com/2022/07/paradise-square-garth-drabinsky-actors-equity-do-not-work-list.html.

CHAPTER 27: AMERICA WILL BREAK YOUR HEART: *WATERFALL*

1. Quoted in Misha Berson, "'Waterfall' Musical at 5th Avenue Blends Thai, Broadway Talents," *Seattle Times*, October 14, 2015, https://www.seattletimes.com/entertainment/theater/waterfall-musical-at-5th-avenue-blends-thai-broadway-talents/.
2. Ibid.
3. The song in question, "Pictures of Life," retains most of its original melody but was largely reharmonized by Shire.
4. David Gordon, "As Their Five-Decade Collaboration Continues, Maltby and Shire Chase a Pre-Broadway *Waterfall*," *TheaterMania*, June 6, 2015, https://www.theatermania.com/los-angeles-theater/news/maltby-and-shire-waterfall-interview_73158.html/.

5. Maltby is quick to add that Viravan came a long way over the course of the show's development. "He didn't understand that what worked for him directing a company of Thai actors looked like chaos to American actors. But he has absolutely learned. He's much smarter about it now."
6. Bob Verini, "'Waterfall' with Thai Pop Star Bie Sukrit," *Variety*, June 12, 2015, https://variety.com/2015/legit/reviews/waterfall-review-musical-pasadena-playhouse-1201517395/.
7. Misha Berson, "'Waterfall' Gushes but Doesn't Keep a Romance Afloat," *Seattle Times*, October 17, 2015, https://www.seattletimes.com/entertainment/theater/waterfall-gushes-but-doesnt-keep-a-romance-afloat/.
8. "America Will Break Your Heart" itself has since been replaced by a different song for the end of Act I, a number known as "Thai Love Song," which is reprised at the end of the show.
9. Haak had also served as musical director for *Sousatzka* in Toronto.
10. Boggess had originated the part of Katherine in a New York lab production of the show in 2014, prior to the Pasadena premiere.
11. Dale Rieling, phone conversation, October 25, 2023.
12. A two-and-a-half-minute promotional video for the production, which can be seen on YouTube, gives a taste of how opulent and thrilling the Bangkok production of *Waterfall* was, including the spectacular waterfall effect itself: https://www.youtube.com/watch?v=wTsmyICv95k.

CHAPTER 28: POSTPARTUM: *BABY* REVIVAL

1. Mandelbaum, *Not since Carrie*, 282.
2. The fairness of including *Baby* in a book about flops is debatable, given its eight-month Broadway run, its popular cast recording, and its still-flourishing afterlife in stock and amateur rentals, but Mandelbaum's point was unquestionably germane.
3. Simon Saltzman, "'Baby' at Paper Mill Playhouse," *U.S. 1 Princeton Info*, April 27, 2004, https://www.communitynews.org/princetoninfo/artsandentertainment/drama-review-baby-at-paper-mill-playhouse/article_2c27473a-46fc-59f0-9917-6a83f70b5c02.html.
4. Sybille Pearson, Richard Maltby, Jr., and David Shire, *Baby* (New York, Music Theatre International, 2005), vii.
5. There are actually very few alternatives of this type in the published script. One of them is a suggested alteration for one of Nick's lines to Pam, which read in its original version: "We got to make him think June and Ward Cleaver are out here waiting for him. You know: two strong, straight, put-together, adult-type parents. So, sshhhh." The script suggests "Cliff and Claire Huxtable" as an alternative to "June and Ward Cleaver." This, however, has not aged well as an option due to the sexual assault scandal that now surrounds Bill Cosby and is unlikely to be used by anyone.
6. Quoted in Chloe Rabinowitz, "See Julia Murney, Robert H. Fowler & More in Rehearsals for BABY," BroadwayWorld, October 26, 2021, https://www.broadwaywo

rld.com/off-broadway/article/Photos-See-Julia-Murney-Robert-H-Fowler-More-in-Rehearsals-for-BABY-20211026.

7. Maltby also says he brought the actors into the writing process and took some specific material from them.
8. The contribution of Ted Tally, as noted in chapter 13.
9. The idea for an older Arlene came from Murney, who was fifty-two around the time of the production.
10. Both "Serena Williams" and "Althea Gibson" are offered as replacements in the first chorus for "Scarlett O'Hara" in the published *Baby* script from 2005, part of the effort to add racial diversity for that revision.
11. Madame Germaine de Staël, not as well known as most of her counterparts in this song but still useful for rhyming purposes, was a French Revolution–era proto-feminist intellectual and political theorist.
12. The gender-swapped production of *Company* ended up winning the Drama Desk Award in the Outstanding Revival of a Musical category.

CHAPTER 29: OH, THAT'S WHAT THOSE SONGS WERE ABOUT!

1. Viviano had been one of the runners-up for the Barrett role in the original production.
2. Eric Grode, "Cellulite and 2nd Chances as the Stuff of a Revue," *New York Times*, June 21, 2012, C14.
3. Riedel, "Closer Than Ever to a Hit."
4. Deniz Cordell suggests the possibility that "Like a Baby" appears on the recording instead of "I'll Get Up Tomorrow Morning" because by the time the decision was made to replace the former with the latter in the production, Michael Starobin had already orchestrated "Like a Baby," so that was the song that went on the album.
5. "Dating Again" was originally written for a compilation revue of Maltby/Shire songs about marriage called *A Time for Love*, which Maltby assembled as a showcase for singer-actress Lois Robbins. Robbins and Brian Sutherland performed the show in 2007 at the Rubicon Theatre Company in Ventura, California, and again later that year at the Studio Arena Theatre in Buffalo.
6. Brad Hathaway, "Closer Than Ever—New Cast Recording," DC Theatre Scene, October 1, 2013, https://dctheatrescene.com/2013/10/01/closer-ever-new-cast-recording/.
7. This event was hosted by the author.
8. Ryan Leeds, "Theater Reviews: Starting Here, Starting Now," *Manhattan Digest*, March 14, 2016, https://www.manhattandigest.com/2016/03/17/theater-reviews-the-last-class-starting-here-starting-now/.
9. Joseph Verlezza, "'Starting Here, Starting Now' at the York Theatre Company, OnStage Blog, March 14, 2016, https://www.onstageblog.com/reviews/2016/3/14/s1iau8ki2iq5tx7powrdo8u8n96fhy.
10. Referred to as *Revue #3* early in its development, the show now has the working title *About Time* (see chapter 30).

CHAPTER 30: THE SONGWRITERS' SONGWRITERS

1. https://www.youtube.com/watch?v=j2ztluDBShU&t=895s.
2. Maltby and Shire can be seen performing "Smart People" on YouTube: https://www.youtube.com/watch?v=z1x_oVFlayU.
3. Or, as Deniz Cordell vividly describes it, "It's about New York eating you for lunch, spitting you out, and forgetting you exist, but then welcoming you back with open, loving arms."
4. The printed program listed the show's title as *Revue #3*, even though the assumption was that it would ultimately be changed.
5. According to Cordell, "To Be Alive," though written for *Love Match*, never actually made it into the show. Shire, however, took the song's refrain and turned it into his theme for the 1974–1975 TV series *Lucas Tanner*.
6. Once again, the illness of a cast member on the day of the show required Maltby to step in at the last minute for one of the leading roles. As John Weidman put it, "If anybody gets sick in a Maltby/Shire show, don't stand between Maltby and the stage."
7. Shire shared the 1979 Album of the Year Grammy win for the *Saturday Night Fever* soundtrack recording.
8. Rob Kapilow, *Listening for America: Inside the Great American Songbook from Gershwin to Sondheim* (New York: Liveright, 2019), 368.
9. Mandelbaum, *Not since Carrie*, 147.

SELECT BIBLIOGRAPHY

Block, Geoffrey. *Enchanted Evenings*. New York: Oxford University Press, 2009.

Brantley, Ben. "An Album of Fosse." *New York Times*, January 15, 1999, E1.

Brown, Jason Robert. "*Songs for a New World* Meets Closer Than Ever." *Jason Robert Brown* (blog), August 4, 2012. https://jasonrobertbrown.com/2012/08/04/songs-for-a-new-world-meets-closer-than-ever.

Brown, Patricia Leigh. "Twenty *Playwrights* Survey Urban Life." *New York Times*, June 19, 1988, section 2, 5.

Canby, Vincent. "A Child Who Exuberantly Finds His Inner Man." *New York Times*, April 29, 1996, A21.

Chattah, Juan. *David Shire's "The Conversation."* London: Rowman & Littlefield, 2015.

Church, Joseph. *Music Direction for the Stage: A View from the Podium*. New York: Oxford University Press, 2015.

Evans, William H. Liner notes. *Starting Here, Starting Now* original cast recording. RCA Victor, 1977.

Filichia, Peter. *Broadway Musicals: The Biggest Hit & the Biggest Flop of the Season 1959 to 2009*. New York: Applause Books, 2010.

Filichia, Peter. *Strippers, Showgirls, and Sharks*. New York: St. Martin's Press, 2013.

Ford, Phil. "Jazz Exotica and the Naked City." *Journal of Musicological Research* 27 (2008): 113–133.

Forte, Allen. *Listening to Classic American Popular Songs*. New Haven, CT: Yale University Press, 2001.

Gilbert, Andrew. "David Shire Is Still Writing Scores That Make Movies Sing." *San Francisco Classical Voice*, March 8, 2019. https://www.sfcv.org/articles/artist-spotlight/david-shire-still-writing-scores-make-movies-sing.

Gopnik, Adam. "The Rules of Rhyme." *The New Yorker*, May 23, 2022. https://www.newyorker.com/magazine/2022/05/30/the-rules-of-rhyme-daniel-levin-becker-whats-good-notes-on-rap-and-language.

Gordon, David. "As Their Five-Decade Collaboration Continues, Maltby and Shire Chase a Pre-Broadway *Waterfall*." *TheaterMania*, June 6, 2015. https://www.theatermania.com/los-angeles-theater/news/maltby-and-shire-waterfall-interview_73158.html.

Gottfried, Martin. "'Now,' a Winner Out of Losers." *New York Post*, March 8, 1977.

Grimes, William. "Placing Big Bets on 'Big,' the Musical." *New York Times*, April 21, 1996, section 2, 8.

Holden, Stephen. "'Closer Than Ever' Is One from the Heart." *New York Times*, February 25, 1990, section 2, 27.

Holden, Stephen. "Review/Cabaret; Of Young Adulthood." *New York Times*, January 20, 1989, C13.

Isenberg, Barbara. *Making It Big: The Diary of a Broadway Musical*. New York: Limelight Editions, 1996.

Jones, Chris. "Big." *Variety*, February 25, 1996. https://variety.com/1996/legit/reviews/big-2-1200444881.

Kapilow, Rob. *Listening for America: Inside the Great American Songbook from Gershwin to Sondheim*. New York: Liveright, 2019.

Kaplan, James. "The Cult of Saint Stephen Sondheim." *New York*, April 4, 1994, 48–54.

Klein, Alvin. "The Good News: 'Big' Is Back. *New York Times*, August 20, 2000, Long Island section, 14.

Lapine, James. *Putting It Together: How Stephen Sondheim and I Created "Sunday in the Park with George."* New York: Farrar, Straus and Giroux, 2021.

Laurents, Arthur. *Original Story By: A Memoir of Broadway and Hollywood*. New York: Applause Books, 2000.

Lindbergh, Charles A. *The Spirit of St. Louis*. New York: Scribner, 2003.

Mandelbaum, Ken. *Not since Carrie: Forty Years of Broadway Musical Flops*. New York: St. Martin's Press, 1991.

Miller, Julie. "*Fosse/Verdon*: Inside Ann Reinking and Gwen Verdon's Unlikely Friendship." *Vanity Fair*, May 7, 2019. https://www.vanityfair.com/hollywood/2019/05/bob-fosse-girlfriend-ann-reinking-gwen-verdon.

Pearson, Sybille, Richard Maltby, Jr., and David Shire. *Baby*. New York: Music Theatre International, 2005.

Pender, Rick. *The Stephen Sondheim Encyclopedia*. Washington, DC: Rowman & Littlefield, 2021.

Rabinowitz, Chloe. "See Julia Murney, Robert H. Fowler & More in Rehearsals for *Baby*." BroadwayWorld, October 26, 2021. https://www.broadwayworld.com/off-broadway/article/Photos-See-Julia-Murney-Robert-H-Fowler-More-in-Rehearsals-for-BABY-20211026.

Rich, Frank. "'Baby,' a Musical Exploring Parenthood." *New York Times*, December 5, 1983, C13.

Rich, Frank. "Conversations with Sondheim," *New York Times Magazine*, March 12, 2000, 38+.

Rich, Frank. *Hot Seat: Theater Criticism for* The New York Times. New York: Random House, 1998.

Riedel, Michael. "Broadway Producer, a Convicted Felon, Is Yellin' at Rehearsal." *New York Post*, January 31, 2017. https://nypost.com/2017/01/31/broadway-producer-a-convicted-felon-is-yellin-at-rehearsal.

Riedel, Michael. "Closer Than Ever to a Hit." *New York Post*, July 6, 2012. https://nypost.com/2012/07/06/closer-than-ever-to-a-hit.

Rousuck, J. Wynn. "'Big' Shrinks, Grows Musical." *Baltimore Sun*, October 5, 1997. https://www.baltimoresun.com/news/bs-xpm-1997-10-05-1997278012-story.html.

Sacks, Oliver. *Musicophilia*. New York: Vintage Books, 2008.

Schiff, Stephen. "Deconstructing Sondheim." *The New Yorker*, February 28, 1993. https://www.newyorker.com/magazine/1993/03/08/deconstructing-sondheim.

Secrest, Meryle. *Stephen Sondheim: A Life*. New York: Alfred A. Knopf, 1998.

Sondheim, Stephen. *Finishing the Hat: Collected Lyrics (1954–1981)*. New York: Alfred A. Knopf, 2010.

Sondheim, Stephen. *Look I Made a Hat: Collected Lyrics (1981–2011)*. New York: Alfred A. Knopf, 2011.

Strouse, Charles. *Put on a Happy Face: A Broadway Memoir*. New York: Sterling, 2008.

Suskin, Steven. *Show Tunes: The Songs, Shows, and Careers of Broadway's Major Composers*. New York: Oxford University Press, 2010.

Swayne, Steve. *How Sondheim Found His Sound*. Ann Arbor: University of Michigan Press, 2007.

Viertel, Jack. *The Secret Life of the American Musical*. New York: Sarah Crichton Books, 2016.

Wasson, Sam. *Fosse*. Boston: Mariner Books, 2014.

Wilder, Alec. *American Popular Song: The Great Innovators, 1900–1950*. New York: Oxford University Press, 1972.

Wolf, David. "Starting Here, Starting Now." In *The Theatermania Guide to Musical Theater Recordings*, edited by Michael Portaniere, 344. New York: Back Stage Books, 2004.

INDEX

For the benefit of digital users, indexed terms that span two pages (e.g., 52–53) may, on occasion, appear on only one of those pages.
Figures are indicated by *f* following the page number